PUEBLOS WITHIN PUEBLOS

PUEBLOS WITHIN PUEBLOS

Tlaxilacalli Communities in Acolhuacan, Mexico, ca. 1272–1692

BENJAMIN D. JOHNSON

UNIVERSITY PRESS OF COLORADO

Louisville

© 2017 by University Press of Colorado

Published by University Press of Colorado
245 Century Circle, Suite 202
Louisville, Colorado 80027

All rights reserved
First paperback edition 2019

 The University Press of Colorado is a proud member of
The Association of University Presses.

The University Press of Colorado is a cooperative publishing enterprise supported, in part, by Adams State University, Colorado State University, Fort Lewis College, Metropolitan State University of Denver, Regis University, University of Colorado, University of Northern Colorado, University of Wyoming, Utah State University, and Western Colorado University.

ISBN: 978-1-60732-690-8 (cloth)
ISBN: 978-1-64642-014-8 (paperback)
ISBN: 978-1-60732-691-5 (ebook)
DOI: https://doi.org/10.5876/9781607326915

Library of Congress Cataloging-in-Publication Data

Names: Johnson, Benjamin D., author.
Title: Pueblos within pueblos : tlaxilacalli communities in Acolhuacan, Mexico, ca. 1272–1692 / Benjamin D. Johnson.
Description: Boulder : University Press of Colorado, [2017] | Includes bibliographical references and index.
Identifiers: LCCN 2017021813| ISBN 9781607326908 (cloth) | ISBN 9781646420148 (pbk) | ISBN 9781607326915 (ebook)
Subjects: LCSH: Communities—Political aspects—Mexico—Texcoco (Region)—History. | Texcoco
   (Mexico : Region)—Colonization—History. | Tezcucan Indians—Mexico—Texcoco (Region)—Politics and government.
Classification: LCC F1219.1.T4 J64 2017 | DDC 972/.53—dc23
LC record available at https://lccn.loc.gov/2017021813

Cover illustration, Core Tlaxilacalli in Tepetlaoztoc, used by permission of the British Museum.

To Ana Paula and Joaquim

To my beloved family

*Es de su propio Señor
tan rebelado vasallo
que convierte en sus ofensas
las armas de su resguardo.*

—SOR JUANA INÉS DE LA CRUZ

Contents

Acknowledgments — ix

A Brief Note on Usage — xiii

INTRODUCTION: HISTORY AND TLAXILACALLI — 3

CHAPTER 1: THE RISE OF TLAXILACALLI, CA. 1272–1454 — 40

CHAPTER 2: ACOLHUA IMPERIALISMS, CA. 1420S–1583 — 75

CHAPTER 3: COMMUNITY AND CHANGE IN CUAUHTEPOZTLAN TLAXILACALLI, CA. 1544–1575 — 97

CHAPTER 4: TLAXILACALLI RELIGIONS, 1537–1587 — 123

CHAPTER 5: TLAXILACALLI ASCENDANT, 1562–1613 — 151

CHAPTER 6: COMMUNITIES REBORN, 1581–1692 — 174

CONCLUSION: TLAXILACALLI AND BARRIO — 203

List of Acronyms Used Frequently in This Book — 208

Bibliography — 209

Index — 247

Acknowledgments

There are so many people I wish to thank for their generous help and support: colleagues, friends, and family.

Many sincere thanks to Emilio Kourí, Dain Borges, Mauricio Tenorio-Trillo, Brodwyn Fischer, Ramón Gutiérrez, and Friedrich Katz at the University of Chicago, as well as to a wonderful group of colleagues from graduate school: Faisal Ahmed, Carlos Bravo Regidor, Patrick Iber, José Angel Hernández, Sarah Osten, Jaime Pensado, Mikael Wolfe, Romina Robles Ruvalcava, Sabine Cadeau, Hank González, Diana Schwartz, Ananya Chakravarti, Casey Lurtz, Ann Schneider, Julia Young, Dora Sánchez Hidalgo, José Luis Razo, Stuart Easterling, Emilio de Antuñano, Jackie Sumner, Aiala Levy, Tessa Murphey, Antonio Sotomayor, Julene Iriarte, Frutuoso Santana, and Josh Beck. I also deeply thank Frank Safford, Robert Lerner, and Jock McLane at Northwestern.

In the realms of Nahautl studies and Mexican history, I am truly grateful for outstanding colleagues such as Caterina Pizzigoni, David Tavárez, Vera Candiani, Luis Fernando Granados, Javier Eduardo Ramírez López, Kevin Terraciano, John Sullivan, Fritz Schwaller and the Northeastern Nahautl Studies collective, Joe Campbell, Frances Karttunen, Louise Burkhart, Jerry Offner and the "Corpus Xolotl" project, Gordon Whittaker, Julia Madajczak, Alan and Pamela Sandstrom, Stephanie Wood, Victoriano de la Cruz, Kelly McDonough, Justyna Olko, Sergio Romero, Barbara Mundy, Mangus Pharao Hansen, Lori Boornazian Diel, Pablo García Loaeza, Federico Navarrete Linares, Margarita Menegus Bornemann,

Katarzyna Mikulska, Amos Megged, Betsey Haude, Mariano Cando Morales, Roger Magazine, Barbara Williams, Octavio Barajas, Fernando Escalante Gonzalbo, Elías Rodríguez Vázquez, Pascual Tinoco Quesnel, Susan Kellogg, Ofelia Morales, Jonathan Amith, and José Omar Tinajero Morales. Sincere thanks to Kirsten Weld and the Harvard Latin American/Caribbean History Workshop, Margarita Salas Aranda of the Centro de Estuios Históricos y Sociales de Texcoco, Eduardo Natalino dos Santos and the CEMA group at the Universidade de São Paulo, Rodrigo Bentes Monteiro and Marcelo Rocha of the Companhia das Índias at the Universidade Federal Fluminense, Leandro Karnal and Silvia Lara of UNICAMP, and Sidney Chalhoub of Harvard. My deepest gratitude goes to the Martínez Pérez family in Mexico City and to Hemenegilda Andrés and Marcos de la Cruz and their family in San Agustín Oapan, Guerrero.

I also want to recognize the skilled archivists and caretakers at the Archivo Municipal of Texcoco, the parish of Santa María Magdalena in Tepetlaoztoc, the Mueso Emeritorio "Fray Domingo de Betanzos" in Tepetlaoztoc, the church of San Sebastián Xolalpan in San Juan Teotihuacan, the diocese of Texcoco, the Archivo General de Notarías del Estado de México in Toluca, the Biblioteca Nacional de Antropología e Historia in Mexico City, the Biblioteca Nacional de México, the Archivo General de la Nación in Mexico City, the Fundación ICA in Mexico City, the Archivo General de Indias in Seville, the Bibliothèque nationale de France in Paris, the Bancroft Library in Berkeley, the Newberry Library in Chicago, the Brown Library in Providence, and the Bentley Library in Ann Arbor, as well as the operators of the Wired Humanities Project at Oregon, the Gran Dicionario Náhuatl and Tlachia sites at UNAM, the Códices and Códice Chimalpahin sites at INAH, Cervantes Virtual, and Amoxcalli.

At the University of Massachusetts Boston I have been fortunate to have wonderful colleagues such as Sana Haroon, Conevery Bolton Valencius, Josh Reid, Monica Pelayo, Heidi Gengenbach, Olivia Weisser, Elizabeth McCahill, David Hunt, Timothy Hacsi, Roberta Wollons, Jonathan Chu, Maryann Brink, Vin Cannato, Paul Bookbinder, Julie Winch, Marilyn Morgan, Ruth Miller, Spencer DiScala, Maria John, Luman Wang, Susan Gauss, Ping-Ann Addo, Jean-Phillipe Belleau, José Martínez-Reyes, Judith Zeitlin, and Ann Blum. A special note of gratitude to Maureen Dwyer, Kelly Ahearn, Kim Ho, and Eddie Sze. I sincerely thank my students for all that I have learned from them.

I also thank UMB's Project Development grant program and the Dean's Research and Travel funds for their generous and ongoing support. Many thanks as well to Jessica d'Arbonne, Laura Furney, Bill and Kristen N. Keegan, Kelly Lenkevich, Beth Svinarich, Cheryl Carnahan, Daniel Pratt, Dan Miller, Darrin Pratt, the University Press of Colorado, and its anonymous readers. All errors remain mine.

Finally, I want to express the greatest appreciation and love to my family: to my parents, Barbara and Rick Johnson; to my sister, Kate Johnson, and to my mother-in-law, Neusa Fernandes de Rezende. I also sincerely thank my extended family—the Vincents, the Clines, the Rezendes, and the Vieiras—and friends close enough to be family: the Koçak Hemmats, the Shafizadeh Santoses, Ivânea Costa, and the Yuilles.

Ana Paula and Joaquim Rezende Johnson are the two greatest gifts in my life. Ana Paula is courageous and loving, thoughtful and true, and she shines more beautifully now than when I first met her over a decade ago. Whether in Texcoco or Cambridge, Salvador or Valladolid, her star guides my way. Joaquim is the best son a parent could hope for: happy, engaged, sincere, open to the world. Every day he surprises me with his joy. I count myself blessed to spend my days with them. Ana Paula, Joaquim: this book is for you. I love you.

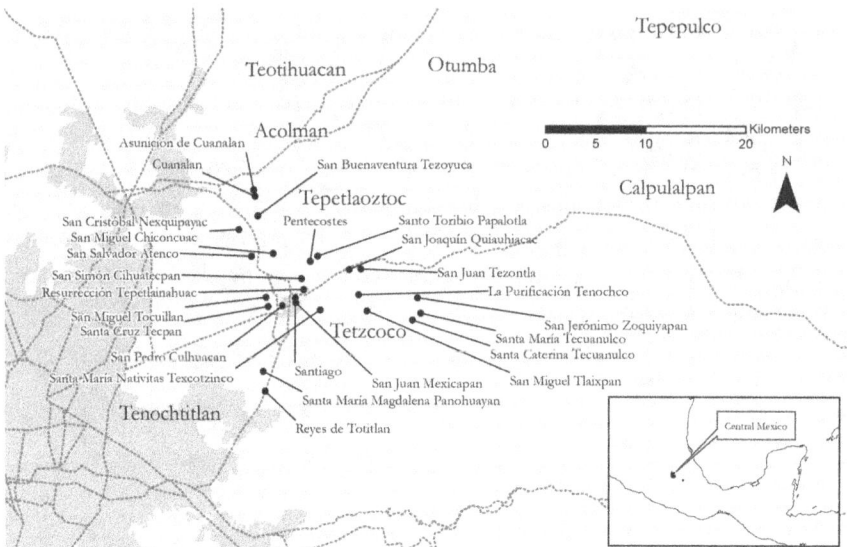

FIGURE 0.1. The Acolhua heartland, overlaid on modern central Mexico. Major altepetl appear in larger font; smaller Tetzcoco-affiliated tlaxilacalli are marked with a dot. Map by Bill and Kris Keegan.

A Brief Note on Usage

This book analyzes localities and institutions over many centuries, meaning that spellings and even pronunciations change. The primary capital of Acolhuacan, for example, appears in the relevant alphabetic sources spelled at least sixteen different ways, from the canonical Tetzcoco,[1] Tezcoco,[2] and Texcoco[3] all the way to Tezioco, Tetzicoco, Catemahco,[4] and Tahui.[5] There is also a glyphic divergence, although most symbols include hill and jar components (figure 0.2). Scholarly convention supports all three traditional spellings,[6] and Tetzcoco is used here because of its predominance in relevant Nahuatl sources. Other names also follow local usage but are occasionally corrected for clarity, giving Otumba, Tlaxcala, and Huexotla instead of Otompan, Tlaxcallan, and Huexotlan but also Huitznahuac instead of Uitznauac. Terms requiring longer discussion, such as Aztec, are addressed in individual footnotes.

NOTES

1. Most Nahuatl sources, from mundane documents to Chimalpahin, prefer Tetzcoco. Divergent spellings of this form include Tetzcohco (*Lienzo de Tlaxcala*, ed. Josefina García Quintana, Carlos Martínez Marín, and Mario de la Torre [Mexico City: Cartón y Papel, 1983]); Tetzcocu (Florentine Codex, book 12, f. 43v, World Digital Library, accessed May 6, 2016, https://www.wdl.org/en/item/10096/); and Tetzcucu (Florentine Codex, book 12, f. 84r).

xiii

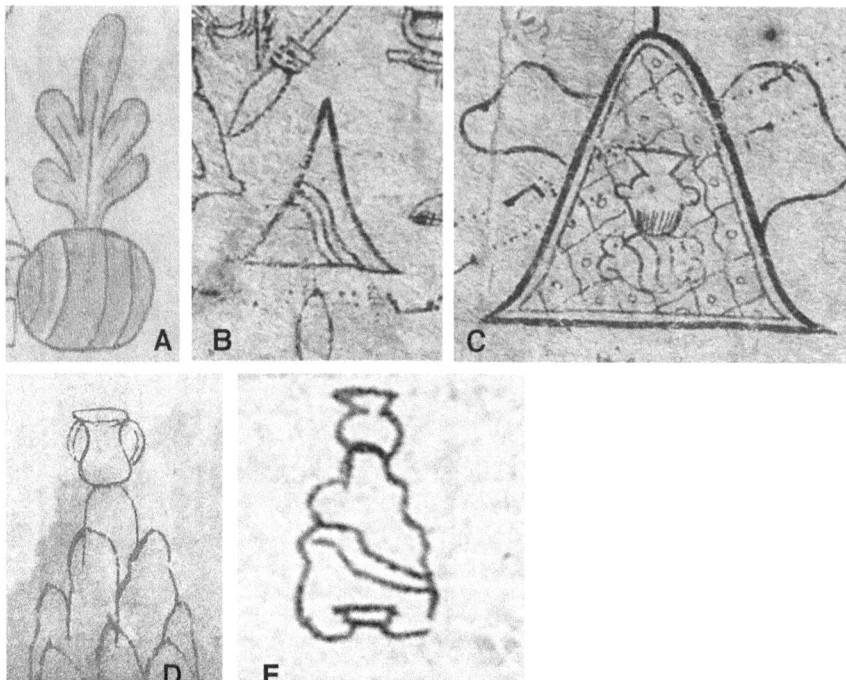

FIGURE 0.2. Glyphs for Tetzcoco. Glyphs from these codices: Azcatitlan, Xolotl (plate 3; *Tlachia* code: X.030.A.23), Asunción, Xicotepec, Plano Topográfico de Texcoco. *Courtesy*, Mme. Claude Stresser-Péan.

2. In his famous "Relación de la ciudad y provincia de Tezcoco," in *Relaciones geográficas del siglo XVI*, vol. 7, ed. René Acuña (Mexico City: UNAM, 1986), Juan Bautista de Pomar uses Tezcoco. Related forms include Tezcuco (Hernando de Alvarado Tezozomoc, *Crónica mexicana*, ed. Gonzalo Díaz Migoyo and Germán Vázquez Chamorro [Madrid: Historia 16, 1997], f. 3r); Tescuco (Alvarado Tezozomoc, *Crónica mexicana*, f. 52v); Tezcucu (Bernal Díaz del Castillo, *Historia verdadera de la conquista de la Nueva España: Manuscrito de Guatemala* [Mexico City: UNAM, 2005], chapter 100); and Tescucu (Hernán Cortés, "Cartas de relación: Segunda relación," *Early Modern Spain Online*, accessed February 4, 2014, http://www.ems.kcl.ac.uk/content/etext/e015.html).

3. Most Spanish-language sources employ Texcoco. Also Texcuco. Cf. Fernando de Alva Ixtlilxochitl, *Obras históricas*, vol. 2, ed. Edmundo O'Gorman (Mexico City: UNAM, 1975), 442.

4. Javier Eduardo Ramírez López, ed., *De Catemahco a Tezcoco: origen y desarrollo de una ciudad indígena* (Texcoco, Mexico: Diócesis de Texcoco, 2017), 320.

5. All of these terms appear in Ixtlilxochitl's discussion of Tetzcoco's name: *Obras*, 140. Another site for Tesuico is Hernán Cortés, "Cartas de relación: Tercera relación," *Early Modern Spain Online*, accessed February 4, 2014, http://www.ems.kcl.ac.uk/content/etext/e016.html.

6. Contributors to the recent edited volume by Jongsoo Lee and Galen Brokaw, *Texcoco: Prehispanic and Colonial Perspectives* (Boulder: University Press of Colorado, 2014), used all three main spellings.

PUEBLOS WITHIN PUEBLOS

INTRODUCTION

History and Tlaxilacalli

This is the story of how poor, everyday central Mexicans built and rebuilt autonomous communities over the course of four centuries and two empires. It is also the story of how these self-same commoners constructed the unequal bonds of compulsion and difference that anchored these vigorous and often beloved communities. It is a story about certain face-to-face human networks, called *tlaxilacalli* in both singular and plural,[1] and about how such networks molded the shape of both the Aztec and Spanish rule.[2] Despite this influence, however, tlaxilacalli remain ignored, subordinated as they often were to wider political configurations and most often appearing unmarked—that is, noted by proper name only—in the sources. With care, however, the deeper stories of tlaxilacalli can be uncovered. This, in turn, lays bare a root-level history of autonomy and colonialism in central Mexico, told through the powerful and transformative tlaxilacalli.

The robustness of tlaxilacalli over the *longue durée* casts new and surprising light on the structures of empire in central Mexico, revealing a counterpoint of weakness and fragmentation in the canonical histories of centralizing power in the region. Empires depended on the supple, responsive power of tlaxilacalli hierarchies—institutions they did not administer and only obliquely controlled—to subdue territories, produce surpluses, manage fragile ecosystems, and metabolize change. For their part, tlaxilacalli continued to act independent of both Aztec and Spanish rule, forging powerful communal ties that outlasted the empires such ties were created to serve.[3] This bottom-up accretion of power explains the rapid and disarticulated growth of Aztec and Spanish imperialism and also the difficulties both powers had incorporating local tlaxilacalli into wider political constructions. Compared to other New World powers, the Aztec empire splintered too quickly for a simple "guns and germs" argument to obtain; the flexible nature of tlaxilacalli arrays is a key missing element. Indeed, Cortés's multivalent armies began receiving tlaxilacalli tribute even before the Aztecs fell.[4]

But it would be unfair to characterize tlaxilacalli as disloyal. Rather, the Aztec empire demanded constant local orchestration, and even self-aggrandizing elites knew it. Tlaxilacalli—too often translated and understood as simply "neighborhoods"—usually submitted to the authority of the sovereign local polity, or *altepetl*, which then scaled up to autonomous mega-provinces (*huei altepetl*) and finally to the entire empire.[5] At each level, submission was traded for autonomy, undercutting any attempt at direct centralizing rule.[6] As the primary site where tributaries joined empires, tlaxilacalli anchored such imperial arrangements. These hierarchical communities, run by commoners administering and even compelling their commoner neighbors, were the very bedrock of empire. When they shifted, the entire arrangement shook.

AIMS OF THE BOOK

Pueblos within Pueblos intervenes in three major debates. First, by placing Aztec and Spanish colonial rule in rare comparative perspective, it unveils an uncanny symmetry between two Mexican empires frequently taken to be un-analyzably distinct from each other. Both the Aztec Triple Alliance and the viceroyalty of New Spain flexed their colonial muscles in local administration but proved paralyzingly disjointed at higher levels of imperial government. Pushing beyond standard approaches to both conquest and continuity, *Pueblos within Pueblos* shows how tlaxilacalli acted independent of imperial rule, reinforcing local ties even as they both bolstered and undermined centralizing alliances. In addition to explaining the rapid rise and fall of the Aztec empire, this focus also illuminates other episodes, such as the popular Mexico City uprisings of 1624 and 1692[7] that provoked broad and long-lasting changes across New Spain.[8] Built flexible from the start, local colonialism began well before Spaniards arrived in Mexico.

Second, the local focus of *Pueblos within Pueblos* makes tributary commoners (*macehualtin*) the protagonists of empire even as it counters recurring scholarly tendencies to homogenize such groups.[9] Specialists often invoke the modular nature of Mesoamerican institutions but have rarely analyzed the constituent polities contributing to such arrays or questioned the implicit framework of such part-whole arrangements. More than "history from below" for its own sake, this book uncovers an ignored causal engine in Mexican history. As they made and remade their nested hierarchies of community and division, local tlaxilacalli built the very backbone of imperial power.[10]

Finally, this book brings the unexamined sinews of Aztec and Spanish imperialism to life for the first time by connecting individuals and households to precise patterns of politics and landscape. Building up from the Acolhua codices Vergara and Asunción (produced ca. 1543–44, the earliest extant land surveys in the Americas), this project models the exact spatial array of tlaxilacalli forms: every commoner household, every plot of land, every excluded ethnic group and starving widow.[11] This final intervention, an advance in both methodology and conceptualization, makes pre-Hispanic and colonial Mexican history at once more human and more precise, more representative and more generalizable.[12]

MARGINAL HISTORIES

Tlaxilacalli appear frequently in Aztec and Hispanic documents, but they are often relegated to the margins of official history. Imperial sources deliberately subsume autonomous and semiautonomous actions to wider narratives, as in the case of Tlalcocomoco and Yopico, two tlaxilacalli that settled the area of Mexico-Tenochtitlan before that altepetl's official founding in 1325. Despite their influence on the ground from the beginning, Tlalcocomoco and Yopico appear as afterthoughts in Aztec histories of the period. The well-known *Annals of Cuauhtitlan*, for example, notes that Mexica migrants "settled in Tlalcocomoco" forty-five years before Mexico-Tenochtitlan "began" and that "a few shacks"—that is, established commoner dwellings—were dotting the landscape before the altepetl's official foundation. After this brief mention, however, the relation veers off to discuss rulers, their altepetl, and their wars, as Tlalcocomoco and Yopico fade from view.[13]

When not overwritten in official histories, tlaxilacalli were exoticized, standing as foils to centralizing power. This is particularly true in early treatments of Acolhua political and legal administration. The Codex Xolotl,[14] for example, shows the Tetzcoca ruler Techotlalatzin sitting commandingly on his royal throne, head erect and weapon in hand, as he welcomes the tearful leaders of four migrant "Tolteca"[15] tlaxilacalli to his growing capital. As the leaders bow their heads, Techotlalatzin emits rulerly speech scrolls, specifying the relationship of the new arrivals to the two tlaxilacalli already present in the altepetl, the long-standing and prominent communities of Tlailotlacan and Chimalpan (figure 0.3).[16]

An exoticizing narrative continues with the later historian Fernando de Alva Ixtlilxochitl,[17] who praises the tolerance the Acolhua ruler Techotlalatzin showed toward the four newly arrived "Tolteca" tlaxilacalli: "The love that Techotlatzin

FIGURE 0.3. New tlaxilacalli. Techotlalatzin welcomes four "Tolteca" tlaxilacalli—Mexicapan, Colhuacan, Huitznahuac, and Tepanecapan—to the two already extant in Tetzcoco, Chimalpan and Tlailotlacan. Also, note the tlaxilacalli reshuffling at the bottom of this figure: the recently arrived Mexicapan and Colhuacan were bundled with older tlaxilacalli, while Huitznahuac and Tepanecapan disappear from the picture. Codex Xolotl, plate 5 (*Tlachia* code: X.050.B/F). *Courtesy*, Bibliothèque nationale de France, Paris.

had for the Tolteca nation was such that, not only did he allow them to live and settle among the Chichimeca [the ethnic majority in what would be come the Acolhua capital of Tetzcoco]; but he also gave them the power to make public sacrifices to their idols and dedicate their temples, which was something that his father Quinatzin had never consented to or allowed."[18] Part of this was likely a Hispanizing move to distance Acolhua Chichimeca from subsequently discredited practices. Regardless of the precise allocation of influence, however, the actions of tlaxilacalli remain striking in their breadth. According to Ixtlilxochitl, the four "Tolteca" tlaxilacalli did not simply arrive in Tetzcoco as meek, submissive migrants. Rather, they bore prime responsibility for introducing fresh trade and political networks and new practices and technologies, as well as public human sacrifice, into the Acolhua realm.[19]

Tlaxilacalli could also appear as telling but easily ignored details to primary narration. In 1521, for example, as Spanish and Tlaxcalteca armies pushed their way into the heart of Mexico-Tenochtitlan, a war leader from the Huitznahuac tlaxilacalli in Tlatelolco forced the Aztec army to keep fighting even when more prominent leaders were ready to surrender. The main priest of Mexico-Tenochtitlan had already declared his imperial deity's acquiescence to defeat—"Huitzilopochtli's command is that nothing happen"—but this message was rebuked by tlaxilacalli fighters: "In this way, they ignored him, and war began again. Tohueyo, the Huitznahuac general, faced them (the invaders) and made the war begin again."[20]

If Aztec communication specialists[21] purposefully marginalized most tlaxilacalli (except their own),[22] a majority of Hispanic authors simply confused or ignored them. Judging by the widespread category errors between tlaxilacalli and altepetl—both of which were frequently described as "pueblos" in Hispanic sources—most Spanish administrators seem to have had little interest in the internal dynamics of central Mexican polities. Other Hispanic appellations—"neighborhood" (*barrio*) for tlaxilacalli and "city" (*ciudad* or *villa*) for altepetl, or "subject town" (*sujeto*) for the former and "head town" (*cabecera*) for the latter—distinguished between these two institutions but confused and flattened the dynamic relationship between them.[23]

This conceptual disconnect, in turn, contributed to the increasing autonomy of tlaxilacalli during the late sixteenth and seventeenth centuries. During the transformative 1624 uprising in Mexico City, for example, Spanish authorities blamed "neighborhood Indians" for organizing and executing the attack on the viceroy's palace without knowing the mechanics of how such a tlaxilacalli-based attack could have unfolded.[24] The same administrative blindness crippled Spanish responses to the comparable 1692 revolt in Mexico City, also directed against centralizing viceregal power.[25]

Despite their profound influence over settlement, religion, and warfare—as well as other key imperial processes discussed later, such as taxation, ecological management, and landholding—tlaxilacalli have remained at the margins of central Mexican history. Once highlighted, however, they can easily be disentangled from totalizing narratives and stand on their own. For example, in addition to its preeminence as a source for Acolhua imperial history, the Codex Xolotl subtly folds into its narration the dynastic histories of two tlaxilacalli of Tetzcoco, Tlailotlacan and Chimalpan (see figure 0.4 for Tlailotlacan and figure 2.4 in chapter 2 for Chimalpan).[26]

Tlailotlacan's dynasty becomes particularly relevant here, for this tlaxilacalli specialized in the information arts, and this Tetzcoca community bore significant (and perhaps sole) responsibility for the creation of the Codex Xolotl itself.[27] Further, just south in neighboring Chalco, the incisive and prolific curator of central Mexican history Domingo Chimalpahin made a similar case regarding the regional pedigree of his home tlaxilacalli of Tlailotlacan, a relative and likely forebear of the one in Tetzcoco:

> [This history] will never be lost, never forgotten. It will always be guarded; we will guard it. We, their children, grandchildren, and younger brothers; their great-great-grandchildren and great-grandchildren; we, their saliva and beards, their eyebrows and fingernails, their color and blood; we, the children of the Tlailotlaca. We who live and were born in the first tlaxilacalli, called Tlailotlacan palace (*tecpan*). It was precisely there, precisely there where they came to govern: all the beloved elders, the beloved Chichimeca *tlatoque* (rulers), the Tlailotlaca tlatoque, the Tlailotlaca lords (*teteuctin*). These words are called "what is kept in the Tlailotlacan tecpan."[28]

Such insistent tlaxilacalli-centered narrations dominate relevant sources. A recent study by Camilla Townsend found similar patterning in a broad range of important early sources, including the Historia Tolteca-Chichimeca, the Codex Aubin, the *Annals of Cuauhtitlan*, the *Annals of Tecamachalco*, and the *Annals of Juan Bautista*, in addition to a now-lost series of court documents from 1553. After noting the piecemeal, segmentary quality of all these sources, Townsend argues that the altepetl, as a contested and changing political project, required the constant accommodation of competing tlaxilacalli demands, which, in turn, produced the "disorderly" format of many early Mexican documents.[29] This model is useful and can be easily generalized. More than modular or even cellular, therefore, the relationship between tlaxilacalli and altepetl was chemical—the former acted as atoms (sometimes freely, more often arrayed in durable mixed forms), while the latter resembled complex molecules, open to profound change as their internal chemistries shifted. Community was multiple, not unitary, just as regional order emerged from local struggle and accommodation more than from command.

FIGURE 0.4. Tlaxilacalli dynasty, Tlailotlacan (Tetzcoco altepetl). Codex Xolotl, plate 5 (*Tlachia* code: X.050.B). *Courtesy*, Bibliothèque nationale de France, Paris.

TLAXILACALLI AND ALTEPETL

Tlaxilacalli predated the Aztec empire and continued well through the Spanish, and scholars have intuited their importance for centuries. Despite this, they have also considered these core institutions too "imprecise" or "difficult" for close analysis.[30] There have been periodic efforts to schematize tlaxilacalli, but most have viewed these hierarchies from the imperial center, as nothing more than unitary and modular administrative building blocks. The diversity and agency of these institutions, together with their face-to-face communitarian orientation, fade when they are summarily classified as simple pieces of a larger whole: "subunits," "sub-communities," "constituent parts," "districts," "barrios."[31] Although there is a certain utility to these descriptive translations, scholars have repeatedly identified serious issues with this approach because such explanatory shortcuts—just like the Spanish and Spanish-influenced sources on which they depend—conflate separate (and sometimes even mutually exclusive) central Mexican institutions.[32]

The easy equivalency of tlaxilacalli and neighborhood can prove problematic, however, particularly regarding the relationship between part and whole. All of the terms identified above, from "subunit" to "neighborhood," imply full dependency between dependent tlaxilacalli and all-encompassing altepetl—a perception confirmed in reigning interpretative paradigms that describe political order as a modular or cellular relationship between these two institutions. Such frameworks imply that one institution cannot exist without the other and, further, that one institution can explain the other: knowing the altepetl, one knows the tlaxilacalli as well.

Nevertheless, there are significant problems with this assertion. First, generic terminology was not always stable, particularly over the multiple centuries and various empires addressed in this book. For example, after about 1680—that is, toward the end of this book's chronology and even beyond—a number of important tlaxilacalli in Tetzcoco began to refer to themselves as "altepetl," despite the fact that they met few, if any, of the standard requisites for customary definitions of this term. Regardless, documents show Nexquipiac calling itself an "altepetl" in 1681, Tlailotlacan using the term in 1707, and Tepetitlan doing the same in 1759.[33]

Despite frequent subordination to wider political structures, therefore, tlaxilacalli also asserted their independence with increasing force entering into the mature Hispanic period—indeed, Bernardo García Martínez estimates that fully two-thirds of eighteenth-century central Mexican "pueblos" had only recently separated themselves from larger political constraints.[34] Part of this owes simply to administrative lag on the part of Hispanic officials: García Martínez and Gustavo Martínez Mendoza note, for example, that Nexquipiac, Tlailotlacan, and Tepetitlan only appeared as independent *pueblos de por sí* in Spanish-language documentation from 1743, and then only partially. Even if they didn't call themselves by this term, preferring perhaps "pueblos" or "altepetl," tlaxilacalli showed themselves to be more insistently autonomous than ever.[35]

PUEBLOS WITHIN PUEBLOS

Such transitions between tlaxilacalli and altepetl have frustrated scholars for decades, leading some to regret having used Nahuatl-based analytical categories at all.[36] As mentioned, category trouble has played a major role in dampening close analyses of tlaxilacalli and other key institutions. While "altepetl" could reference anything from a subordinate community to an entire nation ("the altepetl called Japan"), the

INTRODUCTION: HISTORY AND TLAXILACALLI 11

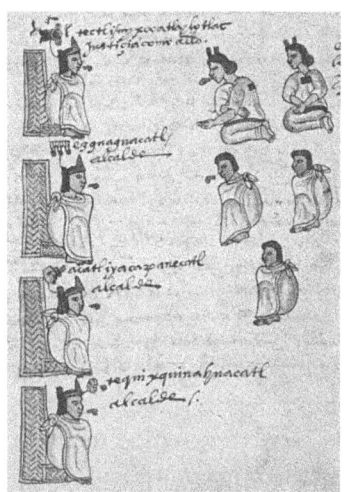

FIGURE 0.5.
Huitznahuac soldier.
Codex Mendoza, f. 67r.
Courtesy, Bodelian
Library, Oxford
University.

FIGURE 0.6. Tlaxilacalli
judges in Moyotlan tlayacatl.
The occasionally mistranslated
Acatlyacapanecatl is third from
the top. Codex Mendoza, f. 68r.
Courtesy, Bodelian Library, Oxford
University.

tlaxilacalli enveloped equally multitudinous worlds.[37] Together with its pseudo-cognate *calpolli*, the term *tlaxilacalli* could reference almost any facet of this core communal institution, including a territorial demarcation, a sacred local landscape, a band of settlers, an ethnic minority, a labor or tribute unit, a collective land endowment, a local political hierarchy, an army division, an Aztec temple, a Catholic parish, or even subdivisions of these aforementioned roles and types.[38]

Seen in a different light, however, the broad semantic field ceded to tlaxilacalli underscores their profound importance to the social and organizational life of central Mexico. Further and much more pointedly, analytical problems such as category confusion only present themselves in the abstract. In the definitive scholarly edition of the Codex Mendoza, for example, the editors unintelligibly translated the imperial warrior class Huitznahuatl, "Huitznahuac resident," as "Thorn Speech" and the judge Acatlyacapanecatl, "Acatl Yacapan resident," as "Lord of the Reed on the Nose"[39] (see figures 0.5 and 0.6). Both of these titles originally referenced attributes of specific tlaxilacalli, which were then generalized—perhaps similar to the expansion of the term *Hollywood* in recent times beyond its original Los Angeles–based referent. Such expansions seem to have been common in local practice: together with their use of general categories, central Mexicans frequently operated in the concrete realm of proper names, opting for the vigorous and precise appellations of specific tlaxilacalli, which then spread across wider conceptual planes.

A tlaxilacalli could bear any grammatically coherent name—many simply evoked the natural or built environment (Huitznahuac, "Among the Thorns"; Acatl Yacapan, "Facing the Reeds"; Apipilhuasco, "Near the Water Pipes")—but in practice, certain designations were repeated again and again across the landscape, exclusively referencing tlaxilacalli. Names could often come from shared historical experience, as in Ixtlilxochitl's comments regarding the migratory tlaxilacalli of Tlailotlacan that then fragmented and spread across central Mexico: "[The Acolhua ruler Quinatzin] gave [Tlailotlaque migrants] a place near Tetzcoco to settle, and the rest he divided between his *pueblos* ('altepetl'), giving each one lands to settle. From here comes the name of the pueblo ('tlaxilacalli') and neighborhood of Tetzcoco, calling itself Tlailotlacan after its first settlers. And so it is for the other pueblos ('tlaxilacalli') named Tlailotlacan within the pueblos ('altepetl')."[40]

Though illustrative of the widespread replication of tlaxilacalli across Acolhuacan, Ixtlilxochitl's narration also belies some of the patent issues with many sources, especially the conflation of Spanish terms such as "pueblos" (tlaxilacalli) and "pueblos" (altepetl). Context demands a separation, but on another level Ixtlilxochitl's analysis makes sense: both tlaxilacalli and altepetl were definable human communities, and their relationships were often stable. Only the former, however, infiltrated the latter.

As noted, the imprecision of Spanish terms for tlaxilacalli and other important institutions has deterred the systematic study of these local communities. As in the Ixtlilxochitl quote immediately above, context can often lead to a definitive answer, but the overlap remains considerable (table 0.1). Note, for example, that pueblo can denote anything between a tlaxilacalli and a huei altepetl.

Despite the multitude of terms listed in table 0.1, the problem of Spanish imprecision can be solved through close attention to proper names. Indeed, the repetition of such names—that is, their projection across various altepetl—anchored the regional scheme of tlaxilacalli; and each word carried a specific, individual weight.[41] Although certain details varied between one altepetl and another, patterns did form: names could denote religious devotion (Huitznahuac to Tezcatlipoca, Chimalpan to Huitzilopochtli),[42] economic specialization (administrators and communication specialists in Tlailotlacan,[43] merchants in Acxotlan), or migratory processes (the Mexica in Mexicapan, Zapoteca in Zapotlan). They could reference founding mythologies, as in the case of the migrations of Tlacochcalco and others from the seven caves of Chicomoztoc, or specific imperial histories, as in the prestige given to Oztoticpac as the site of the Acolhua ruler

TABLE 0.1. Spanish cognates of Nahua institutions

Local Institution	Cognate; Molina 1571[a] Definition	Terms Gleaned from Other Molina Entries	Terms in Other Relevant Sources
huei altepetl	ciudad	ciudad	ciudad, provincia, reino, nación, pueblo
altepetl	pueblo, o rey	pueblo, cabecera, villa, cuidad, común, lo público o real	ciudad, pueblo, villa, cabecera, provincia, nación, gente
tlayacatl	—	barrio	parcialidad, sección, barrio
tlaxilacalli, calpolli	barrio	barrio, collación, cuadrilla	pueblo, barrio, villa, paraje, sujeto, gente, nación, estancia
altepemaitl[b]	aldea, o aldeano; comarca de pueblo	—	paraje, pago, sujeto, estancia, barrio
calli	casa	casa, familia	casa

[a] Definitions come from both the Nahuatl and Spanish sides of Molina's *Vocabulario*.
[b] On the metaphysical meanings of altepemaitl, "hand of the altepetl," see Jerome A. Offner, "Aztec Political Numerology and Human Sacrifice: The Ideological Ramifications of the Number Six," *Journal of Latin American Lore* 6, no. 2 (1980): 212. For the semantic inter-penetration of the "hand of the altepetl" between Nahuatl and Hñähñu, see David Charles Wright Carr, "La sociedad prehispánica en las lenguas náhuatl y otomí," *Acta Universitaria* 18 (2008): 17. The Hñähñu term is *may'ehnini*, "the place of the hand of the polity."

Nezahualcoyotl's outlying palace complex. Table 0.2 provides a brief schematic of some of these canonical names. It is by no means definitive, only listing tlaxilacalli names that repeated more than three times a basic bibliography of central Mexican spatial history.

Precisely because of this intense, face-to-face orientation, tlaxilacalli anchored local identity with an insistence lost to the altepetl. The jaggedly sovereign specificity of each altepetl demanded a unique name, while the intense collective identification of every tlaxilacalli produced shared cultural traits across wider regions. The Yopico tlaxilacalli, for example, structured collective life around its patron deity, Xipe Totec (figure 0.7). "Our Lord the Flayed One," also denominated Yopi, guided this tlaxilacalli's mythic exit from Chicomoztoc and, as mentioned above, Yopico (together with its neighbor Tlalcocomoco, site of Xipe's main pyramid) bore responsibility for this numen's cult in Mexico-Tenochtitlan. Its priests dressed themselves with his distinctive insignia, wearing the conical Yopi hat, carrying the Yopi shield, and even using special Yopi tortillas for ritual practice. Finally, because of the deity's connection to fire and change, this tlaxilacalli also specialized in the transformative arts of gold- and silver-smithing. Given these distinctive signs and practices, it is not surprising that Yopico would also be seen as ethnically distinct

TABLE 0.2. Common tlaxilacalli names in central Mexico

Tlaxilacalli Name	History, Functions, Affiliations (partial list)	Altepetl Where Active (partial list)	Glyph
Acxotlan	Merchants; Quetzalcoatl	Huexotla, Mexico-Tenochtitlan, Tlatelolco, Chalco, Coyoacan, Tlaxcala	
Chimalpan	Migrants from Mixteca; likely provided Tetzcoco's head priest (cihuacoatl), Huitzilopochtli	Tetzcoco, Tepetlaoztoc, Coatlinchan, Chalco, Tlalmanalco, Tlacopan	
Cihuatecpan	Mythic origin in Chicomoztoc; women's organizations; Coatlicue	Tetzcoco, Otumba, Coatlinchan, Mexico-Tenocthtitlan, Tacubaya	
Culhuacan	Mythic origin in Chicomoztoc; Mexica migrants; also the name of an important altepetl	Tetzcoco, Tepetlaoztoc, Coatlinchan	
Huitznahuac	Mythic origin in Chicomoztoc; religious specialists; often associated with the south; Tezcatlipoca/Huitzilopochtli	Tetzcoco, Tepetlaoztoc, Mexico-Tenochtitlan, Tlatelolco	
Mexicapan	Mexica migrants; Huitzilopochtli	Tetzcoco, Huexotla, Coatlinchan, Tizayuca, Ozumba, Azcapotzalco	
Oztoticpac	Early settlement around Tetzcoco; site of imperial palace in Tetzcoco	Tetzcoco, Otumba, Teotihuacan	
Pochtlan	Long-distant traders; Yacateuctli	Mexico-Tenochtitlan, Tlatelolco, Azcapotzalco, Tepozotlan, Ozumba	

continued on next page

TABLE 0.2.—*continued*

Tlaxilacalli Name	History, Functions, Affiliations (partial list)	Altepetl Where Active (partial list)	Glyph
Tepanecapan	Affiliated with Tepaneca power: Azcapotzcalco, then Tlacopan	Tetzcoco, Coatlinchan, Tlacopan, Azcapotzalco, Culhuacan	
Tetzcacohuac	Migrants from mythic Aztlan; magnet school (calmecac)	Mexico-Tenochtitlan, Ecatepec, Itztapalapa, Colhuacan, Chalco, Tacubaya	
Tlacochcalco	Mythic origin in Chicomoztoc; armory	Mexico-Tenochtitlan, Tlaxcala, Ozumba	
Tlailotlacan	Migrants from Mixteca; administrators and communication specialists	Tetzcoco, Teotihuacan, Huexotla, Acolman, Chalco, Ozumba	
Yopico	Mythic origin in Chicomoztoc; goldsmiths; Xipe Totec	Mexico-Tenochtitlan, Tepetlaoztoc, Azcapotzalco, Chiconautla	
Zapotlan	Zapoteca; Xipe Totec; also the name of an altepetl	Mexico-Tenochtitlan, Chalco, Tulancingo	

Sources: Schroeder, *Chimalpahin and the Kingdoms*; Horn, *Postconquest Coyoacan*; Hicks, "Tetzcoco in the Early 16th Century"; Mundy, *Death of Aztec Tenochtitlan*; Codex Xolotl; *Mapa de Coatlinchan*; Memorial de los Indios de Tepetlaoztoc; *Tlachia* website (http://tlachia.iib.unam.mx/); Amoxcalli website (http://amoxcalli.org.mx/); Tetlacuilolli website (http://www.tetlacuilolli.org.mx); Peñafiel, *Nomenclatura geográfica de México*, vol. 2; González y González, *Xipe Totec*; Codex Mendoza; Códice de los Señores de San Lorenzo Axotlan.

from other nearby communities—separate, as all tlaxilacalli were, from their neighbors by specific patterns of lived collective experience.[44]

AGENCY AND ACTION

From the very start, the productive local ethnicity of many tlaxilacalli posed significant challenges to consolidating imperial rule. During the Aztec period, a

FIGURE 0.7. Feast of Xipe Totec in Yopico. Florentine Codex, vol. 1, book 2, f. 20. Florence, Biblioteca Medicea Laurenziana, Med. Palat. 218, c. 204v. *Courtesy*, Ministry for Heritage and Cultural Activities; further reproduction by any means is forbidden.

significant responsibility of upper administration in Mexico-Tenochtitlan consisted simply of managing inter-communal relationships, in making sure that each tlaxilacalli—or, as the capital populations grew, at least that each bundle of tlaxilacalli, each *tlayacatl*—was properly represented in major functions.[45] Each tlaxilacalli bundle had its own separate ritual sections in the main ceremonial complex of Mexico-Tenochtitlan's Templo Mayor; each bundle sent special judges to the main councils of law and war; each tlayacatl had its own warrior divisions that were sent into battle with separate uniforms and insignia; each celebrated its own particular victories with ritual feasts, where only symbolic remains were sent to the ruling center. Aztec rulers also convened imperial councils of both law and war with named representatives from various tlaxilacalli: the Codex Mendoza includes one such tribunal from the tlayacatl of Moyotlan, where four tlaxilacalli judges (called *alcaldes* in the accompanying Spanish text) resolve disputes (see figure 0.6).[46]

Every altepetl, therefore, carried within itself seeds of unfamiliarity and difference, in the multitudinous and diverse tlaxilacalli. This difference could be overt, as during the provocative and exclusionary celebrations staged by the long-distance merchants based in Pochtlan and various other trade-based tlaxilacalli such as Atlauhco and Tzonmolco, or covert, as when Nezahualcoyotl holed up in Tetzcoco's Poyauhtlan tlaxilacalli as a young fugitive. During the Hispanic period, tlaxilacalli bundles also anchored oppositional political movements. In early Hispanic Mexico City, for instance, the tlayacatl of Santa María Cuepopan—center of the altepetl's Hñähñu (Otomí) ethnic minority—staged a massive revolt in 1569 to repulse external meddling by the Archbishop Montúfar in local religious affairs. In their unruly diversity, tlaxilacalli structured both order and division in central Mexico.[47]

Recent scholarship from across Mesoamerica has worked to come to terms with the fractious patterning of regional politics for various periods and situations. In certain key contexts and regions, a strict focus on the actions of the upper elite has broadened to consider the significant power wielded by commoners, who successfully pressed for important public goods such as monumental building, the bureaucratization of financial and legal structures, and the promotion of non-elites within imperial hierarchies.[48] Rural commoners also maintained status vis-à-vis their urban counterparts, accessing the same domestic goods as other tributaries residing closer to the seats of imperial administration.[49]

This is not to say that elite politics were inconsequential; far from it. Indeed, the main contribution of recent theories of collective action lies in the dynamic interactions they posit between relatively stable elite cores and the assertive peripheries swarming around these centers. Up until now, these peripheries have mostly been understood in relation to their respective centers, and one of the aims of the present book is to provide a greater feel for the internal workings of "peripheral" tlaxilacalli, both independent of a referent altepetl and in relation to it.

For central Mexico, tlaxilacalli are key to understanding both collective action and imperial politics over centuries. Because of their robust constitutions, their diversity, and their changeable political rank, tlaxilacalli both anchored and metabolized nearly every imperial project in central Mexico between the thirteenth and seventeenth centuries, while simultaneously churning commoners through their own internal hierarchies. One episode from the early evangelization of Mexico is particularly illustrative of the improvisational power of local tlaxilacalli. The relation comes from fray Diego Durán and is also instructive for its offhanded conflation of tlaxilacalli and neighborhood:

> A very honored padre, zealous in the honor of God and doctrine, with whom I lived and in whose company I served, ordered that a cross be placed in all the neighborhoods ("tlaxilacalli") so that people could go there to say doctrine. All of the neighborhoods placed their crosses except for one, which, as a more devoted people, wanted to press an advantage. They asked to be given license to build a chapel (*hermita*). It was granted and also ordered that the name of the [patron] saint [of the chapel] be either St. Pablo or St. Agustín. They (the tlaxilacalli spokespeople) said they would talk it over.
>
> After fifteen days, they came back and said that they didn't want either St. Pablo or St. Agustín; and, when asked which saint they wanted, they said St. Lucas. I, noticing the pleading and insistence with which they made their request, warned that there might be some evil afoot. I went to the calendar of their [Mesoamerican] idols and saw which feast and sign was the one where St. Lucas's day fell. Knowing this, I went to the leader (*mandoncillo*) of that neighborhood and asked him what his name was and he told me Juan. I begged him to tell me the name he had from the old law, [given according to] the day he was born. He said *Calli*, which means house, and I saw clearly and manifestly that they requested St. Lucas's day because it falls on the day and sign of the house. Even more, two days before is one of the great solemn feasts they had. Rebuking his duplicity and bad intentions in this way, I told him that that superstition was what was moving him and not the mortification of the cross He (Christ) carried when he lived or the great devotion you have for Him.[50]

As is often the case with such sources, Durán's relation obscures key details, but its procedural description of local agency compels attention. The Dominican friar describes tlaxilacalli as a key to early evangelization across a wide spatial and political plane, simultaneously highlighting both rapid compliance and assertive improvisation. Improvisation operated across two levels, both within "St. Lucas" tlaxilacalli and outward toward the evangelizing friars, with the mandoncillo Juan Calli mediating each. Although Durán presents this episode as a victory of missionary vigilance, in another light "St. Lucas" tlaxilacalli achieved its primary goal, that of building a chapel instead of a cross. Although names and feast schedules changed, these seem to have been secondary concerns to the tlaxilacalli, as evidenced by the two-week delay in answering the friars' questions on these topics. Had name or date been a primary concern, "St. Lucas" would have included them in its initial proposal for the chapel.

Here, then, is something of a model of tlaxilacalli interaction with foreign powers (and, by definition, every outside power—from dynastic local ruler to missionary friar—was a foreign power): to begin, tlaxilacalli acted as institutional givens, preexisting even if they were not planted in a given territory. Second, one side or the other (usually, but not always, the centralizing foreign power) demanded action. Tlaxilacalli then coordinated within and among themselves, usually within a cooperative and autonomous framework. The polities then took action, but almost always according to tlaxilacalli processes and schedules, producing significant divergences from the initial foreign demand. Both sides would then debate the meaning and details of the executed action, inventing precedents for future work. This system could also stretch and fray, particularly during periods of crisis or when competing foreign powers fought among themselves for tlaxilacalli allegiance.[51]

Following the shifting interactions between political centers and tlaxilacalli peripheries, this book offers a new periodization of local politics for the Basin of Mexico, based in the core northeastern region of Acolhuacan. A disjunctive break is almost always marked between the Aztec and Spanish periods, for reasons self-evident from an imperial perspective. Local administration, however, retained its logic even as other institutions hemorrhaged. Across multiple centuries, tlaxilacalli built separate arrangements with centralizing powers, kept archives of these proceedings, and then took legal or direct action when these arrangements were infringed—even across the watershed of Spanish and Tlaxcalteca invasion. What emerges is an entire cycle of localized colonial administration—felt from the multitudinous periphery, not the mediating center. The cycle begins with the implementation of tlaxilacalli regimes around the Mesoamerican year One Flint (1272 CE)[52] and continues through the redefinition of these local communities after the population rebound of the mid-seventeenth century.[53]

TRADITIONS AND SCHOLARS

Pueblos within Pueblos culminates a decade of research into the local articulation of imperial politics in Acolhuacan, the most eastern of the three realms constituting the Aztec Triple Alliance. Like all parties to this alliance, Acolhuacan predated the Aztec empire—solidifying through warfare, political marriage, and tlaxilacalli-based colonization regimes for over 150 years before adding its stitches in the years 1426–28 to the patchwork quilt of the emerging Aztec empire.[54]

But even after this imperial pact, Acolhuacan asserted its distinctiveness. Unlike the upswept topknot of Mexica warriors and rulers, Acolhua soldiers and administrators customarily kept their hair loose—tied at the forehead by a broad white band (see figure 0.8).[55] The Acolhua spoke with a different accent and produced different kinds of documents.[56] They passed separate laws and restricted Mexica consumer goods in their markets (ceramics, for example; figure 0.9). As both imperial

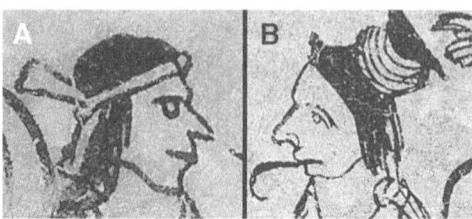

FIGURE 0.8. Acolhua and Mexica men's hairstyles. Códice de Xicotepec. *Courtesy*, Claude Stresser-Péan.

administrators and tlaxilacalli-bound commoners—and, quite often in these commoner-on-commoner hierarchies, as both—the Acolhua remained askance of Mexico-Tenochtitlan.[57]

Despite this marked distinctiveness, *Pueblos within Pueblos* asserts broad comparisons for both the Aztec and Spanish empires in central Mexico, comparisons deriving precisely from the exactitude and rigor of Acolhua information traditions. Acolhua documents allow for the most complete reckoning of tlaxilacalli and their imperial, colonizing politics in northern Mesoamerica. Extant sources from other Mexican regions are almost as good—indeed, much of the advantage of Acolhua information specialists could simply derive from a greater documentary survival rate in the eastern backlands—but extant Acolhua documents still set a gold standard in stitching together demographic, political, economic, agricultural, and territorial information.

Even given these substantial strengths, other aspects of the Acolhua documentary record require further comment. Most pointedly, many of the arguments in this book (particularly those relating to pre-Hispanic eras) rely on documents created under Hispanic patronage, protection, or toleration. Although this context produced patent distortions—distortions that compounded as the documented events passed farther and farther into the distant past—recent scholarship has begun to create a systematic analytical framework for these early Hispanic sources, making them much more accessible for sustained historical research. Scholars have shown certain standardized patterns to Hispanic-era distortions and also illuminated the wider social, political, and intellectual climate in which such documents were produced. They have elaborated the conventions of various early Hispanic genres and cataloged the wider clutches of meaning evoked by once-cryptic symbols and phrases. Further, they have even been able to show the historical development of genre and writing conventions, allowing for change over considerable lengths of time—even allowing for the disruptions of war and colonial rule.[58]

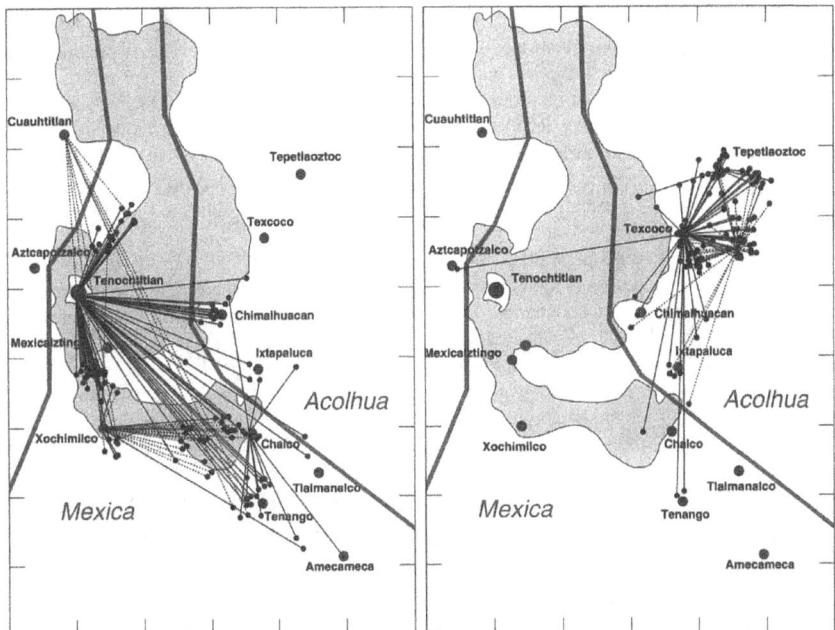

FIGURE 0.9. Separate ceramics markets of the Aztec empire. Minc, "Style and Substance," 363.

Tetzcoca archives burned at least twice during and after the fifteenth-century war for central Mexico. Even before the fall of Mexico-Tenochtitlan, invading Tlaxcalteca forces attacked imperial archives at the palace complex in the Tzillan (or Cillan) tlaxilacalli (sometimes also called Ahuehuetitlan, now known as Los Melones) of Tetzcoco. Some time later, local nobles struck at their own personal collections in fear of religious or political persecution. Decades after these purges the loss still ached, as attested by the early Hispanic historiographer of Tetzcoco Juan Bautista de Pomar:

> They (Tetzcoca) lack the paintings in which they had their histories because when the Marqués del Valle, don Hernán Cortés, and the other conquistadors first entered it (Tetzcoco) sixty four years ago, more or less, they burned them in the royal houses of Nezahualpilli, in a great building that was the general archive of their papers, where all the antiquities were painted. Today, his descendants lament this with great feeling because they were left in darkness, without news or memory of the doings of their ancestors. And those (documents) that had remained in the hands of some principals—some relating to one thing, others to another—(the principals) burned them

out of fear of don fray Juan de Zumárraga, the first archbishop of Mexico, in order to not be accused of idolatry.[59]

But traditions of Acolhua communication survived, even in the face of such systemic damage. Innumerable sources were surely lost, making recoverable history a suggestive patchwork quilt more than a lushly illustrated tapestry. Nevertheless, tlacuiloque and historiographers continued to mobilize canonical sources like the now-lost "Crónica X"[60] and the sources constituting the Codex Xolotl, joining them to robust traditions of oral memory and performance.[61] Pomar makes the same point, arguing that he had to "work harder to seek out and examine" remaining documentary sources, given the losses to imperial Acolhua archives.[62] Indeed, in this later period Acolhua scholars such as Pomar researched, re-imagined, and compiled sources that still shed considerable light on pre-Hispanic history. For the project at hand, the most important such compilations are the Codex Xolotl and a triplex of Tepetlaoztoc sources—the related codices Vergara and Asunción[63] (ca. 1543–44) and the Memorial de los Indios de Tepetlaoztoc (ca. 1554)—produced for an ongoing case against the early Spanish encomendero Gonzalo de Salazar and his son, Juan Velázquez de Salazar.[64]

Scholars as early as Juan Bautista de Pomar in the later sixteenth century have worried about the trustworthiness and validity of extant Tetzcoca sources. Pomar pleads with readers that "if anything seems missing or coming up short" in his history, they attribute this fault to his fragmentary documentary base and "not to a lack of diligence."[65] For Pomar and his contemporaries, however, these diligent efforts flowed through increasingly Hispanic forms and genres, though such forms still depended on local tlaxilacalli. In 1608, for example, the historian Ixtlilxochitl took great pains to verify his narrations with the leaders of seven separate tlaxilacalli in the altepetl of Otumba—Ahuatepec, Tizayuca, Aztaquemeca, Tlamapa, Tepayuca, Axoloayan, and Quatlacinco—all of whom pronounced his work "good and true."[66] Even for the most conservative documents, certain European demands and prohibitions occasionally made their influence felt. The deep stylistic traditionalism of the multivalent Codex Xolotl compendium, for example, expresses certain tendencies toward consolidation, as scribes in Tlailotlacan compiled documents from their archives to face the challenges of the early decades of Spanish rule. Many pre-Hispanic aspects of this and other documents are recoverable, but only in the proper comparative context.[67]

Much like their Hispanic-era scholarly forbears, modern historians have also struggled to assess the veracity of available sources.[68] However, as mentioned earlier, a comparative critical methodology is taking shape. For the specific case of Acolhuacan, scholars such as Patrick Lesbre, Jongsoo Lee, Eduardo de J. Douglas, and Jerome Offner have worked to peel away the distorting layers of Mexica and European influence from Tetzcoca sources, laying bare tentative filaments of early Acolhua historiographical conventions. Others, including Elizabeth Hill Boone, Marc Thouvenot, Gordon Whittaker, Justyna Olko, and Charles Dibble, have laid bare Aztec glyphic and discursive conventions. Still others, particularly Barbara Williams and her various collaborators, have proved the scientific validity of Acolhua information traditions in such fields as mathematics, land surveying, and agronomy. Finally and perhaps most foundationally, increasing collaboration with local historians and experts from the places studied has led to the "ground truthing" of many important documents, placing them at last in their wider spatial context.[69]

All of these practices—local fieldwork, interdisciplinary collaboration, insistent archival research, and critical textual analysis of both alphabetic and image-based communication—undergirds the project at hand. Although sources remain imperfect, they can say much more than they are sometimes given credit for. After the patterned distortions in these documents are accounted for, after they are placed in a wider comparative context and anchored to precise physical forms on the landscape, they become invaluable sources for early Acolhua history. Indeed, particularly for the early period, Acolhua sources are often more reliable than Spanish ones: where the latter speak in vague land measurements such as *fanegas* (the amount of land necessary to plant a certain volume of crop, also called a fanega), the former mark measurements down to the hand span (*matl*), also noting soil type and quality. Context is key, however: because of the complex processes of their formation and use, early Acolhua documents demand vigilant comparison and criticism. They are peerless, but they are also rarely, if ever, sufficient on their own.

CHAPTER OUTLINE AND SUMMARY

The six chapters in this book trace the history of Acolhua tlaxilacalli over time, beginning with their implantation along the northeastern edge of the Basin of Mexico in the thirteenth century and continuing forward through their transformation into bastions of community politics in the sixteenth and seventeenth centuries. They describe the ways a particular pattern of local colonization became a core community institution and how that institution (more successfully than most) responded to warfare and imperialism. *Pueblos within Pueblos* shows how local communities built empires and also how they shattered them.

Chapter 1 shows how tlaxilacalli regimes formed the bedrock of the early Acolhua empire, describing the functioning of each rung of these colonizing hierarchies in detail. It sheds new light on the internal workings of these systems, describing the strong economic and cultural forces, acting across centuries, that pulled agricultural commoners into such arrangements.

Chapter 2 sets this analytical framework in motion, describing the fights to establish the Aztec Triple Alliance and characterizing the powerful tlaxilacalli-based tension at the heart of this empire: local autonomy versus imperial investment. This chapter puts both tlaxilacalli and empire to the test and shows the former stronger than the latter. It briefly recapitulates the foreign (Spanish, Tlaxcalteca, and allies) invasion of the Aztec empire and the demographic and ecological disjunctures this irruption unleashed, the latter of which jostled the spatial array of tlaxilacalli across the Acolhua landscape. More than this, however, it highlights a recurring pattern of central Mexican imperialism, through which Acolhua tlaxilacalli regrouped to support the invading forces of Hernán Cortés and his many allies, in ways strikingly similar to the rapid additive rise of the Aztec empire a century before.[70]

Chapter 3 analyzes one particular tlaxilacalli, Cuauhtepoztlan in the altepetl of Tepetlaoztoc, from the ground up. Beginning with the commoner household or *calli*, it then interrogates the subsequent administrative levels of *tepixque* (people minders), *topileque* (staff holders), and *calpixque* (tlaxilacalli managers), delving deep into the politics and functioning of this hierarchical community. Tlaxilacalli officials administered both ongoing hunger and consistent surplus toward wider political ends. This chapter also shows the ways in which Cuauhtepoztlan reinforced the affective bonds of community, particularly through spatial and religious practice.

Chapter 4 follows with the spatial and metaphysical redefinition of tlaxilacalli in the aftermath of foreign invasion. It shows commoners turning to local tlaxilacalli in times of extreme need and investing them with renewed spiritual and collective power in early Catholic New Spain. This contrasts with the progressive disinvestment of the local nobility in these institutions, which, as shown in chapter 5, placed revitalized tlaxilacalli at the very core of commoner politics by the end of the sixteenth century. Chapter 6 carries this sea change to its seventeenth-century close, showing how these once-imperial institutions came to serve as the primary locus of autonomist and even anti-colonial commoner politics, a politics now so distant from centralizing power that it became nearly invisible to Spanish administrators. The transformation from imperial colonization to unequal community was now complete.

To summarize the main claims of this book: tlaxilacalli were commoner-administered communities that predated and then co-evolved with the Acolhua (later, Aztec) empire and structured its articulation and basic functioning. They were the administrative backbone of both the Aztec and Spanish empires in northern Mesoamerica and often grew into full and functioning existence before their affiliated altepetl. They resembled other central Mexican polities but expressed a local Acolhua administrative culture in their exacting patterns of hierarchy. As semiautonomous units, they could rearrange according to geopolitical shifts and even catalyze changes, as during the additive growth of both the Aztec Triple Alliance and Hispanic New Spain. They were more successful than almost any other central Mexican institution in metabolizing external disruptions (new gods, new economies, demographic emergencies), and they fostered a surprising level of local allegiance despite their structural inequality. Indeed, by the end of the periods covered in this book, they were declaring their local administrative independence from the once-sovereign altepetl. Administration through community and community through administration—this was the primal two-step of the long-lived Acolhua tlaxilacalli, at once colonial and colonialist.

NOTES

1. Classical Nahuatl does not distinguish between singular and plural for inanimate nouns like tlaxilacalli. See, for example, Michel Launey, *An Introduction to Classical Nahuatl*, ed. and trans. Christopher Mckay (Cambridge: Cambridge University Press, 2011), 21.

2. Scholars have been working for decades on the etymology of "tlaxilacalli," but no solution has yet been found. Because of the opacity of this term, some have preferred to refer to the autonomous local communities of the Aztec empire as "calpolli," a partial cognate for "tlaxilacalli" with a cleaner Nahuatl derivation. Despite such historiographical and etymological advantages, this book uses "tlaxilacalli" for two reasons. First, as will be seen later in these notes, "calpolli" and "tlaxilacalli" did not always mean the same thing despite significant semantic overlap. In addition, "tlaxilacalli" appears much more frequently in the relevant sources and has even achieved something approaching parity in scholarly usage. For example, even though James Lockhart follows scholarly convention of the time and uses the term *calpolli* in his monumental *The Nahuas after the Conquest: A Social and Cultural History of the Indians of Central Mexico, Sixteenth through Eighteenth Centuries* (Stanford: Stanford University Press, 1992), he notes that "the word calpolli itself is much less common than tlaxilacalli" (16). Nevertheless, in very particular situations—most frequently, when referring to secondary literature that prefers the term *calpolli*—this book on occasion continues the scholarly practice of conflating tlaxilacalli and calpolli.

3. In addition to tlaxilacalli, other terms also demand definitions at this early juncture: *central Mexico*, *Aztec*, *Mexica*, *Spanish*, and *Hispanic*. *Central Mexico* is a generic term for northern Mesoamerica, roughly bounded by Oaxaca, Michoacan, La Gran Chichimeca, and the Atlantic Ocean. It references neither the imperial capital of Mexico-Tenochtitlan nor the modern nation-state of Estados Unidos Mexicanos. *Aztec* is another particular term, for it only references the centralizing imperial power emanating out of Mexico-Tenochtitlan. This shopworn but effective term is preferable to other, more fashionable terms like *Mexica* or *Tenochca* precisely because of its artificial, and therefore non-ethnic, connotations: the

realm of Aztec Acolhuacan makes more analytical sense than Mexica Acolhuacan, of misleading and ambiguous ethnic affiliation. *Mexica* here refers to the ethnic group emanating from Mexico-Tenochtitlan. *Spanish* and *Hispanic* are two related but distinct terms. The former suggests a stronger connection to Spain, its people, and its administration than the latter, which evokes the local, central Mexican transformations.

4. As recent "New Conquest" historiography has vigorously argued, facile generalizations are impossible for the interlacing wars of sixteenth-century Mesoamerica, which were fought by many sides. Nevertheless, the rapidity of the Aztecs' two-year fall (1519–21) remains a significant outlier. For comparison, the neighboring Purépecha state retained administrative independence for seven years after initial invasion (1522–29), followed by decades of guerrilla warfare. Western Yucatán took a full twenty years for various invading powers to subdue (1527–47), and the Inkas of Tawantinsuyu required forty years (1532–72). Among many other works, a brief introduction to the broad "New Conquest" historiography could begin with Matthew Restall, *Seven Myths of the Spanish Conquest* (Oxford: Oxford University Press, 2003); Susan Schroeder and David Cahill, eds., *The Conquest All Over Again: Nahuas and Zapotecs Thinking, Writing, and Painting Spanish Colonialism* (Sussex: Sussex Academic Press, 2009); along with Restall's review article, "The New Conquest History" *History Compass* 10, no. 2 (February 2012): 151–60.

5. As will be seen in this introduction and throughout the book, tlaxilacalli were quite different from neighborhoods or Spanish barrios. As with the rare equivalence of "altepetl" and the Spanish "ciudad" in Nahuatl documentation, on exceptional occasions relevant sources do conflate "tlaxilacalli" and "barrio." The earliest known example is from 1551, "yn tlacilacal bario Tlamimilolpa," in Teresa Rojas Rabiela, Elsa Leticia Rea López, and Constantino Medina Lima, eds., *Vidas y bienes olvidados: Testamentos indígenas novohispanos* (Mexico City: CIESAS, 1999), 2:92–93. Despite this single early citation, nearly all other mentions come from the later seventeenth century or afterward, as in the repeated switching between "we tlaxilacalli residents" (titlaxilacaleque) and "we barrio people" (tibarrio tlaca) in a 1691 document from Cuauhtepoztlan tlaxilacalli, Tepetlaoztoc. AGN, Tierras, vol. 1610, exp. 3, f. 10r.

As argued later in this book, an entire cycle of tlaxilacalli practice was nearing its end by the 1660s. Among other things, this occasioned a certain improvisational uptick in political terminology: "altepetl" ~"ciudad," "tlaxilacalli" ~"barrio," and the occasional use of such terms as "huicalli" (sujeto, "subject town"—cf. private collection. A digital copy is held in the Archivo del Diócesis de Texcoco. It also appears in Benjamin Daniel Johnson, trans., *Documentos nahuas de Tezcoco* [hereafter DNT], vol. 1, ed. Javier Eduardo Ramírez López [Texcoco, Mexico: Diócesis de Texcoco A.R., 2017], doc. 33) fit into this pattern. At least in Acolhua sources, these trends never became prominent and indeed are so faint that they only appear when dealing with a large and diverse documentary base.

6. Cf. Jerome Offner, *Law and Politics in Aztec Texcoco* (Cambridge: Cambridge University Press, 1983), 284.

7. For the 1624 uprising, see Gibran I.I. Bautista y Lugo, "Los indios y la rebelión de 1624 en la Ciudad de México," in *Los indios y las ciudades de Nueva España*, ed. Felipe Castro Gutiérrez (Mexico City: UNAM, 2013), 197–216; for 1692, see Natalia Silva Prada, *La política de una rebelión: los indígenas frente al tumulto de 1692 en la Ciudad de México* (Mexico City: Colegio de México, 2007), especially 602–4, 613. Following common historiographical conventions, both Bautista y Lugo and Silva Prada use the word *barrio* to describe tlaxilacalli. The regions of Guerrero and Tlaxcala also burned around the same time as the 1692 Mexico City uprising.

8. One such change was the inability of the ten viceroys who succeeded the Marquis of Gelves (deposed in 1624) to restore "order" to the regional administration of New Spain. On the weakness of viceroys in seventeenth-century New Spain, see Jonathan I. Israel, *Race, Class, and Politics in Colonial Mexico, 1610–1670* (Oxford: Oxford University Press, 1975). Earlier scholarship, including Israel, explained viceregal instability through a wider "Decline of Spain" thesis, but John Tutino (*Making a New World: Founding Capitalism in the Bajío and Spanish North America* [Durham: Duke University Press, 2011]) forcibly decouples New Spain from economic reversals in Europe.

Another important outcome of the political crisis of 1624 was the inability of central administration to maintain Mexico City's systems of water management, leading to the catastrophic and transformative flood of 1629. On this flood and its aftermath, see Vera Candiani, *Dreaming of Dry Land: Environmental Transformation in Colonial Mexico City* (Stanford: Stanford University Press, 2014).

9. There were certainly more commoner groups beyond the tlaxilacalli. Afro-Mexicans and mestizo groups, for example, faced many of the same issues as tlaxilacalli. See, for example, R. Douglas Cope, *The Limits of Racial Domination: Plebeian Society in Colonial Mexico City, 1660–1720* (Madison: University of Wisconsin Press, 1994). It is also likely that Afro-Mexicans and mestizo groups participated in indigenous central Mexican society to a greater extent than usually imagined, as was the case in both Guerrero and Yucatán. See, for example, Andrew Bryan Fisher, "Worlds in Flux, Identities in Motion: A History of the Tierra Caliente of Guerrero, Mexico, 1521–1821" (PhD dissertation, University of California, San Diego, 2002); Ben Vinson III and Matthew Restall, eds., *Black Mexico: Race and Society from Colonial to Modern Times* (Albuquerque: University of New Mexico Press, 2009); Matthew Restall, *The Black Middle: Africans, Mayas, and Spaniards in Colonial Yucatan* (Stanford: Stanford University Press, 2009).

10. In recent years, scholars have turned to tlaxilacalli with increased attention, particularly to anchor their documentary analyses. The best of these works deal extensively with tlaxilacalli and even model their spatial array in wider altepetl. See Rebecca Horn, *Postconquest Coyoacan: Nahua-Spanish Relations in Central Mexico, 1519–1650* (Stanford: Stanford University Press, 1997); Barbara E. Mundy, *The Death of Aztec Tenochtitlan, the Life of Mexico City* (Austin: University of Texas Press, 2015). Another important collection of

work makes tlaxilacalli central to the explanatory arguments. See Luis Fernando Granados, "*Calpultin* decimonónicos: Aspectos nahuas de la cultura política de la ciudad de México," in *Actores, espacios y debates en la historia de la esfera pública en la ciudad de México*, ed. Cristina Sacristán and Pablo Piccato (Mexico City: Instituto Mora, 2005), 41–66; Ángel Julián García Zambrano, "Zahuatlan el Viejo y Zahuatlan el nuevo: Trasuntos del poblamiento y la geografía sagrada del altepetl de Yecapixtla," in *Territorialidad y paisaje en el altepetl del siglo XVI*, ed. Frederico Fernández Christlieb and Ángel Julián García Zambrano (Mexico City: FCE, 2006), 422–78; Camilla Townsend, "Glimpsing Native American Historiography: The Cellular Principle in Sixteenth-Century Nahuatl Annals," *Ethnohistory* 56, no. 4 (2009): 625–50. Susan Schroeder's *Chimalpahin and the Kingdoms of Chalco* (Tucson: University of Arizona Press, 1991) also bears mention here: although it deals much more extensively with sub-altepetl "kingdoms" or *tlayacatl* (an administrative layer one rung up from tlaxilacalli, only found in the largest altepetl), its early attention to causal explanations below the altepetl level makes it an obligatory reference. *Pueblos within Pueblos* broadens and deepens this work, harnessing the detailed specificity of Horn and Mundy to the explanatory power of Granados, García Zambrano, Townsend, and Schroeder to create a tlaxilacalli-focused causal engine, firmly anchored to a wide documentary base.

11. Both documents were explicitly produced at the tlaxilacalli level. For specific mention of tlaxilacalli, see Códice de Santa María Asunción (hereafter Codex Asunción), Biblioteca Nacional de México, Sala de Libros Raros, Ms. 1497bis, f. 11v. See also Document cadastral ou Codex Vergara, Bibliothèque nationale de France, Département des Manuscrits, Mexicain (hereafter BnF-MM), 37–39. Both of these documents have been recently published in excellent scholarly editions: Barbara J. Williams and H. R. Harvey, eds., *The Códice de Santa María Asunción: Facsimile and Commentary: Households and Lands in Sixteenth-Century Tepetlaoztoc* (Salt Lake City: University of Utah Press, 1997); Barbara J. Williams and Frederic Hicks, eds., *El códice Vergara: Edición facsimilar con comentario* (Mexico City: UNAM, 2011).

12. Chapter 2 of this book outlines a methodology for connecting specific individuals to precise landforms. Other important close-in work on Aztec cadastral sources includes Eike Hinz, Claudine Hartau, and Marie-Louise Heimann-Koenen, eds., *Aztekizcher Zensus: Zuer indianischen Wirtschaft und Gessellschaft im Marquesado um 1540: Aus dem "Libro de Tributos" (Col. Ant. Ms. 551) im Archivo Histórico, Mexico*, 2 vols. (Hanover, Germany: Verlag für Ethnologie, 1983); Sarah L. Cline, *The Book of Tributes: Early Sixteenth-Century Nahuatl Censuses from Morelos* (Los Angeles: UCLA Latin American Center, 1993); Michael E. Smith, "Houses and the Settlement Hierarchy in Late Postclassic Morelos," in *Prehispanic Domestic Units in Western Mesoamerica*, ed. Robert S. Stanley and Kenneth G. Hirth (Boca Raton, FL: CRC Press, 1993), 191–206; Thomas M. Whitmore and Barbara J. Williams, "Famine Vulnerability in the Contact-Era Basin of Mexico: A Simulation," *Ancient Mesoamerica* 9, no. 1 (1998): 83–98; Mariano Cando Morales, *Tepetlaoxtoc: Monografía municipal* (Toluca: Gobierno del Estado de México, 1999).

Williams and Hicks, in their edition of the *Códice Vergara* (pp. 68–71), give a reconstruction of the sub-district (*altepemaitl*) of Calla Tlaxoxiuhco in Chimalpan tlaxilacalli (Tepetlaoztoc altepetl), but they only site one individual in this array: the noble Pedro Tecihuauh de Castilla.

13. "2 calli ypan inyn xihuitl quimiquanique yn mexitin ynic oncan motlallico tlacocomocco yn tencopa yn colhuaque yquac tlatocati yn tziuhtecatzin colhuacan ... 8 tochtli ypan xihuitl ompeuh yn oncan mexico tenochtitlan çan oc quequezquitetl xacalli quichiuhque yn mexiti ça nonohuian oncatca tolquauhtla yn motlallique." John Bierhorst, ed. and trans., *Codex Chimalpopoca: The Text in Nahuatl* (Tucson: University of Arizona Press, 1992), 26, 31.

Here and elsewhere my translations from Nahuatl differ from previous editions. On the founding influence of the Tlacocomolco and Yopico tlaxilacalli, see Carlos Javier González González, *Xipe Tótec: Guerra y regeneración del maíz en la religión mexica* (Mexico City: FCE, 2011), 96. The author specifically mentions these entities as "calpolli," the partial cognate for tlaxilacalli mentioned in note 2.

14. Codex Xolotl, BnF-MM, 1–10.

15. The "Tolteca" glyph in the Codex Xolotl designates polities and individuals using technologies not employed by Chichimeca, such as sedentary agriculture.

16. Codex Xolotl, f. 5. In his dissertation, Marc Thouvenot read these "house" glyphs as explicitly tlaxilacalli. See "Codex Xolotl: Étude d'une des composantes de son écriture: les glyphs: Dictionnaire des éléments constitutifs des glyphes" (PhD dissertation, EHESS, Paris, 1987), 660–70. However, in his newer *Tlachia* website (tlachia.lib.unam.mx, accessed November 11, 2016), he reads the glyphs as "calpolli." See, for example, his notations for codes X.050.F.08, X.050.F.10, and X.050.F.12.

17. Although earlier scholarly generations frequently criticized the work of Ixtlilxochitl, more systematic readings of both his errors and contributions have led to a recent re-valorization of his work. See in particular Amber Brian, *Alva Ixtlilxochitl's Native Archive and the Circulation of Knowledge in Colonial Mexico* (Nashville, TN: Vanderbilt University Press, 2016); Galen Brokaw and Jongsoo Lee, eds., *Fernando de Alva Ixtlilxochitl and His Legacy* (Tucson: University of Arizona Press, 2015)—especially the chapters by Gordon Whittaker ("The Identities of Fernando de Alva Ixtlilxochitl," 29–76) and Jerome A. Offner ("Ixtlilxochitl's Ethnographic Encounter: Understanding the Codex Xolotl and Its Depdendent Alphabetic Texts," 77–121).

18. "Era tan grande el amor que Techotlalatzin tenía a la nación tulteca, que no tan solamente les consintió vivir, y poblar entre los chichimecas, sino que también les dio facultad para hacer sacrificios públicos a sus ídolos y dedicar los templos, lo que no había consentido ni admitido su padre Quinatzin." Fernando de Alva Ixtlilxochitl, *Obras históricas*, 2 vols., ed. Alfredo Chavero (Mexico City: Editorial Nacional, 1952) 2:75.

19. Ixtlilxochitl also notes that these new tlaxilacalli introduced the cults of two important Aztec deities into Acolhuacan: Huitzilopochtli and Tlaloc.

20. "Auh y yehuatl yn inauatil y Uitzilopochtli cayatle uetzi . . . Auh y ye yuhqui amo mouelcaque, ye no yc peuh y yaoyotl. Ça ye nono oc conixtito conpeualtito yaoyotl Uiznauac tiachcauh Toueyo." Rafael Tena, ed. and trans., *Anales de Tlatelolco* (Mexico City: CONACULTA, 2004), 116.

21. *Tlacuiloque* were more than simply scribes because they were also experts in verbal and performance-based communication. See Katarzyna Mikulska, *Tejiendo destinos: Un acercamiento al sistema de comunicación gráfica en los códices adivinatorios* (Zinacantepec, Mexico: El Colegio Mexiquense, 2015).

22. For an example of local favoritism among tlaxilacalli tlacuiloque, see 8–9, this volume; .

23. The canonical 1571 bilingual dictionary of fray Alonso de Molina—*Vocabulario en lengua castellana y mexicana y mexicana y castellana*, ed. Miguel León-Portilla (Mexico City: Porrúa, 1977)—defines tlaxilacalli as "barrio" and altepetl as "pueblo, o rey." The Spanish term *barrio* is taken as "calpulli. tlaxilacalli" and ciudad as "vei-altepetl." Molina therefore accepts the equivalency of tlaxilacalli and neighborhood but struggles to consistently define altepetl. See table 0.1, this volume; also Lockhart, *The Nahuas after the Conquest*, 56.

24. "Indios del barrio," "Carta de la Ciudad de México, en que se hace relación a S.M. del suceso del tumulto del 15 de enero de 1624," in *Documentos relativos al tumulto de 1624*, ed. Mariano Fernández de Echeverría y Veytia (Mexico City: Imprenta de F. Escalante y Cía, 1855), 2:146.

25. See Silva Prada, *La política*, especially 385–410.

26. In a forthcoming article, Jerome A. Offner describes the negotiation of nobles in Tlailotlacan and Chimalpan as they sought to fulfill both local (tlaxilacalli and tlacamecayotl) and regional (altepetl) responsibilities. Offner, "Apuntes sobre la plancha X del *Códice Xolotl*: cincuenta años más tarde," trans. Agnieszka Brylak, in *Códices del Centro de México: Análisis comparativos y estudios individuales*, vol. 2, ed. Miguel Ángel Ruz Barrio and Juan José Batalla Rosado (Warsaw: University of Warsaw, in press).

27. The evidence for Tlailotlacan authorship consists of the Xolotl's repeated interest in the local history of this tlaxilacalli (particularly dynastic history), combined with Tlailotlacan's long-standing connection with the information arts and sciences. See Offner, "Apuntes." For a critical view on Tlailotlacan's pre-Aztec history, see Eloise Quiñones Keber, "The Tlailotlaque in Acolhua Pictorial Histories: Imitators or Inventors?" *Journal de la Société des Américanistes* 84, no. 2 (1998): 83–96.

28. "Ayc polihuiz ayc ylcahuiz, mochipa pialoz, ticpiazque yn titepilhuan in titeixhuihuan in titeyccahuan in tetemintonhuan in tetepiptonhuan in titechichicahuan in titetentzonhuan in titeyxquamolhuan in titeteyztihuan, in titetlapallohuan in titeheçohuan, in titlayllotlacatepilhuan, in ipan otiyolque otitlacatque in ice tlaxillacalyacatl motenehua Tlayllotlacan Tecpan, y huel oncan catca y huel oncan omotlahtocatillico yn itzquintin in tlaçohuehuetque in tlaçotlahtoque chichimeca, in tlayllotlacattlahtoque in tlayllotlacateteuhctin, inin mitohua inin tlahtolli Tlayllotlacan Tecpan pielli." Domingo Chimalpahin, *Las ocho relaciones y el memorial de Colhuacan* ed. and trans. Rafael Tena (Mexico City: CONACULTA, 1998), 2:272.

29. Townsend, "Glimpsing."

30. Frederic Hicks, "Labor Squads, Noble Houses, and Other Things Called 'Barrios' in Aztec Mexico," *Nahua Newsletter* 49 (2010): 14; Caterina Pizzigoni, *The Life Within: Local Indigenous Society in Mexico's Toluca Valley, 1650–1800* (Stanford: Stanford University Press, 2012), 9.

31. Although he used both tlaxilacalli and calpolli in his classic *Nahuas after the Conquest*, James Lockhart also seems to have recognized a conceptual difficulty in defining these twinned institutions, using a panoply of other names as well, including all of the terms cited above (cf., *The Nahuas*, 36, 50, 53, 56, 57, 61, 65, 122, 128, 147, 188, 196, 197, 219, 487, 490, 607, etc.) *The Nahuas* is much more precise in his treatment of altepetl. It is also careful to avoid the terms *ward*, which it uses as a subsection of a tlaxilacalli, and *neighborhood*, which (unlike barrio) it uses only in Hispanic contexts.

32. Regarding the troubles of an easy identification between tlaxilacalli/calpolli and neighborhood or barrio, see Hicks, "Labor Squads," as well as Luis Reyes García, Eustaquio Celestino Solís, Armando Valenica Ríos, Constantino Medina Luna, and Gregorio Guerrero Díaz, eds., *Documentos nauas de la ciudad de México del siglo XVI* (Mexico City: AGN, 1996), 21–67; Eileen M. Mulhare, "Barrio Matters: Toward an Ethnology of Mesoamerican Customary Social Units" *Ethnology* 35, no. 2 (Spring 1996): 93–106.

33. "ypan altepetl nexquipayac," private collection (a digital copy is held in the Archivo del Diócesis de Texcoco and it also appears in DNT, doc. 33); "ynpani Altepetl Sta Ma tlaylotlaca," private collection (a digital copy is held in the Archivo del Diócesis de Texcoco and it also appears in DNT, doc. 34); "Yn Nican ypa Altepetl Santa Ma purificasion tepetitlan," private collection (a digital copy is held in the Archivo del Diócesis de Texcoco and it also appears in DNT, doc. 40).

34. Bernardo García Martínez, "Pueblos de Indios, Pueblos de Castas: New Settlements and Traditional Corporate Organization in Eighteenth-Century New Spain," in *The Indian Community of Colonial Mexico: Fifteen Essays on Land Tenure, Corporate Organizations, Ideology, and Village Politics*, ed. Arij Ouweneel and Simon Miller (Amsterdam: CEDLA, 1990), 107.

35. Cf. Bernardo García Martínez and Gustavo Martínez Mendoza, *Señoríos, pueblos, y municipios: Banco preliminar de información*, CD-Rom (Mexico City: El Colegio de México, 2012), 1775, 2915, 2658. Despite this base-level independence in civil administration, these three continued to be ecclesiastically dependent on Atenco, Tetzcoco, and Chiautla, respectively.

36. Hicks, "Labor Squads," 14.

37. "Yn ipan altepetl ytocayocan xabon." Domingo Chimalpahin, *Annals of His Time: Don Domingo de San Antón Muñón Chimalpahin Quauhtlehuanitzin*, ed. and trans. James Lockhart, Susan Schroeder, and Doris Namala (Stanford: Stanford University Press, 2006), 62.

38. There has been extensive debate on the relationship between tlaxilacalli and calpolli, with much work left to do. See Pedro Carrasco and Johanna Broda, eds., *Estratificación social*

en la Mesoamerica prehispánica (Mexico City: INAH, 1976); Frederic Hicks, "Tetzcoco in the Early 16th Century: The State, the City, and the 'Calpolli,'" *American Ethnologist* 9, no. 2 (1982): 230–49; Rudolph Van Zantwijk, *The Aztec Arrangement: The Social History of Pre-Spanish Mexico* (Norman: University of Oklahoma Press, 1985); Pablo Escalante Gonzalbo, "La polémica sobre la organización de las comunidades de productores," *Nueva Antropología* 11, no. 38 (1990): 147–62; Lockhart, *The Nahuas after the Conquest*; Pedro Carrasco, *Estructura politico territorial del imperio tenochca: La triple alianza de Tenochtitlan, Tetzcoco y Tlacopan* (Mexico City: FCE, 1996); Federico Fernández Christleib and Ángel Julián García Zambrano, eds., *Territorialidad y paisaje en el altepetl del siglo XVI* (Mexico City: FCE, 2006); David M. Carballo, "Advances in the Household Archaeology of Highland Mesoamerica," *Journal of Archaeoliocal Research* 19, no. 2 (2011): 133–89; M. Charlotte Arnauld, Linda R. Manzanilla, and Michael E. Smith, eds., *The Neighborhood as a Social and Spatial Unit in Mesoamerican Cities* (Tucson: Arizona University Press, 2012).

39. For "Thorn Speech" and "Lord of the Reed on the Nose," see Frances F. Berdan and Patricia Reiff Anawalt, eds., *The Essential Codex Mendoza* (Berkeley: University of California Press, 1997), 208n5, 220n17, respectively. In her recent article for *Estudios de Cultura Náhuatl*, "Las funciones rituales de los altos personajes mexicas," 45 (2013): 42–43, Danièle Dehouve is particularly critical of these misreadings.

40. "Le dió un lugar junto á Texcuco para que lo poblase, y á los demás repartió en sus pueblos, dando á cada uno tierras donde poblase; y de aquí tomó el nombre el pueblo y barrio de Texcuco, llamándose Tlailotlacan por sus primeros pobladores, y asimismo los demás pueblos que hay en los pueblos que se llaman Tlailotlacan." Ixtlilxochitl, *Obras* (1952), 1:124.

41. For an early, if brief, commentary on the similarity of tlaxilacalli names across different central Mexican altepetl, see Van Zantwijk, *Aztec Arrangement*, 54. Also, many of the names mentioned appear as sections of the main Templo Mayor complex in Mexico-Tenochtitlan's ceremonial center, further suggesting the distinct connotations of each name in addition to implying ties with the wider tlaxilacalli. On of these sections, see Florentine Codex, vol. 1, book 2, beginning f. 109v, available through the World Digital Library, accessed May 6, 2016, https://www.wdl.org/en/item/10096/view/1/338/. See also the scholarly edition by Bernardino de Sahagún, *Florentine Codex: General History of the Things of New Spain*, 2nd ed., ed. Arthur J.O. Anderson and Charles E. Dibble (Salt Lake City: University of Utah Press, 1981), 2:179–93.

42. When an illustration in plate 10 of the Codex Xolotl (*Tlachia* code: X.101.L.25) is joined with later commentary by Ixtlilxochitl (*Obras*, 178, 218), it becomes a likely conclusion that Chimalpan also provided the head priest (*cihuacoatl*) for Tetzcoco. See discussion in chapter 2.

43. The semantic reach of Tlailotlacan is particularly broad. Its evocations of power and performative authority became so strong that a separate term *Tlailotlac* (resident of Tlailotlacan) became a generic term for "judge" or "lawgiver"; so, for instance, the head

of Huitznahauc tlaxilacalli could be called "Huitznahuactlilotlac" ("Huitznahuac judge"; lit. "resident of Tlailotlacan who lives in Huitznahauc"). Another telling example is that of Miguel Pochtecatlailotlac—Tlailotlac of the Pochteca—who was tried by fray Juan de Zumárraga's Inquisition in 1539 for allegedly hiding "idols" from the Templo Mayor. See González Obregón, ed., *Procesos de indios idólatras y hechiceros*, 115–39.

44. On Yopico, see González y González, *Xipe Totec*. Regarding the "foreignness" of tlaxilacalli, see Van Zantwijk, *Aztec Arrangement*, 16–21. On tlaxilacalli identity in the Hispanic period, see Horn, *Postconquest Coyoacan*, 20–23, 239–41, and elsewhere across this text.

45. On tlayacatl, see Lockhart, *The Nahuas after the Conquest*, 21–28; Schroeder, *Chimalpahin and the Kingdoms*, 131–36. Because tlayacatl grew out of tlaxilacalli, they occasionally also carried forward tlaxilacalli names. Tlailotlacan (Schroeder, *Chimalpahin*, 131) is one such example from Aztec-era Chalco.

46. The Mendoza judges can be sited at Moyotlan by their tlaxilacalli affiliation, all of which fall into that particular tlayacatl: the Mixcoatlailotlac from Mixcoac, the Ezhuahuacatl from Yopico, the Tequixquinahuacatl from Tequixquipan, and the Acatlyacapanecatl from one of the two subsections of Moyotlan called Acapan. Regarding this final location, Barbara Mundy's extensive listing of tlaxilacalli in Mexico-Tenochtitlan only lists names with Acatl for Moyotlan, both Acatlan. It is likely that Acatl Yacapan was the more complete name for one of these. Cf. Dehouve, "Las funciones rituales"; Mundy, "Place-Names," in *Death of Aztec Tenochtitlan*, 128–67.

The various titles of tlaxilacalli warriors and judges repeat across the various historical and legal books (especially book 8) of the Florentine Codex, as well as in Durán and Tezozomoc. Additional sources include González y González, *Xipe Totec*, on feasts; Dehouve, "Las funciones rituales," for religious representation; and, for the Templo Mayor, Aurélie Couvreur, "La description du Grand Temple de Mexico par Bernardino de Sahagún (Codex de Florence, annexe du Livre II)," *Journal de la Societé des Américanistes* 88, no. 88 (2002): 9–46.

47. According to book 9 of the Florentine Codex (pp. 12, 37 in the Dibble and Anderson edition), tlaxilacalli for long-distance trade included Acxotlan, Ahuachtlan, Atlauhco, Itztolco, Pochtlan, Tepetitlan, and Tzonmolco. See also Lockhart, *The Nahuas after the Conquest*, 192, for a thoughtful reflection on long-standing tlaxilacalli-based work identity. On Poyauhtlan and Chimalpan, Ixtlilxochitl, *Obras* (1952), 187, 209. Chimalpan is well-known, and the "Plano Topográfico de Texcoco" (Bnf-MM, 107) shows that Poyauhtlan is a tlaxilacalli in Tetzcoco, as opposed to some other geographical or political form. On Cuepopan, see Mundy, *Death of Aztec Tenochtitlan*, 178–80.

48. Cf. Richard E. Blanton and Lane Fargher, *Collective Action in the Formation of Pre-Modern States* (New York: Springer, 2008); Lane Fargher, Verenice Heredia Espinosa, and Richard E. Blanton, "Alternative Pathways to Power in Late Postclassic Highland Mesoamerica," *Journal of Anthropological Archaeology* 30, no. 3 (2011): 306–26; David M. Carballo,

Paul Roscoe, and Gary M. Feinman, "Cooperation and Collective Action in the Cultural Evolution of Complex Societies," *Journal of Archaeological Method and Theory* 21, no. 1 (2014): 98–133.

49. For a comparison of "rural" and "urban" commoner consumption, see Michael E. Smith, *Aztec City-State Capitals* (Gainesville: University of Florida Press, 2008).

50. "Un Padre muy honrado y celoso de la honra de Dios y de la doctrina con quien yo vivía y en cuya compañía estaba mandó que en todos los barrios se pusiesen cruces para que allí saliesen á rezar la doctrina. Todos pusieron cruces excto un barrio que como gente mas devota se quiso aventajar y pidieron que se les diese licencia para edificar una hermita la cual les fué concedida y mandado que el nombre del Santo fuese S. Pablo ó S. Agustín ellos digeron que se hablarían. Después de las quince dias volvieron y dijeron que no querían á S. Pablo ni á S. Agustín pues preguntados que Santo querían digeron que á S. Lucas. Yo notando la petición y el ahinco con que la pedían advertí en que podía haber algún mal y fui al calendario de sus ídolos y miré que fiesta y signo era en el que caya San Lucas y considerado fuime al maudoncillo de aquel barrio y pregúntele como se llamaba y el respondióme que Juan. Rogué que me dijese el nombre que tenía de su ley antigua del dia en que había nacido y díjome que en el signo de cally que quiere decir casa y vi clara y manifiestamente pedir el dia de S. Lucas por razón de que cae en el dia y signo de la casa y aun por que dos dias antes es una de las grandes y solenes fiestas que ellos tenían y así reprendiéndole su doblez y mala intención le dige que aquella supesticion le ha el movido y no la mortificación de la cruz que trujo mientras vivió ni la mucha devoción que le tienes." Diego Durán, *Historia de las Indias de Nueva España y islas de la Tierra Firme*, ed. Rosa Carnelo and José Rubén Romero (Mexico City: CONACULTA, 1995), 2:242–43.

51. On all central powers as "foreign" to local communities, see Pedro Pitarch, *La cara oculta del pliegue: Ensayos de antropología indígena* (Mexico City: Artes de Mexico, 2013), 33–34.

52. Evidence for a beginning in exactly 1272 is scarce outside of the Codex Xolotl, making the precise start date less precise than desirable. Given the lack of other candidates, however, this text uses the standard 1272 date.

53. Although the transition from Aztec to Spanish rule remains a prime chronological anchor in central Mexican historiography, a shift from empires to local institutions does tend to reset basic parameters. See, for instance, Bernardo García Martínez, *Los pueblos de la sierra: El poder y el espacio entre los indios del norte de Puebla hasta 1700* (Mexico City: El Colegio de México, 1987).

54. In early sources, the first mention of "Acolhuacan" in a collective or geographic sense comes in plate 2 of the Codex Xolotl (*Tlachia* code: X.020.C.15), in what later became known as the altepetl of Coatlincan or even Coatlinchan-Acolhuacan. As Acolhua power and territory grew, however, this term quickly broadened to its standard meaning, referring to the entire Acolhua realm.

55. Acolhua women appear to have used hairstyles similar to their Mexica counterparts.

56. Even the main historiographer of early Tlaxcala, Diego Muñoz Camargo, stated that the "Tetzcoca language" was more "courtly and polished": "es tenida la lengua . . . tezcucana por más cortesana y pulida." *Historia de Tlaxcala*, ed. Alfredo Chavero (Mexico City: Secretaría de Fomento, 1892), 25. On Tetzcoca painting schools, see Donald Robertson, *Mexican Manuscript Painting of the Early Colonial Period: The Metropolitan Schools* (New Haven, CT: Yale University Press, 1959). In the nineteenth century, Francisco del Paso y Troncoso also noticed a difference in Nahuatl speech from Tetzcoco: "Los náuas de algunas regiones aspiran más que los de otras: donde los de Tlaxcala, por ejemplo, emiten la h aspirada, los de Tetzcoco dejan oir muchas veces el saltillo, y mutua mente se motejan, diciendo éstos de aquellos que hablan como serranos, y aquellos de los de Tetzcoco que son muy afectados en su habla. Pondré como ejemplos los pronom bres nehuatl, téhuatl, yéhuatl, yo, tú, él, pronunciados en Tetzcoco mèuatl, tèuatl, yèuatl, con detención entre la pri mera sílaba y la segunda, como si se tratara de dos mono sílabos." *Descriptión, historia y exposición del códice pictórico de los antiguos Náuas que se conserva en la Biblioteca de la Cámara de diputados de Paris* (Florence, Italy: Salvador Landi, 1899), xxvii.

As part of a wider critique of Alfonso Lacadena's arguments about Nahuatl writing patterns (cf. "Regional Scribal Traditions: Methodological Implications for the Decipherment of Nahuatl Writing," *PARI Journal* 8, no. 4 [2008]: 1–22); Gordon Whittaker ("The Principles of Nahuatl Writing," *Göttinger Beiträge zur Sprachwissenschaft* 16 [2009]: 47–81) has challenged Lacadena's assertion that Acolhua tlacuiloque wrote glyphs differently, presenting cases of "Acolhua"-style writing in other regions. It is possible, therefore, that divergences presented themselves more in pronunciation and genre than in forms of glyphic writing.

57. One interesting aspect of Acolhua regionalism is an inserted "n" in many mundane documents: "tlanlli" for "tlalli," "pinlli" for "pilli," etc. See, for example, DNT docs. 6, 7, 9, 12, 18, 22, 25, and for "tlaxilacanlli" figure 11. Many of these documents are in BNAH, leg. 30, exp. 3 and 8. On warrior hair, see *El Códice de Xicotepec: Estudio e interpretación*, ed. Guy Stresser-Péan (Puebla, Mexico: Gobierno del estado de Puebla, 1995), 43. (Under Mexica pressure, some outlying Acolhua altepetl did adopt Mexica hairstyles; ibid., 120. Although this codex shows Nezahualpilli wearing Mexica-style hair, this is a rarity in Acolhua codices and could be attributed to Xicotepec's large distance from the Acolhua capital.) On Acolhua noble fashion, see Justyna Olko, *Insignia of Rank in the Nahua World: From the Fifteenth to the Seventeenth Centuries* (Boulder: University Press of Colorado, 2013), 222–42. For market separation, see Leah D. Minc, "Style and Substance: Evidence for Regionalism within the Aztec Market System," *Latin American Antiquity* 20, no. 2 (June 2009): 343–74; and Deborah Nichols, "Merchants and Merchandise: The Archaeology of Aztec Commerce at Otumba, Mexico," in *Merchants, Markets, and Exchange in the Pre-Columbian World*, ed. Kenneth G. Hirth and Joanne Pillsbury, 49–84 (Washington, DC: Dumbarton Oaks, 2013). The Acolhua tlacuilo tradition is discussed in note 63. In other aspects Tetzcoco did

synchronize with Mexico-Tenochtitlan. For a Mexica-oriented reading of the Acolhua ruler Nezahualcoyotl, see Jongsoo Lee, *The Allure of Nezahualcoyotl: Pre-Hispanic History, Religion, and Nahua Poetics* (Albuquerque: University of New Mexico Press, 2008).

58. For the project at hand, some of the most important general works of critical methodology include three classics—Robertson, *Mexican Manuscript Painting*; H. B. Nicholson, "Pre-Hispanic Central Mexican Historiography," in *Investigaciones contemporáneas sobre historia de México*, 38–81 (Mexico City: UNAM, 1971); and Lockhart's *The Nahuas after the Conquest*, particularly the fine-grained work in chapters 8 and 9—together with a number of more recent works, including Elizabeth Hill Boone, *Stories in Red and Black: Pictorial Histories of the Aztecs and Mixtecs* (Austin: University of Texas Press, 2000); Townsend, "Glimpsing"; Eduardo de Jesús Douglas, *In the Palace of Nezahualcoyotl: Painting Manuscripts, Writing the Pre-Hispanic Past in Early Colonial Period Tetzcoco, Mexico* (Austin: University of Texas Press, 2010); Pablo Escalante Gonzalbo, *Los códices mesoamericanos antes y después de la conquista española* (Mexico City: FCE, 2010); Olko, *Insignia of Rank*; Brian, *Alva Ixtlilxochitl's Native Archive*; and numerous studies of individual documents, such as Lori Boornazian Diel, *Tira de Tepechpan: Negotiating Place under Aztec and Spanish Rule* (Austin: University of Texas Press, 2008).

In addition, much work (particularly by European scholars) occurs in journals, not monographs. Three of the most important scholars working in these fora are Juan José Batalla Rosado, Gordon Whittaker, and Patrick Lesbre. Representative articles include Batalla Rosado, "Los códices mesoamericanos: problemática actual de su censo," in *Escritura Indígena en México*, ed. Alfonso Lacadena et al. (Madrid, Spain: Cuadernos del Instituto de México en España, 1995), 85–103; Batalla Rosado, "Las falsificaciones de códices mesoamericanos," in *Actas de Primer Congreso Internacional Escrituras Silenciadas en la época de Cervantes*, ed. Manuel Casado et al. (Alcalá de Hanares, Spain: Universidad de Alcalá de Henares, 2005), 363–85; Batalla Rosado, "The Scribes Who Painted the *Matrícula de Tributos* and the *Codex Mendoza*," *Ancient Mesoamerica* 18, no. 1 (2007): 31–51; Whittaker, "The Study of North Mesoamerican Place-Signs," *Indiana* 13 (1993): 9–38; Whittaker, "Principles of Nahuatl Writing"; Whittaker, "Nahuatl Hieroglyphic Writing and the Beinecke Map," in *Painting a Map of Sixteenth-Century Mexico City: Land, Writing, and Native Rule*, ed. Mary E. Miller and Barbara E. Mundy (New Haven, CT: Beinecke Library, 2012), 137–57. Because it deals nearly exclusively with Acolhuacan, Lesbre's work is cited in note 69.

Finally, although some of the work cited here deals specifically with Acolhuacan, note 71 will deal more fully with the specifics of Acolhua historiography.

59. "Faltan sus pinturas en q tenían sus historias, porq al tiempo q el Marqués del Valle D Herdo Cortés con los demás conquistadores entraron la primera vez en ella, q habrá sesenta y cuatro años, pocos más o menos, se las qmaron en las casas reales de Nezahualpiltzintli, en un gran aposento q era el archivo general de sus papeles, en que estaban pintadas todas sus cosas antiguas, que hoy día lloran sus descendientes con mucho sentimiento por haber

qdado como a oscuras sin noticia ni memoria de los hechos de sus pasados. Y los q habían qdado en poder de algunos principales, unos de una cosa y otros, de otra, los qmaron de temor de D Fray Ju Zumárraga, primer arzobispo de México, porq no los atribuyese a cosas de idolotría." Juan Bautista de Pomar, "Relación de la ciudad y provincia de Tezcoco," in *Relaciones geográficas del siglo XVI*, ed. René Acuña (Mexico City: UNAM, 1986), 7:46. Patricia Lopes Don, *Bonfires of Culture: Franciscans, Indigenous Leaders, and the Inquisition in Early Mexico, 1524–1540* (Norman: University of Oklahoma Press, 2010), 4–5, dates this second purge to 1530.

60. Robert H. Barlow's 1945 reconstruction of the hypothetical "Crónica X," together with later scholarship on this same putative source, serves as an example of what can be recovered from the fragmentary extant record. Cf. Barlow, "La Crónica X: Versiones coloniales de la historia de los mexica tenocha," *Revista mexicana de estudios antropológicos* 7 (1945): 65–87. Also, Stephen A. Colston, "A Comment on Dating the 'Cronica X,'" *Tlalocan* 7 (1977): 371–77; Ignacio Bernal, "Durán's *Historia* and the Crónica X," in *The History of the Indies of New Spain*, ed. Diego Durán, trans. Doris Heyden (Norman: University of Oklahoma Press, 1994), 565–78; Sylvie Peperstraete, "La 'Chronique X': Reconstitution et analyse d'une source perdue fondamentale sur la civilisation Aztèque, d'après l'Historia de las Indias de Nueva España de D. Durán (1581) et la Crónica mexicana de F.A. Tezozomoc (ca. 1598)," BAR International Series 1630 (Oxford: Archaeopress, 2007).

61. On wider "graphic communication systems" in central Mexico, see Mikulska, *Tejiendo destinos*.

62. "Tanto más se ha trabajado de buscar y escudriñar lo q se ha hecho." Pomar, "Relación," 47. Key critical guides to these documents are Thouvenot, "Codex Xolotl"; Williams and Harvey, *The Códice*; Williams and Hicks, *Vergara*; Perla Valle, ed., *Memorial de los indios de Tepetlaóztoc ó códice Kingsborough: A cuatrocientos cuarenta años* (Mexico City: INAH, 1992).

An interesting comparison to Tetzcoco's response to its damaged archives can be found in the work of tlacuiloque in the aftermath of the Mexica huei tlatoani Itzcoatl's spate of partisan archival editing. Among a broad bibliography on this topic, see in particular, Federico Navarrete Linares, "Los libros quemados y los nuevos libros: Paradojas de la autenticidad en la tradición mesoamericana," in *La abolición del arte: El Coloquio Internacional de Historia del Arte*, ed. Alberto Dallad (Mexico City: UNAM, 1998), 53–71, on the resiliency of Aztec tlacuiloque. In addition, José Rubén Romero Galván argues that the goal of Itzcoatl's archival destruction was to solidify "la unidad entre los calpulli y la clase en el poder": "La historia según Chimalpain," *Journal de la Societé des Américanistes* 84, no. 2 (1998): 185.

63. Williams and Harvey (*The Códice*, 284) conclude that the missing glyph for Mateo Nauhyotl shows that the *Asunción* was copied from an earlier pictorial document.

64. See Valle, *Memorial*; Barbara J. Williams and H. R. Harvey, "Content, Provenience, and Significance of the *Codex Vergara* and the *Códice de Santa Maria Asuncion*," *American Antiquity* 53, no. 2 (1988): 337–51.

65. "Si en ello pareciere faltar algo y qdar en otras corto, se atribuya a lo dicho y no falta de diligencia." Pomar, "Relación," 47.

66. "Nos Don Martín de Suero, Gobernador, y Francisco Xuárez y Francisco de San Pablo, Alcaldes, y D. Silvestre de Soto, D. Gaspar de Guaman, D. Juan de Suero, D. Bartolomé Pimentel y D. Luis de Soto, Principales, Regidores y Ancianos de la cabecera de esta Provincia de Otumba, y los Alcaldes de los pueblos de Ahuatepec, Tizayuca, Aztaquemeca y Tlamapam, y de las Estan cias de Tepayuca y Axoloayan, decimos: Que ya hemos visto, leído y considerado las Historias y Crónica que tiene escrita D. Fernando de Alva Ixtlilxuchitl, en donde se contienen las historias y crónicas de los Tultecas y Reyes Chichimecas de estas nuevas tierras que ahora se llaman Nueva España . . . todo lo que contienen los diez libros de la dicha Historia y Crónica ha salido muy bueno y verdadero, sin ningún defecto; y la relación que los principales de la ciudad de Texcuco le dieron, está también muy cierta y verdadera . . . Decimos Nos el Gobernador y Alcaldes Regidores Ancianos del pueblo de San Salvador Quatlacinco, que hemos visto y leí do la Historia que tiene escrita D. Fernando de Alva Ixtlilxuchitl, la cual es m u y cierta y verdadera y conforme con nues tras antiguas historias." Ixtlilxochitl, *Obras* (1952), 1:518–19, 521.

67. On the specific case of the Codex Xolotl, see Offner, "Ixtlilxochitl's Ethnographic Encounter." For the broader question of Hispanic influence in Nahuatl literary practices, see Lockhart, *The Nahuas after the Conquest*, chapters 7–9; Escalante Gonzalbo, *Códices*, chapters 4–6, 12.

68. The strongest expression of doubt regarding the reliability of elite-oriented Mesoamerican sources remains Joyce Marcus, *Mesoamerican Writing Systems: Propaganda, Myth, and History in Four Ancient Civilizations* (Princeton: Princeton University Press, 1992).

69. Patrick Lesbre, "Illustrations acolhua de facture européenne (Codex Ixtlilxochitl, ff. 105–112)," *Journal de la Société des Américanistes* 84, no. 2 (1998): 97–124; Patrick Lesbre, "¿Influencias occidentales en el Mapa Quinatzin?" *Revista Española de Antropología Americana* 38, no. 2 (2008): 173–97; Patrick Lesbre, "Le Mexique central à travers le Codex Xolotl et Alva Ixtlilxochitl: Entre l'espace préhispanique et l'écriture coloniale," *e-Spania* 14 (2012), accessed December 2, 2015, https://e-spania.revues.org/22033; Patrick Lesbre, "Oublis et censures de l'historiographie acolhua coloniale: Nezahualcoyotl," *C.M.H.L.B. Caravelle* 72, no. 1 (1999): 11–30; Lee, *Allure*; Douglas, *Palace*; Jerome A. Offner, "Improving Western Historiography of Texcoco," in *Texcoco*, ed. Jongsoo Lee and Galen Brokaw (Boulder: University Press of Colorado, 2014), 25–62; Boone, *Stories in Red and Black*; Thouvenot, "Codex Xolotl"; Whittaker, "Principles of Nahuatl Writing"; Olko, *Insignia of Rank*; Charles E. Dibble, ed., *Códice Xolotl*, 2 vols. (Mexico City: UNAM, 1951); Barbara J. Williams, "Aztec Soil Knowledge: Classes, Management, and Ecology," in *Footprints in the Soil: People and Ideas in Soil History*, ed. Benno P. Warkentin (Oxford: Elsevier, 2006), 17–41; María del Carmen Jorge, Barbara J. Williams, Clara E. Garza-Hume, and Arturo Olvera, "Mathematical Accuracy of Aztec Land Surveys Assessed from Records in the Codex Vergara," *Proceedings*

of the National Academy of Sciences of the United States of America 108, no. 37 (2011): 15053–57; Barbara J. Williams and Janice K. Pierce, "Evidence of Acolhua Science in Pictorial Land Records," in *Texcoco*, ed. Jongsoo Lee and Galen Brokaw (Boulder: University Press of Colorado, 2014), 147–64. Thouvenot has also played a major role in building the *Tlachia* image dictionary (http://tlachia.iib.unam.mx/, accessed April 3, 2016) and other online resources in Nahuatl. Bradley Benton's very recent *The Lords of Tetzcoco: The Transformation of Indigenous Rule in Postconquest Central Mexico* (Cambridge: Cambridge University Press, 2017) came out just as this book went to press and its arguments are not addressed in the text.

Recent examples of "ground truthing" include Davíd Carrasco and Scott Sessions, eds., *Cave, City, and Eagle's Nest: An Interpretive Journey through the Mapa de Cuauhtinchan No. 2* (Albuquerque: University of New Mexico Press, 2007); Williams and Harvey, *The Códice*; Williams and Hicks, *Vergara*; María Castañeda de la Paz, "Nahua Cartography in Historical Context: Searching for Sources on the Mapa de Otumba," *Ethnohistory* 61, no. 2 (2014): 301–27; Mundy, *The Death of Aztec Tenochtitlan*.

70. On patterns of central Mexican imperialism, see Frances F. Berdan, Richard E. Blanton, Elizabeth Hill Boone, Mary G. Hodge, Michael E. Smith, and Emily Umberger, eds., *Aztec Imperial Strategies* (Washington: Dumbarton Oaks Research Library, 1996); Federico Navarrete Linares, "Las dinámicas históricas y culturales de ciclos de concentración y dispersión en las sociedades amerindias," in *Los pueblos amerindios más allá del Estado*, ed. Berenice Alcántara Rojas and Federico Navarrete Linares (Mexico City: UNAM, 2011), 169–99.

1

The Rise of Tlaxilacalli, ca. 1272–1454

The first people to build tlaxilacalli regimes remain anonymous, but their presence stalks the Acolhua landscape. The marks are indelible: new soil types, broader settlement patterns, the reclamation of previously denuded fields, and intensified agriculture, including a return to rigorous maize cropping. All of these marks signal the arrival of a new political and spatial order beginning around the thirteenth century.[1] This order, the order of tlaxilacalli, spread across the Basin of Mexico just ahead of the Aztec empire and contributed directly to its rise. Tlaxilacalli represented an innovative colonization scheme for an ancient landscape and produced the shocking population boom that signaled the rise of a new and imposing Mexican empire.

Humans have lived in central Mexico for many millennia—so many, in fact, that regional history can be sorted into various waves of human consolidation and dispersal, of imperial rise and fall. Scholars know these fluctuations well and often connect them to ecological discussions of carrying capacity: empires stacked people as tightly as they could on the land until there became too many and the ecosystem broke, opening up another cycle of fragmentation and dispersion.[2] Archaeological investigations in Acolhuacan, the Rhode Island–sized northeastern section of the Basin of Mexico, show three such cycles in the 2,000 years leading up to the consolidation of the Aztec empire. The population rise preceding the Aztecs, however, was unique. It demolished previous demographic records for the region, more than tripling the previous mark for peak population and even outstripping modern

DOI: 10.5876/9781607326915.c001

TABLE 1.1. Population trends in Acolhuacan

Time Period	Sites	Area (ha)	Pop. (est.)
500–300 BCE	29	251	9,000
200 BCE–100 CE (Terminal Formative)	52	747	20,200
200–400 CE	37	197	4,000
500–700 CE	23	144	2,675
800–900 CE (Early Toltec)	24	1,059	31,900
1000 CE	59	442	6515
1300–1500 CE (Early/Late Aztec)	110	4,609	116,395
1519–ca. 1600 CE (Early Colonial)	?	?	? (decline)
1960 CE	70	3,219	73,476

Source: Jeffrey R. Parsons, with Richard E. Blanton and Mary H. Parsons, *Prehistoric Settlement Patterns in the Texcoco Region, Mexico* (Ann Arbor: University of Michigan Museum of Anthropology, 1971), 163.

settlement in latter-day Acolhuacan. During the Aztec centuries the number of human settlements doubled, and the total area of human inhabitation rose by a factor of four[3] (table 1.1). Something profoundly changed in the way people lived on the land during the Aztec centuries. They started living in tlaxilacalli.

This chapter profiles the remarkable spread of tlaxilacalli in the early centuries, leading up to the rise of the Aztec empire in the early fifteenth century. Tlaxilacalli, and the economic and demographic booms they catalyzed, proved foundational to the rise and spread of a new form of imperial rule in central Mexico.

THE SPREAD OF TLAXILACALLI

Tlaxilacalli communities diverged markedly from earlier settlement patterns.[4] Data from the Acolhua heartland show, for example, that nucleated arrangements of one kind or another predominated during all periods before the Aztecs, after which they were replaced by a new and more dispersed settlement type, the tlaxilacalli. These communities were unique, spreading large and surprisingly autonomous populations over extensive territories to manage local ecosystems with much greater efficiency. Only decentralized local control allowed for the close-in, rigorous management that proved fundamental for the spread of human settlement across nearly all of central Mexico's varied ecosystems. Tlaxilacalli anchored people on the landscape in new and intensive ways.[5]

In the highlands of the Patlachiuhqui range near the modern Mexican town of Tepetlaoxtoc de Hidalgo, for example, Mary Hrones Parsons has mapped early

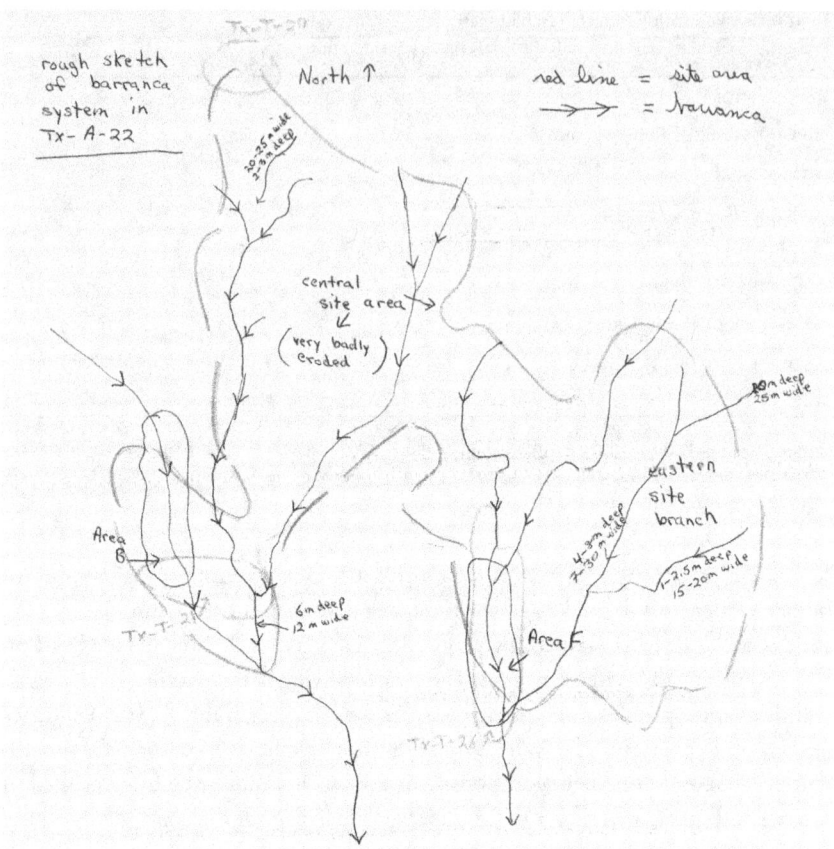

FIGURE 1.1. Settlement disperses and intensifies in the move to the Aztec period. Cuauhtepoztlan Tlaxilacalli, Tepetlaoztoc, Estado de Mexico. This map shows three small Toltec-era settlements (marked Tx-T-26, Tx-T-28, and Tx-T-29) growing into a single, continuous tlaxilacalli, Tx-A-22. (The T notation signifies "Toltec"; A is for "Aztec.") Map by Mary Hrones Parsons, ca. 1968. *Courtesy*, Bentley Historical Library, Ann Arbor, MI, Jeffrey R. Parsons Papers, box 11, vol. Tx-A-22 (I), f. 2r.

settlements ballooning out to cover areas much greater than before. In the lead-up to the Aztec period, three disarticulated settlements grew into a large and dominant tlaxilacalli, Cuauhtepoztlan (figure 1.1), covering an area eight times greater during the move to the Aztec period. These three settlements, previously huddling on a single hilltop and around two small gullies, now crashed together and expanded, filling in the entire upper catchment basin of Huei Tepetl mountain. A primary settlement complex grew up in the center of the new tlaxilacalli, midway between the three earlier sites and presumably drawing from them all. The rest of the area, nearly all of it fed by seasonal streams, formed a contiguous and much more extensive agricultural territory.[6]

Schematizing this work, Carlos Cordova has shown for the wider Acolhua region that settlement shifted from nucleated to thickly settled but dispersed arrangements in the lead-up to the Aztec empire. The intensive, centralizing settlements of the Formative and Toltec eras expanded into extensive, broadly associated communities during the twelfth and thirteenth centuries—patterns that continued as the Aztec empire grew to its height (figure 1.2).[7]

Pre-Aztec tlaxilacalli spread autonomous farming communities over all available land, devolving enough authority to local communities so that each could effectively manage its own specific ecological niche.[8] This, in turn, led to powerful and targeted community investment in productive infrastructure, including successful land reclamation efforts, a return to intensive maize agriculture, the wide use of two different types of anti-erosion dams (maguey and stone), the extensive terracing of uneven hillside plots (figure 1.3), and even the development of a new type of human-managed soil called *tlalcoztli* (yellow soil), a reasonably productive sediment "of moderate depth and fertility" made from the runoff of maguey check dams.[9] In Cuauhtepoztlan tlaxilacalli, these reclaimed soils represented over 20 percent (21.2%) of all assayed soil in the Codex Asunción.[10] Even given the loss of tlaxilacalli landholding in the early decades of Hispanic rule to local mortality[11] and Spanish encroachment, the slightly depleted spatial array portrayed in this codex still represented a large territorial advance over earlier, pre-tlaxilacalli arrangements. The extensive domestication of the local landscape produced a "managed stability" that greatly enhanced the natural carrying capacity of Acolhua territory. This, in turn, set the anchor for later Aztec expansion.[12]

Acolhua rulers recognized the value of tlaxilacalli and their novel agricultural and settlement methods. Although Nezahualcoyotl, the powerful ruler of Tetzcoco and co-architect of the Aztec Triple Alliance, described tlaxilacalli land as "my possessions," he also repeatedly ceded relevant authority to local administrators: "it is theirs, for through their efforts they brought it in."[13] Indeed, tlaxilacalli efforts were far from trifling: the grants cited above describe lands in the vicinity of Nezahualcoyotl's imperial retreat, managed by the tlaxilacalli of Tezontla.[14] Not only were these hillside lands deeply terraced for planting, they also flanked a major aqueduct, which was constructed around the beginning of the Triple Alliance (figure 1.4). These investments were new and robust, flowing through the innovative sinews of Acolhua tlaxilacalli.

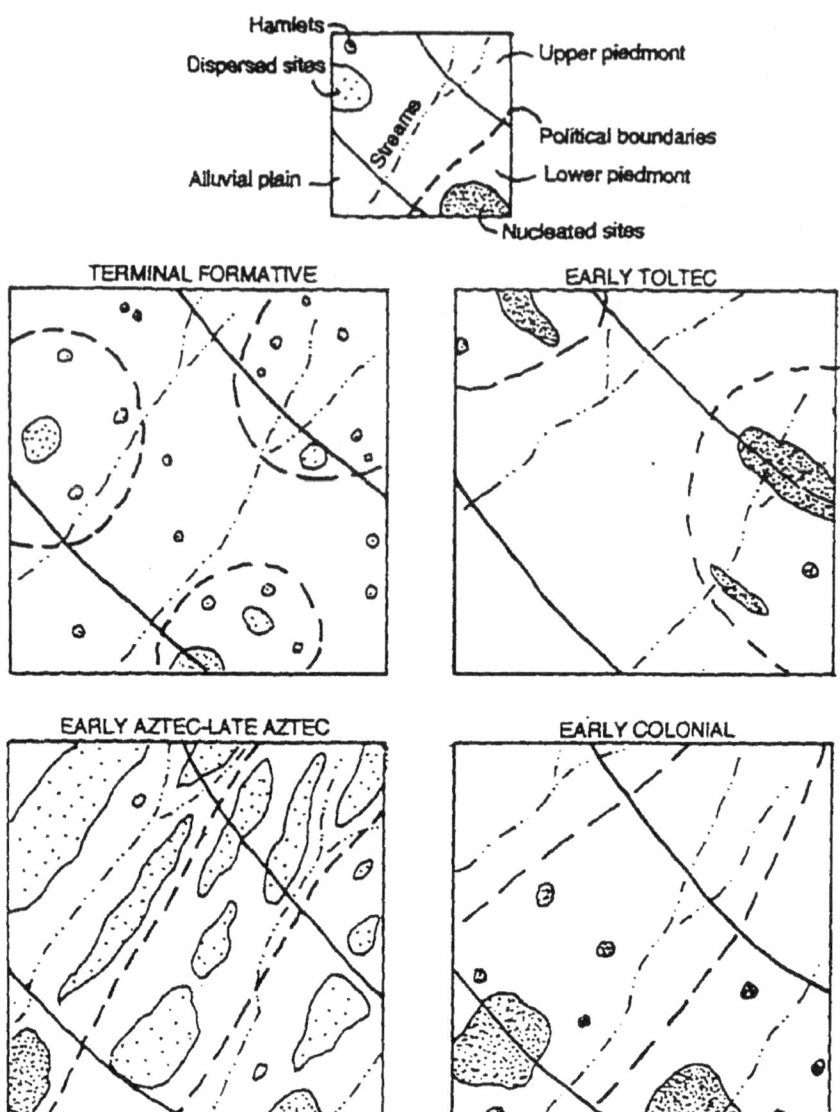

FIGURE 1.2. A schematic of tlaxilacalli expansion. Both before the Aztec period (Terminal Formative, Early Toltec) and after (Early Colonial), settlements nucleated in Acolhuacan. During the Aztec period, however, people spread across the landscape. Cordova, "Landscape Transformation," 466.

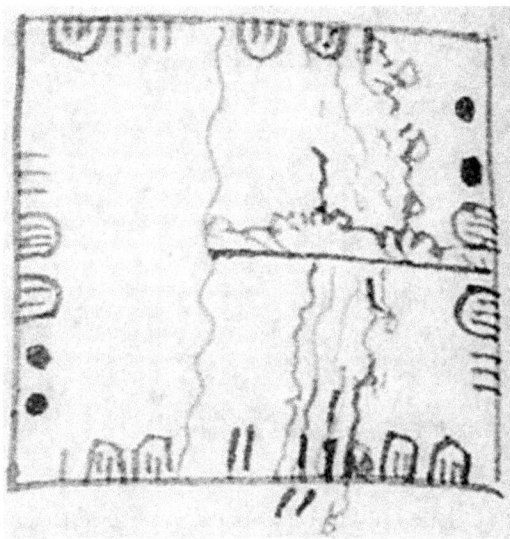

FIGURE 1.3. Stone check dam. Codex Asunción, f. 8v. *Courtesy*, Biblioteca Nacional de México, Mexico City.

TLAXILACALLI COLONIZATIONS

Colonizing tlaxilacalli pulled the Acolhua realm from a chaotic earlier landscape of multiple and diverse mini-polities, the dispersed fragments of the earlier Tolteca empire. After the fiery destruction of the Tolteca capital around perhaps 1000 CE, commoner farmers broke free from imperial tribute bonds[15] and spread across the Basin of Mexico, including areas that would later consolidate into the Acolhua heartland. The archaeological record is so rich that not only does it record the escape of single households from faltering Tolteca control, it also shows the first commoner attempts to organize into locally administered territorial arrays and their first early efforts to reclaim badly eroded landscapes. Tlaxilacalli got their start just after the fall of imperial Tula.[16]

Dispersion meant freedom but also danger, for commoners and others were left exposed to the increasingly frequent raids by mobile war bands, many arriving from the north. One group was led by a Chichimeca invader named Xolotl, subsequently remembered as the founder of Acolhua rule in the region. Xolotl was not Acolhua and did not speak the soon-to-be imperial lingua franca of Nahuatl, but he successfully captured the allegiance of certain vestigial nobles and their dependents and extended a "protective" hegemony over the areas under his control. This control was enough for local nobles to begin to build dependent tribute hierarchies in a few scattered areas and to press for more.[17]

FIGURE 1.4. Terraced hillside fields, just south of Tetzcotzinco. Lands modified and worked by Acolhua tlaxilacalli—perhaps Tezontla?—during the time of Nezahualcoyotl. Photograph by author.

So unfolds the elite-centered founding image of the Acolhua empire, masterfully painted in the Codex Xolotl and other early documents. In its beginning pages, the Xolotl tells the story of the conquest and re-articulation of a part of the old Tolteca tribute empire by new forces from the north. In this first sequence, the newly arrived Xolotl and his companion Nopaltzin reconnoiter the Basin of Mexico and then subdivide its eastern section for invasion, ceding local control to a series of regional "caudillos y capitanes."[18] These captains and their armies then overrun sections along the eastern shore of Lake Tetzcoco, paying tribute to both Xolotl and Nopaltzin in hunted game (identified as such by the glyph of a bound rabbit placed astride a line connecting captain to ruler). The hierarchical relationship between ruler and captain was surely complex, and it bore a territorial connection through ceremonies of possession, such as shooting arrows to the four directions or pulling up clumps of grass and burning them or scattering them to the wind. Even at this early stage, however, the codex clearly distinguishes between the flexible, mixed-use tribute relationships of the war captains and the sedentary tlaxilacalli arrangements of lands farther to the south.[19]

The Xolotl identifies the southern arrangements as Tolteca in origin, but the archaeological work of Cordova and Parsons suggests that these regimes likely emerged later, mostly through joint commoner effort.[20] Regarding such plantings, the Franciscan historiographer fray Juan de Torquemada marks a distinct break with the earlier Tolteca tradition, arguing that ecological depletion and fear of the invading Chichimeca led latter-day farmers to briefly abandon large-scale agriculture in the Basin of Mexico. He then credits the neo-"Tolteca" ruler Xiuhtlato of Cuauhtepec for reintroducing the crop, "spreading [corn] among those of his nation and caste until even the Chichimeca and the Acolhuaque perceived the value of this staple."[21]

Although Torquemada attributes this agricultural recovery to Xiuhtlato alone, the Xolotl shows early "Tolteca" planting beyond Cuauhtepec, particularly in Cholula and Colhuacan. In Cholula, demarcated lands are explicitly marked with a house glyph, strongly suggesting tlaxilacalli organization.[22] Further, in the Colhua fields, *huictli* digging sticks behind the "teeth" tribute glyph also evoke the preexisting action of hierarchically organized local farmers (see figure 1.5 for both images). Particularly because neither Xiuhtlato nor any other elites are shown with agricultural implements (in contrast to plate 5 of the Xolotl, for example), it is likely that this ruler played more of a protective or facilitating role, opening space for tlaxilacalli farmers among the Chichimeca elite, than he did as an actual agricultural administrator.[23]

Regardless of ultimate responsibility for the re-articulation of maize-based agriculture, these regimes soon spread across Chichimeca polities such as Chalco, Zohuatepec, Ahuatlaltepec, and Tlalpiltepec. In these more southern areas, the codex shows Xolotl's various descendants promoting changes through their dependent war hierarchies, changes that would culminate in the broad-scale implementation of tlaxilacalli regimes across the territories now falling under their control. Each of these Chichimeca rulers married "Tolteca" wives and learned techniques of field management from experienced commoner farmers, likely already in tlaxilacalli arrangements. This is particularly clear in the territory of the future Mexico-Tenochtitlan, where the Chichimeca Acamapichtli married the "Tolteca" Ilancueitl of Colhuacan, who brought along specially assigned tribute fields, worked systematically in her own name (figure 1.5b).[24] All of this, therefore, shows migrant elites adopting the styles and techniques of their innovative subjects. Local commoners taught their overlords how to farm, tlaxilacalli style.

Such regimes moved further northward into the lands that would later constitute the Acolhua empire during the reigns of Huetzin of Coatlinchan and Quinatzin of Tetzcoco, who particularly angered his Chichimeca captains by compelling them to plant maize, to group into permanent fixed settlements, and to "follow the order and style of the Tolteca."[25] According to the Xolotl, Quinatzin moved his seat of power to the tlaxilacalli of Oztoticpac around the year One Flint (1272 CE), raising its rank to altepetl and renaming the area Tetzcoco.[26] He also demarcated three new fields in the plains around Tetzcoco for maize-based agricultural regimes (figure 1.6). Quinatzin divided the land around his new capital into three parcels,

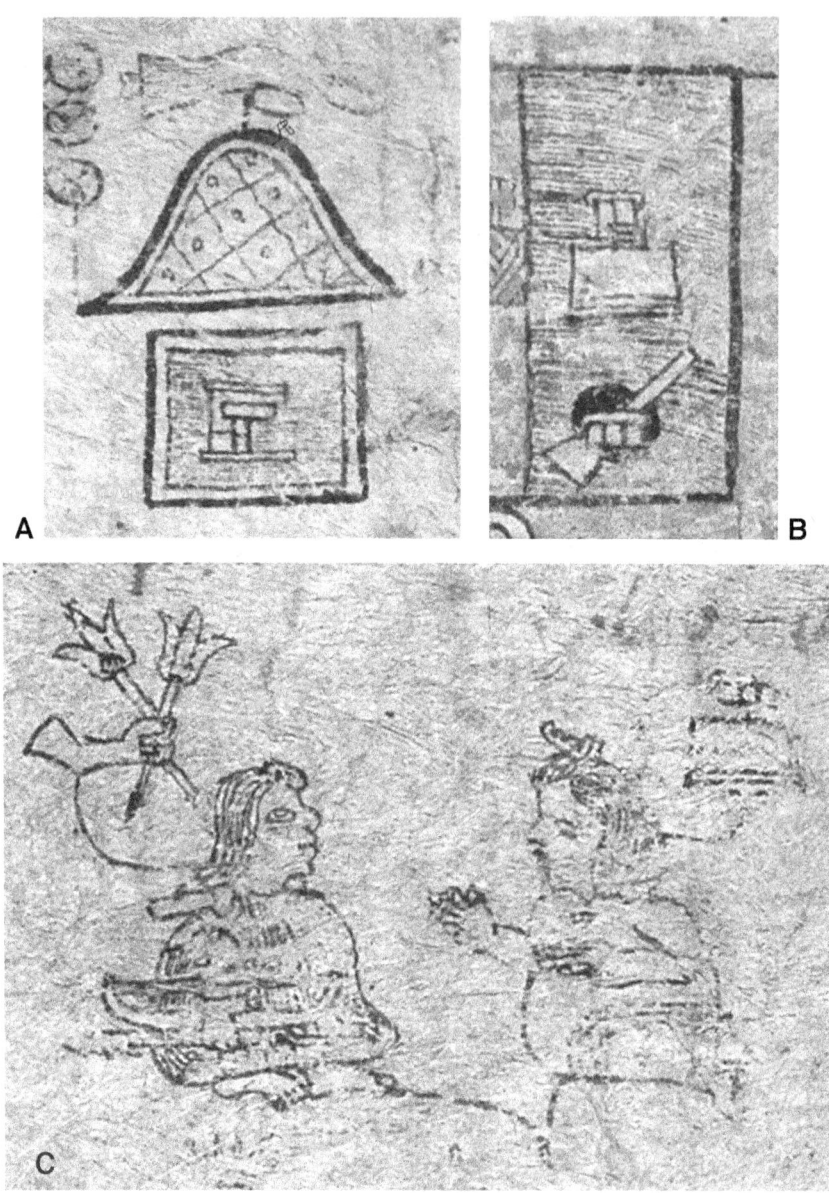

FIGURE 1.5. "Tolteca" agricultural influence. *A*: Demarcated fields with house/tlaxilacalli glyph in Cholula. *B*: Demarcated tributary fields in Colhuacan, with Ilancueitl's name glyph on top. *C*: Ilancueitl and Acamapichtli of Mexico-Tenochtitlan. Codex Xolotl, plate 3 (*Tlachia* codes: X.030.B.12, X.030.I.05+, X.030.G). *Courtesy*, Bibliothèque nationale de France, Paris.

FIGURE 1.6. Land management in the Codex Xolotl. *At center*: Quinatzin, ruler of Tetzcoco, sits on a reed throne above the "cave" glyph for the tlaxilacalli of Oztoticpac. Below him are the three fields he established around Tetzcoco: to the far left is the mixed-use Chichimeca field, and the other two are under intensive maize cultivation, as indicated by the huictli digging stick. The field on the far right includes the floating eye of a local administrator. Note also the same pair of figures—Ocotoch (marked with the "pine rabbit" glyph) and Coacuech (the snake rattle)—placed in the spaces between the separate fields. Separately, *at left*, Yacatzotzolotl of Tepetlaoztoc (identified by the "nose dust" glyph) disputes his levied "rabbit" tribute with Quinatzin. Codex Xolotl, plate 3 (*Tlachia* code: X.030.Z). *Courtesy*, Bibliothèque nationale de France, Paris.

one for transitional Chichimeca tribute and two for "Tolteca" regimes of tlaxilacalli farming. Both the utility and the power of Quinatzin's adopted management regimes come to the fore in the Xolotl's differential treatment of the "Tolteca" and Chichimeca agricultural areas.[27]

In the northern Chichimeca field, demarcated for the first time by Quinatzin, the codex shows a diverse pattern of resource use, including both farming (symbolized by the huictli digging stick) and hunting (represented by the snake, rodent, and rabbit), which persisted despite the efforts of three different rulers to reform and constrain traditional Chichimeca agricultural practices. The southern "Tolteca" areas shared none of this ambiguity. Although also reformed under Quinatzin's rule, the Xolotl shows these areas already under careful oversight. Enclosure produced a more bureaucratic and commodified form of tribute than that of the Chichimeca captains; and this blended hierarchy—autonomous tlaxilacalli with extractive noble overlays—soon became the administrative bedrock of imperial Acolhuacan.

TLAXILACALLI AND TRANSCULTURATION

The tlaxilacalli-guided standardization of once-flexible patterns transformed Chichimeca warlords into Acolhua rulers (even as they retained the title *Chichimecateuctli*, "Chichimeca lord") and profoundly affected the cultural life of their emerging empire. Ever since the ruler Tlotzin choked down his first gulps of maize-based atole, if not sooner, commanding Chichimeca elites experimented with patterns of transculturation—marrying "Tolteca" spouses and raising "Tolteca"-allied children, abandoning Chichimeca languages for the Nahuatl of the highland plains, and adopting the tlaxilacalli-derived cuisine of tamales, tortillas, and pulque, to name but a few important examples.[28] As their empire solidified, however, culture became a sharper tool for both political consolidation and adversarial dissent. At the center of nearly all these fights was the wide diversity of the tlaxilacalli, particularly the nature of their relationship to the consolidating imperial whole.

During the successive reigns of Quinatzin and Techotlalatzin, the primary tlaxilacalli of Tetzcoco took their canonical forms. This settling is often told as a story of in-migration by successive waves of regional "Tolteca" tlaxilacalli—certainly a key occurrence—but the projection and demarcation of Chichimeca lands was just as important. Acolhua rulers had to have somewhere to put the "Tolteca" migrants when they arrived, after all. This territorial reordering privileged "Tolteca" tlaxilacalli at the expense of Chichimeca hunters and captains, but this distinction perhaps best applies retrospectively. Social and political boundaries were redrawn so actively that terms such as *Chichimeca* and "*Tolteca*" soon carried vastly different meanings than they had a few generations before. Nevertheless, boundaries changed and people moved, often violently.[29]

Perhaps most influential, four "Tolteca" groups—explicitly defined in the Xolotl as tlaxilacalli by their characteristic house glyph (see figure 0.3)—were settled close in by Techotlalatzin along the four cardinal directions emanating out of Tetzcoco's growing political and religious center. These four tlaxilacalli (Huitznahuac, Mexicapan, Colhuacan, and Tepanecapan) quickly came to constitute the local administrative bulk of Tetzcoco proper, joining with two other "Tolteca"-derived tlaxilacalli (Tlailotlacan and Chimalpan) settled early in Quinatzin's reign to eventually grow into the six canonical subdivisions (tlayacatl) of the Acolhua capital. Despite Techotlalatzin's move to promulgate Nahuatl as the lingua franca of his small but expanding empire, each tlaxilacalli retained distinct ethnic and religious avocations: the Mexica of Mexicapan worshipped Huitzilopochtli; Colhuaque from Huitznahauc and Tlailotlaca (likely from the Puebla/Mixteca region) from Tlailotlacan followed Tezcatlipoca; Colhuaque from Colhuacan reverenced Tlaloc.[30] Regarding this final deity, the historian and ethnographer Juan Bautista de Pomar states that "the selfsame Colhuaque say that they found [Tlaloc's statue] in this land; and, because the Chichimeca ignored it, [the Colhuaque] began to worship and revere it as god of the waters."[31]

Tlaxilacalli powerfully influenced the wider culture of the growing Acolhua empire. "Tolteca" groups had pressured for public acclimation of their deities since the reign of Quinatzin, and when they conquered additional public space under Techotlalatzin, their influence proved decisive. By the rise of the Aztec Triple Alliance,

Huitzilopochtli and Tlaloc had risen to the top of Tetzcoco's twinned central pyramid, as Tezcatlipoca established himself the tutelary patron of both Tetzcoco and the wider Acolhua realm. Blood sacrifice increased in intensity and frequency. As Acolhua power grew and consolidated, Tezcatlipoca remained the sole responsibility of the tlaxilacalli of Huitznahuac, as it had been since the beginning. The tutelary deity of all of Acolhuacan was housed in its own specific tlaxilacalli.[32]

CHICHIMECA INSURGENCIES

Tlaxilacalli-based transformations in ecology, economics, culture, and administration marked a major break with earlier forms of politics and social organization in Acolhuacan and provoked strong opposition among many key Chichimeca allies, particularly the captains in the contested northern sections of Acolhua settlement. Yacatzotzolotl of Tepetlaoztoc (also known as Yacanex) proved especially vigorous in his opposition, fighting Quinatzin on at least three fronts. He sought to build his own transcultural empire through local marriage alliances, while simultaneously pulling his subordinate Chichimeca hierarchies away from Quinatzin's gathering power base. (See him rejecting tribute payments to Quinatzin in figure 1.6.) Soon after, he declared outright war—donning a spectacularly feathered warrior costume and waging war across the eastern Basin of Mexico.[33]

But as much as Yacatzotzolotl's wider rebellion compelled attention, the smaller story of Quinatzin's deputy Ocotoch is perhaps more illustrative. This Chichimeca captain supervised the promulgation of Quinatzin's noble demands over the southern "Tolteca" sections of Acolhuacan (figure 1.6). According to the Codex Xolotl, Ocotoch also paid hunted tribute to Quinatzin's father and likely to Quinatzin as well. As Quinatzin pushed northward, however, Ocotoch changed sides, joining Yacatzotzolotl's insurgency (figure 1.7) and—at least according to the Tepetlaoztoc-centered partisanship of the Memorial de los Indios de Tepetlaoztoc—successfully detached this altepetl from Acolhua tribute demands for at least five generations. Although Acolhua power later retook Tepetlaoztoc, the surrounding hillsides remained restive, so much so that the historian and ethnographer Fernando de Alva Ixtlilxochitl complained in the early seventeenth century that semi-independent groups occupied the northern hills past Tetzcoco, living as "bandits, not recognizing any king or lord, even down until today."[34]

SPATIAL HISTORIES

While Ocotoch's rebellion takes precedence in the Tetzcoco-oriented (and Tlailotlacan-produced) Codex Xolotl, sources from Tepetlaoztoc remember this

FIGURE 1.7. Ocotoch rebels against Acolhua expansion. Note Quinatzin's speech to him in Chichimeca (marked by the "Chia" glyph). Codex Xolotl, plate 3 (*Tlachia* code: X.030.A). *Courtesy*, Bibliothèque nationale de France, Paris.

warlord in other ways. The Memorial de los Indios de Tepetlaoztoc, for example, describes Ocotoch (and his second, Huei Tonatiuh) as founders of the current ruling dynasty in the altepetl: "Two Chichimeca Indians named Huei Tonatiuh and Ocotoch came to settle the pueblo of Tepetlaoztoc. They settled the pueblo and established its limits and landmarks and ruled the pueblo as natural lords. One of them, the one named Ocotoch, had a son named Tohueyo, who in turn had a son..."[35]

Although the Memorial does not textually declare the specific "limits and landmarks" endorsed by Ocotoch, it does reproduce them in two distinct but related maps spread across its opening pages. The first map is political, the second geographical, but both run flush with tlaxilacalli. Map one (figure 1.8)[36] traces Tepetlaoztoc's frontiers and boundaries and optimistically marks each of these "limits" with the

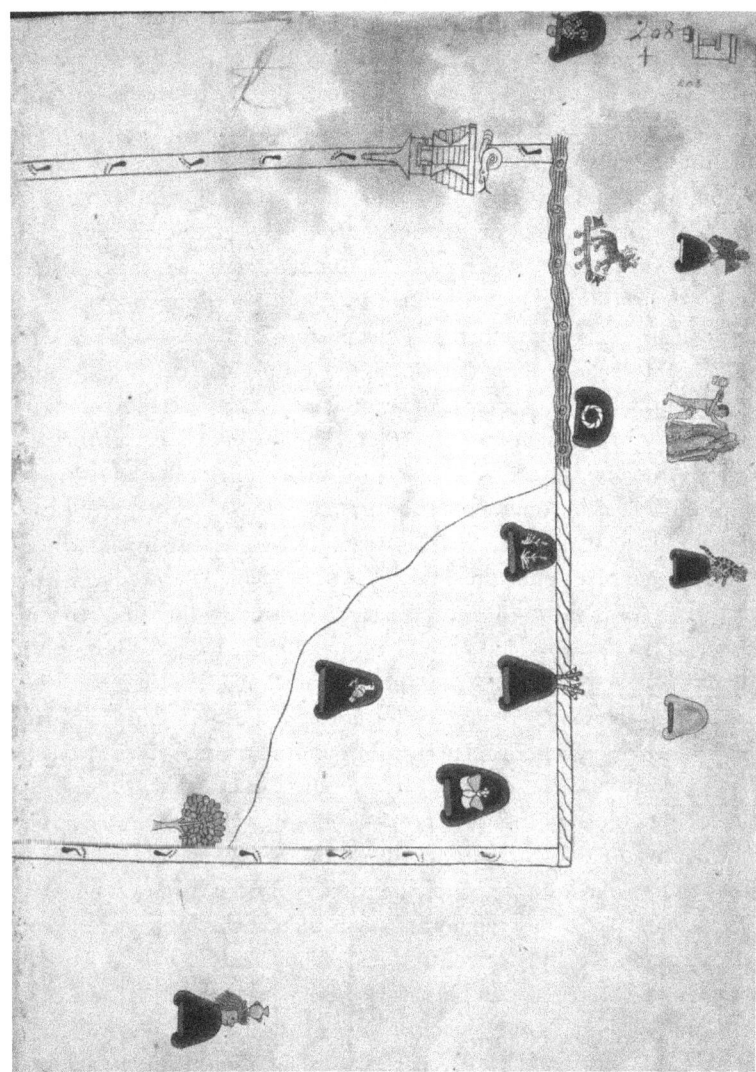

FIGURE 1.8. Boundary tlaxilacalli in Tepetlaoztoc. From *upper right, clockwise*: tlaxilacalli tribute glyph ("house-teeth," partially destroyed), Cuauhchichinolco, Mazaapan ("deer in water," note lack of characteristic "hill" glyph in name), Texcallan, Yahualiuhcan, Ocelotepec, Amalinalco, Xoxoquitepec, Tlamimilolpan, Totoltepec, Papalotla, Tepetzonco, Quauhyacac (tree; no "hill" glyph), Cuauhtepoztlan ceremonial site? (pyramid; no "hill" glyph). Memorial de los Indios de Tepetlaoztoc, f. 1v (map one). *Courtesy*, British Museum, London.

farthest-out tributary tlaxilacalli within the altepetl's orbit. Despite the fact that some tlaxilacalli shifted between Tepetlaoztoc and other abutting altepetl over the centuries—Yahualiuhcan flip-flopped south to Chiautla and back, for example—the Memorial sought to anchor firm administrative claim over them, showing these tlaxilacalli as integral components of the altepetl of Tepetlaoztoc.[37] The second map (figure 1.9) zooms in slightly, nestling local tlaxilacalli within a dense natural landscape. The landmarks in map two include sacred hills and temples, roads and rivers, woods and fields. Again, tlaxilacalli dominate, although the closest-in communities—tlaxilacalli such as Cuauhtepoztlan and Chimalpan—were subsumed into a single glyph for the altepetl of Tepetlaoztoc. The "limits and landmarks" of the Memorial forcefully imply tlaxilacalli, suggesting that, perhaps, Ocotoch recognized the spatial order of these communities even if he rejected Acolhua power.

But the story goes even deeper. Other local codices from Tepetlaoztoc—namely, the related Asunción and Vergara—allow for a still more profound spatial reckoning of local tlaxilacalli. Among other information, these codices record landholding in two close-in tlaxilacalli of Tepetlaoztoc: Cuauhtepoztlan and Chimalpan. Because of the massive population losses that accompanied the production of these codices, the records show a fossilized pattern of landholding that remained visible into modern times: as land pressure dropped, marginal fields such as those in Cuauhtepoztlan were abandoned and their boundary markers left intact.[38]

According to the Codex Asunción, for example, a certain Ciprián Quecil and his household lived on a peculiar twelve-sided plot in the sub-district (*altepemaitl*) of Tlanchiuhcan in Cuauhtepoztlan tlaxilacalli. The irregular shape of Quecil's plot makes it visible in twentieth-century airphotos of the area: in the abandoned area once occupied by Tlanchiuhcan, there appears only one twelve-sided plot of exactly the same dimensions as those demarcated in the Asunción codex (figure 1.10). Particularly given the lack of other twelve-sided fields in the same altepemaitl, the correspondence of this parcel to Quecil's land register becomes undeniable. Around 1540, therefore, Ciprián Quecil and his household lived at the precise coordinates of 19° 35' 47.05" N/ 98° 49' 03.65" W, at the southern tip of his altepemaitl, bordering on the east a small footpath.[39] The use of a similar methodology—that is, building up a model of the entire altepemaitl based on correspondence between codex registers and abandoned modern plots—produces a map of this entire subsection of the tlaxilacalli of Cuauhtepoztlan (figure 1.11).[40]

Through such reconstructions, the spatial history of settlement in Tepetlaoztoc comes powerfully to light. The spatial history of this colonization—at least in the many marginal areas under cultivation—shows noble land claims arriving only after an initial settling push by invading commoners. In the settlement model of Tlanchiuhcan, this pattern becomes particularly clear. To begin, the core residential

FIGURE 1.9. Core Tlaxilacalli in Tepetlaoztoc. From *upper right, clockwise*: Cuauhtepoztlan ceremonial site (pyramid; no "hill" glyph), Tepetlaoztoc (altepetl, not tlaxilacalli), Malinalco, Xoxoquitepec, Tlamimilolpan, Totoltepec, Papalotla, Quauhyacac, Tetlaco, Chicocohuac, Xochitlan, Tonatlan, Ocoxochiyocan, Xacalco, Tototlapan. Memorial de los Indios de Tepetlaoztoc, f. 2v (map two). *Courtesy*, British Museum, London.

56 THE RISE OF TLAXILACALLI, CA. 1272-1454

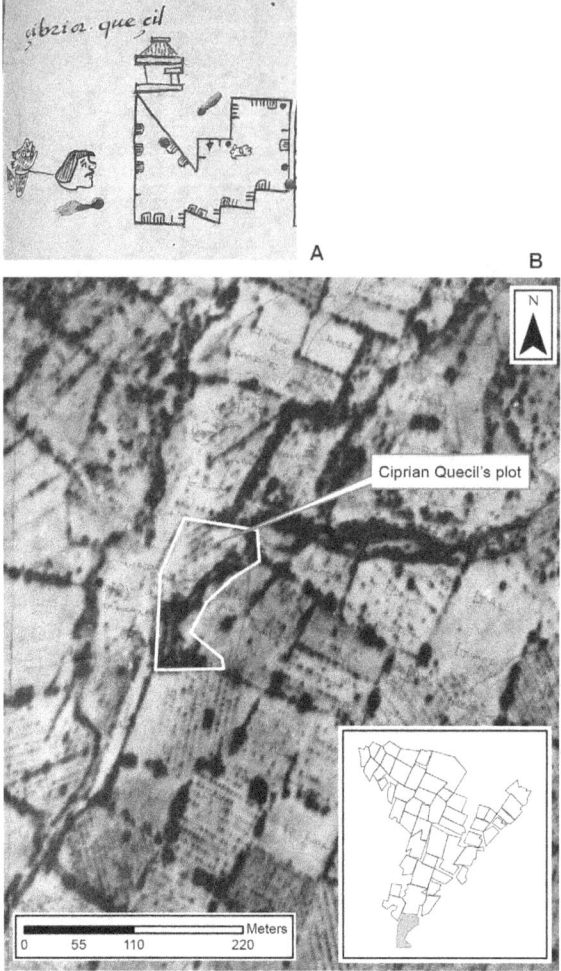

FIGURE 1.10. Ciprian Quecil's plot, in the Asunción codex and a 1968 airphoto. The inset in Map B gives a full reconstruction of Tlanchiuhcan altepemaitl, shown in greater detail in Figure 1.11. *Courtesy*, Biblioteca Nacional de México, Mexico City, and Bentley Historical Library, Ann Arbor, MI.

section contains no elite (dashed perimeter) property. Indeed, all of the central plots of the dominant Nahua group (marked as such by an underlined name on their *calmilli*, or house plot) lay in a continuous run along the main local footpath. Some Hñähñu (Otomí) ethnic minorities such as Ciprián Quecil also lived in

THE RISE OF TLAXILACALLI, CA. 1272–1454   57

FIGURE 1.11. Model of the altepemaitl of Tlanchiuhcan in the tlaxilacalli of Cuauhtepoztlan in Tepetlaoztoc, Mexico. Underlined names mark the site of the house plot (calmilli) of each homestead; dashed borders represent lands held by nobles and worked by dependents. Many tlaxilacalli households held some land independently and worked other lands as dependents. Note that many tlaxilacalli households held some land independently and worked other lands as dependents. Map by Bill and Kris Keegan. Thanks also to Gordon Whittaker for additional help.

this general area but toward the outskirts of the core Nahua settlement, while others lived apart, along the steep edges of the altepemaitl.[41] Also, commoner fields were scattered across the territory—surely the result of the vagaries of inheritance and secondary land markets—but noble landholding was contiguous. Dependent commoners (*mayeque*) lived on noble lands and paid agricultural proceeds to both the local tlaxilacalli and the specific elite owner of the plots they worked.[42]

Taken together, these three spatial features—clustered commoner housing sites, piecemeal commoner landholding, and contiguous elite fields—communicate layers of chronological settlement underlying the wider histories of Tlanchiuhcan altepemaitl, Cuauhtepoztlan tlaxilacalli, and Tepetlaoztoc altepetl. Even from the very beginning of settlement, the tlaxilacalli both structured and reflected local power relations, relations that only become visible once the spatial array is mapped. Judging by housing patterns, Tlanchiuhcan seems to have been settled collectively by a number of commoner households, all arriving to the northern edge of the footpath at roughly the same time, a time before elite interest in the area. These initial colonists and their heirs worked through the local hierarchies of altepemaitl and tlaxilacalli—receiving plots from the collectivity, buying others, gaining still others through marriage or inheritance—to claim distant croplands for themselves, snaking up from the initial core settlement and producing the patchwork of land claims extant in the Codex Asunción. The location of the contiguous elite land—at the edges of the main settlement and climbing steeply up the surrounding hills—suggests that it came later, during the height of mobilization across the wider Triple Alliance, as a forced addition to the core altepemaitl.

The altepemaitl of Tlanchiuhcan—as well as, it seems, the wider tlaxilacalli of Cuauhtepoztlan—began therefore as a self-directed project of Acolhua commoner colonization. However, as Nahua control was firmly established in what had been a Chichimeca stronghold and as the wider push of the Acolhua empire grew in both population and centralizing power, the nobility stepped in and demanded additional hillside planting in Tlanchiuhcan, an endeavor that would further expand the land under cultivation in this altepemaitl. Tlanchiuhcan was therefore both an example and an anomaly, illustrating the general process of commoner colonization as it happened in many Acolhua tlaxilacalli but diverging from this trend in the extent of noble landholding in the area.[43]

In most tlaxilacalli, elites appropriated previously colonized, semi-independent settlements only incompletely and often with considerable difficulty. Marginal colonization—undertaken by a various and shifting group of forward-moving hosts, many of whom bore only passing allegiance to their imperial sponsors—constituted an essential bedrock for later elite efforts toward centralization. These tlaxilacalli colonists brought core institutional forms that eventually facilitated imperial incorporation, but they also opposed later centralizing moves that undermined their local power. Ultimately, this dual pattern of institutional congruence and localist opposition proved decisive to the later structure of Acolhua imperial power.

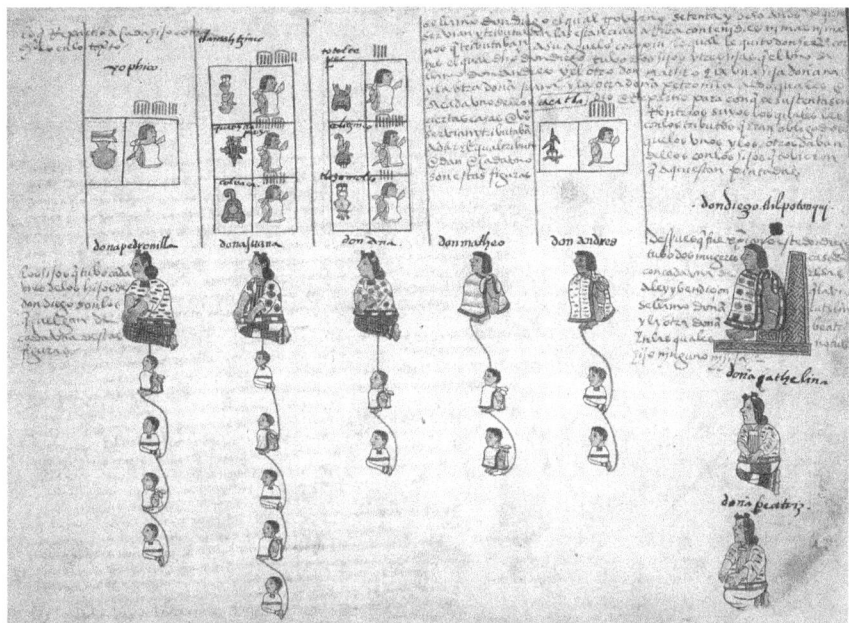

FIGURE 1.12. Noble tlaxilacalli shares in Tepetlaoztoc. Memorial de los Indios de Tepetlaoztoc, f. 3v. *Courtesy*, British Museum, London.

ELITE TLAXILACALLI POLITICS

In late Aztec and early Hispanic Tepetlaoztoc, as elsewhere in central Mexico, a local lord, or *teuctli*, presided over the autonomous confabulation of each tlaxilacalli into the wider structure of the altepetl. The powerful mediating role of these lords is well-known in the scholarly literature: *teuctlatoani*, not the more well-known *tlatoani*, represented the standard category of authority in central Mexico. Indeed, the altepetl-level office of tlatoani simply represented the most powerful teuctlatoani of the confederation, and each tlatoani drew on a specific tlaxilacalli for his (or, occasionally, her) basis of support.[44] During the period described in the Memorial de los Indios de Tepetlaoztoc, for example, the aged tlatoani don Diego Tlilpotonqui appears dividing tribute from eight separate tlaxilacalli among his five children (figure 1.12). Cuauhtepoztlan (the tlaxilacalli modeled above), together with Tlamatzinco and Colhuacan, went to a certain doña Juana; Yopico to doña Petronila; Totoltepec, Colitzinco, and Tlacocomolco to doña Ana; Zacatlan to don Andrés; and none to don Mateo. Aside from certain altepetl-wide privileges accruing to the office of tlatoani, Tlilpotonqui relied on these eight tlaxilacalli for his material and political support. The other twenty-seven tlaxilacalli-based lords consulted and coordinated but did not submit, as the *Memorial* makes plain: "The twenty principles never acquiesced or paid tribute or rent to the aforementioned lord (the tlatoani)." Altepetl-wide power, therefore, grew from the tlaxilacalli.[45]

Even centuries earlier, tlaxilacalli anchored claims to imperial rule. During the early generations of Acolhua power, after the demarcations of Quinatzin and the transculturations of Techotlalatzin, tlaxilacalli had already spread across Acolhuacan. One of the most dispersed of these communities was Tlailotlacan, which had seats in the altepetl of Tetzcoco, Huexotla, Chalco, Acolman, and Ozumba, among many other locations. Since the rule of Ixtlilxochitl Ometochtzin, if not earlier, Tlailotlacan contributed to various ruling *tlacamecayotl* (kin groups) in Tetzcoco.[46]

Countering this power, at least during the time of Ixtlilxochitl Ometochtzin, was the tlaxilacalli of Tepanecapan, which bore the same name as the ambitious political alliance based out of Azcapotzalco, on the western edge of Lake Tetzcoco. Although this tlaxilacalli had arrived in Tetzcoco with four others during the reign of Techotlalatzin, sources suggest it was marginalized from the start. As opposed to Mexicapan and Colhuacan, the two Mexica tlaxilacallli that arrived at the same time, the Codex Xolotl suggests that Tepanecapan was not integrated into existing political regimes in the same way. Whereas the codex shows Techotlalatzin sorting the tlaxilacalli of Mexicapan and Culhuacan together with the already-present Tlailotlacan and Chimalpan, Tepanecapan (as well as Huitznahuac) quickly fell out of the imperial picture (see figure 0.2 in the introduction).[47]

Such a differential welcome was far from innocuous. If the Xolotl is to be believed as a partisan but credible source for pre-Hispanic Acolhuacan—and relevant scholarship increasingly supports this opinion[48]—the separation of Tepanecapan from ruling Acolhua power produced lasting political divisions in Tetzcoco. These breaks came to the fore after the Tepaneca emperor, Tezozomoc of Azcapotzalco, violently overthrew Acolhua power in 1418, killing the huei tlatoani Ixtlilxochitl Ometochtzin. Even the Xolotl's illustration of this assassination shows the divided power of local tlaxilacalli (figure 1.13). In this scene, two assailants—one bearing the glyphs of Tepanecapan and Otumba and the other of Tepanecapan and Chalco—lance Ixtlilxochitl Ometochtzin on the day 10 Eagle. Just to the left of this scene, Chichiquil, the leader of Tlailotlacan tlaxilacalli, recovers Ixtlilxochitl's body a day later and gives it its customary Tlailotlacan-style "Tolteca" cremation. Ixtlilxochitl's son and successor, Nezahualcoyotl, observes the scene from a nearby tree.[49]

There is ambiguity to the "Tepanecapan" glyph cited above—it refers to both tlaxilacalli and empire at different points in the codex—but the idea of tlaxilacalli-based

FIGURE 1.13. Assassination, tlaxilacalli style. Soldiers from Tepanepacan kill Ixtlilxochitl Ometochtzin. The leader of Tlailotlacan then recovers his body. Codex Xolotl, f. 7 (*Tlachia* code: X.070.A). *Courtesy*, Bibliothèque nationale de France, Paris.

conspiracies remains unavoidable. The Tetzcoca historian Ixtlilxochitl notes, for example, that "members from a neighborhood in [Tetzcoco] called the Chimalpaneca killed [Ixtlilxochitl Ometochtzin's] sages and court officials because they were already on [Tezozomoc's] side."[50] Despite Ixtlilxochitl's ongoing conflation of neighborhood and tlaxilacalli, the meaning remains clear: Ixtlilxochitl Ometochtzin was overthrown by the internal machinations of oppositional tlaxilacalli such as Chimalpan. Later on in the Codex Xolotl, Tilmatzin, the leader of Chimalpan, again appears, torturing the aged Acolhua sage Huitzilhuitl with ropes as two Tepanecapan lords goad him on (figure 1.14). Chimalpan and Tepanecapan, and perhaps other tlaxilacalli as well, orchestrated Ixtlilxochitl's fall—from the inside.

TLAXILACALLI AND EMPIRE

Foreshadowing tactics that invading Spanish and Tlaxcalteca forces would employ a century later, the Tepaneca ruler Tezozomoc pulled successive tribute

FIGURE 1.14. Tlaxilacalli machinations. Backed by Tepaneca power, Tilmatzin, the leader of Chiamalpan tlaxilacalli, passes sentence against Acolhua captives. Codex Xolotl, plate 9 (*Tlachia* code: X.090.E). *Courtesy*, Bibliothèque nationale de France, Paris.

hierarchies away from Acolhua control, strengthening his own logistical power at the direct expense of Ixtlilxochitl Ometochtzin.[51] As a result, Acolhuacan completely (if briefly) bent to Tezozomoc's spreading power. Particularly once tlaxilacalli regimes were in place across the Basin of Mexico, tribute became more standardized and commodified, easier to pass between one ruler and the next. But in the end, this rising Tepaneca imperialism would find itself jackknifed by Tezozomoc's successor, Maxtla, who ceded regional hegemony to new upstart powers. Thirteen years after seeing his father murdered by Tezozomoc's allies, the Acolhua leader Nezahualcoyotl joined forces with Mexica tlatoque, Tepaneca dissidents, and intermountain allies from Tlaxcala and Huexotzinco to break Azcapotzalco's dominion in the region. In so doing, he also availed himself of local tlaxilacalli: "He entered in the city with his principals and they all went to sleep in the house of Huitzilhuitl; which, although it was inside the populated area, was at the edge of town, which as I said is where Oztoticpac is" (figure 1.15).[52] After hiding in the cornfields of Oztoticpac, Nezahualcoyotl rallied his troops in the hillside redoubt of Tetzcotzinco and then attacked the ceremonial center of Tetzcoco, expelling the Tepaneca invaders.

Something striking occurs in the Codex Xolotl's narration of this Acolhua retaking of Tetzcoco: tlaxilacalli shoot to the fore while altepetl fade to the background. Although altepetl glyphs for Coatlinchan and Huexotla still appear in plates 9 and 10 as anchors of the major action in central Acolhuacan, the Tetzcoco glyph is noticeably absent—replaced by glyphs for the tlaxilacalli of Tzillan, Chimalpan,

THE RISE OF TLAXILACALLI, CA. 1272–1454   63

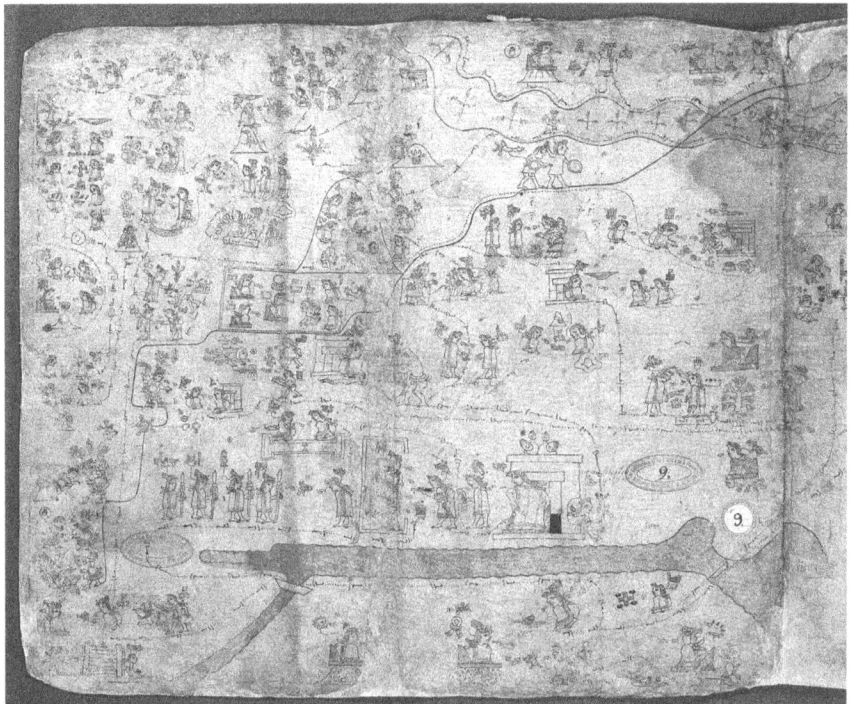

FIGURE 1.15. Tlaxilacalli fill plate 9 of the Codex Xolotl. *Courtesy*, Bibliothèque nationale de France, Paris.

Tetzcotzinco, Oztoticpac, Zacaxochitlan, "Pinolco,"[53] Huilotepec, Coatepec, and Tlanepanolco (figure 1.15).[54] In the Xolotl, tlaxilacalli become the key referents for Tetzcoco's military and political history.

Tlaxilacalli not only constituted the vital stage for Nezahualcoyotl's political action; they also formed the very backbone of his eventual triumph. Just like Tezozomoc before him, Nezahualcoyotl recruited support from various calpixque (tlaxilacalli administrators) across the region, building a network of political support for his coming invasion. According to Ixtlilxochitl, for example, in Pinolco "there was an honorable majordomo (calpixqui) of the Otomí nation who had served his father. When he received word that Nezahualcoyotl was going to sleep in his pueblo, he gathered all the nobles and honorable people from that pueblo and went far out to receive him and treat and console him as much as they could" (figure 1.16). Tlaxilacalli like Pinolco proved vital to Nezahualcoyotl's war effort and structured the politics of the Basin of Mexico for years to come.[55]

FIGURE 1.16. Nezahualcoyotl (obscured by the paper damage but visible in his name glyph) seeks support from the calpixqui of Pinolco tlaxilacalli. Codex Xolotl, plate 9 (Tlachia code: X.090.B). *Courtesy*, Bibliothèque nationale de France, Paris.

DROUGHT YEARS

Nezahualcoyotl's victory consolidated the combined power of Tetzcoco, Tenochtitlan, and Tlacopan in the basin and launched the expansionist profile of what would come to be known as the Aztec Triple Alliance, the great Excan Tlatoloyan. This empire's power was mediated and at times inconsistent, but it also proved to be the most vigorous imperial array in Mesoamerica since Teotihuacan, nearly a millennium before.[56] The new institution of the tlaxilacalli was key to this imperial expansion, both in the flexibility of its administration and the broad extent of its territorial coverage. Tlaxilacalli forced changes across the Basin of Mexico as populations exploded, pushing settlement boundaries to the limit. Nezahualcoyotl's newly reconstituted Acolhuacan was an integral component of this wider imperial drive; and, once again, independent and opportunistic tlaxilacalli hierarchies proved key to the story.

At least this was how things were supposed to go. As misfortune would have it, crops failed miserably beginning in the year Thirteen House (1453). Starvation had hit the Basin of Mexico before, but Thirteen House was particularly bleak. No food remained for either sustenance or ritual, people died in much larger numbers than usual, and the cosmic and temporal orders were called into question. Things became even worse in One Rabbit (1454), and Tetzcoca annals such as the Codex en Cruz recall this and the following year with the image of a naked individual vomiting profusely. Nezahualcoyotl, the huei tlatoani of Acolhuacan at the time, responded as he could. He raised a temple to the Mexica god Huitzilopochtli as a sign of his allegiance to, and leadership within, the consolidating power of the wider Triple Alliance; he sacrificed foreign dignitaries in a plea for full harvests; and he celebrated the eventual return of good yields on the top of the pyramid of the rain god Tlaloc.[57]

The poor cultivators of Acolhuacan, for their part, experienced the drought not as a problem of order but of survival. New expressions entered the Nahua lexicon: *necetochhuiloc* (roughly, "there was One Rabbiting") became a jarring and poetic testament to the horrors of the famine. Across the lake in the Mexica capital, Moteuczoma I erected his notable "hunger stone" monument and freed tlaxilacalli residents from tribute and other commitments to seek survival where they could. Other annals show the twisted forms of commoners lying in the dust as stray dogs scavenged the bodies of the deceased. During these years, death was brutal and survival even more so.[58]

During the lean years, bondage became a viable option for tlaxilacalli commoners and their children. "There was Totonacing," *netotonachuiloc*, is what people said, referring to the rising exchange of captives, both adults and children, for food with the Totonaca people of the Gulf Coast. This trade expanded during the killing famine of 1453–55 and once again during the subsequent appearance of the Thirteen House–One Rabbit calendar sequence in 1505–6 CE. The Codex en Cruz is unmistakable in its reference to Totonacing, depicting a Tetzcoca heading off to the Gulf Coast (marked as such by the distinctive "bird person" visual pun) with a carrying frame and strap, ready for manual service and hauling.[59] Other illustrations are even more explicit, such as those of the Codex Telleriano-Remensis, where a tearful noble laments as a trader carries a bound individual toward the bird people of the lowlands.[60] The Dominican friar Diego Durán, an early Spanish arrival who grew up in Tetzcoco a few decades after the events in question, remarked in the 1570s that "those who left for the land of Totonaca never came back to the cities they left, so that even today you find neighborhoods of (the central Mexican ethnicities)

Mexica, Chalca, Tetzcoca, Xochimilca, and Tepaneca in that land. They went away to live there, and there they remain down to today."[61]

This quote is striking: Durán implies that under the intense pressure of the One Rabbit famine, altepetl ("city" in Durán's retelling) arrangements began to break down across the Basin of Mexico as migratory tlaxilacalli ("neighborhoods") sheared off from wider commitments, heading for Totonacapan. There they remained as tlaxilacalli down to Durán's day, 120 years later. Tlaxilacalli existed before the Aztec empire and anchored its expansion. When this expansion faltered, however, they just as easily detached from these commitments and redeployed, ready for new situations as they evolved. In the end, the Aztecs survived the existential challenge of the "One Rabbit" famine, but tlaxilacalli actions were even more primal: in the case of existential threat, simply detach and reconfigure.

NOTES

1. The use of "first" here simply describes the beginning of the subsequent innovation in local organization that I term *tlaxilacalli*. Local communities, some of them feeding into later tlaxilacalli forms, have a much deeper history in central Mexico.

2. On cycles of concentration and dispersal, see Federico Navarrete Linares, "Las dinámicas históricas y culturales de ciclos de concentración y dispersión en las sociedades amerindias," in *Los pueblos amerindios más allá del Estado*, ed. Berenice Alcántara Rojas and Federico Navarrete Linares (Mexico City: UNAM, 2011), 169–99.

3. Jeffrey R. Parsons, with Richard E. Blanton and Mary H. Parsons, *Prehistoric Settlement Patterns in the Texcoco Region, Mexico* (Ann Arbor: University of Michigan Museum of Anthropology, 1971), 163.

4. Although tlaxilacalli were markedly distinct from earlier forms, comparative research on "typical" Mesoamerican neighborhoods is still useful, particularly because community and spatial divisions have long been important in northern Mesoamerica. Scholarship is particularly vigorous for Classical Teotihuacan. See, for example, the recent edited volume by M. Charlotte Arnauld, Linda R. Manzanilla, and Michael E. Smith, *The Neighborhood as a Social and Spatial Unit in Mesoamerican Cities* (Tucson: Univeristy of Arizona Press, 2012), especially chapters 1–7.

5. Carlos Cordova, "Landscape Transformation in Aztec and Spanish Colonial Texcoco, Mexico" (PhD dissertation, University of Texas, Austin, 1997), 458–59. See also Carlos Cordova, "Pre-Hispanic and Colonial Flood Plain Destabilization in the Texcoco Region and Lower Teotihuacan Valley, Mexico," *Geoarchaeology: An International Journal* 32 (2017): 64–89; Carlos Cordova and Jeffrey Parsons, "Geoarchaeology of an Aztec Dispersed Village on the Texcoco Piedmont of Central Mexico," *Geoarchaeology: An International Journal* 12, no. 3 (1997): 177–210.

6. Archaeological site map by Mary Hrones Parsons, Bentley Historical Library, Ann Arbor, MI, Jeffrey R. Parsons Papers, box 11, vol. Tx-A-22 (I), f. 2r. This work occurred as part of the background preparation for Parsons, Blanton, and Parsons, *Prehistoric Settlement Patterns*, but it was never published.

7. Cordova, "Landscape Transformation," especially chapter 9. Cordova uses the term *dispersed hamlets*, but the array he describes is tlaxilacalli. See the discussion in the previous paragraph for the specific case of Cuauhtepoztlan tlaxilacalli. Toltec here refers to an archaeological era, not necessarily the "Tolteca" farmers who appear frequently in this text.

8. Christian E. Isendahl and Michael E. Smith—"Sustainable Agrarian Urbanism: The Low-Density Cities of the Mayas and Aztecs," *Cities* 31 (2013): 138–40—have recently shown the ecological sustainability of Aztec and Maya urbanism, with the Aztec case anchored in the "calpulli." For their part, Parsons and colleagues repeatedly highlight the importance of what they call "calpulli" but also note that "because of the relatively continuous distribution of dispersed rural occupation in the Tetzcoco Region, we have had little success in delineating on the ground discrete zones of occupation which might be regarded as *calpulli* or *barrio pequeño* units." Parsons, Blanton, and Parsons, *Prehistoric Settlement Patterns*, 230. They do identify one candidate that can be separated out because of the remoteness of its hillside area: site Tx-A-25, just outside Tepetlaoztoc. This, in fact, corresponds to the tlaxilacalli of Tlamimilolpan.

9. For tlalcoztli soils, see Cordova, "Landscape Transformation," 211; Williams and Harvey, eds., *The Códice*, 33. In 2011, Aurelio López Corral ("Los glifos de suelo en códices acolhua de la Colonia temprana: un reanálisis de su significado," *Desacatos* 37: 145–62) challenged the idea of globalizing soil typologies in Acolhua codices. Drawing from a broader evidenciary base, Barbara J. Williams and Janice K. Pierce successfully refuted this claim three years later, in "Evidence of Acolhua Science in Pictorial Land Records," in *Texcoco*, ed. Lee and Brokaw, 147–64, especially 156–60.

10. Regarding land estimates, tlaxilacalli regimes surely lost territory after the fall of Mexico-Tenochtitlan. Spaniards and other foreigners appropriated lands for their own uses (although at this early stage, still often through tlaxilacalli regimes—see chapter 3), and the first wave of demographic collapse also removed laborers from lands. This said, land tenure in the Codex Asunción was only hit by the first wave of demographic collapse, making its registers more conservative than many extant registers. For example, it contains entries for land-poor tlaxilacalli subsections (altepemaitl) such as Tlatozcac, which were quickly abandoned after the fall of the Aztec empire.

11. For a model of population collapse that fits well with available sixteenth-century evidence, see Thomas M. Whitmore, "A Simulation of the Sixteenth-Century Population Collapse in the Basin of Mexico," *Annals of the Association of American Geographers* 81, no. 3 (September 1991): 464–87.

12. All of these characterizations of innovation are from Cordova, "Landscape Transformation," chapters 4, 5, and 9. On the return to maize agriculture from a previous focus

on amaranth and other grains, see Martin Biskowski and Karen D. Watson, "Changing Approaches to Maize Preparation at Cerro Portezuelo," *Ancient Mesoamerica* 24, no. 1 (2013): 213–23; also Martin Biskowski, "Maize Preparation and the Aztec Subsistence Economy," *Ancient Mesoamerica* 11, no. 2 (2000): 293–306.

13. "Oncan ye tlatequipanoloz cemicac quihuallocatiaz in apamitl in cuitlalpitica tepetl, nicahuilia nic nemactia in Taluhpopocatzin Tezontla conizque inipilhuan ihuan ic mopalehuizque, in motequipanozque, za niman ayac huel quincuiliz, can in tlatqui, ca in iciyahuiliztica in oquilhual yacanque." Byron McAffee and R. H. Barlow, "The Titles of Tetzcotzinco (Santa Maria Nativitas)," *Tlalocan* 2, no. 2 (1946): 115.

14. From other documents, it is clear that Tezontla is a tlaxilacalli; see, for example, Biblioteca Nacional de Antropología e Histoira, Terecera Série de Papeles Sueltos (hereafter BNAH-3PS), leg. 7, exp. 218, ff. 10rr.

15. Unless specifically noted otherwise, "tribute" refers to tribute in-kind of various forms, later passing to an admixture of tribute in-kind and cash in the Hispanic period

16. On the dispersion of single houses, see Parsons, Blanton, and Parsons, *Prehistoric Settlement Patterns*, 82–83 (sites Tx-LT-21, Tx-LT-23, and Tx-LT-27); on early reclamation efforts, see Cordova, "Landscape Transformation," especially chapters 5, 6, and 9. Parsons and colleagues (218) also consider "particularly interesting" the "fact that [population] centers grew up in areas where occupation in all preceding periods had been very sparse."

17. The Codex Xolotl and related sources repeatedly privilege Chichimeca experiences of migration, invasion, and dynasty building over local domestic narratives—despite the fact that Tolteca patterns of language, religion, politics, and economics dominated Chichimeca forms across Acolhuacan. In fact, Chichimeca sedentarism appears as an explicit strategy of Tolteca groups—mostly from Chalco, to the immediate south of the future Acolhuacan—to socialize foreign invaders into their local customs and hierarchies. See Federico Navarrete Linares, "Chichimecas y toltecas en el valle de México," *Estudios de Cultura Náhuatl* 42 (2011): 45. Navarrete Linares later broadened this analysis to create an early dynastic history of Tetzcoco in *Los orígenes de los pueblos indígenas del valle de México: Los altépetl y sus historias* (Mexico City: UNAM, 2011), 293–341. On the diversity of Chichimeca, see Rudolf van Zantwijk, "Tlen Quihtoznequi 'Chichimecatl,'" *Estudios de Cultura Náhuatl* 25 (1995): 131–47.

18. Ixtlilxochitl, *Obras* (1952), 1:36. The capture of the southeastern quadrant of the Basin of Mexico by "northern" Chichimeca elites can also be seen in a reorientation of ceramics trade from a southern influence to a northern one. See Destiny L. Crider, "Shifting Alliances: Epiclassic and Early Postclassic Interactions at Cerro Portezuelo," *Ancient Mesoamerica* 24, no. 1 (2013): 107–30.

19. On Acolhua rites of possession, see Ixtlilxochitl, *Obras* (1952), 1:295–96; Michel R. Oudijk, "La toma de posesión: Un tema mesoamericano para la legitimación del poder," *Relaciones: Estudios de historia y sociedad* 23, no. 91 (2002): 97–131. Entering this section based on the Xolotl and related texts, recall both the strengths and limitations of this

and other Hispanic-era documents as sources for earlier history. See introduction, 20–23. See also Jerome Offner's analysis of early tribute flows in Tepetlaoztoc in "Aztec Political Numerology," 208–10.

20. Parsons, Blanton, and Parsons, *Prehistoric Settlement Patterns*, 80–85; Cordova, "Landscape Transformation," chapters 5, 6, 9.

21. "Iba repartiendo por los de su Nacion, y Casta, y de esta fuerte volvio a crecer, y multiplicarse esta Planta, y a cundir por toda la Tierra." Juan de Torquemada, *Monarquía Indiana*, 2nd ed. (Madrid: Nicolás Rodríguez Franco, 1723), 1:67. The detached actions of this ruler from the direct influence of imperial Tula suggest the use of quotes to separate imperial Tolteca from the later "Tolteca."

22. Both Charles Dibble (*Códice Xolotl*, 55: "jardines") and Marc Thouvenot (*Tlachia* code: X.030.B.12: "callalli") read this glyph as only referencing single domestic houses. The broader, altepetl-wide context of every other demarcated field in the Xolotl militates against this interpretation, however.

23. Codex Xolotl, f. 3 (*Tlachia* code: X.030.I.04).

24. On Ilancueitl, see Susan D. Gillespie, *The Aztec Kings: The Construction of Rulership in Mexica History* (Tucson: University of Arizona Press, 1988). On Acamapichtli, see Rudolf van Zantwijk, "La entronización de Acamapichtli de Tenochtitlan y las caracteristicas de su gobierno," *Estudios de Cultura Náhuatl* 15 (1982): 17–26.

25. "compeliendo a los chichimecas no tan solamente a ello [que cultivara maíz], sino a que poblasen y edificasen ciudades y lugares, sacándolos de su rústica y silvestre vivienda, siguiendo el orden y estilo de los tultecas, por cuya causa muchos de los chichimecas se alteraron." Ixtlilxochitl, *Obras* (1952), 2:30; Codex Xolotl, ff. 1r–3r.

Relying on two scenes from the Xolotl, Jongsoo Lee (*Allure*, 77) argues that Quinatzin established his base of power in Tetzcoco with the "permission" of Huetzin of Coatlinchan. It is true that Coatlinchan exercised important power in the region, but Quinatzin appears not to have been completely dependent. The first scene—from plate 2 of the Xolotl, partially excerpted in figure 3.1 of his book—shows Yacatzotzolotl of Tepetlaoztoc and his allies paying tribute to Huetzin of Coatlinchan. This is true as far as it goes, but Lee elides another, richer line of tribute snaking down to Quinatzin and away from Huetzin. Indeed, it portrays Quinaztin sitting on a throne of authority (*icpalli*) while Huetzin sits facing Quinatzin, without the icpalli. Again, on plate 3 of the Xolotl—which Lee (*Allure*, 53, figure 2.3) describes as Quinaztin "asking permission" from Huetzin to found Tetzcoco—Quinatzin again appears on an icpalli while Huetzin does not. (Huetzin does appear on an icpalli in another scene on plate 3; but in the scene Lee cites, the scene involving Quinaztin, he does not.) This said, Coatlinchan and Huexotla did rise to prominence earlier than Tetzcoco.

26. The act of founding is not included in the Xolotl, but the scene quoted in figure 1.6 does include all the necessary glyphs: the year One Flint, the tlaxilacalli of Oztoticpac, and Tetzcoco on a mountain, signifying "altepetl."

27. Codex Xolotl, f. 3.

28. All these adaptations are in the Codex Xolotl. See also Offner, *Law and Politics*, 46.

29. On Techotlalatzin and the smaller territorial extent of Acolhuacan than once imagined, see Jerome A. Offner, "A Reassessment of the Extent and Structuring of the Empire of Techotlalatzin, Fourteenth Century Ruler of Texcoco," *Ethnohistory* 26, no. 3 (1979): 231–41.

30. Offner's "Reassessment" also includes a discussion of ethnic politics, 233–36.

31. "El ídolo y estatua llamado Tlaloc es más antiguo en esta tierra, porq dicen q los mismos culhuaq le hallaron en esta tierra, y no haciendo caso de él los chichimecas, ellos le comenzaron á adorar y reverncia por dios de las agua." Pomar, "Relación," 60. It is possible that the "Colhuaque" in Pomar's text references a wider group of migrants from Colhuacan, but context suggests otherwise.

32. On Tezcatlipoca, see Guilhem Olivier, *Tezcatlipoca: Burlas y metamorfosis de un dios azteca* (Mexico City: FCE, 2004). On Huitznahuac, see Pomar, "Relación," 55. On Techotlalatzin's ethnic (and tlaxilacalli) policies, see Offner, "Reassessment." On sacrifice, see Ixtlilxochitl, *Obras* (1952), 2:35.

33. Codex Xolotl, ff. 3–5.

34. "hechos bandoleros sin reconocer à rey ni señor, como lo están hasta el día de hoy." Ixtlilxochitl, *Obras* (1952), 1:67. The five generations come by counting the rulers between Ocotoch and Cocopin: Memorial de los Indios de Tepetlaoztoc, British Museum Am2006, Drg. 13964, ff. 210v–211r.

35. "vinieron a poblar al pueblo de Tepetlaoztoc dos indios chichimecas que se llamaban Hueytonatiuh y Hocotochtli. Los cuales poblaron el pueblo y establecieron sus límites y mojones y señorearon el pueblo como señores naturales. Uno de ellos, el que se llamaba Hocotochtli, tuvo un hijo que se llamba Tohueyo quien a su vez tuvo un hijo." Memorial de los Indios de Tepetlaoztoc, f. 210v.

36. Valle, *Memorial*, 13–21, also gives a reading of the glyphs in the two maps. Many are useful; some like Coatlinchan, which is sited to the north of Tepetlaoztoc instead of to the far south, are not. Also, José Omar Tinajero Morales, *Imágenes del silencio: Iconología de Tepetlaoztoc* (Mexico City: CEASDP, 2002), 39–42, has been of some use. The author, a local historian from Tepetlaoztoc de Hidalgo, knows the landscape well. In some cases, however, he correctly identifies the location but presents a muddled reading of the glyphs: the double *mitl* (arrow) component in Tlamimilolpan, for example, is absent in this author's reading. In addition, the temple in the two maps is tentatively sited in Cuauhtepoztlan, based primarily on its location in space and the still-existing (if ransacked) ruins of a pyramid in the current ceremonial lands of the modern Asunción cofradía in Tepetlaoztoc, a descendent of Cuauhtepoztlan tlaxilacalli.

37. For one example of Yahualiuhcan as annexed to Chiautla, see Juan de San Antonio's letter in Domingo Chimalpahin, *Codex Chimalpahin: Society and Politics in Mexico Tenochtitlan, Tlatelolco, Texcoco, Culhuacan, and Other Nahua Altepetl in Central Mexico:*

The Nahuatl and Spanish Annals and Accounts, ed. and trans. Arthur J.O. Anderson, Susan Schroeder, and Wayne Ruwet (Norman: University of Oklahoma Press, 1997), 2:236. This is the case of one single tlaxilacalli, not multiple tlaxilacalli with the same name.

38. Across history, boundary markers are among the most conservative human signs left on landscapes. See Timothy Earle, "Archaeology, Property, and Prehistory," *Annual Review of Anthropology* 29 (2000): 51. For the Maya region, see Matthew Restall, *The Maya World: Yucatec Culture and Society, 1550–1850* (Stanford: Stanford University Press, 1999), 105, 146, 200–205.

39. The twelve sides of Quecil's lands measured 26.5 × 4 × 21.6 × 1 × 10 × 16 × 11 × 2 × 10 × 2 × 7 × 3 × 6 × 26 tlalquahuitl, which correspond exactly to the airphoto in figure 1.9. The rest of the altepemaitl was reconstructed in the same way: matching lengths to observable plots. On tlalquahuitl as a historical land measurement, see chapter 2, note 34.

40. Some notes on the methodology of this reconstruction: the map was first assembled by removing all distinguishing political features from each piece, leaving only lengths and soils. These pieces were then placed on the landscape, and field lengths with identical or similar measurements were matched on abutting parcels. This allowed for the landscape to reveal the spatial array of the tlaxilacalli, free from preconceived notions about social or political sorting. It also makes such features as the complete segregation of elite lands all the more striking. Finally, there were two households in this altepemaitl with the same Nahua name, Tecolotl. For clarity one of these Tecolotls uses the given Christian name Damián in the map.

Also, because parts of Cuauhtepoztlan are still under heavy use, a complete reconstruction of the Aztec-era tlaxilacalli was unfeasible. The altepemaitl of Tlanchiuhcan was chosen as a model for a number of reasons. First, unlike the central areas of Cuauhtepoztlan tlaxilacalli, it was abandoned soon after the fall of Mexico-Tenochtitlan, leaving its spatial array intact. It is also the largest of the "fossilized" sub-districts of Cuauhtepoztlan, providing a wider view of a fuller spatial array. The southern half of the "fossilized" sub-district of Tlanchiuhcan still retains nearly all of the boundary markers used in early Hispanic times and can be reconstructed using the same tactics as described for Ciprián Quecil—that is, by matching lengths to observable plots—which gives substantial confidence to the reconstructions. The northern half, where boundary markers are less extant, primarily because of steeper inclines, is more impressionistic. Three other abandoned altepemaitl (Chiauhtenco, Tlatozcac, and Zapotlan) were also modeled and showed similar characteristics to Tlanchiuhcan.

41. On the problematic but common name "Otomí" and the difficulties of choosing another standard term for this diverse ethnic and linguistic group, see David Charles Wright Carr, "'Hñahñu, Ñuhu, Ñhato, Ñuhmu: Precisiones sobre el término 'otomí,'" *Arqueología Mexicana* 12, no. 73 (May 2005): 19. For a history of general Hñähñu history and achievement, the best introduction is Carr, "Los otomíes."

42. Despite work on this problem—see, for example, Pedro Carrasco, "Los mayeques," *Historia Mexicana* 39, no. 1 (July–September 1989): 123–66—the precise relationship of

mayeque to nobles remains inconclusive. What is clear is that these mayeque also participated in tlaxilacalli hierarchies. The Codex Asunción lists mayeque within the normal tlaxilacalli censuses of Cuauhtepoztlan, although its cousin the Codex Vergara marks slightly more separation, listing mayeque at the end of its register of Chimalpan tlaxilacalli.

43. Parsons, Blanton, and Parsons, *Prehistoric Settlement Patterns*, 218, describe this process thus: "There was a general filling in of the Lower and Upper Piedmont zones [that is, of all areas between Lake Tetzcoco and the surrounding mountains] throughout the northern half of the Tetzcoco Region [i.e., Acolhuacan; the southern half was Chalco, a separate realm], with numerous small communities distributed in fairly continuous fashion."

44. On teuctli and the tlaxilacalli-specific office of teuctlatoani, see Lockhart, *The Nahuas after the Conquest*, 16–18.

45. "Los veinte principales nunca tributaron ni acudieron con tributo ni renta al dicho señor." Memorial de los Indios de Tepetlaoztoc, f. 214r. Although the text of the Memorial mentions twenty principales, its pictographic component includes twenty-seven.

46. Codex Xolotl, f. 4. Tlailotlacan's support of Ixtlilxochitl Ometochtzin can be inferred by this tlaxilacalli's recovery and burial of the huei tlatoani's body after his assassination. See Codex Xolotl, f. 7 (*Tlachia* code: X.070.A).

47. Codex Xolotl, f. 5 (*Tlachia* code: X.050.B and X.050.F).

48. Cf. Offner, "Ixtlilxochitl's Ethnographic Encounter."

49. Codex Xolotl, f. 7 (*Tlachia* code: X.070.A); Ixtlilxochitl, *Obras* (1952), 1:168–69. Although the "stone-flag" glyph likely references imperial Tepanecapan more than the tlaxilacalli of the same name, firm divisions between imperial politics and tlaxilacalli communities are often hard to make. In the Tepaneca capital of Azcapotzalco, for example, invading Mexica power was exercised primarily through newly imposed tlaxilacalli, which scaled up to the tlayacatl of Mexicapan. See María Castañeda de la Paz, "Dos parcialidades étnicas en Azcapotzalco: Mexicapan y Tepanecapan," *Estudios de Cultura Náhuatl* 46 (2013): 223–48.

50. "los de un barrio de la ciudad llamados chimalpanecas, mataron los ayos y gente de la recámara del rey por ser ya del bando de los tiranos." Ixtlilxochitl, *Obras* (1952), 2:89.

51. A clear example of this tlaxilacalli appropriation can be seen in plate 7 of the Codex Xolotl (*Tlachia* code: X.070.D), where Tepaneca soldiers accost a calpixqui. On the powerful articulation between imperial elites and local tlaxilacalli, see Isabel Bueno Bravo, "La importancia del faccionalismo en la política mesoamericana," *Revista de Indias* 64, no. 232 (2004): 654–58.

52. "entró dentro de la ciudad con la gente principal y fueron á dormir en la casa de Huitzilhuitzin, que aunque estaba dentro (de la población) estaba al cabo de la ciudad, como tengo dicho en donde es Oztotipac." Ixtlilxochitl, *Obras* (1952), 1:174.

53. The glyph is very deteriorated. Ixtlilxochitl, *Obras* (1952), 1:215, reads it as "Pinolco," but Marc Thouvenot doubts this reading (*Tlachia* code: X.090.B.16).

54. Not all tlaxilacalli glyphs are included in figure 1.15. Some continue on in plate 10.

55. "fue á Pinolco, en donde esjahora Quacoxo, para hacer noche en este lugar, en donde vivía un caballero Mayordomo que había sido de su padre, de nación Otomite, el cual teniendo noticia de que iba á dormir esta noche en su pueblo Nezáhualcoyotl, juntó todos los nobles y gente honrada de aquel pueblo y á buen trecho le salió á recibir y le regaló y consoló todo lo que pudo." Ixtlilxochitl, *Obras* (1952), 1:215.

56. On the Excan Tlatololoyan, see María del Carmen Herrera Meza, Alfredo López Austin, and Rodrigo Martínez Baracs, "El nombre náhuatl de la Triple Alianza," *Estudios de Cultura Náhuatl* 46 (2013): 8–35. For the orchestration of Acolhua power, see Offner, *Law and Politics*.

57. Cf. *Codex en Cruz*, 2 vols., ed. Charles E. Dibble (Salt Lake City: University of Utah Press, 1981). Vomiting evokes starvation because of the nearly inedible nature of desperation foods, which never sat well in the stomach.

58. Judging by its appearance in sources as varied as the Codex Aubin, the Codex Chimalpahin, the Florentine Codex, and the *Anales de Tula*, the term *necetochhuiloc* seems to have been in wide popular usage in the sixteenth century. Matthew D. Therrell, David W. Stahle, and Rodolfo Acuña Soto suggest ("Aztec Drought and the 'Curse of One Rabbit,'" *Bulletin of the American Meteorological Society* 85, no. 9 [2004]: 1263–72) that there was a deeper memory for One Rabbit droughts, reaching back to perhaps even the ninth century. This seems unlikely, however; only a horrible drought would have entered the lexicon as "One Rabbiting," and this term seems to have appeared after 1454. Nevertheless, following this date the stigma of One Rabbit became so troublesome that, according to the Codex Telleriano-Remensis, the younger Moteuczoma postponed the epoch-marking New Fire ceremony (scheduled for One Rabbit, 1505–6) for a year order to avoid the curse. The scavaging dog image comes from the Codex Huichapan, lamina 37. This codex is available online from the Instituto Nacional de Antropología e Historia, accessed August 8, 2016, http://www.codices.inah.gob.mx/pc/contenido.php?id=32.

59. Codex en Cruz. Regarding the "bird person" pun, one of the words for bird in Nahuatl is *tototl*, which shares beginning syllables with the word Totonaca, *totonacatl*. The pierced septum references the Huasteca people, who lived just north of the Totonaca.

60. Eloise Quiñones Keber, in her commentary on the Codex Telleriano-Remensis—*Codex Telleriano-Remensis: Ritual, Divination, and History in a Pictorial Aztec Manuscript*, ed. Eloise Quiñones Keber (Austin: University of Texas Press, 1995), 228—suggests that the bound individual in figure 1.2 is a mummy bundle. This seems unlikely, however, given two important divergences from the canonical form: the eyes are open instead of closed, and the head and feet are uncovered. Particularly given the context, this individual was being taken for sale on the Gulf Coast.

61. "los que salieron para la provincia de Totonacapan . . . nunca mas voluieron á las ciudades de donde auian salido, y así se hallan oy en dia en aquella tierra barrios de mexicanos, chalcas, tezcucanos, xuchimilca, tepanecas, que desde aquel tiempo se fueron á vivir

allí y permanecen hasta el dia de oy. No quisieron voluer más a su natural, temiendo otro semejante suceso y sauiendo que la provincia mexicana carecia de tierras para poder sembrar." Durán, *Historia*, 249. Durán's telling reference to "barrios" as the spatial and political framework for migrants to the Gulf Coast is yet another indication of the importance of tlaxilacalli for the local organization of central Mexicans, even away from their home territories.

2

Acolhua Imperialisms, ca. 1420s–1583

As Nezahualcoyotl rose to command alongside the expanding the Aztec Triple Alliance, most tlaxilacalli quickly fell in line behind his consolidating power. Such reintegration appears clearly in the little-studied final section of the Codex Xolotl, where the canonical tlaxilacalli of Chimalpan and Tlailotlacan make their peace with the new Acolhua huei tlatoani. The sequence begins by profiling Chimalpan's rulers following the exit of the traitorous Tilmatzin, last seen in chapter 1 (figure 1.14) ordering the execution of Acolhua notables. After Nezahualcoyotl's victory, Tilmatzin's sister Tozquentzin, along with her husband, assumed control of Chimalpan and had four sons. The oldest two, Chimalpopoca and Iztaccoyotl, assumed major priestly duties in the altepetl: Chimalpopoca as the head priest (cihuacoatl) of all of Tetzcoco and Itzaccoyotl as the religious leader of Tlailotlacan.[1]

Because of the treachery of their uncle Tilmatzin, the two brothers from Chimalpan sent special emissaries to Nezahualcoyotl to ask for his forgiveness (figure 2.1). As the codex shows, the huei tlatoani received the mission and then conducted a special drinking ritual with one of the emissaries, perhaps of political and metaphysical reintegration. This final section of the Xolotl (the second half of plate 10) is often ignored because Nezahualcoyotl appears only incidentally, breaking a core heroic narrative the codex had been building for half its total extension. Seen from the perspective of Chimalpan and Tlailotlacan, however, the tlaxilacalli most likely to have produced the Codex Xolotl, this final section proves crucial—affirming their loyalty, legitimizing their status, and neutralizing earlier machinations against Acolhua power.[2]

FIGURE 2.1. Chimalpan apologizes. *A*: the post-Tilmatzin dynasty in Chimalpan, including the first two sons, Chimalpopoca and Iztac Coyotl. *B*: Chimalpopoca and Iztacoyotl send emissaries with pulque to Nezahualcoyotl. *C*: Nezahualcoyotl receives the mission. *D*: one of the emissaries celebrates with Nezahualcoyotl in front of the pulque. Codex Xolotl, plate 10 (*Tlachia* code: X.101). *Courtesy*, Bibliothèque nationale de France, Paris.

Such behavior was standard and was repeated again after the fall of the Aztec Triple Alliance. Indeed, it constituted part of the distinct form of tlaxilacalli-based Acolhua imperial strategies—strategies that soon repeated during and after the fall of Mexico-Tenochtitlan. This chapter illustrates many of the patterns of local Acolhua imperialism, taking the sixteenth-century War for Mexico and its aftermath as a key exemplary case. Aztec-era sources are particularly sparse for these questions, but what is recoverable synchronizes well with deeper Hispanic-era documentation. A wider pattern of tlaxilacalli-based imperialism does seem to exist, and when Aztec documentation allows, reference will be made to this wider panorama. This history of local imperialism begins, however, with a rewrite.

ACOLHUA THEORIES OF IMPERIALISM

In the aftermath of Mexico-Tenochtitlan's fall, Acolhua administrators and intellectuals assayed their earlier imperial history and produced a practical working definition of tlaxilacalli-based imperialism, working to apply it to new Hispanic circumstances. Much like the Chimalpan's peace-brokering with Nezahualcoyotl after the Tepaneca War, Acolhua communication specialists also sought to curry favor with their new Hispanic overlords after the fall of Mexico-Tenochtitlan. As much recent scholarship has shown, these tlacuiloque rewrote and reanalyzed available sources to highlight anti-Mexica themes from the start. They even appear to have invented a providential civil war led by the second Ixtlilxochitl (later named Hernando) against centralizing Tetzcoco power leading up to the fall of the Aztec empire. Although Hernando Ixtlilxochitl became tlatoani of Tetzcoco five years after the fall of Mexico-Tenochtitlan, certain sources make him a full huei tlatoani at the eve of the Spanish and Tlaxcalteca invasions.[3] The primary revisionist here was the historiographer Fernando de Alva Ixtlilxochitl, but even he shows his namesake rising to prominence during the fall of the Aztec empire, not before. He contrasts the imputed lone protagonism of Hernando Ixtlilxochitl with the flight of Tetzcoco's huei tlatoani, Coanacoch, to Mexico-Tenochtitlan: "That afternoon, [Coanacoch] embarked with all the lords and gentlemen who were of his opinion. Taking with them their belongings and women, they went to the city of Mexico, abandoning Tetzcoco and causing such rage that the citizens began to riot, some entering into the lake after the king and others ascending the mountains. Ixtlilxochitl was alone and abandoned, trying to retain the people."[4]

Hernando Ixtlilxochitl strove to "retain the people": that is, he worked to redirect tlaxilacalli support toward the invading armies. According to Ixtlilxochitl, the primary contribution of his great-grandfather to the Spanish-Tlaxcalteca war effort was to simply keep Acolhua tribute flowing, only now to different recipients. Other Acolhua histories, such as the Tetzcoca relations appended to the end of the Codex Chimalpahin, also assert that a primary wartime concern of tlatoque should have been the retention of commoners, on whose shoulders the entire imperial structure depended: "If Coanacochtzin had done what the Captain [Cortés] had said, great benefit would have thus been done to the altepetl and the macehualtin. For it is the task of the tlatoque when dangers befall the altepetl to try to determine how they may save the macehualtin, so that it may be well with the altepetl and so that the macehualtin do not, as it were, flee along the roads."[5] Here, distilled to its purest form, is an Acolhua theory of imperialism: retain commoners on the land; tie them through tlaxilacalli regimes to a wider alliance, making sure they are not "ashamed of the altepetl";[6] and then join the various altepetl together through marriage, negotiation, or warfare. It is a recipe for empire; just add tlaxilacalli.

A SHAKEN LOCAL ORDER

The War for Mexico in the years One Reed–Three House (1519–21) initiated a century-long social, demographic, and ecological upending of earlier patterns in the Basin of Mexico. Populations fell drastically, but mostly because of disease and ecological upheaval, not violent conflict. The best current models of demographic collapse give primary destructive weight to epidemics (80% of 1.6 million in the Basin of Mexico dead over the century) and famine (10%), not to homicide or battlefield casualties.[7] Ecosystems crumpled under this biological assault, forcing broad changes to even the most central and centering institutions of collective life—institutions such as the tlaxilacalli.

Nevertheless, tlaxilacalli proved structuring, even under duress. The world-historical onslaught of the Columbian Exchange hit areas far beyond Mesoamerica, but Spanish dominion arrived in the Basin of Mexico with comparative completeness and rapidity. In contrast to nearly every other population center in pre-Hispanic America, central Mexico saw no major revolts against Spanish rule in the first decades after the overthrow of Aztec power—although conspiracies did bubble. Just as remarkable was the pace of victory: imperial occupation in two years instead of the twenty or more spent in comparable regions like Perú or Yucatán. The difference lay in tlaxilacalli regimes, built with the necessary flexibility for precisely such reorganizations. If Nezahualcoyotl could easily reassign lands and tributes, so could Cortés.[8]

Tlaxilacalli hierarchies played a key connective role in both Acolhua imperial practice and its post-epidemic, Hispanic-oriented re-articulation. Although relevant documentation in both Spanish and Nahuatl tends to emphasize heroic biographies over institutional practice, tlaxilacalli influence is pervasive enough that it can be easily extracted from available sources. The Codex Chimalpahin, for example, clearly shows how a new imperial net was pulled from the threads of the old and also the ways in which two related urban hierarchies in Tetzcoco—the new, reordered, and Hispanizing city (ciudad) and the older, imperial huei altepetl—struggled to control local tlaxilacalli.

The anonymous authors of the Tetzcoca material in the Codex Chimalpahin show a fractured response to foreign rule, led by tlaxilacalli administrators (calpixque) in various Acolhua tlaxilacalli—the text mentions Calpulalpan (often taken as an altepetl but treated here as a tlaxilacalli), Yahualiuhcan, Mazaapan, Zoltepec, Coatepec, Itztapalocan, Quauhtlapan, Tlapechhuacan, Hueheutl Itzalan, and Chalco Ocotepec[9]—pulling tribute hierarchies across the region and, remarkably, dragging ascribed nobles along with them. Although the heroic mode of this relation gives initial agency to Cortés and Hernando Ixtlilxochitl,[10] the administrative power of the tlaxilacalli rises toward the end of the narration, separating nobles from traditional claims as land and tribute regimes were renegotiated. This conception inverted standard interpretations of calpixque serving the local nobility, but it is quite possible that the organizational power of the tlaxilacalli overcame the inherited prestige of the nobility—particularly in cases of duress such as the one here. Here is the striking quote, in its entirety:

> The Captain [Cortés] held back all the lands of the tlatoani. Do they really belong to the office of tlatoani (*tlatocayotl*)? And the noble lands, do they belong to Tetzcoco? Do they belong there? When he deprived Ixtlilxochitl of his lands, nobles (*pipiltin*) suffered much in Tlaxcala, in Huexotzinco, in Chalco, everywhere that people work fields for the pipiltin. But the women kept on spinning for them, weaving for them. And the calpixque took [these commoners] from one place to another, along with the pipiltin ascribed to them. Sometimes it was in Otumba that they settled, and sometimes it was in Teotihuacan that they settled, sometimes it was in Tlatelolco that they settled, sometimes it was in Mexico that they settled. For six years, he maintained [the tributaries]. But when Ixtlilxochitl did thus, were benefits done to the altepetl of Tetzcoco? Did he not mistreat the practice of rulership?[11]

In this formulation, local nobles came along as part of the tlaxilacalli—ascribed to, even dependent on, this local bureaucracy. More than this, tlaxilacalli also began to break free from the physical landscape, moving from the core areas of Cortés's logistical support (Tlaxcala, Huexotzinco, Chalco) to early capitals of Spanish power: Mexico City (Tlatelolco) and Hernando Ixtlilxochitl's northern bases in Otumba and Teotihuacan. It is easy to see why Tetzcoca nobles protested their exclusion from this brief windfall of imported tlaxilacalli workers.[12]

During such major changes to the structure of regional power, Hernando Ixtlilxochitl worked to uphold the vitality of Acolhua altepetl as sovereign local entities, struggling to act autonomously of (if in concert with) rising Spanish power. Although he tried to reassure his dependents by evoking an idea of modulated local sovereignty—stating at one point "this is certainly still our altepetl"—this imperial fixer also had to admit that "perhaps they will take your macehualtin away, my children."[13] Nobles bristled helplessly at such a concession, recognizing that without tributaries under their personal control, they would be excluded from the imperial bargaining that molded regional politics. Referencing the foundational bargains of Nezahualcoyotl and other tlatoque who "decided that they would divide the land, eighty-nine years ago,"[14] the nobles attacked recent moves to centralize tlaxilacalli tribute at the central place (*tecpan*), away from local nobles.

Centralization further dislodged noble claims to separate, individualized control over tlaxilacalli hierarchies; and soon enough these hierarchies began to turn on members of the lesser nobility. A later letter in the Codex Chimalpahin from Tepetlaoztoc, signed by Juan de San Antonio in 1564, pointedly describes such interference. Local officials, one of them the calpixqui of the tlaxilacalli of Mazaapan and Yahualiuhcan, arrived at Juan's house with false humility—"My noble, we do not wish to sadden you. We are only stammering macehualtin trying to do our jobs"[15]—and then proceeded to count his belongings and tribute share, returning later to confiscate his land. Should Juan so desire, he was encouraged to lodge a formal complaint with the tlatoani, but the ruler responded with an officious "I have heard your words" and referred him to a lower official.[16] This brought Juan to the brink of desperation, which he expressed in an extended parallel metaphor: "in this way, people just destroyed it; in this way, I was thrown away; in this way, rocks were thrown; in this way, I lost it; in this way, I reproach myself."[17]

As regional politics consolidated around fewer centralizing powers in the Hispanic period, tlaxilacalli themselves became more communitarian and streamlined, ignoring much of the vestigial local nobility that once brokered imperial submission. With few enemies left, with no local wars to fight and no allies to betray, piecemeal imperial negotiations lost their wider regional meaning. The Memorial de los Indios de Tepetlaoztoc is quite blunt on this point, stating that the descendants of local nobility "have come to such poverty and need that they are like any other of the macehualtin of the pueblo."[18]

POWER AND SURVIVAL

This was an overstatement. Despite their political demotions, nobles continued to eat better and die less often than did other tlaxilacalli residents. Nutritional surpluses and better overall health made them less likely to succumb to the successive and killing waves of epidemic disease that battered local communities in the aftermath of invasion, and this altered the demographic balance of tlaxilacalli and their subunits. In the early 1540s, for example, typhus erupted in the altepetl of Tepetlaoztoc, killing nearly two thirds of residents in Cuauhtepoztlan tlaxilacalli (982 of 1,560) even as the codices Vergara and Asunción were being enumerated. Elites, in contrast, fared much better—despite their rapid political marginalization. Indeed, a full three quarters (16 of 21) of the nobles recorded in the Tepetlaoztoc tribute codices survived the deadly epidemic, making them the only group to display any resistance to its relentless onslaught. At least in this case, privilege did buy some measure of survival.[19]

A grim corollary to greater elite survival was a greater mortality rate for the poorest farmers of Tepetlaoztoc, with marginal sub-districts suffering the most. In the rugged, forbidding altepemaitl of Tlanchiuhcan, for example, all members of the ethnic Hñähñu minority working as mayeque died (12 of 12), and this excluded group suffered much higher mortality rates than the dominant Acolhuaque. Even though the wider tlaxilacalli of Cuauhtepoztlan expressed a slight Hñähñu majority at the time of the Asunción's enumeration (48 people in total, compared with 43 Acolhuaque), after the typhus outbreak only 5 people of this ethnicity survived. (Three of these 5 survivors came from the centrally located household of Ciprián Quecil, who, as will be seen in chapter 3, enjoyed the third-largest field allocation in the sub-district.) Five of 7 Hñähñu domestic groups completely disappeared, leaving Quecil's household and that of María, widow of Marcos Tzontemoc, as the only survivors.[20] In total, across both tlaxilacalli of Cuauhtepoztlan and Chimalpan, only 10 percent of Hñähñus survived, compared with 21 percent for Acolhuaque.[21] This second figure is nearly as catastrophic, but it does also show that Acolhuaque survived at twice the rate as Hñähñus. Differential death tolls remade local tlaxilacalli, homogenizing populations as the lower, ethnically marked rungs of these communities died off. Because of epidemic disease, what remained of Tlanchiuhcan became an Acolhua majority sub-district, centered on the only reasonably flat territory ascribed to this altepemaitl.

Retrenchment was therefore also spatial: every single surviving resident of Tlanchiuhcan lived in its least rugged central section, next to the main walking path (figure 2.2). No one living away from this core area survived; even in the best of times, lands were too broken and poor for anything but subsistence, and the pressure of war and disease exterminated the poor farmers struggling to live there. Similar patterns likely obtained for other tlaxilacalli sub-sections in Tepetlaoztoc and beyond. Social and spatial exclusion was once again a matter of life and death. Live in the center or die.

TLAXILACALLI RETRENCHMENT

There was another approach to the stark decisions of the wounded and recalibrating Acolhua hinterland: commoners could simply leave, abandoning tlaxilacalli regimes for new Hispanic institutions. They could become servants or mercenaries or miners or translators or simply marry themselves away. But these options also proved risky and often untested. As the documentary record makes abundantly clear, Hispanizing "Yndians" regularly suffered unwelcome and capricious fates in these early years, despite the fact that commoners did still seek to escape from tlaxilacalli regimes. The new viceregal capital of Mexico City—defined as legally distinct from Tenochtitlan even if its spatial and political array remained basically intact across the Aztec-Spanish frontier of authority[22]—attracted migrants in ways unimaginable during the rule of the factious and internally divided Triple Alliance. Many Acolhua soldiers, allied with Spanish invaders since Hernando Ixtlilxochitl's impromptu self-presentation, followed invading troops north and settled in the new mining towns

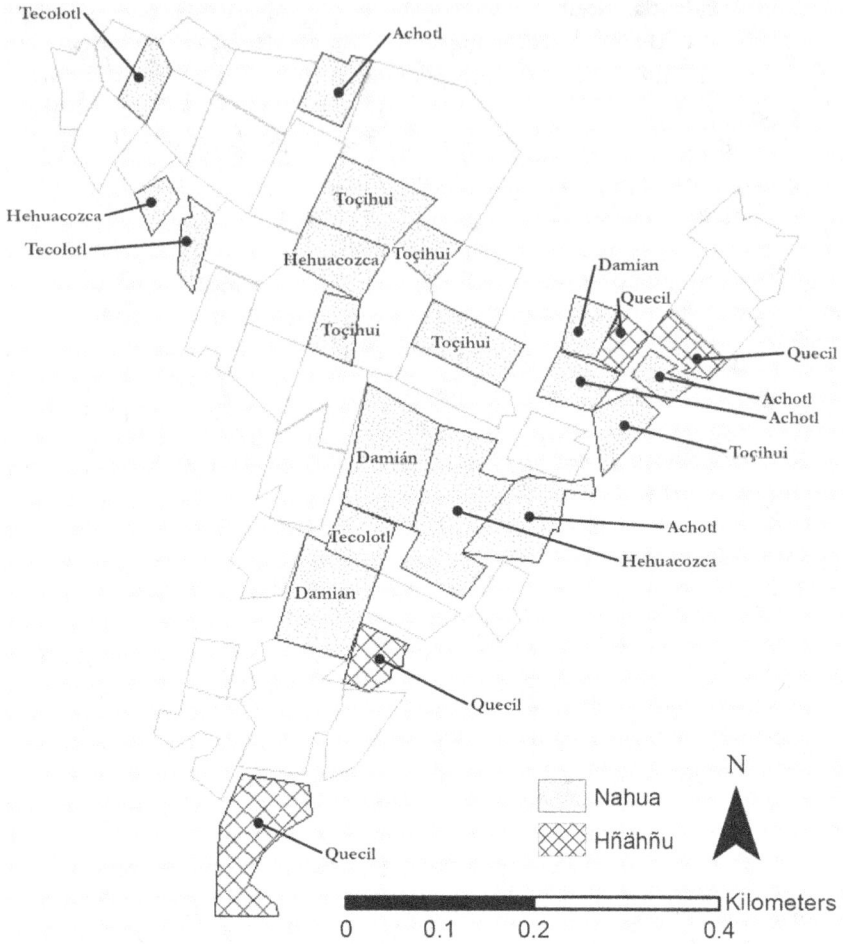

FIGURE 2.2. The spatial array of mortality. Surviving households are listed. In Tlanchiuhcan, only centrally located households survived the typhus epidemic of 1543–44 in Tepetlaoztoc. Map by Bill and Kris Keegan.

such as Querétaro and Zacatecas. Other locals headed east across the old Tlaxcalteca frontier, toward the new settlements like Puebla, and even accompanied the Cabeza de Vaca expedition along the Gulf of Mexico.[23] In like manner, the Codex Asunción shows three early instances of commoner migration to Tetzcoco, clearly indicated by the characteristic footprint next to the glyph for this nearby altepetl. Around 1544, for example, Antonio Coahui migrated from the tlaxilacalli of Cuauhtepoztlan in Tepetlaoztoc to the neighboring altepetl of Tetzcoco (figure 2.3).[24]

FIGURE 2.3. Outflow. The migrant Antonio Coahui (seventh from left), above the glyphs for Texcoco and migration. Codex Asunción, f. 53r. *Courtesy*, Biblioteca Nacional de México, Mexico City.

All of the migrants cited in the Asunción census came from the tiny hillside altepemaitl at the margins of Cuauhtepoztlan tlaxilacalli: one person from Tlaltecahuacan (out of five total households), one from Conzotlan (six households), and one from Zapotlan (four households). Not surprisingly, the small hillside outposts were vacated during the Hispanic period—and the early attestation of migrants from these spatially marginal and politically marginalized altepemaitl suggests that they might have been among the first of such areas to be abandoned. Nevertheless and perhaps surprisingly, these were the only altepemaitl in the wider tlaxilacalli that registered out-migration. All others retained an idea of communal integrity while they hemorrhaged population as a result of epidemic disease.

Even as they retained their base-level identities as anchoring local communities, tlaxilacalli also struggled mightily to accommodate severe environmental disruptions. Archaeological evidence from Tepetlaoztoc, for example, shows tlaxilacalli nucleating to a much greater extent in the early Hispanic period, ceding their characteristic territorial spreads as populations fell away. Demographic and political upheaval made it much more difficult to manage the fragile ecologies of their total spatial arrays, and labor-intensive investments (agricultural infrastructure such as catch dams and terraces) quickly fell into disrepair. This, in turn, damaged other fields through flooding, silting, and runoff. Tlaxilacalli lost significant portions of their productive landscape and had to restructure settlement to accommodate that loss.[25]

Such retrenchments are often ascribed to the colonizing demands of Hispanic rule; but, at least in Tepetlaoztoc, tlaxilacalli shifts predated any standardizing attempts on the part of the recently arrived Spanish, although an early chapel did anchor this altepetl's growing ceremonial center. As seen above, the altepemaitl of Zapotlan was already disintegrating in the early 1540s. Further, archaeological reconstructions mark a drastic spatial reordering after the fall of the Triple Alliance. In Tepetlaoztoc, Carlos Cordova clearly shows how four central tlaxilacalli (likely Cuauhtepoztlan, Chimalpan, Xoxoquitepec, and Chiautzinco, although he doesn't

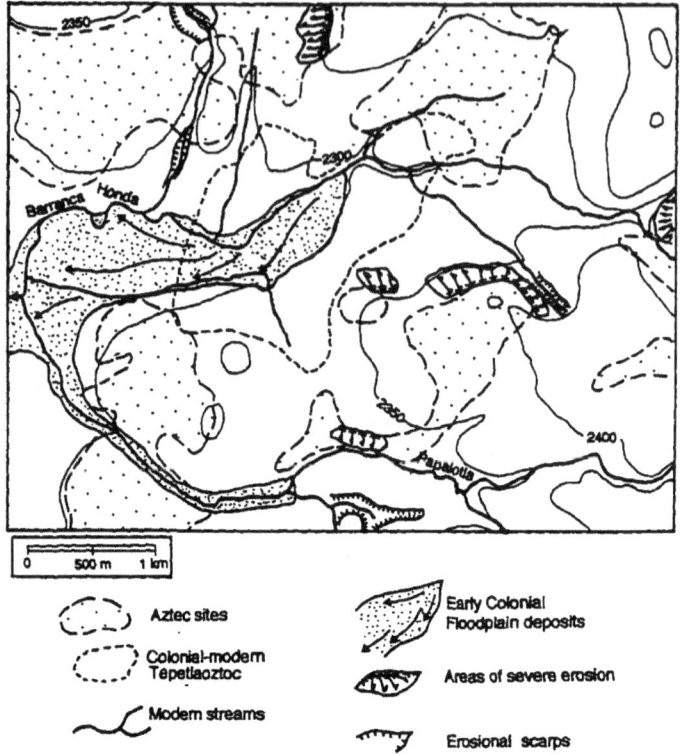

FIGURE 2.4. Four tlaxilacalli consolidating. Four dispersed tlaxilacalli (spotted areas) join together at one center (dotted border). Cordova, "Landscape Transformation," 260.

name them specially) dislodged from their fragile highland territories and consolidated around the altepetl's less erosion-prone ceremonial center, the large altepemaitl of Calla Tlaxoxouhco (figure 2.4).[26] This sub-section of the tlaxilacalli of Chimalpan, attractively located on the flat sides of a riverbank but already experiencing silt runoff from upstream erosion, contained a central market, the noble compound of Pedro Tecihuauh de Castilla, and the newly founded chapel of fray Domingo de Betanzos.[27]

As tlaxilacalli dislodged and moved in space, they retained their separate collective identities: the smaller tlaxilacalli of Papalotla, Malinalco, and Ocoxochiyocan sculpted their own community glyphs into the outer doorway of Betanzos's new chapel as they redeployed nearer to Chimalpan tlaxilacalli (see figure 4.1). Indeed, all tlaxilacalli retained their separate administrative identities even as they crowded

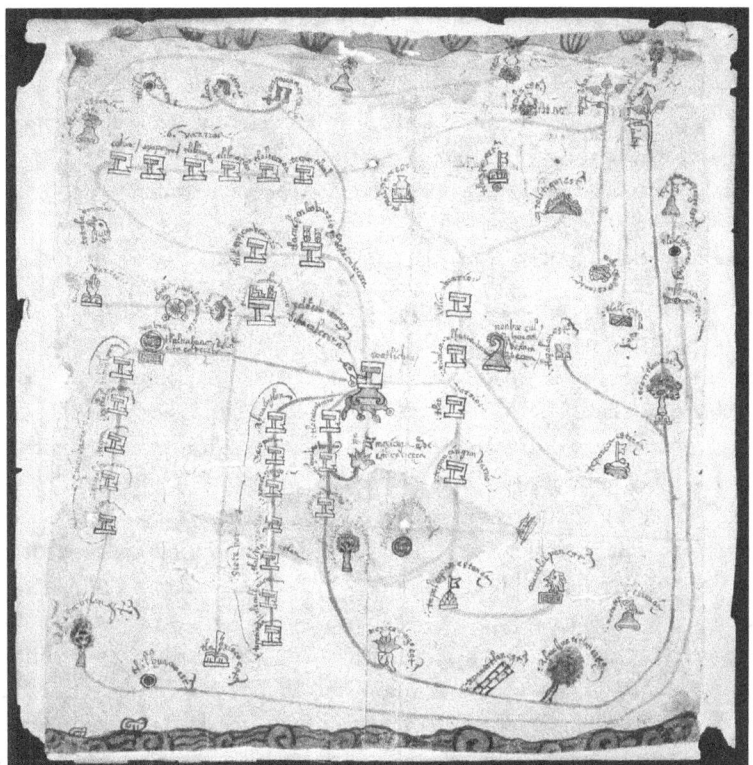

FIGURE 2.5. Early Hispanic tlaxilacalli hierarchies. *Mapa de Coatlinchan.* Note the linked networks of "barrios" and "estancias" connecting into the central glyph of the altepetl of Coatlinchan. *Courtesy,* Instituto Nacional de Antropología e Historia, Mexico City.

closer together on a diminishing acreage of cultivable land. This reflects the experience of other regions, as seen in Ángel Julián García Zambrano's study of the tlaxilacalli of Zahuatlan's continued affective attachment to a sacred barranca of the same name, even after it was dislodged from this landscape during the Hispanic period.[28]

Judging by the calibrated hierarchies of other Acolhua documents from the early Hispanic period, wider tlaxilacalli arrays also retained their logic despite demographic and ecological pressures. Such hierarchical ordering is most present in a remarkable document from just south of Tetzcoco, the Mapa de Coatlinchan (figure 2.5) This map, produced in classic Acolhua style with Spanish alphabetic overlays, details the full political array of the early Hispanic altepetl of Coaltinchan. The Spanish text outlines all four levels of sovereign organization:

- "estancia," denoted by a simple name glyph and corresponding to a tlaxilacalli sub-district, or altepemaitl
- "barrio," marked with house glyph and representing a tlaxilacalli
- "de esta cabecera," shown with a canonical name glyph (Colhuacan, for example) and referencing the tlayacatl layer
- finally, altepetl, denoted by a specialized iconography incorporating the polity's name into the general "water-hill" glyph. No general Spanish or Nahuatl term was used, only the name of the altepetl, Coatlinchan.

Each of these four layers will be described in much fuller detail in chapter 3, through the illustrative case of Cuauhtepoztlan tlaxilacalli.[29]

Although the Mapa de Coatlinchan betrays certain tendencies toward clustering, it also shows tlaxilacalli in their separate vibrant identities. One tlaxilacalli, Chalco Pochtlan, was dedicated to merchants from the altepetl just south of Coatlinchan. Another, Tlilhuacan, sent out two altepemaitl shoots in the neighboring tlaxilacalli of Chimalpan. A different altepemaitl, Ahuehuetitlan, spread itself across five separate tlaxilacalli in the map. In the aftermath of demographic collapse, local politics in Coatlinchan showed itself energized by the fight to retain and re-articulate political hierarchies.

Further, this map lays out each local level along intersecting colored lines, representing a full chain of authority down to each altepemaitl. Although the graphic logic of the map subsumes close-in altepemaitl to wider tlaxilacalli structures and also crashes neighboring tlaxilacalli into each other, the detailed structure of political order remains fully imaginable. The altepemaitl of Oztolitique, for instance, submitted to the tlaxilacalli of Xicolan, which, in turn, appealed to Colhuacan tlayacatl and then Coatlinchan altepetl. All told, the map records twenty-eight altepemaitl, thirty tlaxilacalli, and five tlayacatl in the altepetl of Coatlinchan. No tlayacatl was territorially exclusive; instead, each tlaxilacalli bundle snaked its way among and around its neighbors. Tlaxilacalli politics remained crowded in the early Hispanic period even as tlaxilacalli territory shrunk and nucleated.

SEEKING COMMUNITY

This reordering of territory and politics opened up tlaxilacalli regimes to broader definitions of community. Indeed, so many people died in the first generation following the fall of the Triple Alliance (around 1.1 million of an initial population of 1.6 million, or 69%) that crude birth rates also plummeted: children born after this period were so few in number that they struggled to care for even the reduced number of survivors of the earlier epidemics. For instance, dependency ratios—that is, the number of people relying on each active laborer for basic sustenance—also shifted, combining by the mid-sixteenth century in almost equal measure with total population loss to produce the acute labor shortages that constituted one of the defining characteristics of the first two postwar generations.[30] Acolhuaque quickly noted this decline, writing as early as the 1550s from Tepetlaoztoc that "because of the lack of people in the pueblo, as a result of the excessive tributes and the numerous deaths, [commoners] couldn't pay tributes in the amounts they used to or give as much as the [Spanish] factor would have wanted."[31] But it was administrators, both local and Hispanic, who most strongly felt the visceral pressure of labor scarcity. They could no longer count on the complete levies they had once expected as a matter of course. Numbers mustered no longer matched numbers mandated.

Such labor pressure effectively flipped tlaxilacalli from land-based imperial vanguards to tribute-based commoner polities. Despite the fact that tlaxilacalli still managed access to collective fields through their nested local hierarchies—land pressure remained tight, as foreign ruminants flooded the region—the wider context shifted so drastically that these communities were effectively pulled inside out by demographic crisis. Access to land remained a defining political axis in the tlaxilacalli, but access to laborers soon became an imperative corollary. Complex domestic labor arrangements flowed with even greater intensity through the idiom of kinship. Household arrangements became more diverse and anchored to tlaxilacalli in newly flexible ways.

The experiences of an ecological refugee named Ana, who registered her case before the tlaxilacalli officials of San Miguel Tocuiallan (Tetzcoco) in 1583, prove illustrative across both kinship and tlaxilacalli registers.[32] This one-named protagonist, a wife and mother of one, requested a piece of "precious land" (*ytlaçotlaltzin*) along the saline edge of Lake Tetzcoco after her previous house was destroyed in a flood. She plied tlaxilacalli officials—described with the titles "tlatoque" and "teteuctin," though the reach toward such status was aspirational[33]—with tortillas and alcohol, begged and begged, and eventually received a minuscule 6 × 6 *tlalquahuitl* (~15 × 15 meters)[34] plot of land. (The standard plot, according to the Vergara and Asunción codices, was 20 × 20 tlalquahuitl, or roughly 50 × 50 meters, often given in multiple allotments. Assuming a regular "second-rate" land quality, this measure was also usually enough to support one person's nutritional needs.) Despite its diminutive size, Ana's disbursement was offhand and formulaic, executed with the customary ease of practice:

> Then Juan Francisco said, "Who is going to measure out [the plot]?"
> The teteuctin said, "Who indeed? Other times, wasn't it good ol' Juan? He'll measure it out."
> Then they [the officials] said to him, "Come, good Juan, take the staff (garrote) in your hands and measure it out. Measure out six lengths on all four sides."[35]

After winning this bestowal, Ana cried and embraced the local officials, promising as well to burn candles and incense in honor of San Miguel, patron of the tlaxilacalli. It was through such mundane ceremonies as this that both inequality and community were reaffirmed through the tlaxilacalli, far from the oversight of Spanish officials.[36]

As she tearfully accepted her minuscule apportionment in the tlaxilacalli of San Miguel Tocuillan, Ana promised to burn candles and copal incense for "my beloved father, holy San Miguel, because I am building my house on his land." Once again and in ways very similar to the period of imperial Acolhua rule, tlaxilacalli lands were pledged to a protecting supernatural power. In an earlier period, Tocuillan had unambiguously submitted to Tezcatlipoca, the imperial deity of wider Acolhua power.[37] With the arrival of St. Michael in Tocuillan, Tezcatlipoca was papered over in his tutelary role over this marginal Tetzcoca tlaxilacalli. Functionally, however, San Miguel served a similar role as his predecessor, fitting comfortably into the protective community niche opened up by the "Lord of the Smoking Mirror." Indeed, the tlaxilacalli served in some important ways to domesticate Spanish Catholicism—affixing, for example, the specific location of Tocuillan ("Place of Cranes") to the wider identity of San Miguel. Here, despite the archangel's victory over the Mesoamerican trickster, the wings on St. Michael's back would have almost certainly been made of long white crane feathers.

During an era of wrenching change, local tlaxilacalli managed more than just tribute and land allocations; they also solidified communities. The ongoing investments of commoners like Ana in their tlaxilacalli combined with the residential character of these hierarchies to fill them with wide and contested collective meaning. Particularly after the fall of the Aztec empire—as most local hierarchies crumbled, populations evaporated, and ecosystems deranged—the tlaxilacalli remained a rare bastion of order and autonomy in Acolhuacan. Even as Ana and her kin confronted the harrowing challenge of eking out a living from a plot well below the nutritional demands of even her small household, they simultaneously celebrated their new place in San Miguel Tocuillan's nested hierarchy. Inequality always came with community.

BLENDING KIN

Ana and her kin gained their new house in 1583, right after the last massive epidemic of the sixteenth century, and despite her new house plot, she still depended heavily on her brother. After the flood that forced her from her previous house, she sought shelter with him; given the paucity of her new land grant, it seems plausible that she also relied on her brother's aid to feed herself and her kin into the foreseeable future. Indeed, given both the lack of outbound directional markers in the Nahuatl text and the narrative brevity between Ana's land request (presumably made at her brother's house) and its final measurement, it is plausible that her land grant was either adjacent to or subdivided from her brother's lands. Ana and her brother therefore illustrate one of the key transformations in early Hispanic Acolhuacan: not only were fewer people working, they were also responsible for supporting more dependents than previously.

Domestic arrangements became even more combinatory and flexible in the wake of demographic collapse. As more and more people died and the number of people relying on each adult worker rose, commoners forged new affective bonds, often through revamped tlaxilacalli structures, broadening the meanings of kinship in early Hispanic Acolhuacan. Whereas kinship (or *tlacamecayotl*, a "human rope" of relatives, particularly understood through the links between bride and groom, parent and child) dominated both elite regional politics and the high pronouncements of *Huehuetlatolli* formal speech, belonging and survival were much more present concerns for the commoner households crowding for space in the tlaxilacalli. Foundational household arrangements, though monogamous and formally pledged to local hierarchies, were also changeable and responsive to concerns such as land and labor scarcity. Such transformations were duly recorded as early as the 1540s in the typhus-battered codices Vergara and Asunción.[38]

Once again, the altepemaitl of Tlanchiuhcan provides striking illustrations of these trends (see figure 3.2). The first two census entries for this subdivision, for instance, show more than one line of personal kindred, more than one tlacamecayotl, emanating from the male-female "parental" pairing at the head of the household. The first entry shows Domingo Tozquechol and his wife, Juana, and then records two separate lines of parentage emanating only from Domingo, suggesting that his children—one also named Juana and the other Antonio Tezcapoc—were conceived in two separate situations and most likely with two separate mothers as well. Antonio then married yet another Juana, and a nephew of Domingo's also sought shelter in this same household. The second household, that of Marcos Hachotl and Lucia, shows a different arrangement, including two children conceived and raised collectively, another son (Lucas Xochicozca) from one of Lucia's previous relationships, and that son's wife, Ana.[39]

Populations suffered immense declines during this period, making the breadth and creativity of tlacamecayotl response even more marked. Blended kin groups— where children from previous relations were accepted by both members of the leading couple in a household—represented a full 15 percent of all households in both tribute codices even before the ravages of typhus further complicated arrangements. Blended relations were only one part of a wider and much more varied panorama of domestic diversity in Tepetlaoztoc, including multiple-household homesteads, childless couples, multi-generation arrangements, couples raising only their own children, single parents, abandoned widows, stray relatives, and joint arrangements with no parent-child filial component at all.

Kinship was never to be taken for granted; it had to be constantly reaffirmed. During a commoner marriage ceremony recorded in the *Bancroft Dialogues*, a compendium of Acolhua formal speech from the early Hispanic period, most speakers invoke the risks of failing to affirm the social relations underpinning the ceremony. One describes a break in social relations as "childishness and infantilism," "dust and filth," and "the way of the rabbit and deer." Each of these couplets is well-known discursively: the first invokes immaturity and mental weakness; the second, destabilizing sinfulness; and the last, irresponsible and dissolute wandering. The final couplet is particularly striking, however, for its implicit evocation of marginalized Chichimeca forms of subsistence. Rabbits and deer did represent, after all, the main game of mobile hunters in the region, and a bound rabbit was the glyph for hunted tribute in the Codex Xolotl. This final warning was all the more severe given the ongoing diversity in the Acolhua hinterland, where farmers of marginalized ethnicities increasingly filled in the bottom rungs of tribute hierarchies.[40]

In this connection, one final discursive opposition bears mentioning, and that is the contrast between something that might be called "happiness" and something else akin to "peace of mind." In one section of this dialogue, the unnamed speaker admonishes the groom against "resting in happiness"; later he assures the groom's mother that once the match is confirmed, her "heart can now rest" and her "weeping and sorrow will be recompensed."[41] That is, happiness could be destructive and entropic, lightweight and worthless, while sorrow and labor, the true calling of a commoner, might eventually produce a deeper satisfaction of the heart—gods (and church) willing.

As Acolhua farmers fought to repair and expand their ties of kinship, they simultaneously reinforced the wider ties of altepemaitl and tlaxilacalli. As Ana of Tocuillan sought a new place for herself and her household, she called first on her brother and then, through her brother, on the wider tlaxilacalli. Desperate to belong and to build, survivors of the demographic collapse invented both kin and community within the confines of the early Hispanic tlaxilacalli.

REFILLING THE LANDSCAPE

Foreign invasion, both epidemic and military, destroyed the Triple Alliance and severely challenged Acolhua regional coherence, but not all of the constituent parts of local imperialism suffered a similar fate. In particular, institutions such as the tlaxilacalli quickly came to bolster Spanish rule despite suffering major

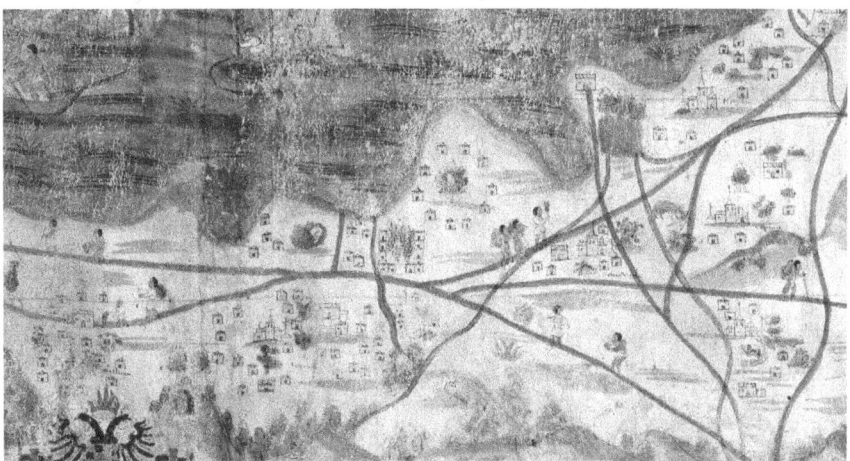

FIGURE 2.6. *Map of Mexico 1550*, showing a subsection of the northeastern quadrant. *Courtesy*, Uppsala University Library, Uppsala, Sweden.

internal stresses. Perhaps surprisingly, these communities successfully metabolized the repeated shocks they suffered, reaffirming and even expanding their place in the local political order. The robust local response to political and environmental change is clearly illustrated in the so-called Santa Cruz map, produced in Tlatelolco around 1555 and currently housed at a library in Uppsala, Sweden (figure 2.6). This exquisitely detailed map, showing people of various social standings going about their lives within a dense physical, spiritual, and political geography, consistently represents the broad changes wrought on the landscape in the generation since the fall of the Aztec empire: churches pop up across the field of vision; just south of Teotihuacan, a Spaniard on horseback directs two native porters and, just below him, another tends to wandering livestock.[42] But these were not the only figures on the landscape: lakeside hunters tend their nets on Lake Tetzcoco as local merchants, pilgrims, and migrants fill the roads of the Acolhua hinterland. A commoner confronts a noble on the way from Tepetlaoztoc, while the earth-monster in this altepetl's name glyph opens its jaws once again. Most important, tlaxilacalli flood the map—127 just in the northeastern section sampled above, each represented by a house glyph specifically arrayed across the landscape.[43]

Tlaxilacalli commoners responded more forcefully to the terrible aftermath of the wars of Spanish invasion than did other leading groups, such as the local elite. Already accustomed to precarious lives, commoners dealt with these tragedies in a more robust and matter-of-fact way, and the tlaxilacalli played an important role in this period of readjustment. It was through these institutions that they began the work of metabolizing Spanish rule for local consumption, setting Acolhua societies back in order—house by house, tlaxilacalli by tlaxilacalli.

NOTES

1. On these sons, see Offner, "Apuntes." See also Charles E. Dibble, "Apuntes sobre la plancha X del Códice Xólotl," *Estudios del cultura náhuatl* 5 (1965): 103–6.

2. Regarding the seldom-described final section, Charles Dibble's scholarly edition only mentions that it has "little relation" to the rest of the plate and then proceeds to quote Ixtlilxochitl's interpretation: *Códice Xolotl*, 117–18. Ixtlilxochitl's comments are useful but brief: *Obras*, 178, 218. Other major studies of the Codex Xolotl, including Lee's *Allure* and Douglas's *Palace*, do not mention this scene.

3. See Patrick Lesbre, "Historiografía acolhua: seudo-rebelión e intereses coloniales (Ixtlilxochitl)," in *Actas del II Congreso Europeo de Latinoamericanistas*, ed. Thomas Brenner and Susanne Schütz (Halle, Germany: Universität Halle-Wittenberg, 1999, published on CD-Rom); Julia Madajczak, "La carrera de Ixtlilxochitl: Una comparación entre fuentes pictográficas y escritas," in *Códices del centro de méxico análisis comparativa y estudios indivduales*, ed. Miguel Ángel Ruz Barrio and Juan José Batalla Rosado (Warsaw, Poland: University of Warsaw Press, 2013), 43–54; Lee, *Allure*; Douglas, *Palace*. For a summary of earlier historiography, see Frederic Hicks, "Texcoco 1515–19: The Ixtlilxochitl Affair," in *Chipping Away on Earth: Studies in Prehispanic and Colonial Mexico in Honor of Arthur J.O. Anderson and Charles E. Dibble*, ed. Eloise Quiñones-Keber (Lancaster: Labrynthos, 1995), 235–39.

4. "luego aquella tarde se embarcó con todos los señores y caballeros que eran de su opinión: llevando consigo sus haciendas y mujeres se fueron a la ciudad de México, desamparando la de Tetzcuco, con cuyo desmán los ciudadanos se comenzaron a alborotar, entrándose unos tras del rey por la laguna y otros por la montaña, quedándose solo y desamparado Ixtlilxóchitl deteniendo la gente." Ixtlilxochitl, *Obras* (1952), 2:241–42.

5. "yntla yuh quichihuani yn coanacotzin yn quito capitan ca cenca ynceliloca yc mochuazquia yn altepetl yhuan yn macehuali ca yehuatl yn intequiuh tlahtoque in ohui ypan mochihua altepetl, yn huel quiyeecoa yn canpa ye huel quimaquixtizqu macehuali ynic huel yez ymaltequh, yn ma yuhqui hotli camo ye in qui[to]tocti in macehual." Chimalpahin, *Codex Chimalpahin*, 2:192. This document was recently acquired by the Instituto Nacional de Antropología e Historia and is now online at http://www.codicechimalpahin.inah.gob.mx/, accessed September 15, 2015.

The phemonenon of commoners "fleeing along the roads" is clearly illustrated in Codex Xolotl, f. 7 (*Tlachia* code: X.070.B) for the earlier episode of the Tepaneca invasion of Acolhuacan. Tlaxilacalli fled for the hills.

6. "ahu in macehuali hace ic quimamatizque yn altepetl." Chimalpahin, *Codex Chimalpahin*, 2:194.

7. Thomas M. Whitmore, "A Simulation of the Sixteenth-Century Population Collapse in the Basin of Mexico," *Annals of the Association of American Geographers* 81, no. 3 (1991): 464–87.

8. On this reassigning, see Nezahualcoyotl's dispositions in "The Titles of Tetzcotzinco," 112–17.

9. Chimalpahin, *Codex Chimalpahin*, 2:194. Although Calpulalpan is often treated as an altepetl and could even have been one at the writing of this codex, all the other entities mentioned were tlaxilacalli. Two of these tlaxilacalli, Quauhtlapan and Ocotepec, were administered as "war lands" (*yaotlapan*) in and around Chalco. (See Carrasco, *Estructura Político-Territorial*, 232.) Two others, Yahualiuhcan and Mazaapan, were frequently disputed tlaxilacalli in Tepetlaoztoc (see figs. 1.8 and 1.9) Following later trends that led to the full independence of some tlaxilacalli, Itztapalocan is now an independent Mexican municipio (Ixtapaluca).

10. On the benefits of Ixtlilxochitl's work to the Acolhua nobility, see Peter B. Villella, "The Last Acolhua: Alva Ixtlilxochitl and Elite Native Historiography in Early New Spain," *Colonial Latin American Review* 23, no. 1 (2014): 18–36.

11. "in quicahualti in capitan yn ixquich tlatocatlalli Cuix maqu itechpohui in tlatocayotl, yhuan in pipiltin inmil Cuix mac ytech pohui in Tetzcuco. pohuia Cuix mac oncan pohui. Ca oyh quitecahualti yn ixtlilxochitzin ca cenca ye quiiyohuia in pipiltin in tlaxcalla in huexotzinco in chalco ye nohuia ompa teyeElimiquilia in pipiltin auh yn Cihua ye ommotetzahuililia teyquitilia auh ȳ calpixque. Ca hahuicpa q'nhuica yhuā in pipiltin intech pohuia in quēma ompa in otonpa in ōmotlalia. Auh yn quēma ompa in teotihuicā in ōmotlatla. auh in quēma tlatelolco in ōmotlalia. Auh un quēma mexico in ōmotlalia ca ye yuh chiquace xihuitl. Yuh quīnemitia ȳ. In tequitque auh yn iuh quichihuin. In ixtlilxochitzin cuix icneliloca mochiuh yn altepetl. Tetzcuco cuix amo çā quitolini in tlatocayotl." Chimalpahin, *Codex Chimalpahin*, 2:198. Local community structures in Tlaxcala and Huexotzinco, called *teccalli*, were slightly different than the tlaxilacalli studied here.

12. The quote also employs a Nahuatl phrase for nobles attached to tribute lands, *itech pohua* or *itech pohuia* (translated here as "ascribed to"), that was used above in the same document to refer to tributary commoners tied to lands. It is possible that this is simply a coincidence, but it is more likely that the landed tribute hierarchy determined the array of both commoners and nobles across a landscape. In this accounting, when the tlaxilacalli was pulled, both nobles and commoners followed.

13. "mach oc tauh macho oc totepeuh ye yc namechnoceccahualtilia aço quimonanaquihui yn amomacehualhuā yn nopilhuā." Chimalpahin, *Codex Chimalpahin*, 2:200.

14. "ynic quimonxelhuique tlalli yn ye napohualxihuitl. ypan chiucnauhxihuitl. Axcan." Chimalpahin, *Codex Chimalpahin*, 2:190.

15. "nopiltzintzine timitztotequipachilhuizque ma xicmocaquiti, ca çan tequitl timaceualtin ca tiquauhque telimicque." Chimalpahin, *Codex Chimalpahin*, 2:218. Later on the same page, one commoner is explicitly named as calpixqui: "yn, tocol calpixqui yaualiuhcan yhuā ȳ maçaapan." The letter also mentions the tlaxilacalli of Chimalpan and Papalotecapan. Although the letter mentions the influence of Tetzcoco nobles, all the tlaxilacalli mentioned are in Tepetlaoztoc, many listed in the maps from the Memorial de los Indios de Tepetlaoztoc. See figures 1.8 and 1.9. (The only tlaxilacalli that is not listed, Chimalpan, is profiled in the Codex Vergara.)

16. "ca oniccac ȳ motlatol." Chimalpahin, *Codex Chimalpahin*, 2:218. The ruler later returns to this theme, stating "I have heard your words. Many times I have heard what you were saying."—"ca oniccac ym molatultzin yhuan ca ye quezquipā niccaqui yn tinechmolhuilila." Chimalpahin, *Codex Chimalpahin*, 2:232.

17. "ca çā iuhquī in tlapopulhuililoc çan iuhquī ninotlatlaxililoc çā iuhquī noca nemomotlaloc ca çan iuh nonnotlahuelcauh çan iuh nonnotlahuellali." Chimalpahin, *Codex Chimalpahin*, 2:218–20.

18. "Pero se les quitó la mayor parte de ello a causa de los excesivos tributos que el encomendero les ha pedido de manera que los descendientes de estos principales han venido a tanta pobreza y necesiadad como cualquiera de los maceguales del pueblo, porque también tributan al encomendero como los macehuales." Memorial de los Indios de Tepetlaoztoc, f. 214r.

19. Four individuals of eight survived in Martín Izcoatl's compound, six of seven for Pedro Tecihuauh de Castilla, and all six for Vicente Aoctlacuani. All heads of household survived.

20. Codex Asunción, ff. 47r–48r.

21. Codex Asunción; Codex Vergara.

22. Cf. Mundy, *Death*.

23. Cf. Álvar Nuñez Cabeza de Vaca, *Naufragios* (online edition), accessed December 9, 2014, http://www.cervantesvirtual.com/obra-visor/naufragios-0/html/feddcf8e-82b1-11df-acc7-002185ce6064_2.html#I_8_.

24. Codex Asunición, ff. 53r, 54r, 55r.

25. Cordova, "Landscape Transformation," 259–65.

26. On the spatial reordering of Tepetlaoztoc, see Cordova, "Landscape Transformation," 259–62; Marisol Pérez-Lizaur, *Población y sociedad: Cuatro comunidades del Acolhuacan*, 2nd ed. (Mexico City: Universidad Iberoamericana, 2008), 89–90.

27. Barbara Williams and Frederic Hicks provide a reconstruction of Pedro Tecihuauh de Castilla's compound in their edition of the *Códice Vergara*, 71.

28. García Zambrano, "Zahuatlan el Viejo."

29. *Mapa de Coatlinchan* (Mexico City: Instituto Nacional de Antropología e Historia, sección codices), accessed June 15, 2016, http://www.codices.inah.gob.mx/pc/contenido.php?id=9.

30. Whitmore, "Simulation," 478–79.

31. "A causa de la falta de gente que había en el pueblo, debido a los tributos excesivos y a las numerosas defunciones, no pudieron dar tantos tributos ni en la cantidad que solían dar y como el factor hubiera querido." Memorial de los Indios de Tepetlaoztoc, f. 28a. See also Pomar, "Relación de Tezcuco," 83–85. On dependency ratios, see Whitmore, "Simulation," 479. Remarkably, in neighboring San Juan Teotihuacan, the Spaniard who composed the geographic relation for this altepetl remarked that "the comfort that (locals) now have is the cause of their illness" (el regalo que ahora tienen es la causa de enfermedad). "Relación de Tequizistlan y su partido," in *Relaciones*, ed. Acuña, 2:237.

32. Ana's case has been widely analyzed in the specialized literature, but never within the context of tlaxilacalli. See, for example, Pilar Mayanez, "Documentos de Tezcoco: Consideraciones sobre tres manuscritos en mexicano del ramo 'tierras,'" *Estudios de Cultura Nahuatl* 22 (1992): 325–43; James Lockhart, "Y la Ana lloró: Cesión de un sitio para casa, San Miguel Tocuilán, 1583," *Tlalocan* 8 (1980): 21–33; James Lockhart, "And Ana Wept: Grant of a Site for a House, San Miguel Tocuillan, 1583," in *Nahuas and Spaniards: Postconquest Central Mexican History and Philology*, ed. James Lockhart (Stanford: Stanford University Press, 1991), 66–74; Lockhart, *The Nahuas after the Conquest*, 455–59. Another version of this document appears in Matthew Restall, Lisa Sousa, and Kevin Terraciano, eds., "Nahuatl Grant of a House Site in San Miguel Tocuillan, 1583," in *Mesoamerican Voices: Native-Language Writings from Colonial Mexico, Oaxaca, Yucatan, and Guatemala* (New York: Cambridge University Press, 2005), 100–102.

Other Acolhua documents clearly show Tocuillan as a tlaxilacalli in Tetzcoco. See DNT docs. 29 and 32. Things are particularly clear in document 29, where Tocuillan appears in the same grammatical plane as well-known tlaxilacalli such as Tlailotlacan and Mexicapan.

33. For Lockhart's skepticism about the title of these officials, see *The Nahuas after the Conquest*, 86.

34. Following a conversion given by the early seventeenth-century Tetzcocan historiographer don Fernando de Alva Ixtlilxochitl, Barbara J. Williams and H. R. Harvey define tlalquahuitl as measuring 2.5 meters in Acolhuacan. Cf. Williams and Harvey, eds., *The Códice*, 27. The tlalquahuitl measurement was long used in Acolhuacan, with manuscript attestations into the seventeenth century. In addition, Williams—in "Mexican Pictorial Cadastral Registers: An Analysis of the Códice de Santa María Asunción and the Codex Vergara," in *Explorations in Ethnohistory: Indians of Central Mexico in the Sixteenth Century*, ed. H. R. Harvey and Hanns J. Prem (Albuquerque: New Mexico University Press, 1984), 107—reports that rope was sold in this region by 2.5 m sections through the mid- to late twentieth century Further, according to Lockhart, the tlalquahuitl (which he called simply "quahuitl") measure was equivalent to the *matl* used in Colhuacan farther south. "Matl" is very rare in Acolhua documents, but it does show up on rare occasion. Cf. Lockhart, notes in the file "Land and Economy"—accessible at the Wired Humanities Project online Nahuatl dictionary under the search term "matl," accessed February 25, 2016, http://whp.uoregon.edu/dictionaries

/nahuatl/index.lasso. It is possible that the long staffs used by topile officeholders could be the length of one tlalquahuitl. See the section on topileque in chapter 3, 105–6.

35. "[tic]monequiltia cuix mica cuix noço nepa capa." "niman oquimitalhui y jua françizcotzin aqui quihualtamachihuaz niman oquitoque y teteuhti aquinel amo yepa yehuatl y tlaocole y juatze quitamachuhuaz niman oquilhuique y tlaocole xihualauh juate xocona [*sic*] y caRocha momtica xictamachihua nauhcap[a] cuiquase caRocha xictamachihua." AGN, Tierras, vol. 2338, exp. 1, ff. 8r–9v. The garrote used here was likely of the standard tlalquahuitl measure.

36. Although this document eventually entered Spanish archives, it only did so 150 years later as a part of a local land and inheritance dispute. It was filed as a part of "household papers" presented by one of the sides in the case and likely served as a local land title for tlaxilacalli officers before this time.

37. Indeed, an Acolhua prayer from Tepepulco, dedicated to Tezcatlipoca, makes specific reference to a place called Tocuillan: "At Tocuillan, the God Enters" (ya Tocuilitla teuaquj), Primeros Memoriales, Museo del Real Palacio, ms. 3280, f. 274r.

38. Elite male polygamy did influence regional politics during the Post-Classic and continued through the early Hispanic period, when the tlatoani of Tepetlaoztoc married "each of his wives by law and [Christian] blessing" ("casado con cada una de ellas a ley y bendición," Memorial de los Indios de Tepetlaoztoc, f. 3).

39. Codex Asunción, f. 47r.

40. "in pīpīllōtl in cōcōnēyōtl"; tĕuhtli tlàçolli"; "mānēn tōchtli maçatl iòhui anquitocatzin." Karttunen and Lockhart, eds., *Bancroft Dialogues*, 110 (first two couplets), 108 (wider phrase).

41. "àmo ticochtoz àmo tipāctoz"; "aço onixtlāhuiz in amochōquiz in amotlaōcol in amēlcìcĭhuiliz . . . aço īntech ozcēhuiz in amīx in amoyōllo." Karttunen and Lockhart, eds., *Bancroft Dialogues*, 108, 110.

42. On the role of livestock in ecological change, see Elinor G.K. Melville, *A Plague of Sheep: Environmental Consequences of the Conquest of Mexico* (Cambridge: Cambridge University Press, 1994).

43. Although this map is occasionally known as the Santa Cruz map and erroneously attributed to the Spanish cartographer Alonso de Santa Cruz, the authorship is clearly Mesoamerican. Miguel León-Portilla and Carmen Aguilera suggest Tlatelolca. Cf. León-Portilla and Aguilera, *Mapa de México-Tenochtitlan y sus contornos hacia 1550* (Mexico City: Celanese, 1986). The Uppsala University Library, where the document is housed, characterizes the map simply as *Map of Mexico 1550*. Note as well that the figure of 127 tlaxilacalli comes from the entire northeastern quarter of the map, not the subsection reproduced in figure 2.6.

3

Community and Change in Cuauhtepoztlan Tlaxilacalli, ca. 1544–1575

Tlaxilacalli served as an anchor for the re-articulation of Acolhua society after the fall of Mexico-Tenochtitlan. Because of their mediating role between domestic units and regional alliances, they promoted the reintegration of broken social relations and then tied these newly reformed bonds into supple political building blocks. This chapter analyzes the bottom-up integration of one early Hispanic tlaxilacalli, Cuauhtepoztlan in Tepetlaoztoc (profiled in the Codex Asunción),[1] showing how its particular land and production hierarchies led to the re-creation of local community. In this tlaxilacalli, community and compulsion went hand in hand, reinforcing both affective and political ties against a background of profound demographic and ecological change.

HUNGER IN CUAUHTEPOZTLAN

Early Hispanic Cuauhtepoztlan resembled many tlaxilacalli in both Aztec and Hispanic times, as its basic functioning wove together hunger and community. Hunger compelled people to join, but community—the basic human need to participate and belong—made their joint actions worthwhile, even treasured. Simple caloric need, however, proved a strong incentive to participate in tlaxilacalli regimes: careful estimates from Cuauhtepoztlan suggest that both surplus and scarcity were endemic to this tlaxilacalli even after the initial demographic and ecological crises of the Spanish and Tlaxcalteca invasions of 1519–21.[2] Although the tlaxilacalli

DOI: 10.5876/9781607326915.c003

produced much more than was needed for basic social reproduction (141% of necessary calories), fully one-sixth of the population, 16 percent, consistently went hungry. Under normal climatic conditions, 84 percent of residents ate well, 60 percent with a surplus. Things became precarious in poor harvest years, when 61 percent of the tlaxilacalli population faced undernourishment, with 52 percent at risk for famine. Nevertheless, another two-fifths (39%) remained well-fed, and 20 percent retained a surplus. These estimates show persistent structural inequalities in Cuauhtepoztlan, marked by how well people ate. At the top were those who never starved; at the bottom, those who rarely had enough to eat.[3]

Of all marked groups in the Codex Asunción, only one stands out for its persistent and extreme caloric shortfalls: the Hñähñu ethnic minority. Despite representing a significant subsection of the population recorded in both the Asunción and Vergara codices (22%, an estimated 275 individuals of 1,242 total), Hñähñus suffered both spatial and political marginalization within Cuauhtepoztlan tlaxilacalli. They lived at the periphery of community settlements, fighting for subsistence on unproductive lands as either dependent fieldhands (mayeque) or the poorest of local tributaries.[4] Figures from the Asunción suggest that Hñähñu farmers produced only 19 percent of the calories needed for social reproduction, a stark reminder of their profound marginalization: 114 people made do on just under 4 hectares of poor land. Farming must have been supplemented by other subsistence strategies, therefore—which helps to explain reports from other areas of the Basin of Mexico describing Hñähñus eating desperation foods such as grass and larvae.[5] Further, the Asunción and Vergara marked Hñähñu marginalization with a differential house glyph showing a pitched thatched roof instead of a flat adobe one.[6]

Despite poor lands and the broad disruption of its carefully managed ecological array, therefore, mid-sixteenth-century Cuauhtepoztlan still produced in excess for a majority of the population, fed five-sixths of its members, and left a persistent (largely Hñähñu) minority starving. Most residents still fell in between, however, and this gave tlaxilacalli their compulsive bite.

THE ADMINISTRATION OF HUNGER

Because land flowed through the local tlaxilacalli, the easiest way to access more of it was to assume administrative functions within this local hierarchy—most often by overseeing the production of immediate neighbors.[7] Asunción registers show, for instance, the poor Hñähñu Ciprián Quecil—the farmer precisely matched to the landscape in chapter 1 (55–57)—receiving 30 percent more productive land than his immediate neighbor (generating 12,428 daily Kcal versus 9,478) in exchange for oversight of this neighbor and another large but land-poor mayeque household, which produced a whopping 35,355 daily Kcal for themselves and their landowner. But, as was often the case in the bottom rungs of tlaxilacalli administration, Quecil's advantage over his neighbors was illusory. Militating against any comparative accumulation for this lowest of baseline managers were the three separate kin groups he supported on his homestead. Extra land meant extra occupancy; and all Quecil received for his work was authority over (and help from) his two neighbors and administrative influence over his homestead.[8] Despite equivocal benefits for commoner taskmasters, the advantages were clear for the institution of the tlaxilacalli and its elite beneficiaries: thanks to Quecil, an extra 7,821 square tlalquahuitl (4.89 hectares) of soil fell under intensive cultivation. Commoners became ready overseers of their peers, while Aztec and then Spanish elites reaped the benefits.[9]

But at least Quecil didn't starve—if barely. His wider household (consisting of his own six-person tlacamecayotl, his older sister, and a young couple led by the wife) produced just over 85 percent of the necessary calories for nutritional well-being, only a slight fraction above the World Health Organization's (WHO) modern cutoff for food security crisis.[10] Quecil's household relied on the production of the two other domestic groups under his purview, for his neighbor's small three-person household cultivated 165 percent of their daily caloric needs and the other eight-member mayeque household produced a surplus of nearly two-and-a-half times their nutritional requirements. The best way for commoners like Quecil to ensure their own nourishment, it seems, was to reapportion a bit of food from their neighbors on either side before passing calories up the hierarchy.[11] In the reasonably fed centers of the tlaxilacalli, household allocation and consumption occurred along precise gradients of food security and nutritional well-being.[12]

These gradients were named and standardized and can be recovered from data in the Codex Asunción. The next section provides a rung-by-rung descriptive analysis of early Hispanic tlaxilacalli hierarchies, based on information for the specific case of Cuauhtepoztlan as contained in this document. Although certain details might diverge across the wider extension of Acolhuacan, formulaic registers such as land titles, legal filings, and baptismal records suggest a strongly marked general pattern, building from household (calli) to patio group, from patio group to sub-district (altepemaitl), from sub-district to tlaxilacalli, and from tlaxilacalli on up to altepetl and empire.

CALLI AND HOUSEHOLD

As seen earlier, the calli anchored local responses to the large-scale disruptions of the 1520s, and it continued to play this role for centuries.[13] It anchored political, social, and ecological regimes across Acolhuacan. Indeed, community—that potent mixture of hierarchy and solidarity—began in the homestead, or calli, in the sometimes tense, sometimes loving interactions among spouses, children, relatives, and dependents.[14] Artificial but still lifelike samples of these interactions explode across the pages of compendia of commoner speech such as the Primeros Memoriales: a woman, for example, rebuffs another with a brusque "how can you pick a fight with me? Are you my husband? Are you my man?" suggesting that the proper site for conflict was the domestic calli, not the public sphere. She continues, asking, "Do I live thanks to you? Do you serve me? Do I eat thanks to you?" further signaling the ties of obligation and nourishment mediated by the commoner household.[15]

Despite marked patriarchal overtones in such documents as the Primeros Memoriales, women seem to have generally held their own in Acolhua household economies and to have done so in marked contrast to ethnicity-based exclusions of the Hñähñus.[16] Crucially, women householders do not appear to have been penalized calorically in tlaxilacalli-wide allocations of productive land, continuing to receive the standard allotment of 400 square tlalquahuitl (~0.25 hectare) per capita.[17] Also, and most particularly among the poorest commoners, women served as anchors of household survival. In Cuauhtepoztlan's worst-quality lands (the 42% of soils identified as third-class), for example, women's maguey production accounted for over half of household calories in the form of drinkable pulque and aguamiel and the assorted edible parts of this plant.[18]

The collective aspect of household life also comes surprisingly to the fore in the Codex Asunción, particularly in a sequence of seemingly offhanded glyphs connected to the couple Lucía and Toribio Nauhyotl. In nearly all registers, whether in the Asunción or elsewhere, the male appears first in the household listing, bearing a name glyph. In the specific case at hand, however, Lucía appears first, as the widow of Toribio Nauhyotl (figure 3.1) The Asunción lists her as the head of a domestic unit, facing her late husband, who still carries the name glyph Nauhyotl, or "Four." Lines connect Toribio to a woman's head just below the four defining marks, and this serves as Lucía's glyph in other entries in the Asunción.[19] Lucía appears to have inherited the Nauhyotl glyph from her deceased husband, suggesting that perhaps this was a household name glyph instead of an individual one. (Indeed, the use of name glyphs continued for generations after the fall of the Aztec alliance; data from Tepetlaoztoc show use through the 1570s).[20] If this was the case—which is likely, since Lucía was not the only woman to inherit glyphs in the Asunción—household belonging took precedence over individual identity, even for the adult male marked as its head.[21] Further, land claims also appear to have passed seamlessly to Lucía and other widows, for they retained land allocations approaching standard holdings—around 350 square tlalquahuitl for every household member.[22]

FIGURE 3.1. Lucía, widow of Toribio Nauhyotl. She has no name glyph in the initial census enumeration (*A*) but assumes her husband's "four" sign, seen fully in the boundary counts of her lands (*B*). Asunción, ff. 52r, 63v. *Courtesy*, Biblioteca Nacional de México, Mexico City.

Names likely continued to pass as inherited identities during later periods, although Hispanic surname practices and inheritance laws soon obscured local patterns of transmission. Nevertheless, certain patterns of name inheritance continue to demand attention. Specifically, certain Christian first names begin to pass from parents to children, likely carrying with them specific evocations of affection and identity. In the Antecontla subsection of Cuauhtepoztlan tlaxilacalli, for example, the passing of the name Juana from mother to daughter seems to be far from trivial (figure 3.2a). Circumstantial but intriguing evidence suggests that the mother, called doña Juana in the Asunción codex, was in fact the daughter of Tepetlaoztoc's tlatoani, don Diego Tlilpotonqui.[23] Recall from chapter 1 (see figure 1.12) that a

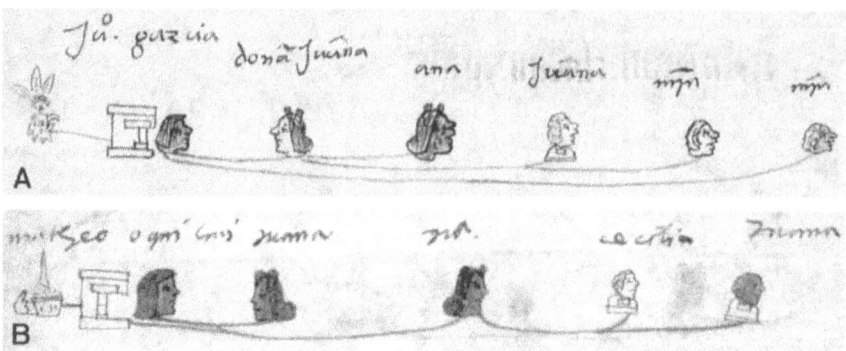

FIGURE 3.2. Transfer of the name Juana in Cuauhtepoztlan. *A*: the noblewoman doña Juana bequeaths her name to a daughter. *B*: a commoner household passes the name across three generations. (The middle figure uses the abbreviation "ju^a" for Juana.) Codex Asunción. *Courtesy,* Biblioteca Nacional de México, Mexico City.

certain doña Juana inherited the tlatoani's tribute share from Cuauhtepoztlan, and it would stand to reason that doña Juana gave her Christian name to her oldest daughter to bolster that daughter's claims to later inheritance. Lower-status households also followed this practice: in the same sub-district of Antecontla, two mothers also passed along names to their daughters, making three of twenty-two total; and in another sub-district of Cuauhtepoztlan, the name Juana traversed three generations: from grandmother to mother to daughter (figure 3.2b). Names were a powerful inheritance, anchoring people in the symbolic and spatial arrays of their local tlaxilacalli.[24]

"PEOPLE MINDERS," THE TEPIXQUE

One step up from the vital struggles of the calli, local tepixque such as Ciprián Quecil served as the first rung of community-based compulsion in rural Acolhuacan. Commoners like Quecil oversaw the collection of two or three neighboring houses and, in exchange, received a small bit of additional land or food, mitigating their frequent hunger. Indeed, the borderline nutritional crisis plaguing Quecil and other tepixque added extra insistence to their administrative and collective efforts; and this shows up in tribute records. When the level of famine analysis in the tlaxilacalli of Cuauhtepoztlan is widened to tepixqui-headed arrays or "patio groups," levels of overall hunger fall considerably, so that only 3 percent of such wider groupings faced a risk to their food security in normal years. (In bad years, however, 61% of groups still starved while 39% still ate—exactly the same figure as the household-level analysis.) Tepixque pulled food from their neighbors for themselves and their bosses, sitting at the top of this sophisticated array.[25]

The techniques of tepixque compulsion were marginal and diffuse enough to largely escape archival capture, but something of their practice appears in the conflict-laden commoner dialogues of the Primeros Memoriales. In one scene a macehualli, likely a lowly tepixqui, arrives at the house of an acquaintance and starts to push him around, yelling "step aside, you stupid lout, you fat ungrateful wretch!" The householder responds to these assaults by calling the tepixqui a fool, a drunkard, a drug fiend, an adulterer, "a house enterer, one who lives with others, an obstructer, a two-tongued one who exaggerates things to others, a people watcher." People watcher, house enterer, unreliable accountant, overbearing administrator: all accusations of coercive local administration. The householder continues his attack: "Can you become an altepetl, you little commoner? Shut up! What will you do to us? How will you conquer us? Are you our *topile*, our tlatoani? You're just a dog, a turkey. Your home is shit; you live in the dirt!"[26] Shooting through these insults are the small administrative distinctions between one poor commoner and another. Neither one held local power like a *topile* (head of a sub-district) or wielded sovereign rule like a tlatoani. Both were poor, often starving. But one was charged with collecting food from another, and on this simple action empires were built.

Here as well, however, there still appeared opportunities for community and even solidarity. As tepixqui of a minority ethnic group, Quecil likely aided the entry of his subordinates into a crowded social and territorial plane and could also have aided his subordinates in accessing tlaxilacalli or altepemaitl-wide goods. The spatial array of Quecil's altepemaitl of Tlanchiuhcan suggests how something like this might have occurred in Cuauhtepoztlan tlaxilacalli (figure 3.3). In the model in the figure, Quecil's homestead appears at the very bottom of the altepemaitl. The homesteads of the two neighbors under his immediate oversight are also marked.

When placed in this specific spatial context, telling details come to the fore. First, Quecil did not live directly adjacent to his tribute dependents, although he did plant a field near to one of them. More profound, the tepixqui Quecil and the dependent households of Pedro Tlaocol and Marcos Cozcacuauh appear as later minority Hñähñu additions to the early group of Acolhua colonists, settling at the margins of the core homestead area. Particularly given the marginal situations of his dependents, Quecil might have aided his Hñähñu subordinates in finding space in Tlanchiuhcan, the first domestic group tucked into an edge of the main Acolhua settlement group and the other a later arrival working as mayeque on elite land.[27]

The two dependent households living under Quecil's protection also suggest something about the early processes of insertion within a local hierarchy. The

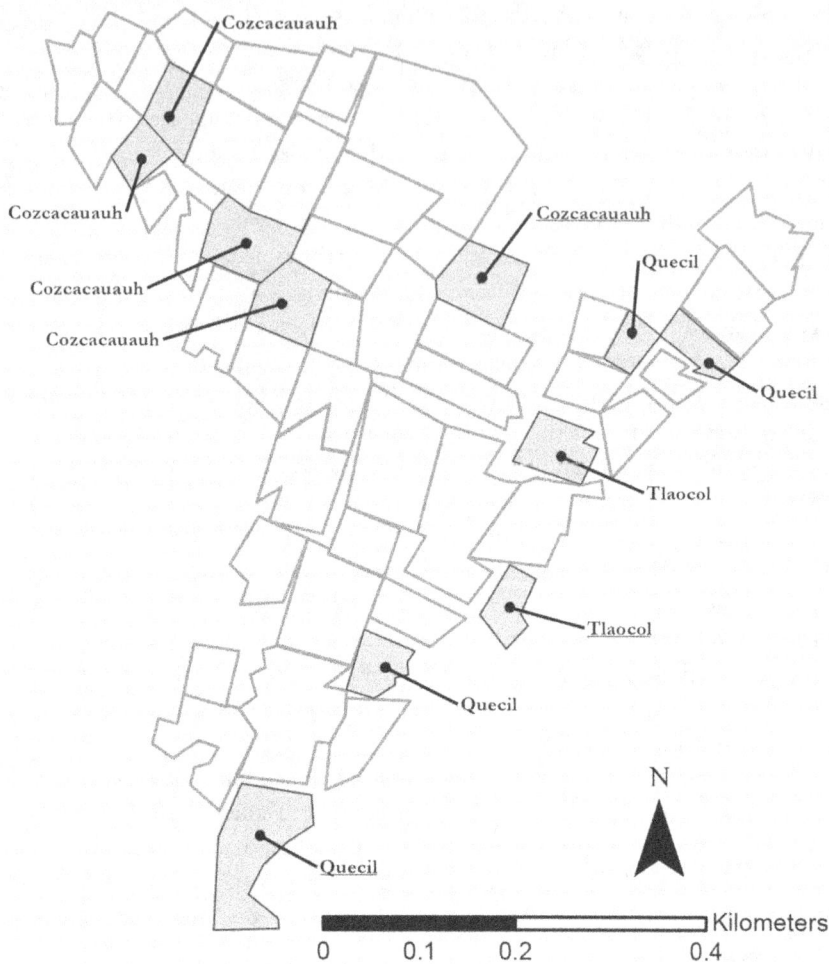

FIGURE 3.3. One patio block unit in Tlanchiuhcan altepemaitl: Ciprián Quecil, Pedro Tlaocol, and Marcos Cozcacuauh. Homesteads, or calmilli, are also marked in underline. Map by Bill and Kris Keegan.

household of Pedro Tlaocol, for instance, already managed its own land, while the mayeque group of Marcos Cozcacuauh had none to its name. It is possible to infer, therefore, a many-stage process by which marginal commoners could work themselves into a local hierarchy and then up through its ranks. At the bottom of this pyramid would be households such as Cozcacuauh, who lived under the direct protection of a low-level tepixqui like Quecil. One step up from this would be Tlaocol, with a separate independent homestead and assigned land but still under Quecil's direct oversight. The local tepixqui occupied the next rung higher, managing others from the edge of the main settlement. In addition to mustering tribute up the local hierarchy, therefore, Quecil could have also served as a poor person's intermediary, managing the submission of dependent Hñähñus within the workings of the altepemaitl and, by extension, the wider tlaxilacalli.[28]

"STAFF HOLDERS," THE TOPILEQUE

Within the wider sub-district of Tlanchiuhcan, the Hñähñu tepixqui Ciprián Quecil himself submitted to another commoner, a member of the Acolhua majority named Damián Tecolotl. This head of the altepemaitl was called topile, or staff holder, and his long rod of authority could have perhaps served as a standard tlalquahuitl measurement for land apportionment in his sub-district—recall, for example, the measurements of "good ol' Juan" in the apportionment of Ana's land in Tocuillan.[29] Topileque often enjoyed privileged land allotments. For example, not only did Tecolotl enjoy the largest amount of land of anyone in the altepemaitl,[30] but his homestead was placed at the very center of the core settlement clusters. Tecolotl, like Quecil, was also one of the few residents who did not work elite lands to make a living. Tecolotl's field allocation was the largest in the sub-district—2,549 square tlalquahuitl to feed 5 people, or 510 tl^2 per person, roughly 25 percent more than the standard per capita field allocation—and it provided nearly two-and-a-half times the daily calories needed for well-being. It was at this level of sub-district management that local administrators began to enjoy the privileges of their office. In addition to a major caloric surplus, Tecolotl's oversight of the entire altepemaitl earned him the coordination of 121 dependents.[31]

Each altepemaitl also expressed its own strongly marked collective identity, represented through a distinct territorial demarcation, a separate name glyph, and a specific religious avocation. Such signs are readily recoverable for Tlanchiuhcan, the subdivision of Cuauhtepoztlan tlaxilacalli modeled above, and other neighboring sub-districts. This altepemaitl's bounded territorial array has been analyzed more than once in this book (see figures 1.10, 2.2, and 3.3), and its complex glyph appears in the pages of the Codex Asunción (figure 3.4). It recognized a spiritual anchor in the nearby mountaintop of Huei Tepetl, and during the early Hispanic period it bore a specific vocation to the Lord of the Resurrection.[32]

Territorially, symbolically, socially, and metaphysically, each altepemaitl stood alone, pulling together within the wider sociability of the tlaxilacalli. Some altepemaitl, such as Tlatozcac, were minuscule, containing only six households along a single mountainous outcrop; others, such as Cuauhtepoztlan, were much

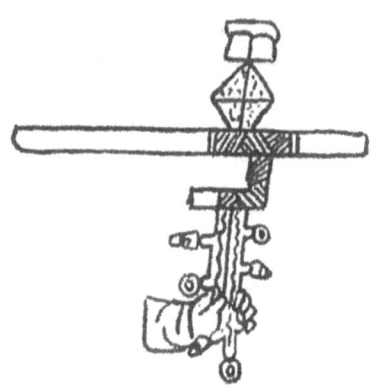

FIGURE 3.4. Tlanchiuhcan glyph.
Codex Asunción, f. 55v. *Courtesy*,
Biblioteca Nacional de México,
Mexico City.

larger, dominating a broad plain with seventy-nine total households.[33] Some altepemaitl—particularly the Texcalticpac of Martín Izcoatl or the subsection of Calla Tlaxoxiuhco where Pedro Tecihuauh de Castilla had his noble compound (see below)—served almost as miniature sectional fiefdoms; others, such as Tlanchiuhcan, belied earlier commoner colonizations subsequently overtaken by imperial nobles. Despite these local diversities, none of these altepemaitl exercised administrative independence. Only by joining together as tlaxilacalli did they exercise considerable local power.

TLAXILACALLI MANAGERS, THE CALPIXQUE

Regardless of the specificities of altepemaitl—large or small, remote or central, favored or marginalized—all joined together at the core level of local community, the tlaxilacalli. Here, administration became more powerful and institutionalized; across the periods in question, the tlaxilacalli served as the primary organizing force in local politics. In addition to tribute collection, this was the institution that managed key questions of local administration: land tenancy and assignment, population and tax records, and collective religious and political affiliation. This is where people lived: early documents register people's residence by tlaxilacalli, employing either the form *-pohui* (counted as a part of) or *chane* (householder), while later registers listed locals by tlaxilacalli and foreigners by altepetl.[34] The center of the tlaxilacalli housed the temple of local devotion and also contained the local armory, where community battalions formed for military engagements. Each tlaxilacalli was administered by a calpixqui (literally "housekeeper," but more like a majordomo; pl. calpixque) who, although a commoner, stood above all others in the locality.[35]

The calpixqui stalked the apex of the tlaxilacalli tribute hierarchy, and in Cuauhtepoztlan this official's name was Martín Tozpan. Occupying the first position in this codex (the first entry of the first altepemaitl), Tozpan controlled massive personal lands, clearly marking his dominion over 1,242 direct dependents in the tlaxilacalli. His holdings totaled 7,941 tl², or nearly 5 hectares in total—50 percent larger than any other allocation in Cuauhtepoztlan. These holdings approached the entire territorial extent of smaller altepemaitl such as Zapotlan (population 34) and Cuitlahuac (pop. 33) and broke down to 882 tl² for each member of his 9-person household, twice the per capita allotment. In total, these lands produced almost 50,000 daily calories, more than three times the nutritional needs of his household. Such largesse allowed Tozpan to maintain houses on two separate plots, where Tozpan and his wife, Juana, built an expansive single tlacamecayotl (string of relatives) totaling 7 children. Despite Tozpan's commoner status, this large single household stood as one of the sharpest distinctions between the calpixqui and his dependents, who were most often cast across small and fractured domestic groups. Poor commoner lands would support nothing larger.[36]

Despite his comparative wealth, Tozpan remained dependent to the highest-level tlaxilacalli administration, the noble *teuctlatoani*, the "lordly speaker" in the tlaxilacalli, discussed immediately below. In 1545 he "was given" the title *tlacateuctli*, "lord of people," by some unknown power—likely the teuctlatoani, although the tlatoani is another possibility.[37] Although evoked in some compendia of Nahua thought as standing in poised opposition to the teuctlatoani, the powerful but still dependent rank of tlacateuctli began as a commoner military office and grew during the early years of Hispanic administration to encompass civil responsibilities as well.[38]

These commoner leaders orchestrated tlaxilacalli activity along many different lines of collective endeavor; but in specialized realms, official experts (such as the role of *achcauhtin*, or generals, in war) also exercised important leadership roles within the tlaxilacalli.[39] For quotidian political administration, calpixque like Tozpan turned to an occasionally changing group of local elders called *huehuetque* (elders; sing. *huehue*), prominent for their experience as well as their comparative wealth in landholding. In Tozpan's tlaxilacalli of Cuauhtepoztlan, this group would have likely included the topileque Toribio Yaotl (5,154 tl², the second-largest household allocation across the tlaxilacalli) and Antonio Ehecatl (4,308 tl², the third-largest) and perhaps Albino Tlilcoatl as well, who headed a domestic economy of 6,331 tl², spread across three independent households. More than loyal subservience, therefore, huehuetque were prominent for their political skill, demonstrated by their large territorial apportionments, which often lay outside the otherwise carefully calibrated land and tribute hierarchies of the Codex Asunción. Huehuetque knew how the system worked, and they shared this experience with the local calpixqui.[40]

THE LORDLY SPEAKERS, TEUCTLATOQUE

At the very top of tlaxilacalli hierarchies, anchoring the spatial and political array of each community and reaching up to pretensions of altepetl-wide influence, sat a noble who consumed subordinate tribute streams and served broader functions in regional political alignments. These nobles were called teuctlatoque, and the hierarch from the most powerful local tlaxilacalli became, in turn, the sovereign tlatoani for the entire altepetl.[41] All of this makes intrinsic sense, but Cuauhtepoztlan presents a minor difficulty because of the incompleteness of its register. Assuming that the doña Juana cited above in the section on name inheritance is indeed the tlatoani's daughter set over Cuauhtepoztlan, it is impossible to calculate the extent of her landholdings because these pages were ripped from the Codex Asunción some time in the past. (This does, however, suggest the possible extent of her land titles, which would have been a target for her rivals.)[42]

This conceptual gap can be filled by moving just south to the tlaxilacalli of Chimalpan, where the teuctlatoani Martín Itzcoatl managed a personal compound of 50 dependents and a whopping 26,086 square tlalquahuitl—over three times the holdings of both the calpixqui Martín Tozpan and lower lords like Vicente Aoctlacuani and Pedro Tecihuauh de Castilla (see below). Izcoatl's compound occupied a full quarter of the entire territorial extension of the large altepemaitl of Texcalticpac and surpassed the total extension of many smaller altepemaitl such as Zapotlan and Tlatozcac. Not all of this land was held in Itzcoatl's name (his single household had 6,759 tl²), but the complete lordly holdings of Texcaltipac, complete with attached mayeque and secondary nobles, did fall directly under the teuctlatoani's purview.[43]

Two other lords (teteuctin; sing., teuctli) also lived in Chimalpan tlaxilacalli, both in the large central sub-district of Calla Tlaxoxiuhco: Vicente Aoctlacuani (household: 6,608 tl²; compound: 8,999 tl²; 17 total dependents) and Pedro Tecihuauh de Castilla (household: 998 tl²; compound: 8,029 tl²; 24 total dependents). The comparatively small household allocation to Tecihuauh de Castilla reinforces the idea that the local nobility did not need to plant to secure their sustenance. This was instead the tribute hierarchy's job. Williams and Hicks also show that the various plots of these noble compounds were contiguously allocated, and they plot the spatial extension of one such "lordly place," or tecpan, that of Tecihuauh de Castilla.[44] (All noble inhabits of a tecpan, both leaders and dependents, fell within the widest and most common category of nobility, that of *pilli*; plural, *pipiltin*.) The same can also be said for the large compound in Oztoticpac tlaxilacalli profiled in the Oztoticpac Lands Map.[45]

Despite the contiguous nature of most noble landholding—recall the spatial separation of noble lands in the altepemaitl of Tlanchiuhcan (58)—nobles fit

FIGURE 3.5. Martín Itzcoatl's head glpyh, complete with ruff. Codex Vergara, f. 42v. *Courtesy*, Bibliothèque nationale de France, Paris.

uncomfortably within the wider structure of tlaxilacalli regimes. Their compounds mapped territorially within wider spatial arrays; but, as in the case of Aoctlacuani and Tecihuauh in Calla Tlaxoxiuhco, they often weighed heavily on lower levels of administration, particularly the altepemaitl. Occupying forty-eight separate plots, the compounded holdings of Tecihuauh surely influenced the practice of tribute mobilization among his immediate neighbors, perhaps leading to a particularly vigorous practice of oversight in this sub-district. Calla Tlaxoxiuhco did, in fact, have its own topile, a certain Juan Coacuech, but the nobles Aoctlacuani and Tecihuauh dominated the immediate locality.[46]

This said, pipiltin such as Tecihuauh and Acotlacuani did serve certain integrative functions. It is well-known that noble compounds anchored the wider politics of both the altepetl and other regional arrangements, most particularly in providing marriage partners for people-hungry imperial tlacamecayotl. Beyond this role, nobles also operated on the lower ends of local hierarchy, offering small amounts of land and autonomy to poor sharecroppers at the lowest levels of tlaxilacalli hierarchies. Tecihuauh, for his part, included three mayeque households in his wider compound, in addition to other, more independent commoners who worked his fields in addition to their own. Nobles, therefore, served an important if predatory function in the tlaxilacalli, mediating alliances both above and below the community's compulsive core.

FEAR AND RESPONSIBILITY

As the teuctlatoani of Chimalpan, Martín Itzcoatl wielded considerable autonomous power within the tlaxilacalli under his purview. Befitting this higher status in early Hispanic Tepetlaoztoc, Itzcoatl, alone among residents in Chimalpan, wore a Spanish ruff in his head glyph, which, together with his receding hairline and toothless jaws, completed a picture of experience and prestige. As teuctlatoani, Itzcoatl could punish crimes with banishment or execution; and he could remove officials from their posts, shaving their distinctive and supernaturally charged haircuts: "thus fear spread; people were then very obedient."[47]

Every "year" of the 260-day *tonalpohualli* divinatory calendar, on the day One Reed, the date specially devoted to rulership, teuctlatoque like Izcoatl gathered the "total collectivity" of their various dependents (often combining various tlaxilacalli for this single purpose), split them by office and gender, and then scolded them on proper behavior within the tribute hierarchy. During this yearly ceremony, tlaxilacalli rulers spoke with the voice of the sovereign altepetl and its tlatoani: "the teuctlatoque represent the mat and the throne (rulership)."[48]

Taking a clump of copal incense in his hand, a teuctlatoani would step before a flaming brazier, throw the copal incense over the coals, and spin a vision of hierarchical acquisition: "Be diligent. Clear the soil; make ridges; work the land; break up the earth; plant the magueyes; sow cacti. In this way you will become rich. You will have good meat. You will buy people. You will bathe (sacrificial victims). You will eat (psychedelic) mushrooms. You will build yourselves houses; your home will be in a good place. This, this is living."[49] Such a "living" demanded inequality: riches required a corresponding category of poverty; slaves implied owners and sacrificial victims, the sponsors of sacrifice. Tlaxilacalli hierarchies identified precisely whom to compel in the pursuit of well-being.

THE CUAUHTEPOZTLAN HIERARCHY, TOP TO BOTTOM

Very schematically then, the tlaxilacalli hierarchy of Cuauhtepoztlan seems to have consisted of four separate, articulated levels below the sovereign altepetl, each dependent on the vigilance of one macehualli over others. At the top of this commoner hierarchy and giving its name to the entire arrangement was the tlaxilacalli, headed by a calpixqui or *calpollec* (calpolli holder), who occasionally consulted with his supporting huehuetque. The wider tlaxilacalli was then supported by subordinate "hands"—called here altepemaitl but also occasionally termed *calmaitl* (house hands) or *tlalmaitl* (land hands), led by section bosses, or topileque. These "hands" were then set over patio blocks, each led by a favored householder, the tepixqui. Finally, at the very root level of this system, each house (calli or *xacalli*, depending on ascribed ethnicity) organized itself into a flexible arrangement of kin, anchored by lands and a distinctive name glyph (or, much later, surname).

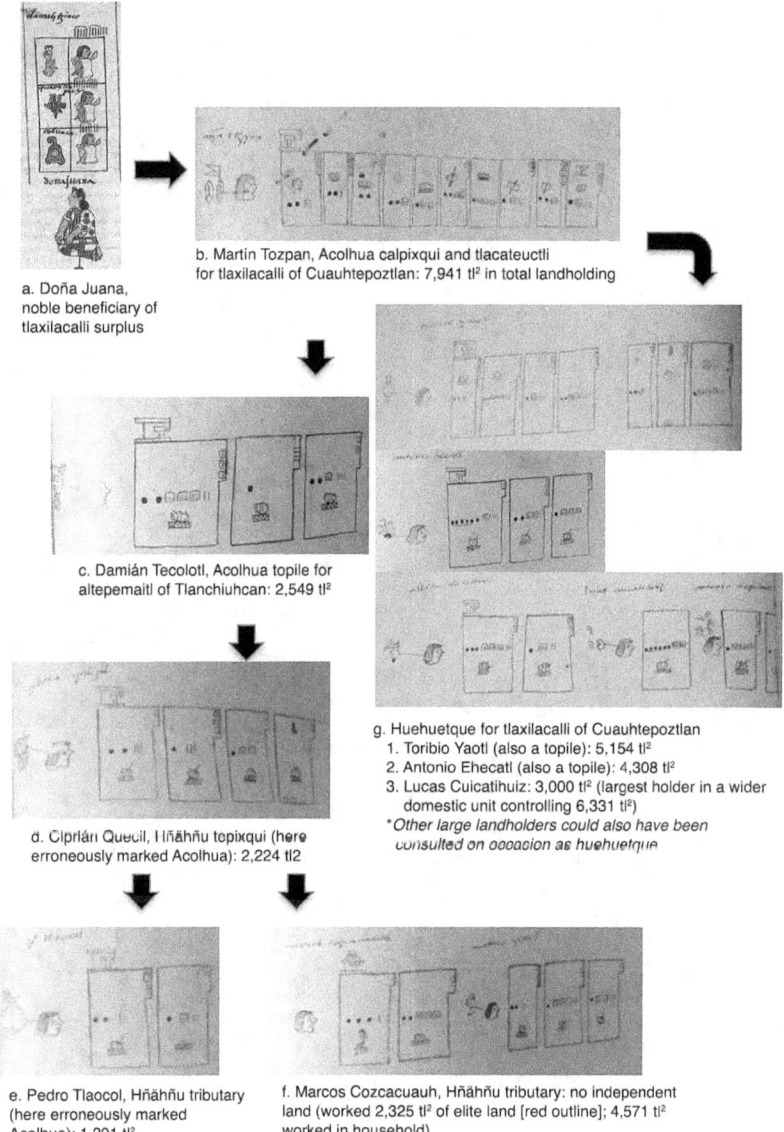

FIGURE 3.6. An illustrated hierarchy of Cuauhtepoztlan tlaxilacalli, ca. 1545.

As an illustration, a slice of the entire hierarchy of the tlaxilacalli of Cuauhtepoztlan is modeled in figure 3.6, showing the articulation across all four levels of its local administration.

FIGURE 3.7. Community religion. *A*: the ruins of the local pyramid of Cuauhtepoztlan tlaxilacalli. *B*: ten meters to the north, on the same plot of land, is a sign proclaiming the religious vocation of the Asunción cofradía. On August 15, the large feast day of the Assumption of Mary Magdalene is still celebrated in the same field. Photos by author.

Finally, despite the autonomous operation of each tlaxilacalli as both a separate political hierarchy and a distinct social entity, they did also interact and even coordinate with their local counterparts. Textual hints from the codices Asunción and Vergara, for instance, suggest that tlaxilacalli were not atomized or divorced from their immediate neighbors. Williams and Hicks, for example, show for the Codex Vergara that the altepemaitl of Topotitlan, tributary to the tlaxilacalli Chimalpan, was fully inserted within the spatial array of the next-door tlaxilacalli Cuauhtepoztlan.[50] These two tlaxilacalli neighbored each other and inter-penetrated territorially. Autonomy was different than isolation.

THE LOCAL COSMOS OF THE TLAXILACALLI

Nevertheless, tlaxilacalli remained distinct across the periods in question, with a communal autonomy stretching in one form or another from the Mesoamerican Post-Classic deep into the subsequent centuries of Hispanic rule. This autonomy changed markedly over time, beginning as an ecological imperative and then morphing into a later array of political administration and social belonging. Across this transformation, however, certain practices retained coherence even as wider parameters shifted. Religion was one of these realms, perhaps the most important across the centuries of tlaxilacalli administration. It anchored community, mobilized collective action, and connected the local landscape to the wider cosmos.

This connection was physically marked in Cuauhtepoztlan by its community pyramid, or *momoztli*, the ruins of which remain an important communal site for the *cofradía* of Santa María Magdalena Asunicón in modern-day Tepetlaoxtoc (figure 3.7).[51] In the early sixteenth century, it is possible that this temple land was cared for in some way by the calpixqui Martín Tozpan, perhaps in his role as tlacateuctli. Among the lands ascribed to this calpixqui in the Codex Asunción appears one plot that only occurs in the *milcocolli* perimeter count, written in a second line above Tozpan's other lands.[52] It bears an image of a woman's head above crossed conch shells and next to a sacrificial spine (figure 3.8). It is possible that this is nothing more than a name glyph; but the conch shells are out of place for this use, occupying the area usually employed in the Codex Asunción for additional commentary, such as the mention of migration. It is more likely, therefore, that this glyph could evoke the female priesthood of the *cihuatlamacazque* through reference to their ritual objects of performance and self-sacrifice.[53] This evocation of locally oriented female spiritual leadership becomes even more intriguing after Tozpan's tlaxilacalli built its first chapel to Santa María Magdalena Asunción, commemorating another woman's bodily transformation and sacrifice.[54]

FIGURE 3.8. Possible evocation of the cihuatlamacazque priesthood. Codex Asunción, f. 8v. *Courtesy*, Biblioteca Nacional de México, Mexico City.

Among the worship of various female deities, the cihuatlamacazque could also reverence male deities, including Tezcatlipoca.[55] This connection to the "Lord of the Smoking Mirror" is particularly important because Cuauhtepoztlan tlaxilacalli appears to have had a special connection to this Mesoamerican numen during the Aztec and early Hispanic periods. Based on naming patterns, Cuauhtepoztlan expressed a marked devotion to this shadowy and primal supernatural being, often invoking specific appellations or attributes, such as Miquiztli (death), Yaotl (enemy), Yohualli (night), Yohualecatl (night wind), Tlilhua (the blackened one), Xochihua (flower bearer),[56] Tecolotl (owl), Mazatl (deer), Huitzitl (hummingbird), and even Tezcapoc (smoking mirror). Deities closely related to Tezcatlipoca were also evoked in commoner names: Coatl (snake) for Quetzalcoatl and Ozomatli (monkey) for Xochipilli, while the cloud-serpent Mixcoatl and the rain bringer Tlaloc appeared under their own names, with Tlaloc also receiving numerous invocations as Quiahuitl (rain, also associated with Tezcatlipoca). But elsewhere in the wider tlaxilacalli there was also one macehualli named Juan Ichan Teopan Nemi, "Juan, his home is in the church." Things were indeed changing, processed once again from within the tlaxilacalli.[57]

During the early period of tlaxilacalli-based religious reinvestment—perhaps in the 1560s or 1570s, judging by textual clues[58]—administrators in Cuauhtepoztlan took stock of their community and its lands, elaborating an important alphabetic document within the pages of the Codex Asunción. This "Asunción Land Title," often read as a simple demarcation of space, came also to serve as an evocation of the community and its sacred landscape, enumerating the metaphysical extension of the tlaxilacalli through reference to its sacred mountains.[59] The eastern mountain Ayauhcalli sets the stage, and the narration then begins in a counterclockwise direction following Mesoamerican spatial practice, mentioning a range of peaks including Coyotianguiztli (Coyote Market), Amiltepetl (Mountain of the Irrigated Milpas, dedicated to St. Mary of the Assumption), Xoxoqui Tepetl (Green Mountain), and finally, Huei Tepetl (Big Mountain, dedicated to the Lord of the Resurrection). Fittingly, a cross stands at the end of this range, serving as the next boundary marker of the tlaxilacalli. After this, the land flattens out and the divisions change to lines of trees, ravines, rivers, and a road.[60]

After the mountain sequence, Cuauhtepoztlan's lands also begin to run into their borders with neighboring tlaxilacalli—specifically, Tetexocotlan and Los Reyes to the west, Acxotlan to the southwest, San Gerónimo Chimalpan and Huei Xochitl to the south, "the land of the tlatoani don Martín de Sevilla" to the southeast, and, completing the sequence, San Vicente to the east with one final mountain, Tetepayo (Walled Enclosure). Supernatural, natural, human, and social entities—separable here in only the most schematic analyses—dominated a landscape still crowded with both neighbors and meaning despite the wrenching population and ecological disruptions that occurred almost simultaneously with this remapping of the Cuauhtepoztlan tlaxilacalli.[61]

NOTES

1. Although the codices Asunción and Vergara share almost all structural similarities, the Asunción provides more historical information because of its ongoing use in Cuauhtepoztlan tlaxilacalli after its initial enumeration. It contains, therefore, precious additional information through the 1570s, while the Vergara only retains information to the early 1540s. Further, although there are not enough data to state whether the data for Cuauhtepoztlan are representative of all Acolhua tlaxilacalli, its organization does seem of a standard pattern. There are, for example, traces of similar tribute documents in Acolhuacan, but most seem to have been lost over time. See, however, the *Ramírez cadastral fragment* (BNAH, Colección Antigua 213); also Patrick Lesbre, "Dos manuscritos pictográficos tezcocanos desconocidos del siglo XVI—escrituras y nobleza acolhua colonial: Tezcoco y Atenco, 1575," *Estudios de Cultural Náhuatl* 41 (2010): 231–57.

2. Whitmore and Williams, "Famine Vulnerability." Another bit of supporting evidence for persistent hunger in Acolhuacan comes from skeletal analyses of other Post-Classic central Mexican areas, such as Cholula. See Lourdes Marquez Morfin, Robert

McCaa, Rebecca Storey, and Andes del Angel, "Health and Nutrition in Pre-Hispanic Mesoamerica," in *The Backbone of History: Health and Nutrition in the Western Hemisphere*, ed. Richard H. Steckel and Jerome C. Rose (Cambridge: Cambridge Unviersity Press, 2005), 307–40.

3. Whitmore and Williams, "Famine Vulnerability." In addition to its treatment of systematic hunger, this article also provides useful information on carrying capacities, crop selection, and land use. The authors explicitly state that this article supersedes Barbara J. Williams, "Contact Period Rural Overpopulation in the Basin of Mexico: Carrying-Capacity Models Tested with Documentary Data," *American Antiquity* 54, no. 4 (October 1989): 715–32. On Tepetlaoztoc's historically poor soils, see Parsons, Blanton, and Parsons, *Prehistoric Settlement Patterns*, 102; Cordova, "Landscape Transformation," chapters 5 and 6. Although these models account for both staple agriculture and important forms of secondary farming, such as intercropping and the full exploitation of crops (maguey as both pulque and consumable fiber, for example), they do not address other forms of subsistence, such as foraging, lacustrine extractions, or trade.

4. For wider patterns of exclusion in Nahua thought, see Justyna Olko, "El 'otro' y los estereotipos étnicos en el mundo nahua," *Estudios de Cutura Náhuatl* 44 (2012): 165–98.

5. Estimates instead of exact figures are used for the percentage of Hñähñus because of a missing census for the Huitznahuac section in the Codex Asunción. Hñähñu caloric production comes from the Codex Asunción, following the methodology of Whitmore and Williams in "Famine Vulnerability." Two ambiguously identified households (Hñähñu in one register, Acolhua in another) were included in these figures, but an extra name was omitted that appeared in one register without a corresponding face glyph. These are marginal cases and do not much influence the overall pattern of Hñähñu exclusion one way or another. On desperation foods, see Charles Gibson, *The Aztecs under Spanish Rule* (Stanford: Stanford University Press, 1964), 30.

6. These thatched-roof houses were, quite literally, shacks. The English word *shack* derives through Spanish from the Nahuatl *xacalli*; and the Hñähñus lived, by definition, in these mosquito-plagued structures. Although the *Oxford English Dictionary* (oed.com, accessed January 8, 2014) calls the etymology of shack "obscure," the derivation is clear: xacalli → *jacal* (Sp.) → shack. (In addition, the Nahuatl term for mosquito was *xacalmoyotl*, "shack fly"; see Frances Karttunen, *An Analytical Dictionary of Nahuatl* [Norman: University of Oklahoma Press, 1992], 321.)

7. Modern scholarly editions of both the Asunción and the Vergara provide a schematic analysis of land equality in certain altepemaitl of both Cuauhtepoztlan and Chimalpan tlaxilacalli. See Williams and Harvey, *The Códice*, 48–50; Williams and Hicks, *Códice Vergara*, 53.

8. Jerome A. Offner ("Archival Reports of Poor Crop Yields in the Early Postconquest Texcocan Heartland and Their Implications for Studies of Aztec Period Population,"

American Antiquity 45, no. 4 [October 1980]: 848–56) has questioned these calculations based on low tribute incomes noted for Chiconautla and four other altepetl in the Contaduría section of the Archivo General de Indias. Whitmore and Williams ("Famine Vulnerability," 87–88) show, however, that field production regularly included more than simply maize, particularly intercropped maguey. Further, because these registers are counted as "tribute" (cf. AGI/ Contaduría/662), it is possible that they only account for a fraction of total production. This being said, Offner rightly mentions that much more work is needed on patterns of individual land tenure, particularly in the tlaxilacalli. See his "The Future of Aztec Law," in *Legal Encounters on the Medieval Globe*, ed. Elizabeth Lambourn and Carol Symes (Kalamazoo, MI: ARC Humanities Press, 2016), 2, no. 2, article 3.

9. Codex Asunción, ff. 47v, 57r, 70r. Figures for Quecil and his neighbors are based on Whitmore and Williams, "Famine Vulnerability." Excluding elite-owned fields worked by others, the total land held independently in Ciprián Quecil's tribute group was 3,515 square tlalquahuitl, or about 2.2 hectares.

10. Although the WHO standards come from modern developmentalist work, human biology has not changed enough in four-and-a-half centuries to warrant rejection of these standards as a general benchmark of well-being. Whitmore and Williams, "Famine Vulnerability," also use this benchmark.

11. This reapportionment also included food for festive and communal commemorations; see the discussion of tepixqui-headed "patio groups" below.

12. In total, the caloric needs for Quecil's household were 14,696 daily Kcal. The needs of the two dependent households were 5,759 for the farmer Pablo Tlaocol and 14,736 for the tenant farmer Marcos Cozcacauh. These figures do not include protein or important nutrients, so many commoners could still have been undernourished even if they did get sufficient calories. Regarding mayeque, the precise arrangements between these farmers and landowners are still unknown for both Acolhuacan and Mesoamerica more broadly.

13. On the calli, see Robert McCaa, "The Nahua Calli of Ancient Mexico: Household, Family, and Gender," *Continuity and Change* 18, no. 1 (2003): 23–48. For the later Hispanic period, see Pizzigoni, *The Life Within*.

14. For an in-depth analysis of Nahua kin terms, see Julia Madajczak, "Nahuatl Kinship Terminology as Reflected in Colonial Written Sources from Central Mexico: A System of Classification" (PhD dissertation, University of Warsaw, Poland, 2014).

15. "ma nachca quê tinechpevaltia cuix tinonamic cuix tinoquichvi . . . cuix no ze mopal ninemi cuix tinechtlaecoltia cuix mopal notlatlaqua." Primeros Memoriales, Biblioteca de la Real Academia de la Historia, ms. 9-5524, f. 71r. (The Primeros Memoriales document is divided in two. Hence, where the citation includes a mention of the "Academia" it refers to this part of the document.) For concise treatments of gender conceptions, see Susan Kellogg, *Weaving the Past: A History of Latin America's Indigenous Women from the Prehispanic Period to the Present* (Oxford: Oxford University Press, 2005), 19–29; Louise M. Burkhart, "Mexica

Women on the Home Front: Housework and Religion in Aztec Mexico," in *Indian Women of Early Mexico*, ed. Susan Schroeder, Stephanie Wood, and Robert Haskett (Norman: University of Oklahoma Press, 1997), 25–50. For Acolhuacan, see Elizabeth M. Brumfiel, "The Quality of Tribute Cloth: The Place of Evidence in Archaeological Argument," *American Antiquity* 61, no. 3 (July 1996): 453–62. For an intense engagement with Nahuatl gendered discourse, see Madajczak, "Nahuatl Kinship Terminology."

16. See in particular Madajczak's discussion of "mother as matrix" in "Nahuatl Kinship Terminology," 152–56.

17. For women household heads, see Codex Vergara, ff. 27r, 29r, 32r, for María, wife of Lucas Cipac, whose head glyph always comes first but whose husband's name is attached to fields even when his wife is the only head glyph listed; a similar pattern obtains in the dependent noble household of Cecilia and Alonso Telpozaca and the commoner homestead of Cecilia Mimich: Codex Vergara, ff. 38v, 40v, 44r, 46r, 51r, 53r; the same might have also been the case for Cecilia, wife of Lucas Chochol, but the data are incomplete: Codex Asunción, f. 34v. Within wider patriarchal domestic groups, there were also dependent households led by women with no independent landholding, such as María, wife of Antonio Mixcoatl: Codex Asunción, ff. 6r, 15r, 24v.

18. Whitmore and Williams, "Famine Vulnerability," 87–88.

19. Codex Asunción, ff. 51v, 63v, 68v.

20. In the Nahuatl language alphabetic glosses of the Codex Asunción, Lucía is not called Nauhyotl but rather *lucia ycnoçihuatl*, "the widow Lucía."

21. For inherited glyphs, see Codex Asuncion, ff. 52r and 77r, for Luisa icnocihuatl Nauhyotl; Codex Vergara, f. 19v, for Margarita icnocihuatl Coconetl; Codex Vergara, ff. 4r, 9v, 17r, for Magdalena icnocihuatl in huepol Chapan, who inherited the name from her brother-in-law. Francisca icnocihuatl and Ana icnocihuatl, Codex Vergara, ff. 4r, 9r, 17r, 35r, 37r, also inherited complex glyphs, but the males' names are unknown.

22. Including her deceased (but still enumerated) husband in the calculations, Lucía's household of five worked a total of 1,781 square tlalquahuitl (tl^2,) which gives a per capita allocation of 356.2 tl^2. More broadly, 400 tl^2 per capita does seem to be the standard allocation. Its quarter-hectare measurement is nearly identical to the 0.24 ha calculated by Whitmore and Williams, "Famine Vulnerability," 91, as the average per capita allocation for caloric well-being. Further, 400 tl^2 is a nice full number for the base–20 counting system (20-by-20, square) used in tlaxilacalli tribute regimes. Additional confirmation of this standard allocation is the corncob glyph placed only on fields under this value in the calculation of surface area.

23. Williams and Harvey (*The Códice*, 64) suggest that doña Juana was the daughter of don Diego Tlilpotonqui but provide little evidence to support this claim. Supporting evidence includes the early use of the Spanish honorific "doña," which was restricted to the upper elite at this time; the Hispanic last name García attached to her male companion; and

the missing pages for what should have been her land titles in the Codex Asunción, suggesting an attempt to curtail what could have been large individual holdings.

24. On later naming patters, see Lockhart, *The Nahuas after the Conquest*, 117–30.

25. Whitmore and Williams, "Famine Vulnerability," 90–91; Karttunen and Lockhart, eds., *Bancroft Dialogues*, 110.

26. "cuix teoa tatiz titepitiz ỹ timecevaltontli ma nel cēca oc itla xiquito cuix i quē titechivaz cuix ic titechpopoloz cuix tevatl titopil itotlatocauh ca ça no titzcutli titotoli cuitlapā tlaçolpā mocha monemiya." Primeros Memoriales (Academia), f. 70v.

27. Regarding Ciprián Quecil's social and political status, it seems likely he also spoke Nahuatl well because he was identified as Acolhua twice in the codex. Codex Asunción, ff. 47v, 70r.

28. Regarding insertion within a specific tlaxilacalli, documents like the *Ramírez cadastral fragment* prove that macehualtin could hold land in more than one altepemaitl. However, even here, each commoner was inscribed within a single, specific tlaxilacalli. Also, Marcos Cozcacuauh's second name demands attention, for it resembles the name of a famous noble tlaxilacalli in imperial Tetzcoco, Cozcacuauhco. Could Marcos, a recent arrival in Tepetlaoztoc, have fled fields in Cozcacuauhco after the fall of the independent Acolhua empire?

29. The roughly 2.5 meter length of a tlalquahuitl staff might appear large, but Central Mexican iconography often shows extravagantly long rods of authority. See, for example, figure 4.4 in this book.

30. Like most levels of administration below the altepetl, there is no standard term for a tlaxilacalli sub-district. Michael E. Smith—"Houses and the Settlement Hierarchy in Late Postclassic Morelos: A Comparison of Archaeology and Ethnohistory," in *Household, Compound, and Residence: Studies of Prehispanic Domestic Units in Western Mesoamerica*, ed. Robert S. Santley and Kenneth G. Hirth (Boca Raton, FL: CRC, 1993), 191–206—prefers *chinamitl*, but this term carried a different meaning in many Nahuatl documents, referring instead to either chinampa agriculture or walled enclosures. See the long entry for "chinamitl" in the Wired Humanities Project's online Nahuatl dictionary: http://whp.uoregon.edu/dictionaries/nahuatl/index.lasso, accessed August 8, 2016. David Charles Wright Carr—"Los otomíes: cultura, lengua, y escritura" (PhD dissertation, El Colegio de Michoacán, 2005), 157—uses altepemaitl and suggestively connects altepemaitl, "hand of the altepetl," to the related Hñähñu term *ma'yehnini*, "place of the hand of the polity." Later Acolhua documentation suggestively uses the term *calpolli* for a tlaxilacalli sub-district, but this distinction needs to be proved more convincingly to be effective. One rare example from 1732 reads "here, before the people of the tlaxilacalli of Santa Catarina Chimalpan, in the calpolli of Tianguiztenco: we, the tlatoque, the officals of the *república [de indios]* in the huei altepetl of San Agustín Acolman . . ." (ynica ytlacatlantzin co ynipa tlaxilacali Sta catarina ximalpan ypan calpoli tiaquiz teco tehuan tintlatoqu de tualos de republica ypan huey altepetl S. Augustin Acolman). DNT, doc. 38.

31. Tecolotl's four-person household produced 17,361 daily Kcal for an estimated subsistence need of 7,368. Codex Asunción, ff. 47r, 69v.

32. Codex Asunción, ff. 55v, 73r.

33. Altepemaitl like Tlatozcac were so small that they were entered jointly in the accounting of the Codex Asunción. In contrast, the largest altepemaitl of Cuauhtepoztitlan was so influential that it nearly shared its name with the entire tlaxilacalli of Cuauhtepoztlan; only the small but transformative particle -ti- modified the altepemaitl's name from the one used by the wider tlaxilacalli.

34. An extensive series of documents from late sixteenth-century Tetzcoco provides a good panorama of these terms. Citations for the "-pohui" form are common. Cf. BNAH-3PS, exp. 2–40, ff. 8r, 11r, 15r, 23r. "Chane" is less common; cf. BNAH-3PS, exp. 2–40, ff. 8r, 16r. "Chane" was also used by elites to refer to their residence in the city of Tetzcoco. See the differential use of "chane" in this example, for example: "Señor Joan de pomar. pilli. chane ynicā ypan omoteneuh çiudad [Tetzcoco] omononotzque yn yehuatl pedro de san franco. Sant Sebastian puhui. hotlatlitic chane." BNAH-3PS, exp. 2–40, f. 17r. On the separation of tlaxilacalli locals and altepetl foreigners, see Archivo del Diócesis de Texcoco, *Casam[tos] Baptis[s] y Difuntos Desde 16 de Março de 1670: Cuanala* #2, 1670–91, Varios YN.

35. On tlaxilacalli armories, Ross Hassig—*Aztec Warfare: Imperial Expansion and Political Control* (Norman: University of Oklahoma Press, 1995), 95—describes "weapons . . . stored at the entrances to the temples, apparently in each barrio."

36. Codex Asunción, ff. 1r, 18r. Also, as above in the calculation of the percentage of Hñähñus in the tlaxilacalli, the estimate of 1,242 for the total population of the tlaxilacalli of Cuauhtepoztlan is the result of a missing census for the altepemaitl of Huitznahuac in the Codex Asunción.

37. "años 1545. quimacaq mīn tozpā tlacatecuitl." Codex Asunción, f. 17v. A later notation from 1565 in the same section mentions Gabriel de Galicia being "given justice" (omacoc justiçia) by the long-serving alcalde Andrés Ortiz, suggesting a slight but believable slippage in the grantor of the office. A certain Antonio Tlacateuctli is also named as an alcalde in 1550 (f. 12v), reporting to the tlatoani don Luis de Tejeda.

38. A quote from the Floretine Codex nicely summarizes this point: "there are two teuctlatoque, one military, one noble. The one from the military is the tlacateuctli" (*vme in tecutlato, ce quappan, ce pilpan: ce quappan, tlacatecutli*). Florentine Codex, Dibble and Anderson, eds., book 6, 110.

39. For the case of the teachcauh Tohueyo (a singular form of achauhtin), see page 7 in the introduction. On the wider subdivisions of responsibility and jurisdiction, see Jerome A. Offner, "The Distribution of Jurisdiction and Political Power in Aztec Texcoco: Subgroups in Conflict," in *Five Centuries of Law and Politics in Central Mexico*, ed. Ronald Spores and Ross Hassig (Nashville, TN: Vanderbilt University Publications in Anthropology, 1984), 5–14.

40. Codex Asunción, ff. 36v, 75r, 79v. Williams and Harvey, *The Códice*, 399, note that Lucas Cuicatihuiz appears to be missing a "twenty-count" black dot; I accounted for this in my calculations. Also, it is impossible to specify the final decimal place for this count because of the tightly sewn binding of the codex.

41. This distinction is even more tenuous in the first Asunción Land Title, which refers to the head of a neighboring tlaxilacalli as "the tlatoani of Los Reyes," "yn reyes tlatohuani d. Juã palacala." Codex Asunción, f. 21r.

42. Cf. Lockhart, *The Nahuas after the Conquest*, 16–18. Frederic Hicks, "Governing Smaller Communities in Aztec Mexico," *Ancient Mesoamerica* 23, no. 1 (2012): 47–56, also gives a useful summary of some of the responsibilities of what he calls "lordly executives." His sources, however, are strongly influenced by "Eastern" central Mexican sources (Huexotzinco, Tlaxcala), which only partially apply to the "Western" Acolhua case. Hicks does not discuss the difference between "Eastern" and "Western" sources; nor does he cite Lockhart's important work on this distinction.

43. Codex Vergara, f. 42v.

44. Williams and Hicks, *Vergara*, 71.

45. On the Oztoticpac map, see Howard F. Cline, "The Oxtoticpac Lands Map of Texcoco, 1540," *Quarterly Journal of the Library of Congress* 23 (1966): 77–115; Howard F. Cline, "The Oztoticpac Lands Maps," in *A la Carte, Selected Papers on Maps and Atlases*, ed. Walter W. Ristow (Washington, DC: Library of Congress, 1972), 62–98; Herbert R. Harvey, "The Oztoticpac Lands Map: A Reexamination," in *Land and Politics in the Valley of Mexico: A Two Thousand Year Perspective*, ed. Herbert R. Harvey (Albuquerque: University of New Mexico Press, 1991), 163–86; Xavier Noguez, "El Mapa de Oztoticpac de la Biblioteca del Congreso de Washington: Una edición facsimilar," in *Códices y Documentos sobre México: Segundo Simposio*, ed. Salvador Rueda Smithers, Constanza Vega Sosa, and Rodrigo Martínez Baracs (Mexico City: INAH, 1997), 2:301–10.

46. Codex Vergara, f. 14r.

47. "ynic mauhcamanca. Auh cenca vel ic otetlacamachoc." Primeros Memoriales (Academia), f. 64v.

48. "in tecutlatoque in mvteneva in petlapan in icpalpa." Primeros Memoriales (Academia), f. 62r.

49. "ma ye mel xiçacamo, xitlacuentoma, xitlacuentlapana ximeteca xictlaça in nopalli yehoa yc timotlamachtiz, ticpiaz in tonacayutl titecoaz titealtiz tinanacaquaz timocaltiz qualcã yez in mochan: o yeva y o yehoa I, yn nemoaloni." Primeros Memoriales (Academia), f. 64r.

50. Williams and Hicks, *Vergara*, 66.

51. The feast day is August 15. See Cando Morales, *Tepetlaoxtoc*, 51. The rubble remaining at the site of the local pyramid of Asunción is a fraction of its earlier volume. Stones were removed for moden civic construction in Tepetlaoztoc.

52. On the milcocolli annotation system, see Williams and Pierce, "Evidence of Acolhua Science," 149–53.

53. On the cihuatlamacazque, see Pilar Alberti Manzanarez, "Mujeres sacerdotisas aztecas: Las cihuatlamacazque mencionadas en dos manuscritos inéditos," *Estudios de Cultural Náhautl* 24 (1994): 171–217.

54. Alberti Manzanarez, "Mujeres sacerdotisas aztecas." Thanks to Mariano Cando Morales, member of the Asunción cofradía in Tepetlaoztoc, for showing the location of this field and to Barbara Williams for orienting the field in the Codex Asunción.

55. Alberti Manzanarez, "Mujeres sacerdotisas," 181.

56. Pete Sigal extensively discusses the term "Xochihua" in relation to queer performance in his "Queer Nahuatl: Sahagún's Faggots and Sodomites, Lesbians and Hermaphrodites," *Ethnohistory* 54:1 (2007): 9–34.

57. "juº ychā teopanemi." Codex Asunción, f. 49r.

58. The main evidence for this mid-century estimate is the presence of don Juan Diego Hernández, an administrator active at this time, as a signatory in the Asunción Land Title.

59. On mountains and tlaxilacalli, see Garcia Zambrano, "Zahuatlan el viejo."

60. Codex Asunción, ff. 1v, 5v, 21r, 35v.

61. Williams and Harvey (*The Códice*, p. 4) show that most of these mountains conserved the same names through the twentieth century. The fieldwork supporting this book also confirms their observation.

4

Tlaxilacalli Religions, 1537–1587

Even as Cuauhtepoztlan tlaxilacalli projected itself once again across its surrounding landscape, it also began to incorporate new symbols of belief within its basic operational practice. Entering the second generation of Christian-inspired devotion in Tepetlaoztoc around 1560, members of Cuauhtepoztlan were already tying the universalizing saints and images of Catholic religiosity into a renovated sacred and productive landscape. The Codex Asunción records an early mobilization of its local hierarchy in service of Christian religious patronage. The process begins with the calpixqui of Cuauhtepoztlan, don Juan Diego Hernández, and his counterpart in Hispanic administration, the alcalde don Dionisio de la Cruz, apportioning local land for the new tlaxilacalli patron, "the noble lady tlatoani," Santa María Asunción. The action then proceeded to the topile of Tlatozcac altepemaitl, don Cristobal de Santa María, who, in turn, called on "the dear Martínezes" (likely local tepixque) to distribute the land to their dependent cultivators to "pay tribute" to the tlaxilacalli patron.[1]

Tlatozcac was one of the steep, foothill altepemaitl, and the grant specifically notes that the ground is in the wooded upland (*quauhtlali*). From the perspective of the early Hispanic tlaxilacalli, a donation of such land could usefully serve two ends at once. Because the land was steep and brushy and the marginalized Tlatozcac was also losing population, a donation here would not severely impact the tribute income from more productive lands. Equally important, land here approached the peaks of two neighboring hills, Ocoyo and Ayauhcalli. As mountains were regularly understood as sustaining foundations for local community, it made perfect sense to firmly lodge Cuauhtepoztlan's new patron saint in this wider spiritual landscape.

A later donation by the same calpixqui, don Juan Diego Hernández—here in concert with his younger brother, don Juan Diego de la Cruz—makes the entire process even more explicit. This second land donation occurred in the altepemaitl of Tlanchiuhcan, and here the mountain Huei Tepetl served as reference point. The narrator's voice is also distinct, assuming a mid-level position of authority, receiving a land donation and then reassigning it: "At the foot of Huei Tepetl in Tlanchiuhcan, dear Matías the carpenter works serving the (Lord of the) Resurrection. He will go beating the little magueyes to buy *ocote* incense for the remembrance of Easter. The huehuetque, don Juan Diego de la Cruz and the elder don Juan Diego Hernández, teachcauh of Quahuetzquixochititlan,[2] gave it to me [the local official, perhaps a topile] in the year 1575."[3] A tlaxilacalli artisan was charged with procuring traditional incense for local celebrations of Easter, and he did so at the base of Huei Tepetl—tapping magueys to make pulque for the market, where he also bought the ocote. The reconstituted sacred landscape was also one of popular commerce, where the new accouterments of devotion were mustered and sold through the market—linking in a new way the sacred landscape of a tlaxilacalli to the wider economics of its altepetl and region.

One final land grant in the Asunción codex describes an even more permanent economic association between tlaxilacalli locals and the local church of Santa María Asunción. It is undated and describes how the narrator, his children, and his brother, Miguel Espíndola, were given flat land and magueys of the local church in exchange for them "working for and repaying" the self-same chapel.[4] Here the process of spatial reconstruction comes full circle: the tlaxilacalli continued to function in the key areas of land distribution and labor mobilization, but this labor was now understood as also benefiting the church, as an anchor of the community's sacred landscape. Produce and labor continued to flow out of the tlaxilacalli, but their destination was now much more local, often no farther than the community chapel. As seen here in the case of Cuauhtepoztlan, tlaxilacalli regularly paid for their own transformations into local parishes—a fitting investment, as it would turn out.[5]

Landed, community religiosity was already a vital component of commoner lives—each particular tlaxilacalli carried its own patron deity in imperial Acolhuacan, after all—but the recodification of these practices was nevertheless crucial because it opened the way for tlaxilacalli to articulate themselves up through the emerging Catholic hierarchies of early New Spain. This chapter describes religious and political shifts in a regional context, showing first how Christian evangelization and Inquisitorial persecution flowed through tlaxilacalli networks and then how such networks reconstructed both the spiritual and physical architecture of community life in early Hispanic altepetl.

TLAXILACALLI RELIGIOUS NETWORKS

Repeated testimony from the early Mexican Inquisition shows that tlaxilacalli-based ritual specialists continued to orchestrate both spiritual practice and the physical upkeep of important religious instruments across central Mexico well into the first generation of Hispanic rule.[6] In the Acolhua region, a certain Mocauhque, the local "pope" (religious expert) from the "barrio subjeto" (tlaxilacalli) of Izpan (Tulancinco altepetl), asserted in 1539 that "everyone (in the tlaxilacalli) obeyed him and gave him everything he requested," including feathered shields, masks, clothing, and conch shells.[7] Mocauhque further noted that he himself was a "disciple" of another ritual specialist, Tenancatl, from the neighboring altepetl Tepepulco.[8]

Nothing else is known about Tenancatl, but the articulation of Mocauhque through wider religious networks appears robust and ongoing, just one illustration of a much wider process of tlaxilacalli-based spiritual practice. Examples of such regional articulation abound, including the affiliation of two local specialists to the tlacateuctli of Xalataco tlaxilacalli (Tula altepetl), religious artifacts spread across the tlaxilacalli of Azcapotzalco, the marriage ceremonies performed by officials in four separate tlaxilacalli of Ocuituco, and the care for and construction of religious effigies in the same tlaxilacalli of that altepetl.[9] Later, Cristóbal, the "principal" of Ocuituco, was asked about other "idol guardians." After describing a series of "sorcerers and magicians" who were still active in the region, Cristóbal then explained the specifics of tlaxilacalli-based religious responsibility in his region:

> In the barrio of Miguel, the principal of this pueblo (altepetl), lives an Indian named Tecpatetl who, during the time of unbelief, used to guard the demons with his father; perhaps he will know where some idols are. In the barrio of the tlacatecatl (a military office), there is an old Indian named Teucatl who is from Tonacacinco, who used to be in the devil's house called Coamiahuatl guarding, taking care of his trumpet. Likewise, in the same barrio lives another Indian called Tetlatla who used to be guard and herald of another devil called Macuilxochitl. Likewise, there is another Indian named Cuetlan who lives with don Juan, the former cacique of this pueblo. He used to be the guardian of a devil called Icnopilli. These are the ones who will know where there are idols.[10]

A related but much more spectacular example of tlaxilacalli-based religious coordination concerns the diffusion and care of religious articles rescued from the Templo Mayor after the fall of Mexico-Tenochtitlan. Across a series of Inquisition cases, Spanish officials sought articles stored in tlaxilacalli in the altepetl of Colhuacan and the tlayacatl of San Juan Moyotlan in Mexico City. (There were also fleeting mentions of Tlacopan, Xaltocan, Xilotepec, and Chalco.) In one such raid, the tlatoani of Colhuacan was asked, after extensive questioning, whether there were "any other idols" left to be uncovered. The tlatoani, Don Baltasar Toquezquauhyotzin, cited at least ten separate tlaxilacalli by name, each with its own metaphysical secret, although he was unaware of the full extent of such activity: "he has heard tell that there are things of the devil and he doesn't know what they are."[11] Such unfamiliarity is remarkable, for don Baltasar himself was deeply enmeshed in the network striving to protect religious articles and activities from rising Spanish persecution. Part of this protection likely included leaving tlaxilacalli free to continue their own local spiritual practices even as he supported wider collaboration on other fronts. Tlaxilacalli-based religious activities remained only partially visible, even to a local and collaborating tlatoani. It was probably better for both that way.

Following this pattern but also seeking to expand it in the aftermath of Mexico-Tenochtitlan's defeat, some religious specialists sought to fashion new tlaxilacalli-based networks of supernatural affiliation.[12] Two of the most famous attempts in the Acolhua hinterland were those of the powerful Martín Ocelotl, who enjoyed purpose-built houses in tlaxilacalli in both Tetzcoco and Mexico City,[13] and the upstart Andrés Mixcoatl, who was apprehended while still in the process of building his network of dependents. The latter case is particularly illustrative: witnesses described Mixcoatl stalking various tlaxilacalli in Tetzcoco, Tepetlaoztoc, and Chiautla, in addition to his later work in the Sierra Norte de Puebla, and threatening officials with death if they did not produce tribute. In the Sierra Norte, Mixcoatl sought out the tlacateuctli of Atneztla, a "barrio subjeto" of the altepetl of Cuauhchinanco, asking for material support. When this official did not comply, Mixcoatl asked the tlacateuctli "why did you not come when you knew I was arriving" before telling him that "he must die."[14]

But Mixcoatl did find success in other tlaxilacalli. For example, the calpixqui of Atliztacan in Cuauhchinanco, a certain Ocelotl by name, was impressed by Mixcoatl's claims of rain making and collaborated with three other tlaxilacalli (Metepec, Zacatepec, and Apipilhuasco) to build Mixcoatl a local base of operations: "because they believed he was a god, each barrio came to build his house in the aforementioned barrio of Atliztacan."[15] According to Ocelotl, his physical support of Mixcoatl also included food, paper, and rubber for sacrifice; five loads of maize, and eight loads of ocote pine. The other tlaxilacalli offered similar contributions.[16] Here is a wider accounting of some calpixque from Cuauhchinanco who supported Mixcoatl, taken from Inquisition records:

> Witnesses: Juan (Indian name: Xochicalcatl), resident and tezcacoacatl[17] of Xocopan; Huitzilhuitl, resident and tlacateuctli[18] of Metepec; all the principles of that pueblo[19]

and of Zacatepec; Totococ and everyone from that pueblo; Ocelotl, who is in charge of Atliztacan and all from that pueblo; and the province of Tototepec,[20] and Huei Acocontlan, and Acatlan, and many other pueblos that I don't mention here—all know how the aforementioned Andrés (Indian name: Mixcoatl), passed himself off as a god, how he made it rain. They do all things for him. He asked them to sacrifice many things for him.[21]

CONFLICTING AFFILIATIONS

Such sacrifices, remarkably, could still be organized hierarchically fifteen years after the fall of Aztec power in central Mexico, and missionary friars took note. These friars, together with others in the Church, encouraged a religious recodification of Acolhua communities. The Franciscan missionary Toribio de Benavente Motolinia, active in the early years in and around Tetzcoco, highlighted the key role of tlaxilacalli in his nostalgic retrospective of early missionary work, stressing the logistical advantages of evangelization through community. His narration references Mexico-Tenochtitlan and Tlatelolco specifically, but it can just as easily apply to Tetzcoco, site of the first permanent Christian mission in central Mexico. Note as well the customary conflation of tlaxilacalli and neighborhood common in Spanish documents of the time: "In the first year that the friars arrived in this land, the Indians ... began to collect, those of one neighborhood and parish one day and those of another neighborhood another day, and there the friars went to teach and baptize children. And within a short time everyone gathered on Sunday and feast days, every neighborhood at its head town (*cabecera*, 'altepetl'), where they had their old chambers because there were still no churches."[22]

As populations fell and institutions buckled under epidemic disease and ecological disruption, these regimented performances also shifted. In early June 1539 in the altepetl of Chiconautla, friars encouraged locals to perform a series of public "processions, supplications, and disciplines" to call for rain and a reprieve from recurring epidemics. Looking on at what seems to have been a significant group of participants, the Tetzcoca noble don Carlos Ometochtzin called aside an associate named Francisco, calpixqui of the local tlaxilacalli of Yopico, and began to criticize his collaboration with the friars: "Poor you ... You want to make them believe what the padres preach and say, but you are wrong."[23]

Later, in the house of his brother-in-law the tlatoani, Ometochtzin called together a series of high-ranking tlaxilacalli officials and continued his attack. Again, he specifically targeted Francisco from Yopico. He praised the spiritual insight of his forbears and then sought to rebuff the attempts of the Spanish administration to coordinate with Yopico: "And if the viceroy, or the bishop, or the provincial superior tells you something, don't say anything; just keep it to yourself."²⁴ He finished by evoking the special status given to local officials: "Look, I'm saying this here among ourselves because we are *principales*."²⁵

Much has been written about don Carlos Ometochtzin and his infamous trial by the Holy Office, but the participation of tlaxilacalli has been repeatedly ignored as part of this story.²⁶ The witness who first denounced Ometochtzin to the Inquisition was Francisco of Yopico, and one of the main points of contention seems to have been this calpixqui's coordination with local Spanish officials. Other tlaxilacalli officials also found themselves ensnared in Ometochtzin's case. Among the many collaborators denounced with don Carlos can be found some individuals with clear tlaxilacalli titles, including Juan Tlailotlac and Lorenzo Mixcoatlailotlac. During a later period, Lorenzo Huitznahuatlailotlac and Juan Tlacochcalcatl were called to muster their tlaxilacalli (likely Huitznahuac and Tlacochcalco, judging by the names) to destroy statues and other artifacts found during the Ometochtzin case. Much more than previously imagined, tlaxilacalli found themselves at the heart of fights over religion and community in early Hispanic central Mexico.²⁷

BUILDING BELIEF

Tlaxilacalli proved central to the rival region-wide push of local evangelization. Indeed, it was through tlaxilacalli labor musters (*coatequitl*)²⁸ that calpixqui such as Lorenzo Huitznahuatlailotlac and Juan Tlacochcalco organized the construction of churches and the destruction of temples.²⁹ This is most strikingly illustrated in the first early chapel built around 1528 in Tepetlaoztoc under fray Domingo de Betanzos's supervision.³⁰ Here, remarkably, three tlaxilacalli of this altepetl—Papalotla, Malinalco, and Ocoxochiyocan—proudly molded their community glyphs into the outer wall of the church complex, right above the entrance (figure 4.1).³¹ The glyph for the altepetl of Tepetlaoztoc is notably absent, as is the sign of Chimalpan, the tlaxilacalli housing the new chapel. Perhaps the three extant glyphs above the entryway posit a joint claim to church ownership, together with that of the hosting tlaxilacalli. A spatial array is also present in this reckoning for Papalotla, Malinalco, and Ocoxochiyocan were located along Tepetlaoztoc's borders—southwest, east, and northwest, respectively, to be precise—marking divisions with neighboring altepetl. Even as the altepetl transformed and redeployed, the mark of tlaxilacalli on early Christian Tepetlaoztoc remains undeniable.

Farther south but still skirting the Sierra Madre foothills, a later appendix to the "Titles of Tetzcotzinco" records how "all the macehualtin" were mustered in 1537–39 to build the new parish church Santa María Nativitas, connected to the tlaxilacalli of Tetzcotzinco.³² Monumental building now became the main work of this tlaxilacalli:

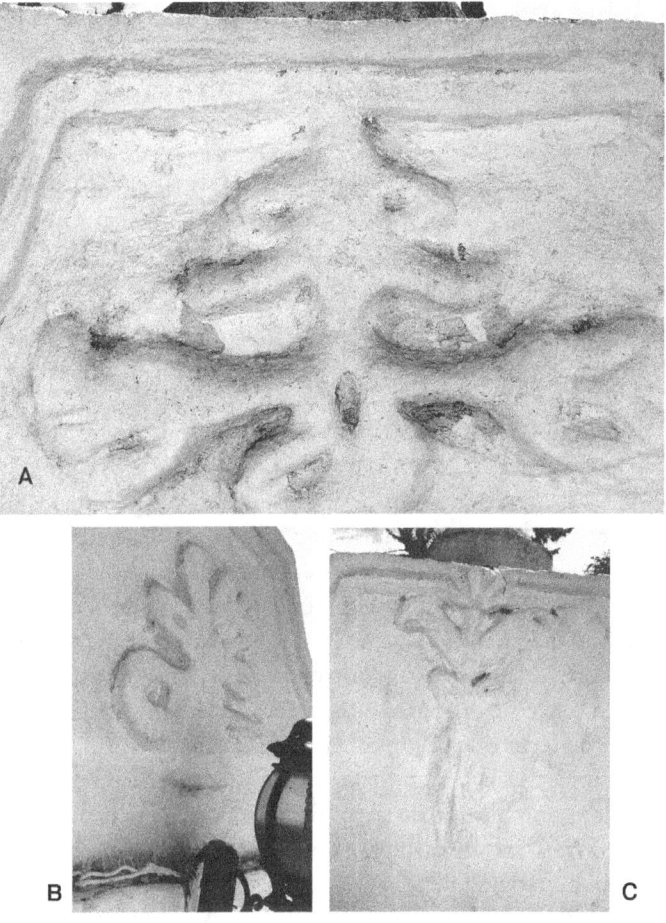

FIGURE 4.1. Tlaxilacalli-based religious building. Glyphs of the tlaxilacalli of Papalotla, Malinalco, and Ocoxochiyocan on outer wall of the Emeritano fray Domingo de Betanzos, Tepetlaoztoc. Photos by author.

the appendix to the "Titles of Tetzcotzinco" resoundingly states that "not a single Spaniard was present or made an offering" in the construction. And, although "they worked very hard," it notes with pride that "no one forced" the macehualtin to work: "they were only reminded of God, of the Holy Spirit, of the *huehuetque*, and of their wives and children." That is, they were called to duty by the ties of their dependence: to elders, to their households, and to the new religious order. This scalar and minute motivation was the genius of imperial tlaxilacalli, the means by which poor commoners pulled labor from their impoverished neighbors.[33]

At the very same time, 1539, "the Indians who went with the principales" in this tlaxilacalli—in all likelihood, the self-same commoners who were simultaneously building the parish church of Nativitas—were sent up the surrounding hills of Tetzcotzinco to Nezahualcoyotl's temple to "destroy the [sculpted religious] figures and break them. For those that can't be broken, burn them, so that after burning them, they could be broken and destroyed."[34] This temple had previously been ascribed to don Carlos Ometochtzin, and its destruction was more than a simple case of idol breaking; it was one more way to fully erase this tlatoani's spiritual links to a tlaxilacalli specifically tied to a history of rulership in Tetzcoco. In Tetzcotzinco as likely elsewhere as well, the work of re-creating a local religious landscape involved a double motion of leveling and raising, articulated once again through the actions of early Hispanic tlaxilacalli.

Small, tlaxilacalli-sized chapels spread across the landscape in the 1540s, leading Motolinia a few decades later to optimistically count 2,000 churches in the core areas of Acolhuacan: 1,000 for Tetzcoco and environs; another thousand for the northern reaches between Otumba and Cempoala. Although likely exaggerating the reach of early missionary success, the Franciscan explicitly mentioned the locally motivated nature of local building, which produced churches for the "pueblo," "parish," "neighborhood," and "noble"—that is, for the tlaxilacalli:[35] "In the pueblos there are many well-adorned churches. There are pueblos without monasteries that have more than 10 churches, each with its not-insignificant church bell or bells. In the [regional] circuit [of evangelization] there must be 500 churches, big and small; and if the Indians hadn't been contained—if they had had freedom to build—it isn't too much to imagine that there would have been 1,000 churches because each parish and each neighborhood and each noble wanted their church to build."[36]

The collective skill for monumental construction, organized and mustered by tlaxilacalli, could be applied toward various ends, as evident in another section of Motolinia's *Memoriales*, where he describes the rapid reconstruction and repair of Mesoamerican temples that had been damaged by the early persecutions of the missionary friars. Notice again the reference to the widely diffused nature of skilled trades and the regular conflation of "neighborhoods" with tlaxilacalli in reference to the main sites of religious building. "Pueblos" here likely means altepetl:

> They made these aforementioned altars with awnings and with steps in many places along the road, in the hills and in the neighborhoods of their pueblos and in many other places, like oratories where they have many idols. And for many days these public sites could not be completely destroyed because there are many of them in different places and also because they made others again every day. After having razed many

(temples) to their patios, in just a few days they (wrecking crews) happened to find again other ones, or only a fewer. There was no need (for those who wanted to reconstruct the temples) to look for master stoneworkers or engineers to make them, or for chipping hammers and those who sharpen them. Many of them are masters and they work one rock with another. You can't wear them out or run them down.[37]

Once again, in this Franciscan's retelling the work was quick, precise, and anonymous. Thanks to tlaxilacalli control in these early decades, labor musters became an expected input for centralizing regional administration. But such decentralized control also reinforced tlaxilacalli autonomy, allowing communities to shape the local meanings of Christian imagery in remarkable ways.

IMAGES OF FAITH

The early modern stylings of Motolinia's Spanish prose repeatedly obscure the artisans and laborers who built and destroyed public architecture in early Hispanic Acolhuacan, and this omission was more than a simple accident of usage. Throughout the early periods of religious building and turmoil, elites—both Acolhua and Spanish—saw commoners as objects of conversion and mobilization instead of active participants in regional fights over evangelization. Nevertheless, commoners did the work of making and unmaking the landscape and provided the vast majority of heads to be baptized, bodies to be gathered, and souls to be fought over. Because of the hierarchical organization of both Acolhua society and Catholic missionary work, however, elite testimonies still often served as guiding statements on such matters as religious organization and collective belief. This, in turn, structured both the practices of early Mexican evangelization and the stories told about the period in question.[38]

Such favoritism is perhaps unsurprising, but it still produced pattern difficulties for elite missionary endeavors. Many evangelists recognized that their first attempts at rushed, hierarchical baptisms produced masses of converts they later deemed unacceptable according to the expected conventions of Iberian Catholic belief. Friars even retracted and criticized their own early efforts. Motolinia again is a source of record: "They [the missionaries; Motolinia includes himself in this grouping] thought that everything was done, since the idolatry of the devil's temples was removed and some people were even coming to baptism; but then they encountered that which was most difficult, that which needed more time to defeat and destroy."[39]

Inter-religious conflict and dialogue remains a vital and thoroughly studied topic in Mexican and Mesoamerican historiography, and this layering did not begin

FIGURE 4.2. Amimitl. Primeros Memoriales, f. 264v. *Courtesy*, Real Biblioteca de Madrid.

with the arrival of Catholicism. In the Primeros Memoriales from Tepepulco, for instance, Acolhua ritual specialists performed entire invocations in Chichimeca languages despite the fact that they did not know the full meaning of the words. "*Çani aueponi, çani çani teyomi*," they would repeat, giving a bit of Nahuatl interpretation: "This means, he set forth from Chicomoztoc. 'Çani aueponi' are Chichimeca words—Çani aueponi, çani çani teyomi." But for other songs, even interpretation failed. The performance dedicated to the hunter Amimitl, for instance, was also "said to really be a Chichimeca song." However, the specialists declared that "there was no way to make what it says understandable in our Nahuatl language."[40]

As both Mesoamerican religious specialists and Catholic evangelists knew, language could be difficult to translate and therefore often appeared in a secondary (if still important) register—a particularly important demotion given the multilingual practices of nearly all Acolhua polities. Although the religious specialists of Tepepulco could not translate all of the invocation of Amimitl into Nahuatl, they could precisely describe his full array of clothing, jewelry, makeup, and accessories (figure 4.2). Part of this was the belief that such costumes could effectively summon the immediate presence of the deity.

The array of Amimitl:
His facial paint is chalk.

FIGURE 4.3. Cross pendant. Memorial de los Indios de Tepetlaoztoc, f. 25r. *Courtesy,* British Museum, London.

His paper earplugs.
His headdresses of leather thongs.
His quetzal feather tuft.
He is painted with [vertical] stripes of chalk.
His paper stole.
His small bells.
His sandals.
His net carrier.
In his hand is his cactus spear.[41]

Perhaps in a similar way to the re-appropriation of the Chichimeca deity Amimitl in Tepepulco, Tepetlaoztoc artisans also mobilized wider symbolic registers to create some of the earliest extant Christian iconography in central Mexico. This production included crosses, which were made locally as tribute for the Spanish encomendero and therefore displayed comparatively little missionary influence. Despite the demands of this tribute recipient, however, the artisans made the crosses according to their own conceptions of utility and display, placing them on items, such as a pendant, rarely used in Hispanic fashion. At least in this early case, Christianity was made and worn according to local ideas of performative devotion.[42]

Listed in the Memorial de los Indios de Tepetlaoztoc as a part of tribute goods paid to the encomendero Gonzalo de Salazar in the early 1540s, the pendant consisted of an obsidian cross outlined in gold, standing on top of a golden step pyramid (figure 4.3). The cool aquatic symbolism of the obsidian instantly suggests Tezcatlipoca, the "Lord of the Smoking Mirror," and this link is confirmed by the small peanut-shaped bells hanging from each arm and the base of the cross.[43] This "cross of Tezcatlipoca" proves a fitting reference to both the recent fall of empire and the mysterious cycle of rebirth through Christ signaled by the cross shape itself.[44] The pyramid, a synecdoche for both the wider community and its surrounding landscape of spiritual mountains, served as both the support and the stage for the transformations acting through the obsidian cross.

After this and other early essays by Tepetlaoztoc's artisans—such as a red-eyed monkey scaling a cross on a hairpiece, for example—a new canon for religious imagery emerged. Precisely because of the power of early Catholic symbolic communication, image continued to trump exegesis well into the periods of Spanish rule—seventeenth-century Tetzcoca documents, for instance, express the wider Nahuatl convention of seeing Latin Mass as opposed to hearing it: "on Sunday . . . we go to the church to see Mass." The spoken words were, after all, meant to be a mystery.[45]

RELIGION AND REBELLION

Despite the sacramental focus of the early missionaries, religion remained a daily practice in the tlaxilacalli, not a weekly one. For all the importance given to a few hours each week of formal liturgy, the evangelists left to others almost all of the wider symbolic acts involved in connecting human lives to a disconcertingly fragile and often inchoate cosmos. Once again, tlaxilacalli were key. Motolinia remarks that "celebrations to the devil" were most regular when commoners "planted their maize fields and when they harvested them"[46]—that is, when agricultural labor became collective on a local level—and the Tetzcoco-raised Dominican Diego Durán goes even further, recalling that "in the churches,[47] I myself have heard the public announcement, when all the pueblo was present, that the time of the harvest has come. They all rush off to the fields with such haste that neither young nor old remain behind. They could have gathered the crop earlier, at their leisure; but since the old diviner found in his book or almanac that the day had come, he proclaimed it to the people, and they went off at great speed."[48] Harvest, as a key process of the cosmos, required special metaphysical care, even after local parishioners had built their own chapels for Christian worship. Tlaxilacalli prayed for the maize to ripen and then deployed to gather it in.

Labor remained a central point of conflict in the early evangelical history of Acolhuacan and even sparked a major riot in the northern altepetl of Teotihuacan between the years 1557 and 1559. During the first years of Catholic administration in Teotihuacan, the altepetl found itself under the irregular care of Franciscans, whom locals seem to have regarded favorably. Nevertheless, evangelization was slow. In contrast to the zealous temple busting in places such as Tetzcoco, Mexico City, and Cholula, the formidable pyramid complex in Teotihuacan attracted comparatively little missionary attention, and no attempts were made to raze or repurpose its sanctuaries.

In the years 1557 and 1558—corresponding to the worrisome Thirteen House–One Rabbit sequence in the Mesoamerican calendar—Teotihuacan was a minor stop along the missionary circuit of itinerant Franciscans; so minor, in fact, that the Spanish viceroy Luis de Velasco el Viejo decided to switch its evangelical care to the neighboring Augustinian order, based only a few kilometers away in the new fortress-like monastery at Acolman.[49] As the new monastery grew, its construction earned broad local distrust for its violent and unsophisticated methods of labor capture. After the Augustinians were granted dominion in Teotihuacan, they demanded a similar church, built with similar methods. Teotihuacan instantly refused, both as an elite hierarchy and a general polity, and conflict exploded.[50] Augustinians complained to Mexico City that "no Indian man or woman" showed up to even "give them a jar of water," let alone hear their preaching. In response, the Augustinians appealed to the capital for stern punishments. The calpixque of Teotihuacan's various tlaxilacalli were beaten bloody while their subordinate topileque had their staffs of authority broken, in addition to the whipping. "Church Indians"—that is, locals specifically tasked to the local chapel—were stripped naked by the Augustinians, physically bound, and forced to attend Mass.[51]

After this less than auspicious beginning, the Augustinians covered the newly occupied local church with images of their order, which were promptly defaced. The missionaries accused a certain Juan Martín—the church guardian, *teopan tlapixque*, according to the Codex San Juan Teotihuacan—and beat him and others "mightily." Juan Martín and his compatriots, however, soon dug their way through a wall and escaped. Others, both nobles and commoners, were then similarly arrested, but all escaped with considerable outside help. In the measured and consistent organization belying the work of local hierarchies, various prisoners were able to dig holes in the walls of their cells and escape while the Augustinians heatedly petitioned the viceroy to install a puppet tlatoani for the altepetl.[52] Here is the subsequent narration of the Franciscan historian fray Gerónimo de Mendieta: "When this [new ruler] arrived in San Juan [Teotihuacan], he arrested some nobles and others from the common people and put them in jail, bound in chains and stocks. But because almost the whole pueblo ('altepetl') was of a single voice and opinion, by night they dug through the jail and released all the prisoners and set them free. At this time, there were only five or six people on the friars' side."[53]

Losing not only popular support but also the coercive power to imprison, the Augustinians decided to pursue the altepetl's tlatoani, don Francisco Verdugo Quetzalamamalitzin, who had fled to the marginal tlaxilacalli of Santa María Coatlan with a group of nobles. The rest of the population of the inner altepetl also fled the ceremonial and civic center and retreated to the backcountry—likely to outlying tlaxilacalli such as Coatlan—where they spent over a year away from their houses and fields. Nevertheless, even at this point of extreme dislocation, social control continued to operate, as locals shot arrows at anyone from the altepetl who tried to approach or help the Augustinians and even threatened banishment. Starving and besieged, the friars finally abandoned the altepetl, which returned to Franciscan oversight.[54]

Mendieta comments that up until the flight of Quetzalmamalitzin, the Augustinians did not know that the tlatoani and the various teuctlatoque of Teotihuacan "were against them," thinking instead that "it was the generality of the pueblo that was rebelling, not the heads."[55] This small but illustrative comment suggests that the overall organization of the uprising might not have come from the top of the altepetl but from the bottom and the middle, from the administrative and tributary macehualtin. This supposition gains strength at the end of the conflict, when commoners from Teotihuacan left for the viceregal capital of Mexico to negotiate with the viceroy, ending the conflict. Here again is the Franciscan's version:

> Many Indian men and women of the poor people joined together and more than 400 of them went to Mexico. They entered before the viceroy and the *audiencia real* just as they had left (Teotihuacan), shabby and miserable, calling in a single voice for justice, describing the large grievance that was done them by making them die in this way of hunger and wandering for so much time away from their houses ... (The viceroy then) issued a general pardon to the whole pueblo (altepetl) and particularly to don Francisco (Quetalmamaliztin) and the nobles and [gave] permission for them to attend whichever catechism they wished.[56]

Mendieta's prejudices—as well as those of the heroic history mode in general—led him to emphasize the poverty of the commoner negotiators instead of their successful diplomacy or organizational strength. When reference to local organization became unavoidable, Mendieta reflexively denied its existence ("the generality was rebelling, not the heads") or highlighted the actions of the tlatoani and nobles. Despite all this, it is impossible to ignore the active participation of macehualtin in this uprising, both during the armed phase of expulsion and in the ensuing negotiations with the viceroy. At the end of his narration, Mendieta arrives at the moral of his story, a paean to his Franciscan order: "It is true that [the macehualtin] suffered all that came their way, even to the death of them all, so that they could achieve what they desired, which was having friars of St. Francis in their pueblo. And when they achieved this, their joy was so great that they forgot all their past anguish and, with great pleasure, made in a few days a pious monastery and a good stone and mortar church. They are happy and receive catechism."[57]

Seen in another light, however, the moral is quite different: it was the commoners who rose up "heedlessly" against the Augustinians and expelled them. It was they who survived away from their houses for over a year and who negotiated peace with the viceroy. They built the new monastery for their altepetl. If any doubt remained about the influence of tlaxilacalli regimes over all this, the collective work of building the church and monastery in "a few days" belies a profound influence. In Teotihuacan, tlaxilacalli defeated the Augustinians.[58]

LEVELS OF REBELLION

Mendieta is not the only source for this rebellion, and the historian even mentions that people in Teotihuacan "made a report of all that happened and sent it to Spain," convincing King Felipe II of the necessity of changing the religious oversight of the altepetl.[59] Nevertheless, this royal decision arrived after the accord the viceroy had already negotiated with the macehualtin. Tlaxilacalli regimes proved more agile than Spanish imperial deliberations. It is unknown whether the remarkable Codex San Juan Teotihuacan (figure 4.4) was the same "report" mentioned by Mendieta, but it is indispensable for understanding the underlying politics of the 1557–59 uprising.

The codex was produced by the local tlaxilacalli nobility, the teuctlatoque, who appear in the first line of this document with papers in hand and chains on their feet. The subsequent lines faithfully report the different layers of local administration: the nobility, led by tlatoani don Francisco Verdugo Quetzalmamalitzin and his brother, don Lorenzo; the calpixque; and then the sub-district-level topileque. (Middling officials, such as the tepixque, are omitted, suggesting their lowly positions in the overall hierarchy.) The distinctions are precise: the nobility carried the honorific "don" before their names, the following group is specifically identified as "calpixque," and each topile carries the defining staff of office (*topilli*) in his hand. At each level, the authorities suffer repression. For the tlatoani and the higher nobles, the punishment was cuffs and chains and for lesser nobles, the indignity and strain of hard work. For the calpixque, it was the bloodying blows of Augustinian whips and for the topileque, the breaking of their staffs and the assault of a Spanish soldier's cat-o'-nine-tails.[60]

Although noble patronage guided the preparation of this codex, elite roles and actions receive secondary attention across the document. The calpixque and the topileque, in contrast, show themselves central to the action. Even though the higher nobles present the petition and the lesser nobles carry the beams of the future monastery, the Augustinians themselves only appear on the subsequent line of the codex, negotiating with the calpixque and reinforcing their foundational importance for the orchestration of collective work across the altepetl. When this support waned, as it quickly did, the Augustinians jumped to direct violence, exercised by themselves and allied Spanish soldiers over tlaxilacalli hierarchies and their sub-districts.

FIGURE 4.4. Four levels of local administration. Tlatoani and teuctlatoque (top line and then again leading the line of noble beam carriers); lesser nobility (second line, carrying beams); calpixque (third line, with bloodied backs and hands raised in prayer); topileque (fourth line, carrying staffs, which are then broken). Note also the paper in the hands of the nobles in line one, the two jailbreaks in lines two and three, the soldier beating a calpixque at the right edge of line two, the Augustinian meeting on line three to the right, and the raised cat-o'-nine-tails, just visible above the large hole in line four. Codex San Juan Teotihuacan. *Courtesy*, Instituto Nacional de Antropología e Historia, Mexico City.

The central position of these local administrators is remarkable in its consistency, while the friars and nobles stalk the margins of the document.

Following this initial treatment of local administration, the Codex San Juan then provides a detailed accounting of the friars' tribute demands: loads of corn, wheat, fish, and cotton; rocks and stone masons for construction projects; the tribute of 400 local macehualtin. It is after this that the population flees to the countryside, and the codex includes an eloquent scene of a noblewoman holding a baby hidden among maguey plants as another pilli (her husband?) listens to the scoldings of an Augustinian. Head counts above the scene record the 60 men and 20 women who died during the year of Teotihuacan's flight to the countryside.

The final section of the codex surveys aspects of the Christian geography of the region, showing a full catechism in one of Tetzcoco's old public buildings—perhaps part of the tecpan—and empty churches in both Teotihuacan and Acolman. Male and female nobles kneel (before a Franciscan?—the obscure figure is not dressed as the other friars) outside the vacant church in Teotihuacan, and Augustinians congregate outside the one in Acolman. Off to the side, a robed and turbaned Spaniard wanders amid a blurred inscription that includes the words *teopan* (church) and *matililztli* (teaching). Appended to the codex are some obscure fragments that might relate to the San Juan codex or might not, containing male and female head counts (tlaxilacalli registers?) and a few listings of individual names.

REMAKING THE SPRITIUAL LANDSCAPE

The empty churches in Teotihuacan and Acolman evoke the ongoing unease in both altepetl regarding the place of churches in commoner lives, but this unease did not generalize. Tetzcoco's church complex appeared full and, as seen in chapter 3, tlaxilacalli in Tepetlaoztoc quickly adopted church construction and incorporated Catholic landholding, imagery, and festivals into local administration. In the intermountain Acolhua altepetl of Tepepulco, site of the Primeros Memoriales, the documentation for community Catholicism shows itself to be even more vibrant.

While people in Teotihuacan were rebelling against Agustinian oversight, locals in Tepepulco threw festive and pyrotechnic community celebrations in the plaza outside the walls of their Franciscan convent (figure 4.5). Sixteenth-century graffiti etched into this convent's inner walls crowds the visual plane with festivities, anchored by a celebration involving the popular *volador* spectacle, during which four specially trained acrobats (accompanied by a fifth logistical and musical aide) hang headfirst from an impressively tall pole and spin themselves down to the crowd below. In the graffiti, drums resound; fireworks explode; clowns satirize; the devil provokes illicit sex; a man draws his sword; horses run wild.[61]

The volador component is particularly remarkable because it carries a profound significance in Mesoamerican spirituality, far beyond Christian connotations. The breadth of this ceremony across a wide regional scope—attested by early Hispanic sources among the Nahua, Hñähñu, Tutunacu, Teenek, and Hamasipini (Tepehua) peoples in northern Mesoamerica; the K'iche', Kaqchikel, Achi, and Tz'utujil in the Maya region; and the Pipil-Nicarao in lower Central America (Nicaragua)—suggests a diverse and occasionally conflicting range of meaning; but all sources agree that the dance of the voladores evokes fertility and renewal. At the height of the Aztec empire, a precursor of this dance was celebrated during the month of Tlacaxipehualiztli and devoted to Xipe Totec, master of the bloody renewal of life on earth. Strikingly, the Tepepulco convent includes graffiti of an ocelot-warrior in full battle array, ready for the "striping" ceremony of this same month whereby captives were systematically scratched in mock combat before being led up the pyramid steps for their final, sacrificial end.[62]

FIGURE 4.5. Festive graffiti from the Tepepulco convent, with the volador pole at center. Also note the convent to the left of the pole, anchored by its arch and belfry; the drum and the procession of clowns to the right; the well-realized horse and rider behind the pole; and the two devils in the upper left corner inciting a couple to illicit love. Rodríguez Vázquez and Tinoco Quesnel, *Grafitis*, photo 112.

All this was part of a broader array of supernatural powers that infringed on the sacred geography of the Tepepulco convent. The supreme Mesoamerican rain deity, Tlaloc, shared billing with a mermaid of European stylistic form, although this latter icon also conjured images of local varieties of female water spirits such as the *alamantzin, cihuatlacamichin,* and *tlanchana*.[63] Further, as Alessandra Russo has noted, the Tepepulco convent also includes significant astronomical observations in graffiti, such as the solar eclipse of 1587, connected in local medical thinking to a worry over birth defects. Finally, in addition to its frequent and repeated representations of church architecture, the corpus of Tepepulco graffiti also includes Mesoamerican step temples in its repertoire, complete with accompanying drummers.[64]

In addition to its festive, documentary, and architectural functions in Tepepulco, the Franciscan convent also anchored an interlocking network of "all the churches in the pueblos subject to this head-town"—thirty-nine in total, and eleven within less than an hour's walk from the main convent in Tepepulco.[65] This network, carefully elaborated not only by Christian name but also by extensive travel notes, accompanied a now-lost map attached to the 1581 geographic relation of Tepepulco. Although

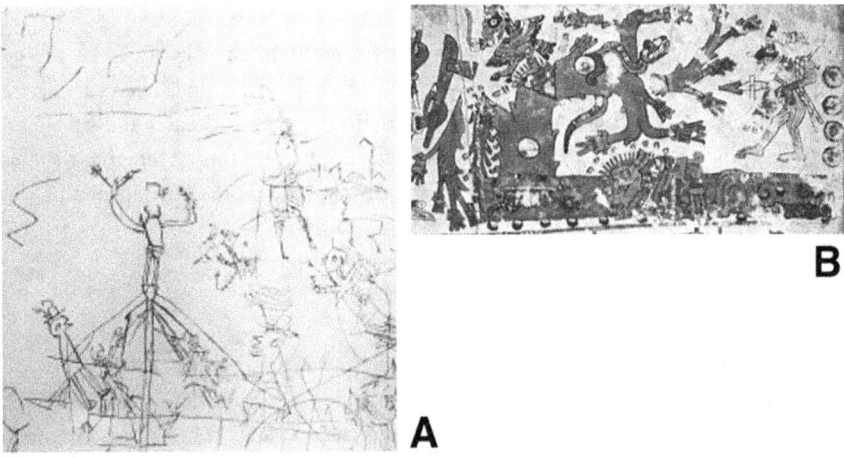

FIGURE 4.6. Voladores and Tamoanchan. *A:* another set of volador graffiti from the convent of Tepepulco. Rodríguez Vázquez and Tinoco Quesnel, *Grafitis*, photo 14. *B:* Tamoanchan. Codex Borgia, 19. The wounded tree in Tamoanchan references a core Mesoamerican myth. Note as well the eagle above the tree: voladores strove to represent birds during their flying displays.

always referencing the central altepetl, this network quickly branched outward to the links between various tlaxilacalli: "From this pueblo of Tepepulco to the pueblo of Acopinalco, and to the pueblo of San Martín, and to the pueblo of Santa María Magdalena, and to the pueblo of San Sebastián: one good league of paths, twisting in parts; and all the way, a very rough and gullied path, along some low hills."[66] The paths were multiple, connecting various chapel-bearing tlaxilacalli, each of which was within an hour's walk of the others. By the early 1580s, dense tlaxilacalli networks had largely reconstituted themselves, both spatially and as anchors of collective identity.

Returning to the wider place of the volador dance, which reaches beyond the specifics of imperial Aztec religion in both territorial and chronological breadth, Martha Ilia Nájera Coronado has noted that this ceremony always occurred during liminal points of inflection: Tlacaxipehualiztli during the Aztec period, when old skins are shed for new ones; Carnaval, that point in the Christian calendar when the world turns upside down; as well as baptisms, solstices, periods of drought, and the beginning and end of the agricultural year.[67] She likens the planting of the volador pole in the symbolic and functional center of the polity to the fertilizing actions of human sexuality and the spinning of the voladores around this pole to the rotatory exchanges in Tamoanchan, "the place of the flowering tree," "the place of the tree of the beyond."[68]

More than just a festive component to accompany Hispanic fireworks, therefore, the volador dance outside the convent in Tepepulco served to reestablish connections to deeper Mesoamerican processes of renewal and to re-found spiritual geographies—now emanating outward from the main plaza in front of the Franciscan monastery across a dense network of chapel-bearing tlaxilacalli (figure 4.6). To be sure, the voladores now wore crucifixes on their breasts and brimmed hats on their heads, but the wider act of recreating community remained incontrovertible. New social, political, and metaphysical networks sprung out of the renewed bonds between local communities.

NOTES

1. "xexelhueque yn mattitzin . . . ypan tictotequipan ilhuzque yn tlatoca zihualpilli azupziō." Codex Asunción, f. 47v. Don Dionisio was alcalde (~calpixqui) of Xahuetenco.

This chapter focuses primarily on the politics and sociability of tlaxilacalli religions. For a treatment of religious specialists in tlaxilacalli and calpolli, see Miguel Pastrana Flores, *Entre los hombres y los dioses: Acercamiento al sacerdocio de calpulli entre los antiguos nahuas* (Mexico City: UNAM, 2008).

2. This might be a reference to, or a more elaborate alternate name for, the tlaxilacalli of Xochitlan in Tepetlaoztoc.

3. "ycxitla yn huitepetl tlachiuhcan yn matiaztzin ypā quimotequipanelhuiz yn resorecçiō quimictizaz in metoti yc quicohuaz ocotzitli ypan ylnamicocatzi yn pazqua onech momaquilique yn huetque ȳ don jo diego de la cruz ihuan ytiachcatzi do jo diego ernandez quahuetzquexochititla huehue ypā xihuitl 1575." Codex Asunción, f. 73r.

4. "ypan tlatequipanozque quixtlahuatzque." Codex Asunción, f. 36r.

5. Lockhart (*The Nahuas after the Conquest*, 28) notes that in the first decades of evangelization, missionaries often demarcated parishes by altepetl. These large, region-wide divisions quickly broke down, so by the 1570s, tlaxilacalli-sized parishes were common. Barbara E. Mundy (*The Mapping of New Spain: Indigenous Cartography and the Maps of the Relaciones Geográficas* [Chicago: University of Chicago Press, 2000], 128) sees parishes correspoinding to calpolli in Cholula by 1586; Kevin Terraciano (*The Mixtecs of Colonial Oaxaca: Ñudzahui History, Sixteenth through Eighteenth Centuries* [Stanford: Stanford University Press, 2001], 106) notes that in his administrative work, the renowned sixteenth-century missionary grammarian fray Alonso de Molina used *perrochia* (parrish) as a stand-in for tlaxilacalli or calpolli, not altepetl. Lockhart (*The Nahuas after the Conquest*, 209) does note for a later period that "an impressive calpolli church could be an argument for a new parish."

In theory, a lack of priests might have been a hindrance to tlaxilacalli-sized parishes, but local administration quickly filled this gap. The Codex Asunción suggests something of this robust action. It was tlaxilacalli officials who measured and demarcated church land, for instance. Cf. Codex Asunción, ff. 12v, 15r.

6. I thank David Tavárez for help with the finer points of argument in this and the following section. Relevant works by Tavárez on the issue of indigenous networks of religious devotion include *The Invisible War: Indigenous Devotions, Discipline, and Dissent in Colonial Mexico* (Stanford: Stanford University Press, 2011); "Escritura y disención: Resistencia y cosmologías alternas en el México colonial," *Revista de Indias* 69, no. 247 (2009): 81–104; "Archivos, narrativas y silencios historiográficos sobre la extirpación de idolatrías en Nueva España," *Jahrbuch für Geschichte Lateinamerikas* 46 (2009): 43–60.

7. "toda la gente le obedecía y le daban todo lo que pedía." "Procesos de indios idolatras y hechiceros," *Publicaciones de la Comisión Reorganizadora del Archivo General y Público de la Nación*, ed. Luis González Obregon (Mexico City: AGN, 1912), 3:72; the original source is AGN, Inquisición, vol. 38, exp. 7.

8. "Procesos de indios," 72. See also Guy Stresser-Péan, *Sol-Dios y Cristo: La cristianización de los indios de México vista desde la Sierra de Puebla* (Mexico City: FCE, 2011), 87–88.

9. "Procesos de indios," 10, 157–58.

10. "en el barrio de Miguel, principal de este dicho pueblo, vive un indio que se llama Tecpatetl que solía andar con su padre en guarda de los demonios en su infidelidad, y que quizá él sabrá de algunos ídolos dónde están y que en el barrio de Tlacatecatl, vive un indio viejo que se llama Teucatl, que es de Tonacacingo, que solía estar en la casa del diablo que se llamaba Coamiavatl, en su guarda, por su trompeta; y que asimismo vive en el dicho barrio otro indio que se dice Tetlatla, que solía ser guarda y trompeta de otro diablo que se llamaba Macuyxuchitl, y que así mismo un indio que vive con Don Juan, cacique que solía ser de este dicho pueblo, que se llamaba Cuetlan, solía ser guarda de un diablo que se llamaba Ycnopili, y que de estos se podrá saber dónde hay ídolos." "Procesos de indios," 159.

11. "ha oído decir que hay cosas del demonio y que no sabe lo que es." "Procesos de indios," 178.

12. For a wider discussion of this phenomenon, see Stresser-Péan, *Sol-Dios y Cristo*; Serge Gruzinski, *Les hommes-dieux du Mexique: pouvoir indien et société coloniale XVIe–XVIIIe siècles* (Paris: Éditions des Archives Contemporaines, 1985).

13. For Martín Ocelotl, see AGN, Inquisición, vol. 38, exp. 4. See also Leon García, "The Return of Martin Ocelotl: A Nahua Eschatological Discourse in Early Colonial Mexico" (PhD dissertation, University of California at Los Angeles, 2010); Patricia Lopes Don, "Franciscans, Indian Sorcerers, and the Inquisition in New Spain, 1536–1543," *Journal of World History* 17, no. 1 (2006): 34–47; J. Jorge Klor de Alva, "Martin Ocelotl: Clandestine Cult Leader," in David Sweet and Gary Nash, eds., *Struggle and Survival in Colonial America* (Berkeley: University of California Press, 1981), 128–41.

14. "yendo el dicho Andrés Mixcoatl á Atneztla, que es un barrio subjeto á Quahuchinanco, dice este testigo que no le salió á recibir el tacacutly de aquel pueblo al camino; enojado el dicho Andrés, díxole al tlacatecutly: 'por qué no veniste, pues sabías que yo venía agora; bien sé lo que te ha de venir'; diciendo que había de morir." "Procesos de indios," 69.

15. "como creían que era dios le vinieron á hacer cada barrio su casa al dicho barrio de Atliztaca." "Procesos de indios," 57.

16. In his *Sol-Dios y Cristo*, Stresser-Péan specifically notes (84–88) that Mixcoatl "found support and understanding among the less important chiefs, called the *achcauhtin*, who were perhaps less depenent on Spanish authorities." Achcauhtin, it will be recalled, occupied the main military posts their tlaxilacalli.

17. Echoing the confusion about the titles Tlailotlac and Huitznahuatl mentioned in the introduction to this volume, the Spanish scribe in this section of the Inquisition record confused the tlaxilacalli-derived title Tezacoacatl (military judge; literally, Tezcacoac resident) for a personal name. The convoluted phrase "Juan Tezcacoacatl (Indian name: Xochicalcatl), resident of Xocopan" (Joan Tezcacoacatl, en nombre de indio Xuchicalcatl, vecino de Xucupa) records the title Tezcacoacatl before the given name Xochicalcatl. On the title Tezcacoacatl, see the entry for this term in UNAM's online *Gran Diccionario Náhautl*, accessed August 4, 2016, http://www.gdn.unam.mx/diccionario/consultar/palabra/tezcacoacatl/id/65533, which itself derives from the Florentine Codex and the works of Hernando de Alvarado Tezozomoc, among other canonical sources.

18. The scribe expresses similar confusion about the title tlacatecutli. The punctuation in the phrase "Huitzilhuitl, resident of Metepec; Tlacateuctli, de Metepec" (Uizcicitl, vecino de Metepec, Tlacatecutli, de Metepec) appears to reference two different people, but tlacateuctli is a title and only rarely a name.

19. Although the term first used in this record is *pueblo*, barrio appears one page later in the same context, making the reference to tlaxilacalli unavoidable: "y de otro barrio otras cinco cargas, y de Metepec otras dos cargas, y de otro barrio una carga, y de otro barrio, que se llama Apipilhuasco, dos cargas." "Procesos de inidos," 57. Usage in the rest of the narration slips between "pueblo" and "barrio."

20. Here, however, use of the word *provincia* is an explicit reference to altepetl, not tlaxilacalli. The modern site is Tutotepec, Hidalgo. Other cited altepetl are the modern towns of Huayacocotla, Veracruz, and Acatlan, Hidalgo. All three are in the Sierra Norte region, which also includes northern Puebla.

21. "Testigos: Joan Tezcacoacatl, en nombre de indio Xuchicalcatl, vecino de Xucupa; Uizcicitl, vecino de Metepec, Tlacatecutli, de Metepec; todos los principales de aquel pueblo y de Zacatepec, Totococ, y todos los de aquel pueblo; Ucelutl, que tiene carga de Atliztaca y todos los de aquel pueblo, y la provincia de Tototepec, y Ueyacucutla, y Acatla, con otros muchos pueblos que aquí no pongo, saben como el dicho Andrés, y en nombre de indio Mixcoatl, *se hacía dios, y cómo por el llovía, y se hacen todas las cosas, y pedía muchas cosas para que le sacrificasen*" (original italics). "Procesos de indios," 56.

22. "En el primer ano que a esta tierra llegaron los frailes, los Indios de Mexico y Tlatilolco se cornenzaron a ayuntar los de un barrio y feligresia un día, y los de otro barrio otro día, y alli iban los frailes a enseñar y bautizar los niños; y desde a poco tiempo los

domingos y fiestas se ayuntaban todos, cada barrio en su cabecera, adonde tenian sus salas antiguas, porque iglesia aun no la habia." Toribio de Benavente Motolinia, *Historia de los indios de la Nueva España*, ed. Edmundo O'Gorman (Mexico City: Porrúa, 1969), 109.

23. "pobre de ti . . . quieres tú hacer creer a estos lo que los padres predican e dicen, engañado andas." *Proceso inquisitorial del cacique de Texcoco*, ed. Luis González Obregón (Mexico City: AGN, 1910), 2. It is clear that Francisco was an official in Yopico; calpixqui is an inference from his high rank. (He was allowed to stay when don Carlos Ometochtzin expelled lower-ranking officials from his later discussions.) The refrence is "Francisco, indio, que estaba en el barrio de Yopico"; *Proceso*, 5.

24. "e si alguna cosa te dijere el visorey, el obispo, el provincial, no lo digas a nadie, sino guárdalo para ti." *Proceso*, 6.

25. "y mira que esto te digo aquí entre nosotros que somos principales." *Proceso*, 6.

26. See, for example, Patricia Lopes Don, *Bonfires of Culture: Franciscans, Indigenous Leaders, and the Inquisition in Early Mexico, 1524–1540* (Norman: University of Oklahoma Press, 2010); Ethelia Ruiz Medrano, "Don Carlos de Tezcoco and the Universal Rights of Emperor Carlos V," in Lee and Brokaw, eds., *Texcoco*, 165–85; León García Garagarza, "The 1539 Trial of Don Carlos Ometochtli and the Scramble for Mount Tlaloc," in Amos Megged and Stephanie Wood, eds., *Mesoamerican Memory: Enduring Systems of Remembrance* (Norman: University of Oklahoma Press, 2012), 193–214.

27. *Proceso*, 11. The others mentioned likely also had specific tlaxilacalli offices, but it is impossible to tell what they were based on through the names given.

28. For a recent study of coatequitl, see David M. Carballo, "Labor Collectives and Group Cooperation in Pre-Hispanic Central Mexico," in *Cooperation and Collective Action: Archaeological Perspectives*, ed. David M. Carballo (Boulder: University Press of Colorado, 2013), 243–74.

29. In her *Murmillos de antiguos muros: Los inmuebles del siglo XVI que se conservan en el Estado de México* (Toluca: Instituto Mexiquense de Cultura, 1994), Margarita Loera Chávez makes this connection clear, noting that beginning in Tetzcoco around 1535, there was a concerted effort to destroy local temples toward the goal of obtaining building materials for new Hispanic constructions.

30. The date comes from Loera Chávez, *Murmillos*, 57.

31. In 2013, Roberto Rivera Pérez identified the glyphs of six "comunidades" on this same outer wall: Apipilhuasco, Chiautzinco, Xolalpan, Nopalan, Tlalmimilolpan, and Totolapan. See his dissertation, "Bandidos, arrieros y machos contempoáneos del Acolhuacán septentrional: Múltiples espacios para la construcción de la masculinidad" (Universidad Autónoma Metropolitana–Iztapalapa, Department of Anthropology, 2013), 84. It is possible that the others have been lost in the ongoing renovations of this complex. Indeed, the visible glyphs are covered very thickly in various layers of paint, making readings of these signs somewhat tentative. Fieldwork in August 2015 discovered only the three glyphs mentioned here. Both

the director of the site, Lorena Rivero, and a local historian, Jose Omar Tinajero Morales, stated that the only glyphs at the site were the three above the main entrance. The naming of specific tlaxilacalli comes from a comparison with local place glyphs.

32. The administrative ordering of Catholic parishes was in considerable flux during these early years. Tlaxilicalli affiliation, though also undergoing important changes, provided an important administrative backstop for these Catholic reorderings.

33. "yeica ayac ce caxtiltecatl oman, omo huentica. Zan huel oquimaxcahuique mochintin in macehualtin... ayac oquin cuitla huilti zan oquinmolnamictili in Dios Espiritu Sancto in huehuetque ihuan in innacihuan ihuan in inpilhuan... in hual chicahuac in otequitihuac." "Titles of Tetzcotzingo," 122–24. Interestingly, although this document refers to the tlaxilacalli of Tetzcotzinco as a little altepetl (ialtepetzin), it also describes a dependent relationship to the city (ciudad) of Tetzcoco.

34. "fué a la sierra que se dice Tezcucingo, en la cual había muchas figuras de ídolos esculpidas en las peñas, á las cuales su Señoría mandó deshacerles las figuras e quebrallas, y á las que no se pudiesen quebrallas, que les diesen fuego, para que después de quemarlas se pudiesesn quebrar y deshacer; é por su mandado los indios que iban con los principales los comenzaron a quebrallas." "Procesos de indios," 29.

35. As seen above, each of these Spanish terms evokes in one way or another the idea of tlaxilacalli. Some, like pueblo, can also apply to altepetl; others, such as parish or neighborhood, cannot.

36. "En los pueblos ay muchas yglesias e muy adornadas; pueblo ay fuera de los que tienen monesterio de más de diez yglesias, y en cada vna su campana, no pequeña, o campanas. Abrá en este çercuyto que digo quinientas yglesias entre chicas y grandes y si no les ouieran ydo a la mano a los yndios y tuuieran libertad de edificar, no es mucho que ouiera oy dia mill yglesias porque cada perrocha y cada barrio y cada prinçipal quería su iglesia edificar." Toribio de Benavente Motolinia, *Memoriales; o, Libro de las cosas de la Nueva España y de los naturales de ella*, ed. Edmundo O'Gorman (Mexico City: UNAM, 1971), 296.

37. "Hazían de aquellos altares ya dichos cubiertos y con gradas en muchas partes del camino, y en los altos y en los barrios de sus pueblos y en otras muchas partes como oratorios, a do tenían diuersos ýdolos. Y estos públicos en muchos días no los pudieron acabar de destruir, ansí por ser muchos y en diversas partes, como porque hazían otros de nueuo cada dia, que auiendo quebrado en vn patio muchos. Dende a pocos días que tornauan á hallar de nuevo otros tantos, ó pocos menos, porque como no avían de buscar maestros canteros o ymagineros que los hiziesen, ni escoda y quien se la afilase, sino que muchos dellos son maestros e vna piedra labran con otra. No los podian agotar ó acabar." Motolinia, *Memoriales*, 155.

38. See, for example, Robert Ricard's iconic and still cited, *La "conquête spirituelle" du Mexique: Essai sur l'apostolat et les méthodes missionaires des ordres mendiants en Nouvelle-Espagne de 1523-24 à 1572* (Paris: Institut d'ethnologie, 1933). The religious history of New

Spain has progressed greatly in the eighty-five years since this book's publication. Useful publications over the past generation include Louise Burkhart's *The Slippery Earth: Nahua-Christian Moral Dialogue in Sixteenth-Century Mexico* (Tucson: University of Arizona Press, 1989); Louise Burkhart, *Before Guadalupe: The Virgin Mary in Early Colonial Nahuatl Literature* (Austin: University of Texas Press, 2001); Osvaldo F. Prado, *The Origins of Mexican Catholicism: Nahua Rituals and Christian Sacraments in Sixteenth-Century Mexico* (Ann Arbor: University of Michigan Press, 2004); Martin Austin Nesvig, ed., *Local Religion in Colonial Mexico* (Albuquerque: University of New Mexico Press, 2006).

39. "Ya que pensauan que por estar quitada la ydolatría de los templos del demonio y venir a la doctrina algunos y al bautissmo, era todo hecho, hallaron al más dificultoso y que más tiempo fue menester para vençer y destruir." Motolinia, *Memoriales*, 151.

40. "cani aveponj çani, çani, teyomj q. n. chicomoztoc onivallevac çani aveponi, ichichimectlatol. çani aveponj çani, çanj teyomj . . . Jn amimitl icuic yuh mitoa in veli chichimecacuic amo vel caquizti in tlein quitoa in tonavatlatol ypa." Primeros Memoriales, ff. 276v, 277v. As the comments of these ritual specialists suggest, religion was about much more than words and their meanings. Wider religious experiences depended on reading and writing and on much else, such as verbal performance; the plastic, scenic, musical, and discursive arts; material culture and the physicality of space; group and individual human interactions; violence and joy; attraction and repulsion; the enactment of memory and experience; the presence or absence of sex, food, and intoxicants; the influence of climate and the heavens; and landscapes both familiar and mysterious, to name only a few central aspects.

41. "amimitl inechichiuh, yaxval tiçatl, y yamanacoch ytzoncutlax. yquetzaltemal motiçavavanticac. y yamancapeanal. ytzitzil ycac ymatlavacat ytzivactlacuch yn intac icac." Primeros Memoriales, f. 264v.

42. Memorial de los Indios de Tepetlaoztoc, ff. 251, 49v.

43. Elizabeth Baquedano, "Tezcatlipoca as Warrior: Wealth and Bells," in *Tezcatlipoca: Trickster and Supreme Diety*, ed. Elizabeth Baquedano (Boulder: University Press of Colorado, 2014), 113–33. The bells are very similar to the image quoted in figure 4.3, this chapter.

44. On Tezcatlipoca, see Olivier, *Tezcatlipoca*.

45. "ynipan domingo . . . tihui yn iglesia yn Misa tonita." AGN, Inquisición, vol. 301, exp. 19, f. 2. On the evangelical utility of music and theatre, see Prado, *Origins of Mexican Catholicism*; Fernando Horcasitas, ed., *Teatro náhuatl*, 2 vols. (Mexico City: UNAM, 2004).

46. "Y era que de noche se ayuntauan y llamauan y hazían fiestas al demonio con muchos y diuersos rritos que tenían antiguos, en especial quando sembrauan sus maizales y quando los cogían." Motolinia, *Memoriales*, 151.

47. The use of the plural here, together with the later evocation of "pueblo," strongly suggests tlaxilacalli.

48. "yo lo he muchas veces oido apregonar en las iglesias cuando el pueblo está junto y acuden tan á una y con tanta priesa que no queda chico ni grande que no acuda habiendo

podido coger antes y de espacio pero como el sortílego viejo halló que el día era llegado que en su libro y calendario halló dio aviso y luego acudieron sin ninguna dilación." Durán, *Historia*, 2:232–33.

49. Constantino Reyes Valerio, in his *El pintor de conventos: Los murales del siglo XVI en la Nueva España* (Mexico City: INAH, 1989), 18, estimates that the Acolman convent required 10,781 separate trips to simply bring the basic materials necessary for the 10,000 cubic meters in its construction. He estimates a similar value for the convent in Teotihuacan and calculates 225,385 total trips for a wider list of 25 early convents.

50. There are a number of Spanish sources for the Teotihuacan riots, but most derive from Gerónimo de Mendieta, *Historia eclesiástica indiana*, 2 vols., ed. Antonio Rubial García (Mexico City: CONACULTA, 1997). Also see Fray Agustín de Vetancurt, *Teatro mexicano* (Mexico City: Porrúa, 1971); Manuel Gamio, ed., *La población del Valle de Teotihuacán: Representativa de las que habitan las regiones rurales del Distrito Federal y de los estados de Hidalgo, Puebla, México y Tlaxcala*, 3 vols. (Mexico City: Dirección de Talleres Gráficos, 1922).

In addition, it is tempting to see the nearly contemporaneous Juan Teton uprising as an Acolhua story, as Guilhem Olivier suggests: Olivier, "Tlantepuzilama: Las peligrosas andanzas de una diedad con dientes de cobre en Mesoamérica," *Estudios de Cultura Náhuatl* 36 (2005): 245–71. A detailed examination of the place names, however, suggests the region of Toluca, not Tetzcoco.

51. "no hubo indio ni india que les diese un jarro de agua." Gerónimo de Mendieta, *Historia eclesiástica indiana*, book 3, ch. 59, available at Cervantes Virtual, accessed December 12, 2013, http://www.cervantesvirtual.com/obra-visor/historia-eclesiastica-indiana-0/html/.

52. On the cacicazco of San Juan Teotihuacan, see Guido Munch, *El cacicazgo de San Juan Teotihuacan durante la colonia* (Mexico City: INAH, 1976); William T. Sanders and Barbara J. Price, "The Native Aristocracy and the Evolution of the Latifundio in the Teotihuacán Valley, 1521–1917," *Ethnohistory* 50, no. 1 (Winter 2003): 69–88; Jongsoo Lee, "Colonial Writings and Indigenous Politics in New Spain: Alva Ixtlilxochitl's Chronicles and the Cacicazco of San Juan Teotihuacan," in *Ixtlilxochitl and His Legacy*, ed. Brokaw and Lee, 122–52.

53. "Llegado este á S. Juan, prendió algunos principales y otros algunos de la gente popular, y los puso en la cárcel con prisiones y en cepos; mas como casi todo el pueblo era de una voz y opinion, de noche horadaron la cárcel y sacaron todos los presos y pusiéronlos en salvo. En este tiempo habia en el pueblo solos cinco ó seis indios de parte de los religiosos." Mendieta, *Historia*, accessed December 12, 2013.

Mendieta finished his *Historia* in the convent of Huexotla, right outside of Tetzcoco. See Luis González y González, *Jerónimo de Mendieta: Vida, pasión y mensaje de un indigenista apocalíptico* (Zamora: El Colegio de Michoacán, 1996), 44–50, and Gabriela Urquiza Vázquez del Mercado, *Convento Huexotla: Reflejo de la mística franciscana* (Mexico City: Plaza y Valdéz, 1993), 47–49.

54. Mendieta, *Historia* (accessed December 12, 2013), calls Coatlan a "visita" of the "pueblo" of Teotihuacan.

55. "el comun del pueblo era el que se alborotaba sin las cabezas." Mendieta, *Historia*, accessed December 12, 2013. Pueblo here references the altepetl.

56. "juntáronse muchos indios y indias de la gente pobre, y fueron á México mas de cuatrocientas personas, y entraron así como iban desarrapados y miserables ante el virey y audiencia real, clamando todos á una voz y pidiendo justicia, diciendo el grande agravio que se les hacia trayéndolos así muertos de hambre, peregrinando tanto tiempo fuera de sus casas. Respondiéronles que se volviesen á ellas y que se les haria justicia... [El virrey] envió un perdón general a todo el pueblo, y en particular a don Francisco y a los principales, y licencia para que fuesen a la doctrina a do ellos querían." Mendieta, *Historia*, accessed December 12, 2013.

57. "es cierto que padecieran todo cuanto se les ofreciera, hasta morir todos ellos, ó alcanzar lo que deseaban, que era tener frailes de S. Francisco en su pueblo. Y cuando lo alcanzaron fué tanta su alegría, que olvidaron todas las angustias pasadas, y con gran contento hicieron en pocos dias un devoto monesterio y una buena iglesia de cal y canto, y están en paz y tienen doctrina." Mendieta, *Historia*, accessed December 12, 2013.

58. To be sure, living for over a year in spatial and economic dislocation could not have been comfortable for either Teotihuacan's thousands of residents or their various neighbors. If Mendieta's calculations are to be believed, the altepetl consumed 10,000 pesos—in both community and "individual" savings, whether "lost or stolen"—during its year of dislocation. This amounted to roughly ten times the amount spent by the tlaxilacalli of Tetzcotzingo a decade earlier in the three years it consumed building its church under Tetzcoco's sacred hills. This becomes an understandable sum given the difference in scale between altepetl and tlaxilacalli. Cf. Mendieta, *Historia*, accessed December 12, 2013; "Titles of Tetzcotzingo," 124–25.

59. "hicieron una informacion de todo lo pasado y enviáronla á España." Mendieta, *Historia*, accessed December 12, 2013; Códice San Juan Teotihuacan, Biblioteca Nacional de Antropología e Historia, Códices 35–69.

60. The calpixque are identified as such later in the document. One was not a calpixque but a teopan tlapixque (church minder). A mangled note mentioning "calpolli" is also visible. The codex as a document is well-worn, filled with holes and illegible annotations, but many of the nobles' names can still be deciphered or at least guessed at: Toribio Sánchez, Pedro Tomás, Pablo Ocelotl, and possibly the surnames Sánchez, Martín, and Lorenzo. Among the calpixque, many names are partially legible: Tomás Coatl Tonal, Damián Bravo, Juan Colotl, Damián [Aoc...?], Julián Toledo, the church guard Juan Martín, a certain Antonio Mamatililo (?), Martin Quinmecatl (?), and two others who bear no recorded names.

61. Alessandra Russo, *The Untranslatable Image: A Mestizo History of the Arts in New Spain, 1500–1600* (Austin: University of Texas Press, 2014); Elías Rodríguez Vázquez and Pascual Tinoco Quesnel, *Graffitis Novohispanos de Tepeapulco, Siglo XVI* (Pachuca, Mexico: Universidad Autónoma del Estado de Hidalgo, 2006).

62. Russo, *Untranslatable*, 74–76, 149–50; Martha Ilia Nájera Coronado, "El rito del 'palo volador': Encuentro de significados," *Revista Española de Antropología Americana* 38, no. 1 (2008): 51–73.

63. All of these appear in the final catalog of images in Rodríguez Vázquez and Tinoco Quesnel, *Graffitis*.

64. Russo, *Untranslatable*, chapter 6.

65. "todas las iglesias de los pueblos sujetos a esta cabecera, cuyos nombres estan escritas al pie de las iglesias de cada uno." "Relación de Tepeapulco," in *Relaciones geográficas*, ed. Acuña, 7:181.

66. "Hay deste pueblo de Tepeapulco al pueblo de Acopinalco, y al pueblo de San Mtín y al pueblo de Santa María Magdalena y al pueblo de San Sebastián, una buena legua de caminos torcidos en partes y, todo, de camino muy áspero y barrancoso, por una sierra rasa." "Relación de Tepeapulco," in *Relaciones geográficas*, ed. Acuña, 7:182.

67. Martha Ilia Nájera Coronado, "El rito del 'palo volador': encuentro de significados," *Revista española de antropología americana* 38, no. 1 (2008): 51–73.

68. Translations for Tamoachan are tentative; even the original language of this word remains unknown. See Patrick Johanssen K., "Tamoanchan: una imagen verbal del origen," *Estudios de Cultura Náhuatl* 49 (2015): 59–92. See also Alfredo López Austin, *Tamoanchan y tlalocan* (Mexico City: FCE, 1994).

5

Tlaxilacalli Ascendant, 1562–1613

The core Mesoamerican idea of intertwining creation—of disparate but joined powers weaving together as they converge toward a center—reached far beyond the virtuosity of the voladores even as it was symbolized by their pole-top ceremony. Around the same time Tepepulco was throwing raucous parties in front of its Franciscan convent, the Tetzcoca noble Juan Bautista de Pomar collected an impressive song cycle he titled *Romances de los Señores de la Nueva España*, a broad repertoire of Nahua vocal performance from early Hispanic Acolhuacan. In one of these songs, a singer calls out from the "flower tree of Tamoanchan," exhorting his friends to whirl to the drummer's *to-to-ti* triple beat. The singer then continues, evoking the fleeting beauty of flowers and calling out an unnamed noble by both tlaxilacalli and ethnicity: "Where we go, where we go to die, do we yet have life? Is there yet a place of pleasure, yet a pleasure land, O Lord our God? Delicious flowers, perhaps, are only here on earth. And songs. On earth. It's true, yes, true: we pass away. *Ohuaya ohuaya* [melodic verbalization] . . . You Tlailotlac,[1] you Acolhua! No one will rule an altepetl, no one will be left on earth. *A ohuaya ohuaya*."[2]

This song was popular, spreading from singer to singer across the performance networks of early Hispanic central Mexico, and it appears with slight variations in the *Cantares Mexicanos* compendium collected in Tlatelolco/Mexico City around the same time Pomar was gathering his *Romances* in Acolhuacan. In addition to evoking classic elite themes of despair, abandonment, and stoicism, this song proved particularly relevant across the late sixteenth century for the uncertainty it expressed regarding local administrative authority, sovereign jurisdiction, and the very persistence of human life in community: who would rule the altepetl in the aftermath of its demographic implosion? Would life, let alone the altepetl, even exist as bodies of the local dead stacked higher and higher? Such doubt was largely an elite preoccupation for both the Acolhua and the Spanish: local macehualtin soon came to their own strategic conclusions regarding the structure of imperial power in early Hispanic Acolhuacan and developed their own methods of dealing with their dead. But this is a later story, and elite disarticulation sets it up.[3]

This chapter compares two ways the living dealt with communities, living and dead, in late sixteenth-century Acolhuacan: one elite and kinship-derived; the other, commoner and tlaxilacalli-based. The former—ever more a province of translated deeds, titles, and testaments—found itself increasingly distorted by Spanish legal codes and ideas of male primogeniture; while the latter, anchored in the physicality of burials and in the ruggedness of survivors, produced new, vital patterns of remembrance and continuity—patterns that set important precedents for decades and even centuries to come.

TRANSLATION AND TRANSFER

Patterns of elite disarticulation are well illustrated for mid-century Teotihuacan, still basking in its victory over the Augustinians, but the story was similar in many places across Acolhuacan. In 1563, a mere four years after its successful uprising, San Juan—as Teotihuacan was now also coming to be known—faced a transition in power. The savvy and independent-minded tlatoani, don Francisco Verdugo Quetzalmamalitzin, lay on his deathbed, dictating his final will in Nahuatl and bequeathing to his wife and daughter income from "all the lands of the altepetl, all the lands of the calpolli," which was "divided in seven ways, through which the macehualtin pay tribute." Important for a ruler, Quetzalmamalitzin anchored his claims in legal precedent, distinguishing nine separate types of tlatoani landholding, including lands won through conquest (*tepehuatlalli*) and appropriated from enemies (*yaotlalli*); those designated for domestic service (*tequitcatlalli*) and for local bureaucracy (*tecpantlalli*); those pledged to the office of the local ruler (*tlatocatlalli*), held for the huei tlatoani of Tetzcoco (*tetzcocatlatocatlalli*), or given in dowry when his daughter married into the Teotihuacan line (*cihuatlalli*); and, finally, those supporting the lord's spiritual force (*itonal in tlacatl*) and deriving from his noble station (*pillalli*). Further, in these bestowals, Quetzalmamalitzin evoked the specific management of his possessions, distinguishing irrigated lands (*atlalli*) from those left fallow (*tlacahualli*) and parsing those lands and palaces that derived from the institution of rulership (*tlatocayotl*) from those that emanated from the metaphysical avatar (*-ixiptla*) of the tlatoani himself.[4]

During this process, Quetzalmamalitzin called an ally, the Franciscan friar Alonso de Vela (a indigenist firebrand who reportedly had argued from the pulpit against local tribute payments to all Spaniards, including to the king) to translate the will into Spanish.[5] For the most part, this "beloved father" exercised care and skill in the translation work, but even the most ardent Hispanic allies did not communicate everything Quetzalmamalitzin intended. Indeed, friar Vela's omissions are telling: he did not translate the tlatoani's indications regarding irrigation or fallowing of the land, and he was much less vigorous than Quetzalmamalitzin in defining the specific legal status of the inheritance—he did not distinguish fields deriving from the rulership itself (tlatocayotl) from those emanating out of the palace bureaucracy (tecpan), for instance. The Franciscan also diffused the fraught spiritual associations of the term -ixiptla by simply saying that such lands "represent my person." Finally, although Vela took pains to distinguish complete tlaxilacalli (translated as "barrios") from their constituent elements, the friar's use of a sterile word like *partes* (parts) to evoke root-level altepemaitl hierarchies presented these community institutions as simple landscape elements.[6] In these small changes, fray Vela subtly but consistently shifted reference from the diverse and spiritualized ties of a tlatoani and his property into a staid and instrumental assay of a local noble's property.[7]

A similar Hispanizing move was afoot in the realm of tribute. Although, with Vela's help, Quetzalmamalitzin was able to transfer much of his sovereign property into an inheritable Hispanic estate (*mayorazgo*), his broad and varied tribute shares declined precipitously, from eleven daily payments drawn from seven separate tlaxilacalli in 1543 to ten weekly payments a decade later. Further, land specifically designated as his "tribute land" (tequitcatlalli) diminished from a broad legal concept of "lordly energy" (itonal in tlacatl), evoking the primal concept of *tonalli* life force, to a demarcated 400 by 200 tlalquahuitl plot in 1552. Regarding dependent labor, his quota of female cooks and male woodsmen fell from ten daily to three a week. Food allocations also declined, but he did now receive forty pesos quarterly, a rather robust sum—enough, for instance, to buy a very large section of farmland.[8]

Such Hispanizing transfers only grew after Quetzalmamalitzin's death as payments passed to his daughter, doña Ana Cortés. In her first year of tribute receipts, cash income fell to sixty pesos yearly, a mere 38 percent of her father's share. Just as damaging, however, was the erosion of the legal bases for her institutionalized landownership. The viceroy Enríquez ruled that doña Ana's sixty peso payment would be the only benefit deriving from the office of rulership (tlatocayotl) in Teotihuacan and that all her properties would be held separately, as a private Hispanic estate, or mayorazgo. Other members of the local elite complained loudly and repeatedly about this land privatization, arguing that if the office-based holdings designated as either tlatoani or palace lands (tlatocatlalli, tecpantlalli) could not remain a tlatoani prerogative, they should at least be divided among the nobility. These demands, however, were consistently rebuffed by three separate levels of Hispanic administration (the viceroy, the real audiencia, and the local juez)—so much so that "a great penalty" was imposed on the pipiltin so they would "never more lie to themselves" about their legal standing.[9]

To be sure, the private holdings of Ana Cortés and her favored kin remained intact, with title passing down at least partially for centuries, but they were now dependent on institutions and forces far removed from the politics and precedents of the altepetl. Mexico City now mattered in a way Mexico-Tenochtitlan or even Tetzcoco never did. A telling detail of this transformation comes in the career of the Tetzcoca historian Fernando de Alva Ixtlilxochitl, a grandson of doña Ana who inherited parts of this estate. Although this local judge and historian defended his claims, by the end of the seventeenth century his descendants found themselves offering Ixtlilxochitl's remarkable personal archive (including codices such as the Xolotl, Quinatzin, Tlotzin, and Tepechpan) to the savant don Carlos de Sigüenza y Góngora in gratitude for his legal services in defense of their property. Quite literally, then, this tlatoani's heirs traded historical patrimony for legal guarantees, secured now by Spanish rule.[10]

EROSIONS OF MEANING

Despite his personal success negotiating Hispanic laws and institutions, Ixtlilxochitl also perceived the significant imperial transformations reordering the Acolhua hinterland. In one of his histories, this Tetzcoca historian lamented that Hispanic reorganizations of tribute schemes placed an "insupportable weight" on the vestigial Acolhua nobility, focusing his entire attention on their changing relationship with tlaxilacalli regimes. Here is Ixtlilxochitl's complaint, quoted at some length:

> Of all the pueblos and lands and control that we had, they have left us only the head town (cabecera) of Tetzcoco with four or five dependencies (sujetos). And even these, seeing the little favor that we are given and how lowly we are taken to be, want to rise against us and stand for themselves. They have taken from us the pueblos of our chamber, where we had our haciendas and inheritance in those self-same pueblos—which we made and populated, and from which we have received and continue to receive notable insult. We live poor and needy, without any income, and we see that the pueblos that were ours, our very lands—where the people were our sharecroppers (*renteros*) and tributaries and the calpixque were the ones that we had placed—we see that now they are lords of possession, even though they were macehualtin. Now they have the income of these pueblos and we, being the lords, are poor and without anything to eat.[11]

It is clear that the processes of interchange and translation between Spanish and Mesoamerican paradigms were far from value-neutral. Instead of a benign but persistent mis-recognition of the other—Lockhart's "double mistaken identity" argument[12]—it seems more likely that actors of all sorts fought to cast filmy tissues of conjectural improvisation across the mid-century void: tissues that could, through luck and practice, eventually be conjured into precedent and tradition.[13] Fray Antonio de Vela does seem to have sought to defend the rights of Teotihuacan's nobility through his verification and translation of Quetzalmamalitzin's will; but it is also true that Vela, to the extent he was able given the constraints of Quetzalmamalitzin's deathbed oratory, anchored these noble rights in Spanish understandings of lineage and primogeniture, not in the pagan heat or institutional prerogatives accruing to the ruler from his possessions as the physical embodiment of a metaphysically charged and closely arranged landscape.[14]

As both legal and supernatural meanings leached from noble landholding and, even more, as dependent workers continued to die in the fields, local lands were often understood by the nobility as little more than the fungible asset they were taken for in Hispanic contexts. For the remaining nobles of Acolhuacan, particularly those cut off from the first-born mayorazgo or *cacicazgo* inheritances of tlatoani holdings, land soon became nothing more than fields, a transferable economic input. Without an army of dependent farmers to work their lands and enjoying little sovereign control over their localities, Acolhua nobles largely cashed out of local "palace economies" by the 1570s and moved to the viceregal capital if they had the means. Across the final decades of the sixteenth century, therefore, there was a veritable sell-off of noble lands, particularly around the increasingly marginalized former capital of Tetzcoco—which, in the words of the royal physician Francisco Hernández, was by the 1570s only home to "mediocre" citizens "because they lack mines of gold and silver."[15]

TRANSLATING TITLE

Such a reordering marks a significant departure from earlier noble understandings of the agricultural hinterland. Indeed, during the Aztec empire, huei tlatoque had to force Acolhua nobles to live close-in near the capital—and Nezahualpilli executed one of his sons who refused to abandon his personal palace. Power emanated from the broad network of local tlaxilacalli building across Acolhuacan; indeed, a prime struggle of imperial statecraft was to forcibly concentrate this power at the political-religious center. By the turn of the seventeenth century, however, this conception had reversed: power spread from the center, and the difficulty was to make it reach the now distant hinterlands.[16]

Some pipiltin still held on to their estates, however. For instance, a Tetzcoca noble named doña Angelina fought over decades to, as she memorably put it, "secure my food" after the death of her husband in 1562. This husband was one of the innumerable children of the Acolhua emperor Nezahualpilli; he died during the great wave of "privatization" of noble lands in the 1560s, leaving his widow in a position of significant risk. Doña Angelina, however, met this challenge with steely determination, declaring "although I am a woman and never hunted, never went to war . . . I can still order my mayeque to plant the land." And this she did for twenty-seven years, "spreading the macehualtin" across her possessions.[17]

By 1589, however, all of Doña Angelina's fieldhands had died, and she herself had become "old, without faculties to work any longer." The noblewoman therefore "had a talk with myself, in my heart" and decided to donate her house and fields and granary in the altepemaitl of Oztochyacan to her "beloved" nephew—the historian, ethnographer, businessman, and land speculator Juan Bautista de Pomar, compiler of the beautiful song cycle that opened this chapter. Between the late 1570s (the date of the last killing epidemic of the sixteenth century) and the 1590s, Pomar, the historian and intermediary, mediated the sale of at least nine separate properties around Tetzcoco, often buying them himself.[18]

This was a fundamentally different process than Quetzalmamalitzin's consolidation of his various lands into a single Hispanic mayorazgo, because Pomar constructed his holdings piecemeal from the wreckage of Acolhua noble landholding. One reason, it seems, the Tetzcoca elite preferred Pomar as their intermediary of choice was his kinship connection to these once-illustrious noble lands. A sale from 1596 expresses something of this trust and affection, where the noble don Miguel de Carbajal effusively praised Pomar as his relative and confidant: "I give him (the land) because he is truly one of us, he is a relative. Truly, we are one. In this way, I show my great love for my beloved cousin ['primo hermano'—a Spanish borrow] because I give him (the land). It will no longer be counted as my milpa. Forever, eternally, it will be counted as his."[19]

Pomar's acquisitions included a former imperial garden (*xochimilli*) and a decommissioned woman's palace (*cihuatecpan*), both in the tlaxilacalli of San Esteban Tlailotlacan, in addition to various houses and fields in multiple other tlaxilacalli, some of which seem to have been purchased from local non-elite intermediaries. A later Tetzcoca report of Pomar's activities even states that he "laid out the boundaries of the head palace, the home of Nezahualpilli" in the tlaxilacalli of Tlaixpan—lands this surveyor claimed for himself "because it's been thirty or more years since he began to buy them from Yndians and Spaniards."[20] Pomar's mediating knowledge served the local Acolhua elite, emerging Hispanic interests, and—just as often—himself.[21]

FINANCIAL TRANSLATIONS

Juan Bautista de Pomar epitomized the Hispanizing transformation of noble landholding even as he catalyzed its spread. On numerous occasions, he bought or inherited noble lands and then re-deeded them according to Hispanic protocols, plucking these compounds from their surrounding tlaxilacalli contexts and then accommodating the holdings into expanding networks of Spanish-derived property rights. Crucially, Pomar and other land speculators bought lands from nobles almost exclusively, which meant that commoner-based tlaxilacalli holdings were largely exempt from this wide-scale noble retreat from rural landholding—although they were also threatened by Hispanic property regimes and other major environmental and economic dislocations.

Beyond the specific concerns of each negotiation, Pomar followed standard patterns in his land purchases. His primary work consisted of transferring Acolhua-backed land claims into Hispanic ones. Despite nostalgia for his grandfather Nezahualpilli's imperial sovereignty, Pomar firmly ensconced himself in the Hispanizing sociability of the urban Tetzcoca elite. The examples are multiple: he married a Spaniard, socialized with Spaniards (including the inimical Jácome Passalli; see chapter 6 for a wider reckoning of this sweatshop owner's various misdeeds),[22] and identified his home as the "city of Tetzcoco," never adhering to the regular custom (even among elites) of mentioning a home tlaxilacalli. Only once did he describe himself as a pilli in Nahuatl documents, generally preferring the Hispanic title "señor." Like other nobles across New Spain, it was Pomar's deep connections to an Acolhua imperial past that allowed him to more fully enter into elite networks of Hispanic prestige.[23]

The single document in which Pomar claimed pilli status is noteworthy in itself because it deals with ruined idols near the tlaxilacalli of Santa María Nativitas, destroyed in the time of don Carlos Ometochtzin (see chapter 4). In 1582, Pomar bought a large (~8.6 ha) "piece of land that lies at the crossroads, beside a hill, next to a broken stone altar." This land, in the tlaxilacalli of Cozcacuauhco (figure 5.1), was defined in 1575 as "belonging to the community" (an interesting formulation addressed later in this chapter) and forcibly privatized in that year by the noble don Lázaro de la Cadena and his equally formidable mother. They pressured a local official named Pedro de San Francisco Tlaocol, perhaps the calpixqui, to buy this land from them for an inflated price of 20 pesos.[24]

This was clearly not standard practice, for when Tlaocol heard the price, he "looked at (don Lázaro) with fear and didn't dare" respond. After heated negotiations that lasted five rounds, don Lázaro eventually accepted the price of 17 pesos, 3 tomines, and then proceeded to bicker over payment schedules. Eventually, Tlaocol took possession of the fields over the protests of other noble land speculators and ratified his

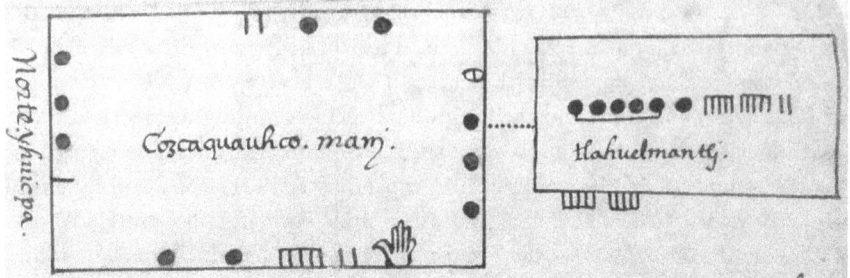

FIGURE 5.1. Map of the Cozcacuauhco field under dispute, 1575. Note calculations for both perimeter (*left*) and surface area (*right*): balls equal 20 tlalquahuitl; joined lines, five; and lines, one. BNAH-3PS, leg. 3, exp. 2–27, f. 15r. *Courtesy*, Instituto Nacional de Antropología e Historia, Mexico City.

title before the local "tlatoque"—that is, the tlaxilacalli-level "alcaldes and regidores" of Tetzcoco, likely don Lázaro and his associates.[25] The calpixqui held this field for seven years and then passed ownership to his son, who sold it for just under half the price (8 pesos) to Juan Bautista de Pomar in 1582. It is only in relation to these lands that Pomar assumes the title of pilli, perhaps to better conform to the history of Cozcacuauhco as a tlaxilacalli known in Aztec times for its noble compounds.[26]

Pomar held this property for a generation and bequeathed it and other holdings to his wife, the Spaniard doña María de Ibarburen, before his death in the early seventeenth century. Doña María subsequently remarried and ceded the property rights to her new husband. In 1613, upon the husband's death, title passed to his daughter and son-in-law. Finally, this couple sold the estate, together with two other parcels of land, for the staggering price of 13,000 pesos—an astronomical increase, given that the estate in Cozcacuauhco had been bought for 8 pesos only three decades before. To be sure, the other two parcels could have made up the lion's share of the total selling price, but the question remains the same: what could have provoked such an extreme fluctuation—from 8 pesos to some fraction of 13,000 pesos—in little more than a generation?[27]

The answer begins with New Spain's changing silver economy. By the beginning of the seventeenth century, all of Mexico's major mines were active, flooding the world economy with specie. Silver had been scarce in Acolhuacan and remained a chore to procure for many commoners, but large Hispanic actors in the area now had relatively easy access[28] to *iztac teocuitlatl* (white gold), the Nahuatl term for this metal.[29] Rising liquidity for elites, together with royal demands in the 1560s requiring tribute payments in only silver or corn, meant that this metal also increasingly organized commoner labor in the area, a move that further detached tlaxilacalli hierarchies from their imperial beneficiaries. Inflation and "financialization" combined with new forms of capital investment (like a water wheel in Cozcacuauhco) to further raise the price of Pomar's holdings. What were once sacred ruins of the imperial Tetzcoca elite now became fungible real estate holdings, easily traded in the new economy for white gold, the motor of the export economy in New Spain.[30]

During the final decades of the sixteenth century, central Mexican nobles, in their various and shifting factions, fought among themselves and against equally splintered Spanish administrators across an ecological landscape still shocked by the joining of two hemispheric ecosystems. Much has been written about the manifold ways clashing native elites and factionalized Spanish administrators disputed control of sovereign Mexican polities in the ongoing aftermath of war, disease, and ecological upheaval. In central Acolhuacan, the change came in two steps. First, the nuanced details of noble control over tlaxilacalli were abstracted and standardized through both financial and legal means. After these initial shifts had drastically reduced the value of local hierarchies to the vestigial local nobility, these elites then rapidly sold off their land titles in exchange for greater currency in the new silver economy. Land was worthless to the local nobility without its attached labor hierarchies.[31]

DEBATING LANDSCAPE

As Spanish thought and bureaucratic practice increasingly detached nobles from their claims to land and tribute, these sources of wealth often began circuitously drifting toward Hispanic economies. Clearly, some property remained attached to local nobility, with lands held in mayorazgo and cash payments ascribed to a tlatocayotl or a Hispanic cacicazgo. These privileges often accrued to increasingly Spanish-oriented urban kin groups, such as the Alva y Cortés clan of Teotihuacan—who boasted in Nahuatl as early as 1610 of marrying "gachupines."[32] Tribute income also fell away in the demographic and ecological disruptions of the sixteenth century: there were fewer commoners to pay tribute or work extensive estates. Finally and most interesting for purposes here, some lands and tributes were reassigned to other hierarchies, other overlords, other institutions. As seen with such invaders as Tezozomoc and Hernán Cortés and also in the case of Acolhua rulers like Nezahualcoyotl and Hernando Ixtlilxochitl, such reassignments have a deep regional history. However, early Hispanic reassignments were comparatively piecemeal, confused, and equivocal—one cause for the absolute glut of land disputes filling the Tierras branch of Mexico's general archive down to today.[33]

A primary reason for this confusion derived from divergent understandings of land and ownership in early Hispanic Acolhuacan, a topic that is still not completely understood for northern Mesoamerica. The tlaxilacalli, for example, seem to have held final "ownership" over their constituent territory and reassigned lands in response to various changes, including the sale of plots by residents. Residents likely enjoyed semi-permanent and alienable usufruct of their enumerated territories, which, in turn, was confirmed by their participation in and payments to their tlaxilacalli. Nobles, particularly the teuctlatoani, claimed income from subordinate members of these communities and therefore could also stake a claim for tlaxilacalli "ownership."[34]

As seen above in the case of Quetzalmamalitzin and Vela, Hispanic law distorted and translated the diverse and often competing categories of land tenure in Acolhuacan. This fraying of the ties linking the local nobility to their subordinate hierarchies led many nobles—even those who resisted land alienation—to eventually seek the services of a broker such as Juan Bautista de Pomar, whose knowledge of and kin connections in Tetzcoco also gave him significant advantages as he competed with Spanish interlopers for lands.

Take the case of Pomar's 1591 dispute over three *caballerías* of land (around 128 ha) with the Spanish herding barons Marcos and Pedro Mejía de Bocanegra, which he waged jointly with various noble allies in Tetzcoco. The Mejía de Bocanegras characterized their opponents specifically but imprecisely as "Juan de Pomar, for himself, and don Pedro de Alvarado and consorts, and Luis de San Sebastián and other Yndians." Each of these defendants attacked the Mejía de Bocanegras' proposed grant of pastureland in a different way: Luis de San Sebastián and other administrators of the "barrios" of Moyotepec, San Juan Olopan, and Apantzinco described themselves as "retainers (*terrazgueros*) working and cultivating those lands"; Alvarado and his noble allies asserted ownership since the times of Nezahualpilli; and Pomar claimed direct inheritance from his aunt, the same doña Angelina who hustled for decades to "secure food" after her husband's death.[35]

A central dispute in the Mejía de Bocanegra case centered on the nature of ownership: was the fight over lands and their titles or over communities and their labor?[36] Both the Mejía de Bocanegras and, to a lesser extent, the noble group led by Alvarado argued that the primary anchors for these four place names were the "empty" mountains named Moyotepec, Olopan, Apantzinco, and Patlachiuhqui despite nearby residential quarters (*vecindades*), containing "houses of Yndians," as well as their corrals, sweatbaths, and livestock pens. They recognized the settlements but argued that although there were "ten or twelve Yndians living in three areas of the foothills and divisions of the aforementioned hills, in all their places they only plant two *almudes* [somewhere between two and four liters] of corn." Despite this, Marcos Mejía de Bocanegra argued that "they try to defend all of the mountains and summits." Alvarado and company argued against Mejía de Bocanegra's claims, but they accepted the premise that the primary argument was over lands and mountains, not communities and dependents. This conceptualization was further supported by a detailed map annexed to the process that placed the names in question on the top of each indicated mountain.[37]

Pomar argued the opposite: although recognizing his inheritance from doña Angelina as fields and geoforms, not people, he asserted his right to these holdings based on the work of his dependents: "I have a great quantity of cultivated lands, as clearly manifested by the work of those who keep them." In Pomar's argument, labor meant usufruct meant ownership. It was not his own labor, however, that secured Pomar's claim but rather that of his organized subordinate hierarchies, "my Yndians and dependents."[38]

Moving now to these laborers themselves, to the "natives of the barrios" of Moyotepec, San Juan Olopan, and Apantzinco, they explicitly asserted their status as dependent farmers, as "terrazgueros who work and cultivate" the lands under their control, and declared simply and definitively that "there is no space to anchor a (new) land grant" for the Mejía de Bocanegras. Strikingly, in one of their declarations, these laborers fully evoked the multi-level hierarchical array of tlaxilacalli regimes, effectively proving the ongoing activity of these patterns of organization—even after the demographic and ecological disruptions of the sixteenth century. Here is their declaration at length. Note once again the use of "neighborhood," this time to describe a tlaxilacalli sub-district:

> Juan Pascual, Francisco Porres, Diego de San Juan, and José de Morales, macehual Yndians and natives of this city (Tetzcoco), from the neighborhood and homesteads of Moyotepec, in the case regarding Marcos Mejía [de Bocanegra]'s request (for a land grant) in the name of Pedro Mejía de Bocanegra: we say that the aforementioned place where they are requesting (the grant), on Patlachiuhqui hill in our neighborhood of Moyotepec, is where we have our houses and farmlands and magueyes; it's where we live. We live as terrazgueros of the principals of [the Tetzcoco tlaxilacalli of] Chimalpan—just as our fathers, grandfathers, and ancestors left for us. Despite being under this regime, we pay tribute to your Majesty and (fulfill) our personal labor requirements. If our aforementioned area is subjected to (the land grant) we will have no other recourse than to abandon our houses and lands.[39]

Beyond their tribute-based submission to the imperial center and their generations-deep evocation of landscape, the "macehuales and natives" of Moyotepec insist on their subordination to the core Tetzcoca tlaxilacalli of Chimalpan. In other words, the "barrio" of Moyotepec was in fact an altepemaitl, a far-flung sub-district of a Tetzcoca tlaxilacalli—a conclusion confirmed by the "mestizo" map of the case,[40] which shows that Moyotepec consisted of only three houses among

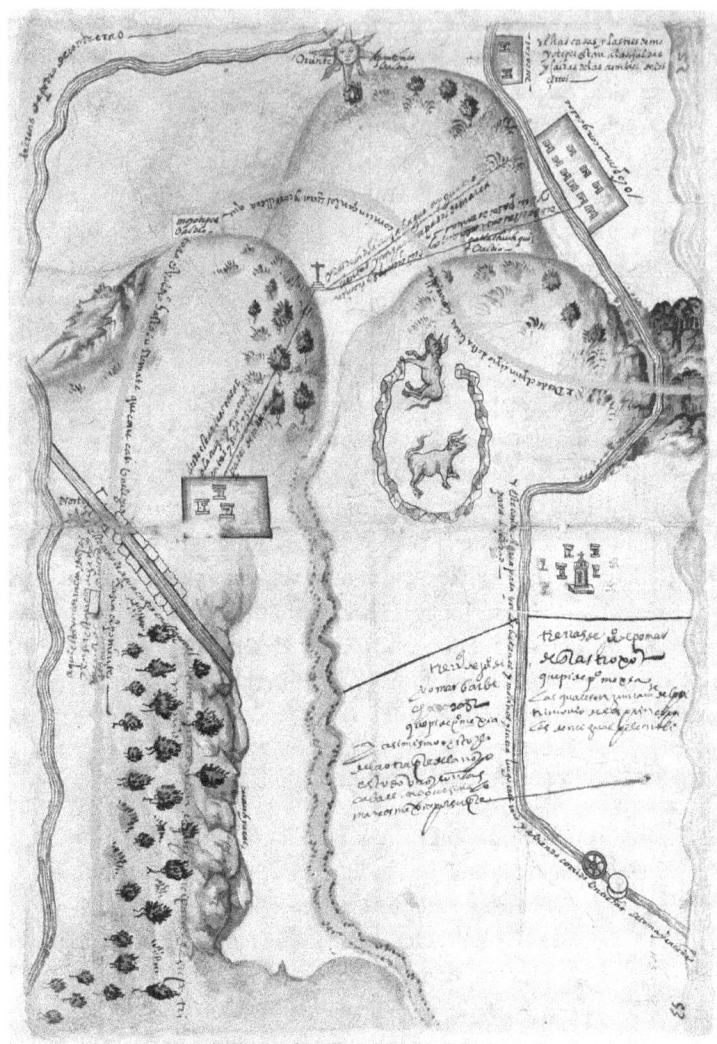

FIGURE 5.2. Mountaintop sub-districts of Chimalpan tlaxilacalli. Moyotepec is represented by the three houses at the center of the map; Olopan (nine houses) and Apantzinco (two) appear in the upper right. Referencing the wider spiritual geographies of the area, the distances to each altepemaitl are measured from the central hillside cross. The extensive lands of Juan Bautista de Pomar straddled the river on each side, just above the water mill. The four extant houses and chapel just above Pomar's lands were also likely his, as could have been the six erased (ruined?) housing structures. Finally, note the lands of Pedro de Contreras at the upper left and the corral at center. *Courtesy*, Archivo General de la Nación, Mexico City.

"the slopes and ridges on the summits of the hills."[41] (Olopan had only nine houses; Apantzinco, though unnamed, seems to have had just two.) Despite their minuscule populations, Moyotepec and its sister hierarchies serve as one of the clearest examples of proof that multi-level tlaxilacalli hierarchies continued to function well into the Hispanic period and beyond the demographic free-falls of the sixteenth century. Tlaxilacalli mightily resisted the extinctions facing other local institutions, as did the constituent micro-hierarchies.

DEEPER HISTORIES

These arguments eventually won over the viceroy, don Luis de Velasco el Mozo, who denied the Mejía de Bocanegras' land grant and cited both Pomar and the "natives" of Tetzcoco in his decision—but such rulings were far from uniform and always trailed the often violent physicality of occupation. Indeed, only a year later and in the exact same region, Pedro de Contreras (noted in the upper left corner of the map in figure 5.2) successfully attacked the sub-district of San Gerónimo Amanalco, just north of Moyotepec, legally appropriating the lands and "causing more than twenty villainies; robbing not only chickens and corn and other stuffs but also forcing [himself on] our daughters and wives, among other dirty things." This tactical and gendered violence, together with a late-striking epidemic, forced farming households from the hills they first populated "by order of the revered Nezahualcoyotl" in the first decades of the Aztec empire. After these expulsions, Contreras filled the now-empty farmlands with "dependents, whether natives (*gañanes*) or mulatos . . . who are strangers and do not know the value of this land."[42]

The value of this land: in both the Mejía de Bocanegra and Contreras cases, local altepemaitl claimed centuries-deep patterns of dependence on larger hierarchies, hierarchies that stretched across the chasms of foreign invasion and demographic loss. Not only did they know the political and economic value of the land, they also knew its precise characteristics—with measurements down to the hand span and a detailed reckoning of its soil content. Even in the 1590s, the primary value of lands flowed from the hierarchies that worked them. In both of the hillside cases, however, powerful recent arrivals moved against these claims, seeking *tierras baldías*, lands empty of both people and history, to anchor their new enterprises. Marcos Mejía de Bocanegra was particularly insistent on this point, arguing that "the aforementioned (hills), especially Patlachiuhqui, Moyotepec, and Apantzinco, are empty, without any use or advantage—nor have they ever had such in ten, twenty, thirty, forty, fifty years in this place. After so much time, the memory of men is not [reliable]. So they are, and have been, ownerless."[43] Not even Mejía de Bocanegra trusted these assertions about the universal habits of local memory, for on the very same page he also attacked the specific historical claims of his tlaxilacalli-based opponents, asserting that "they don't have a claim to the aforementioned hills, neither to the fields. Their writings must be read in this way—they must be someone else's—because they say that the hills belong to the macehuales and the fields to the heirs of Nezahualpilli, so there is a contradiction in their custom and practice."[44]

But the nested hierarchies invoked by the macehualtin constituted the anchors of land tenure in Acolhuacan. To own land meant to exploit it, and exploitation flowed through the semi-independent tlaxilacalli hierarchies that managed their own internal hierarchies of settlement and access. The apparent contradiction of "dual ownership" argued by Mejía de Bocanegra was in fact the very proof of *uso y costumbre*, of custom and practice, and the legal basis for ongoing local ownership of the fields and hills under dispute.

Mejía de Bocanegra and Contreras, like most foreign arrivals in this period, ascribed an empty topography and crumbling traditions to the Acolhua hinterlands they attempted to remake into rural Spanish hamlets. Pomar, in turn, saw the social landscape and knew the histories, which he worked to translate into exploitable Hispanic registers. Local tlaxilacalli, however, opened up a surprising third approach to imperial rearticulation, dealing directly and often independently with emerging regional hierarchies. Sometimes this approach worked (as in the case of Chimalpan's hillside dependents), other times it did not (as in Pedro de Contreras's violent takeover of Amanalco), and on still other occasions this approach produced something entirely new and unexpected. So it happened that the northwestern boundary of Tetzcoco, just south of Tepechpan, where the tlaxilacalli of Tezcatzonco Tlanelocan succeeded in forcing its own patterns of hierarchical submission, its own history and landscape, against both the Hispanic administration and the intermediary Juan Bautista de Pomar. This, in turn, raises an important final point about wider patterns of early colonial Spanish administration.

FORCING NEW ORDER

The story begins, as do most from this period, with the final massive epidemic of the sixteenth century, in the years 1576–81. Hierarchies buckled once again during this period of demographic hollowing and agricultural failure; and, as almost always in the immediate vicinity of Tetzcoco, Juan Bautista de Pomar was there to seek an advantage. Tezcatzonco Tlanelocan appears to have been particularly hard-hit, and Pomar arrived in this tlaxilacalli around 1582, in the immediate aftermath of the epidemic, to request vacant land for his dependents in the neighboring tlaxilacalli of San Gregorio Tlaquilcan. In a later petition, various topileque of Tezcatzonco Tlanelocan, writing for themselves and "everyone else" from this locality, described what happened next:

Truly, in this way, he separated us from our land by deceit. We say again before you that a year ago we received our land. So mandated the former tlatoani, don Antonio de San Francisco, gobernador. But the señor Juan [Bautista] de Pomar pleaded with us, saying: "My grandchildren suffer. With your permission, today they will plant your milpa. There they will harvest it, and then they will return it to you." All this was done with the lands of Tezcatzonco...

Today we arrive at the third year in which they harvest that milpa; and again they say, "I'm only planting it." In such a way, they mock the land, and our help, with their words.[45]

As might be expected, San Gregorio fought back with its own petition—but this document differed from that of Tezcatzonco Tlanelocan in both form and feeling. Adopting a Hispanizing discourse of absence and forgetting, San Gregorio argued that "nobody still remembers to whom [the land] belongs" and asserted that the milpas had been fallow for twenty years, so that tall grasses now grew "where we will put our tributary milpa." They claimed that landscape should be defined by convenience above history, so the lands that were "far from where people live" in Tezcatzonco Tlanelocan should accrue to San Gregorio because "it lies beside our houses; we cleared it." Purchase should secure ownership above labor; so San Gregorio, which bought the land (from Pomar?), would hold title above Tezcatzonco Tlanelocan, which shared in the fieldwork. Finally and crucially, San Gregorio saw its ownership as deriving principally from Spanish authority and serving Hispanizing ends. It was to work the land so the city of Tetzcoco could be fed after the killing regional epidemic:

> Lucas Hernández, Matco Juárez, Lázaro Méndez, and Melchior Díaz, counted as part of San Gregorio Tlaquilcan, here in the city of Tetzcoco, appear before you, pleading your powerful sovereignty in the name of His Majesty. We say that by the law of the Real Audiencia, we truly confirm and administer the wide milpa. We paid for it, and it belongs to the community...
>
> People must be reminded of what we said a year ago: the Justice and Rulership [*cabildo*] ordered us to work the milpa for two years; they let us have it. With our heart, for another year we will stay, until the end of the year [15]86. How can the land be another's if we are always cleaning it and clearing it? How can we lose it?
>
> Today we ask you, we implore you, and we say with all our heart that we will take our wide milpa for another year. May you desire this. In this way, you ordered us two years ago; you requested this so that the city here may be served, may be sustained.[46]

The contrasts between San Gregorio and Tezcatzonco Tlanelocan were indeed striking. Whereas the former reverenced Spanish authority—from the king on down to the local council—and Spanish authority only, the latter also evoked the separate office of the tlatoani, tlatocayotl, in its pleas to the cabildo. San Gregorio relied deeply on its ties to nobles such as Juan Bautista de Pomar, while Tezcatzonco prided itself on its commoner-based administration, even going so far as to disqualify its opponents in San Gregorio on the basis of hierarchical politics, commenting dismissively that "they are not macehualtin." The two sides clashed over usage and definition of the precise Spanish legal term *comunidad*, community, with San Gregorio claiming the term referred to the collectively held central lands of an altepetl (*fundo legal*) and Tezcatzonco Tlanelocan defining it as the private, inheritable lands of the tlatoani.[47]

Matters then became even more surprising. Tezcatzonco Tlanelocan reached into its own tlaxilacalli-based local archive, "investigating the colored and the black (i.e., the ancient painted documents), the dictates of the lord tlatoani Nezahualcoyotl, made 170 years ago, a long time ago," to bolster its arguments.[48] Such mention of tlaxilacalli-specific archives is not unknown, but it rarely appears in the specialized literature. It is clear, however, that the specific, detailed nature of local tlaxilacalli administration required its own institutional memory—a memory largely ignored by the Spanish administration.

More remarkable than even this, however, was the reason for such research. Reaching back to early imperial Aztec politics—and not only ignoring the subsequent century-and-a-half of political upheaval but also completely redefining the parameters of ownership flowing from this source—the commoner tlaxilacalli of Tezcatzonco Tlanelocan staked a claim to the personal lands of Tetzcoco's tlatoani, arguing that "the palace . . . [and] all the lands of the tlatoani are ours" through the gifts of "our great-grandfathers, grandfathers, and fathers" and that "the extension of milpas belongs to the community (comunidad)." This evocation of community-held tlatoani land innovated on at least two levels. First, it upended the causality of ownership, so tenant farmers could claim the lands of their overlords. In addition and just as powerfully, it pulled the Spanish legal definition of comunidad out of its urbanizing colonial context and submitted it to the rule of a tlaxilacalli. Access to "community" land, even in Spanish times, would be through the tlaxilacalli, not the city (ciudad) or the altepetl.[49]

Tezcatzonco Tlanelocan seems to have been aware of its innovations. Though maintaining the precise conventions of polite Nahuatl address, this tlaxilacalli chided the cabildo for its ambivalence while looking toward the structure of future administration in the area. Its alternating lines of deference and insistence deserve to be quoted at length: "Leave us title to the land . . . May we have your rule as tlatoani. This will confirm the hearts of your macehualtin—our children and grandchildren—when we look to the future. For this reason, we solicit you. All your macehualtin prostrate themselves before you. We, the people of Tezcatzonco

Tlanelocan, bow down (before you). May you learn, oh our teteuctin, oh tlatoque! We kiss your hand and feet. We plead [for] justice."⁵⁰

Remarkably, Tezcatzonco Tlanelocan won—and resoundingly so. The cabildo first remanded the dispute back to the disputing tlaxilacalli "to listen and consult ... and come to an accord, so as to never again give trouble about this." Nevertheless, after a back-and-forth involving at least four tlaxilacalli, Tezcatzonco Tlanelocan pressured the cabildo again. This time, the council fully endorsed this brash tlaxilacalli's claims, citing a previous decision in 1576 but also seconding its redefinition of tlatoani lands as belonging to this "community," which it understood as the commoner residents living in Tezcatzonco Tlanelocan. Further, the cabildo severely rebuked San Gregorio (and, at least implicitly, Juan Bautista de Pomar) for stirring up "disorder." In this specific case, therefore, the deep history of tlaxilacalli communities overran the expedient forgetfulness of Hispanizing land speculators even as wider regional politics continued to bend toward new patterns of submission and marginalization. But even here, change flowed both ways—tlaxilacalli changed, but so did Spanish ideas and institutions. Comunidad would never be the same.⁵¹

Change rocked Acolhuacan as assertive tlaxilacalli such as Tezcatzonco Tlanelocan grabbed more and more agency from faltering imperial institutions, particularly the local nobility. Once again, the flexible and creative actions of tlaxilacalli set them at a comparative advantage compared to other local structuring institutions. As the nobility cashed out their stakes in local administration, tlaxilacalli like Tezcatzonco doubled down on their political commitments. Tezcatzonco was not alone; indeed, there were cases of assertive tlaxilacalli pushing for lands and privileges before cabildos and other regional tribunals. Through these actions and many others executed with varying degrees of success, local politics in rural Acolhuacan was progressively reborn, piece by hierarchical piece.

NOTES

1. As discussed in the introduction, note 45, Tlailotlac generalized into a broader term evoking administrative leadership.

2. "xochicuahuitlo ... y tamohuâchā .... cano tihui hue cano tihui om timiqui oc nelo yn tinemi oc ahuiyaloya oc ahuiltilano yehuaya *totecoyo* i Dios i acā çāniyo nicann i tlalticpacqui huelic xochitli yhuān i cuicatl yhuān i tlalticpac ye neli ye nel tihui ohuaya ohuaya ... i tlaylotlaquin i tacolihuatsin ... ayac tepetiz ayac mocahuaz - yn tlalticpâc a ohuaya ohuaya." John Bierhorst, ed. and trans., *Ballads of the Lords of New Spain* (Austin: University of Texas Press, 2009), accessed December 3, 2014, http://www.lib.utexas.edu/books/utdigital/book/index.php?page=songs.php&pagenumber=11; http://www.lib.utexas.edu/books/utdigital/book/index.php?page=songs.php&pagenumber=12.

A few notes about Bierhorst's version of this text: first, it greatly improves earlier translations, particularly regarding precision. In addition, it is accompanied by a beautiful online component, including high-quality scans of the original document and recorded drum beats to match the cadence of the songs. Indeed, the online features vastly outstrip the offerings of the print version. Also, my translation differs from Bierhorst's in important ways: his final line of this quote reads "O Arbiter! You! Father-keeper at the Waters! None shall have a city. No one shall be left on earth." Nevertheless, it still remains an advance over earlier work.

3. John Bierhorst, ed. and trans., *Cantares Mexicanos: Songs of the Aztecs*, (Stanford: Stanford University Press, 1985), 346.

4. "yn ixquich altepetlalli calpollalli chiconcan quiztica ypā tlacalaquia maçehualtin." AGN, Vínculos y Mayorazgos, vol. 232, exp. 1, f. 21r.

5. A further indication of Quetalmamalitzin's affinity for Franciscans was his stipulation in his will (f. 11r) that he be buried in a habit of St. Francis.

6. On the metaphysical connection among the altepetl, the ruler, and images of the hands and feet, see Offner, "Aztec Political Numerology."

7. AGN, Vínculos y Mayorazgos, vol. 232, exp. 1, ff. 26r–39r. See also García Martínez, *Los pueblos*; Robert Haskett, *Visions of Paradise: Primordial Titles and Mesoamerican History in Cuernavaca* (Norman: University of Oklahoma Press, 2005), especially chapter 4. Such a redefinition would also help Quetzalmamalitzin's inheritors in Spanish courts of law.

8. "Los primeros señores de Teotihuacan y sus comarcas," BnF-MM, no. 242. The plot increased to 400 × 400 tlalquahuitl in 1553.

9. "Auh huel huei penatlaliloque in pipiltin ica in acmo ocçecpa motelhuizque." *Tanto ddel testamento de Dn Franco Verdugo Quetzalmamalictzin*, BnF-MM, no. 243. Note the early borrow of the Spanish word *pena* (punishment) here.

10. Cf. AGN, Vínculos y Mayorazgos, vol. 232, exp. 1, ff. 261r–262v. There has been much recent scholarship on Ixtlilxochitl, including this bequest. See Brian, *Alva Ixtlilxochitl's Native Archive*; Amber Brian, "The Alva Ixtlilxochitl Brothers and the Nahua Intellectual Community," in *Texcoco*, ed. Lee and Brokaw, 201–18; Lee, "Colonial Writings"; and an entire special issue of *Colonial Latin American Review* 23, no. 1 (2014).

11. "se nos han quitado todos los Pueblos y tierras y mando que teníamos, y nos han dejado solamente en la cabecera de Texcuco con cuatro ó cinco sujetos, y aun los cuales viendo el poco favor que se nos dá y en cuan poco somos tenidos, se nos quieren alzar y poner por sí, y se nos han quitado los Pueblos de nuestra recámara, de donde teníamos nuestras haciendas y heredades en los propios Pueblos que nosotros de nuestra gente hicimos y poblamos, de lo cual hemos recibido y recibimos notorio agravio, y vivimos muy pobres y necesitados sin ninguna renta, y vemos que los Pueblos que eran nuestros y nuestras propias tierras, la gente que en ellos estaba eran nuestros renteros y tributarios, y los Calpixques que nosotros teníamos puestos, vemos que ahora son Señores de dones, siendo como eran Mazehuales y

tienen renta de los dichos Pueblos, y nosotros siendo Señores, nos vemos abatidos, y pobres sin tener que comer." Ixtlilxochitl, *Obras* (1952), 1: 445.

12. Lockhart, *The Nahuas after the Conquest*, 445–46.

13. For an example in early Hispanic law in New Spain, see Offner, "The Future of Aztec Law."

14. Lockhart, *The Nahuas after the Conquest*; see also García Martínez, *Los pueblos*.

15. "las fortunas de los ciudadanos son mediocres, porque como carecen de minas de oro y de plata, dedican todo su tiempo a comercio, a la agricultura, al ganado lanar y a otras cosas semejantes." Francisco Hernández, *Antigüedades de la Nueva España* (Madrid: Dastin, 2003), 138.

16. Ixtlilxochitl, *Obras* (1952), 2:169; see also Susan Toby Evans, "Aztec Palaces and Other Elite Residential Architecture," in *Palaces of the Ancient New World*, ed. Susan Toby Evans and Joanne Pillsbury (Cambridge, MA: Harvard University Press, 2009), 7–58.

17. "auh ynicnilçihuatl ahmo nicmahaçia ahmo nontlayecoua ya. ye hica yncenca miac tlalli yhuan ypampa yzcenca miaccan texti toc. chachayacatoc/ auh ynin oconcatca ynmacehualtzizintin toma yecauan ynoquichihuaya auh ynaxcan aocaque omochnemiquilique." BNAH-3PS, leg. 9, exp. 3–9, f. 21r.

18. "yhuan ypampa ynoçenca ninilamatili çanniman aocmo nihuiliti yn nictequipanoz. auh caoninononotz mochica noyollo ỹnicnomaquilia cemih cac nicnaxcatilia yn nopilotzin Jhoan de pomar." BNAH-3PS, leg. 9, exp. 3–9, f. 21r.

19. "Auh ynic nicnomaquilia ypampa caçan tiçeme tiçentlaca caçantite huantin ynicnoprimo hermano ca oc hualca ynitechmotlaçuhtilia ympampa ynnicno tlauhtilia caahtle ypā pouqui yn nomil. Auh mochipa çemihcac ytetzinco pouhtaz." BNAH-3PS, leg. 9, exp. 1–35, f. 19r. This document is also interesting because of its publishing history, for James Lockhart used this deed for the cover art of at least three of his books: *Nahuas after the Conquest*, *Nahuas and Spaniards*, and *Nahuatl as Written*.

20. "in Juan de Pomar in quichiuh traSacion in izompa tecpan in ichan neçahualpiltzintli." AGN, Intestados, vol. 268, f. 316v. (This report also criticized Pomar for being incomplete in his survey work.) "son del dicho Pomar porque a más de treinta y más años que las comenzó a comprar a indios y españoles." AGN, Tierras, vol. 2726, exp. 8, f. 39r. Other purchases by Pomar can be found in BNAH-3PS, leg. 7, exp. 2–21, f. 19r; exp. 2–32, f. 18r; 2–36; exp. 2–37, f. 21r; exp. 2–40, f. 23r.

21. For a good summary of Pomar's intermediate position, see Patrick Lesbre, "Un représentant de la première génération métisse face à l'aristocratie acolhua: Juan Bautista Pomar, Tezcoco (fin XVIe–début XVIIe siècle)," in *Transgressions et stratégies du métissage en Amérique colonial*, ed. Bernard Lavallé (Paris: Sorbonne Nouvelle, 1999), 183–200.

22. On the links between Pomar's widow and Jácome Passalli, see AGNM-T, caja 1, leg. 1, ff. 71r–77v.

23. Pomar married a Spaniard, doña María de Ibargueren, and conducted frequent trade with Spanish businessmen, importing 192,000 Guatemalan cacao beans and 300 fanegas of maize into Tetzcoco over a single month between December 29, 1575, and January 19, 1576, for example. Cf. Archivo de Notarías del Estado de México, Texcoco no. 1 (hereafter AGNM-T), caja 1, leg. 1, ff. 12v–13r, 35r–35v. When Pomar died, doña María inherited most of his assets. She then remarried—to another Spaniard, Bartolomé de Tramasaguas—and effectively consolidated her inheritance through lineage-based Spanish titles.

24. "niquitohua canicnocohuj. tlaltzintli oncā ȳmani tlanacazco. tepantitlan tapalcamomoztitlā ini huicpa comonidad." BNAH-3PS, leg. 3, exp. 2–27, f. 15r. On the deeper history of this property, Ixtlilxochitl (*Obras* [1952], 1:112) mentions that Cozcacuauhco was earlier one of the "gardens" of Nezahualcoyotl.

25. "auh çā nicmauhcayttac. hao ninotlapalo." BNAH-3PS, leg. 3, exp. 2–27, f. 15r. The reference to "alcaldes and regidores" also evokes the local cabildo of the altepetl, but only functionaries from Cozcacuauhco were active in this transaction. On the Hispanic cabildo more widely, see Robert Haskett, *Indigenous Rulers: An Ethnohistory of Town Government in Colonial Cuernavaca* (Albuquerque: University of New Mexico Press, 1991).

26. Pomar bought more land in Cozcacuauhco in 1587: BNAH-3PS, leg. 3, exp. 2–23, f. 13r. This one measured much less than his earlier purchase; it was comparatively insignificant in size, perhaps a third of the other purchase.

27. AGNM-T, caja 1, leg. 7, ff. 182r–189r.

28. See, for example, the extensive transactions recorded in AGNM-T, beginning in 1575.

29. Because the etymology of teocuitlatl literally derives into "white divine excrement," a pun becomes unavoidable; see Cecilia F. Klein, "Teocuitlatl, 'Divine Excrement': The Significance of 'Holy Shit' in Ancient Mexico," *Art Journal* 52, no. 3 (1993): 20–27.

30. Charles Gibson, *The Aztecs under Spanish Rule* (Stanford: Stanford University Press, 1964), 200.

31. The literature on early Hispanic local nobility is extensive and includes Gibson, *Aztecs*; Margarita Menegus, *Del señorío indígena a la república de indios: El caso de Toluca, 1500–1600* (Mexico City: CONACULTA, 1994); Margarita Menegus and Rodolfo Aguirre Salvador, eds., *El cacicazco en Nueva España y Filipinas* (Mexico City: Plaza y Valdés, 2005); Lockhart, *The Nahuas after the Conquest*; Haskett, *Indigenous Rulers*; Jose Luis de Rojas, *Cambiar para que yo no cambie: La nobleza indígena en la Nueva España* (Buenos Aires: Editorial SB, 2010); Arij Ouweneel, "From Tlahtocayotl to Gobernadoryotl: A Critical Examination of Indigenous Rule in Eighteenth-Century Central Mexico," *American Ethnologist* 22, no. 4 (November 1995): 756–85; Susan Kellogg, *Law and the Transformation of Aztec Culture, 1500–1700* (Norman: University of Oklahoma Press, 1995).

32. "Yn d.n Fran.co de Navas Peres de Peraleda quimonamicti in d.a Maria Caballero Caxtillan cihuatl cachopina." "Tanto ddel testamento de D.n Fran.co Verdugo Quetzalmamalictzin," BnF-MM 243, f. 9r.

33. *Tanto ddel testamento de Dn Franco Verdugo Quetzalmamalictzin*, BnF-MM, no. 243. On the Alva y Cortés inheritance, see Guido Munch, *El cacicazgo de San Juan Teotihuacan durante la colonia* (Mexico City: INAH, 1976); Sanders and Price, "Native Aristocracy."

34. Nevertheless, and despite these legal precedents, recall Jerome Offner's insistence that land sales were common in Acolhua tlaxilacalli. Cf. Offner, "On the Inapplicability of 'Oriental Despotism' and the 'Asiatic Mode of Production' to the Aztecs of Texcoco," *American Antiquity* 46, no. 1 (1981): 43–61.

35. "Juan de pomar Por si y don pedro de Albarado y consortes y luis de san Sebastian y otros yndios . . . los naturales de los barrios de moyotepec Apantzingo Y San Juan Olopan que como Terrazgueros labran y cultivan aquellas tierras." AGN, Tierras, vol. 2726, exp. 8, f. 181r.

36. Another question relates to the invasion of ruminants in these agricultural fields. For grazing, see Melville, *Plague*; also Gibson, *Aztecs*, 278; Brian P. Owensby, *Empire of Law and Indian Justice in Colonial Mexico* (Stanford: Stanford University Press, 2008), 116.

37. "que DieZ y doze Indios que estan poblados en tres partes a las faldas y Remates de los dhos cerros que entre todos y en sus lugares apenas siembran dos almudes de mays en las tierras que tienen labradas por cuyo Respecto pretenden defender el todo de la serrania y cumbre . . . la veZindad y Casillas de Indios . . . corrales de Indios temasCales y maJadas . . . por la veZindad propinqua . . . caserias de yndios." AGN, Tierras, vol. 2726, exp. 8, f. 140r.

38. "tengo mucha cantidad de tierras cultivadas como claramente consta por la labor q las tienen q son las q se dizen xicotepetenco temochco y otlatlitec . . . yndios y Criados mios." AGN, Tierras, vol. 2726, exp. 8, f. 191r.

39. "Luis de san sebastian Augustin de galizia franco porres benito de santa maria y por luis maldonado munoz por lo que A Cada Uno e nos toca y por los naturales de los barrios de moyotepec Apantzingo Y San Juan Olopan que como Terrazgueros labran y cultivan aquellas tierras . . . en Los dichos Lugares de apantzingo y San Juo Olopan que por El Auto esta declado no aver lugar de sembrar ninguna md . . . Juan pascual franco porres Diego de san Juan y Joseph de morales yndios maceguales y naturales desta çiudad del barrio y casio de moyotepec en lo que tiene pedido marcos mexia En en nobmre de P mexia de bocanegra sobre El sitio de Era que pretnede se le hagamos en el çerro de patlachiuqui y en nrō barrio de moyotepec Dezimos que En el dho lugar tenemos nras Casas. Y tierras de sementeras y magueyales donde vivimos Ya vivimos Como terrazqueros de los principales de chimalpan Segun Y como nros padres aguelos y antepassados nos deJaron y sin embargo destar debajo deste titulo pagamos Los tributos A Su magd Y nrās servicioS personales y se se suJete nros Dho su sitio de sanar en la dha parte no Tenemos Otro rremdio sino desamparar Las dichas nrās Casas y Tierras por que no ay quinientos pesos." AGN, Tierras, vol. 2726, exp. 8, f. 211r.

40. On "mestizo" maps and artistic styles, see Russo, *Untranslatable Image*.

41. "estas casas y las tres de moyotepec estan a las faldas y Caidas de las cumbres de los çerros." AGN, Tierras, vol. 2726, exp. 8, f. 161r. Cordova, "Landscape Transformation," 189–91, also briefly mentions this case.

42. "la contradiçion q los naturales de dicha ciudad hizieron, y Jhoan de Pomar por las tierras . . . @tes viniese la mortandad cocoliztli los indios acostumbrados [a] beneficiar la dicha tierra . . . or mādado de nezaualcoyotzī . . . está . . . haciendo más de veinte vellacerias en robar no solo gallinas y mayz y otras cosas antes en tener q hazer a ntras ijas y mugeres y otras cosas suzias . . . y decimos que los criados, ansi gañanes como mulatos de dicho pedro de contreras son estraños y forasteros q no saben la qualidad desta tierra." AGN, Tierras, vol. 2726, exp. 8, ff. 181r–v.

43. "los dhos especialmte patlachiuhqui moyotepec apantzinco son baldios sin Suso ni aprovechamto Alguno ni Jamas la antenido de DieZ, beynte, treynta, quarenta, cinquenta anos q a esta parte y tanto tiempo que memoria de hombres noes en contres[?] y ansi an estado y estan sin dueño." AGN, Tierras, vol. 2726, exp. 8, f. 38r.

44. "no tienen parte en los dhos cerros ni en las dhas tierras y aSi Se Colege de su escripto Pues alegan de Ser ageno diZiendo ser los dichos cerros de maçeguales y las dhas tierras de los herederos de Necahulpiltzintli, de manera que la contradiZion es por uso y Costumbre." AGN, Tierras, vol. 2726, exp. 8, f. 38r.

45. "Antonio de sant Raphael yhuan francisco de la cruz yhuan mathias de santiago yhuā gaspar nuñez yhuan thomas de aquino yhuan yn octiçequintin tezcatzonco tlanelocan . . . caycaxacan çexxihuitl yn tech cauilizquia. totlal. cahuel quin monahuatilli. yn tlahtoani. catca don Antonio de Sant franco gounernador auh caçayehuatzin. yn señor Joan de pomar. ynic techmotlatlauhtilli quinihtalhui. motolinia yna mocnihuan çahueliuhti ynaxcā. cōtocazq. amo mil. oncā onpixcazq. niman amechcauilizque. ynixquichquichiua tezcatzonco tlalli. yhuinin ynquimihtalhui. auh ynaxcan yeotahçico ynic Ehxxiuitl oncapix ca millpā yenocuel çentlamantli ynquihtua. caçanictoca mocacayaua yhuinin ynotlananquilique. tezcatzonco tlaca. auh yntlaquilcan tlaca yenelli ynamo quicahualiz tlamati. tlanlli. miyec ynintlahtol ynic otla nanquilique." BNAH-3PS, leg. 7, exp. 2–18, f. 10r.

46. "Lucas hernandez matheo xuarez Lazaro mendez melchior diez san gregorio tlahquilcan tipohui ynincanipan çiudad tetzco Amixpantzinco. tineçi tictotlatlauhtilia yn amomahuiztlatocayotzin ynicatzinco su magd+ tiquihtoua ynitlanauatiltzin Real audiençia huel ticneltilia tictequipanoua yn milmanalli toconixtlaua ynco mūd pouhqui . . . auh yetechiuiliznequei yctitoteilhuique ȳ yeçexiuitl auh ynic techmonauatili Justa Regimio caoxxiuitl yntoconchihuazq milli toconcauazque auh yuhcatoyollo caoçcexiuitl yntiquitz tiui ypan ynictlaniz año de ochenta yseis aos auh maço yn tlal queniuh nenti otictochipahuilique oticçacamoque cemiac ypan oticpoloque Etc ypampa ynaxcā çenca tamechtocnotlatlauhtilia titlaytlami tiquitoua cayuhca toyollo ynoccexiuitl oncā toconcuizq tomilmanal mayuhxicmonequiltiq auh yn tlatoçoc oxxi huitl onitechmonemactilizq ypampa caomocotechmonequi caz çiudad ytlayecoltiloca ynticneltilia." BNAH-3PS, 3ª Série de Papeles Sueltos, leg. 7, exp. 2–20, f. 11r.

47. "amomaçehualhuan." BNAH-3PS, 3ª Série de Papeles Sueltos, leg. 7, exp. 2–19, f. 10v.

48. "tictepotztocatihui yn itlil yn itlapal ynitlatecpantzin yn tlacatl tlah tohuani yn neçahualcoyotlzin yn ye chicuehpohualxihuitl yhuan ȳ yemah tlacpohual xihuitl." BNAH-3PS,

leg. 7, exp. 2–18, f. 10r. There is an error in this chronology because Nezahualcoyotl had not yet assumed rulership in 1415. Such an evocation of deep archival practice remains striking, however.

49. "ynocyenepa yehuecauh xihuitl maçan yuh ya yniuhmopia tlahtoca tlalli ynixixquich tetechpopouhtica yn santa ynes yhuan santa cruz yhuan tezcatzonco yhuan tlahcuilcom macamoye huatl tlanenelo tlamomoyaua yn comūd pouhqui milcmanalli." BNAH-3PS, leg. 7, exp. 2–18, f. 10r.

50. "matechoncahuililcam canel topial yn tlalli . . . auh matic piacom yn motlahtoca tlanauatiltzin ynic moyollalizque ynamocnomaçehualhuan yn topilhuā yn toxhuiuam yn compa titztihui Etc. ypampa yna axcan tamech tocnotlatlauhtilia amixpantzinco mopechteca ymixquichtin ymmaçehualhuan yntiquinpachoua yn tiquinayaca tezca tzonco tlanelocan tlaca maximocnotlamachinticom totecuiyohuane tlahtoquee tictenamiqui amomatzin amocxitzi tiquihtlani Jus.a." BNAH-3PS, leg. 7, exp. 2–18, f. 10r.

51. "ynic notzalozq Santa hynestlaca yhua Sant gregorio tlahquilcan tlaca ymotlamanixtin quicaquizq ynpeticion yniuh moteil huia tezcatzōcotlanelocan tlaca ynitechpayntlal nahuatilozq ynic aocmo ytechonmayahuizq." BNAH-3PS, leg. 7, exp. 2–19, f. 10v.

6

Communities Reborn, 1581–1692

On June 9, 1581, midway through the final year of the last killing epidemic of the sixteenth century, the residents of the backwoods tlaxilacalli San Joaquín Coapanco in the Tetzcoco hinterlands gathered in their local graveyard to celebrate ancestors and community. "Many principal Yndians and natives," the record states, "congregated and joined together to hear Mass in the patio and cemetery of the monastery of the lord Saint Francis." From this monastery—actually a small local chapel pledged to the distant central convent in Tetzcoco—tlaxilacalli members launched a claim to both collective identity and joint sustenance, demanding formal recognition of hillside lands they used to both plant maize and bury their dead.[1]

This particular blurring of culture and agriculture, of community and work, was new to tlaxilacalli members but also known—or at least easily comprehended. Although cremation and cave-based burial were fading as funerary customs, locals quickly adopted both the practice and logic of underground burial. Graveyards became sites of community affiliation, resting places of the beloved dead, as tlaxilacalli members simply extended the Nahuatl verb "to plant" (*tōca*) to include the new techniques of Christian burial, now doubly fertilizing their land with both sustenance and memory. As they presented their petition to local Hispanic authorities, 154 household heads, "together with everyone else from the aforementioned barrio" of Coapanco, added their names to the community demand for the lands in question.[2]

At almost exactly the same time, another tlaxilacalli—this time from the neighboring altepetl of Tepetlaoztoc—launched competing claims over the same lands

DOI: 10.5876/9781607326915.c006

along the eastern flank of Tepetloxto hill. Here, "many Yndians, men and women, congregated in the church"[3] of the equally remote San Martín Tetlicac to collectively apportion a 400 by 400 *braza* (~740 by 740 meters) grant to the local religious brotherhood (cofradía) of the Rosary, of which many locals were members. Were it not for the matter-of-fact quotidian tone in both of these contrasting demands, such commotion over very poor land in a marginal area would come as a surprise. This was, after all, the demographic nadir of post-invasion central Mexico: better lands were supposed to be readily available, local institutions too weak to fight, and community life in disarticulated shards.

Despite the ragged aftermath of demographic collapse, tlaxilacalli such as San Joaquín Coapanco and San Martín Tetlicac battled mightily not only to survive but also to expand their reach. Even in the local fight described above, five additional "pueblos and neighborhoods" (i.e., tlaxilacalli) from both Tetzcoco and Tepetlaoztoc joined the struggle over Tepetloxto hill's eastern terrain: San Gabriel (Nahuatl name unknown), San Pedro Chiautzinco, San Andrés Contlan, Santiago Ticoman, and San Gerónimo Amanalco. Throughout these and other fights of rebuilding, tlaxilacalli members expanded the meaning of land and ownership to include both territory and community—demanding, as with Coapanco, the right to harvest their "ancestral sites" and also, as with Tetlicac, to "gather on Saturdays, and on the eve of the solemn celebration and greeting of Our Lady, and on other stipulated days to say universal Masses or have them said, and for the burials of the brothers" of the cofradía of the Rosary, "where a lot is spent."[4]

The competing tlaxilacalli of Coapanco and Tetlicac not only illustrate the vital work of rebuilding taking place across the Acolhua hinterland, they also provide two strikingly different experiments in early Hispanic tlaxilacalli reconstruction. Coapanco presented itself as an ancestral homeland, while Tetlicac asserted its identity as a fully Catholic religious sodality. Neither definition was exclusive or all-encompassing, but Tetlicac's innovative argument proved more successful in Spanish courts of law—rebuffing not only rival tlaxilacalli but a voracious Spanish interloper and the mediating Juan Bautista de Pomar as well. As confirmed in later conflicts over this same land, cofradía ownership proved decisive to Tetlicac's victory; but this tlaxilacalli was also buttressed, as were so many others across this period, by a previously ignored clutch of settlements ascribed to its hierarchy, "some houses that seem to be of the comunidad of the pueblo."[5]

This chapter carries the history of battle-hardened Acolhua tlaxilacalli to its culmination, opening toward a new cycle of local politics in the region. Over this period, tlaxilacalli such as Coapanco and Tetlitec grew stronger and more expansive—sometimes by default, as the best of a set of limited options, but even here their comparative force vis-à-vis other local institutions astounds. Indeed, by the mid-seventeenth century, tlaxilacalli were so independent that they were refusing to pay profits to the center and even claiming altepetl status themselves. These local communities increasingly understood themselves as independent polities.

CATHOLIC KINSHIP

Religious brotherhoods, such as the victorious cofradía of the Rosary in San Martín Tetlitec, are traditionally understood as something separate from, but inter-penetrating with, tlaxilacalli communities. And yet, it was the cofradía of the Rosary that rose to the defense of Tetlitec against Juan Bautista de Pomar, Spanish interlopers, and rival tlaxilacalli. It was the same cofradía that not only managed planting and fallowing but also analyzed land quality, planned irrigation, and kept administrative records. Further, these officials evoked movement and transformation, blurring conceptual lines between local community and religious brotherhood, when they began petitions with formulations such as "the gobernador, alcaldes, and regidores; for themselves and for all the brothers who are in [the cofradía], and for all the pueblo and community that is joining together..."[6]

To be clear, "pueblo" here meant tlaxilacalli, not altepetl—a later mention of "the congregation and pueblo of San Martín" confirms this beyond a doubt—and the early Hispanic relationships between these two levels of autonomous local administration flowed with increasing vigor through the structures and sociability of domesticated Catholic religion. Land apportionment, for example, often happened right after Mass. Field measurement—of both the close-in fundo legal (core section) and outer graveyards and more distant planting sites—also came to be anchored by the chapel of the tlaxilacalli and through this to the people of the cofradía. At least in Tepetlaoztoc's cofradía of the Rosary, anchored in the tlaxilacalli Tetlitec and its chapel of San Martín, locals officiated their own religious ceremonies and burials in the likely event that they did not hire an outside priest to preside.[7]

In San Martín, members even tactically declared that they, as "natives," were "too poor... to continue [giving] alms to sustain the cofradía." This was ultimately part of their successful play to win the contested hillside lands of Tepetloxto. (As will be seen, the religious brotherhood continued strong well into the seventeenth century and beyond; sustaining the cofradía turned out not to be much of a problem.) At base, the entities of church, comunidad, and religious brotherhood—each theoretically separate and distinct in Hispanic law—inter-penetrated so powerfully that San Martín Tetlicac became something of a network hub, with formal distinctions leading in and out but blurring at the collective center of connection.[8]

Entering the mid-Hispanic period, similarly thick connections reached as well from tlaxilacalli to altepetl, once again anchored through the architecture of local

Catholicism. In 1634, having outgrown the initial Dominican hermitage and its various out-buildings—that is, the same hermitage still conserving tlaxilacalli glyphs on its outer wall—the altepetl of Tepetlaoztoc built itself a monumental new church. It was a collective effort, and, as such, every comunidad gave its part. As recompense, each tlaxilacalli claimed a niche in the wider structure and decorated it with telling expressions of local affiliation. Local cofradías managed the upkeep of these images and facilitated important feast days of the tlaxilacalli.

The current artwork in the niches of Tepetlaoztoc's central church, though of more recent fabrication, illustrates (if anachronistically) something of how the altepetl-wide performance of tlaxilacalli identity might have happened centuries ago. For example, the niche reserved for the current neighborhood[9] of La Columna, once the residential core of the Calla Tlaxoxiuhco altepemaitl of Chimalpan tlaxilacalli, displays a painted cloth *lienzo* of the Christ at the Column. The space of present-day Santa María Magdalena Asunción, the vestigial component of Cuauhtepoztlan, displays the resurrection of Christ, of which St. Mary Magdalene was the first witness. The southern barrios of Santo Tomás Apipilhuasco, San Pedro Chiautzinco, and San Vicente are collectively represented by a joint painting of St. Thomas, St. Peter of Verona, and St. Vicente Ferrer—together with the early evangelist St. Hyacinth of Poland. Finally, the adjoining modern neighborhoods of Calvario and Santísima share a niche with Christ encountering the Holy Spirit. In many ways, both more recently and in the deeper past, community was belonging was public religious display.[10]

BELOVED LANDS

Such commoner reinvestments in local tlaxilacalli came during a period of great restructuring in the Acolhua hinterlands. By the early seventeenth century, local populations were largely bottomed out, and many traditional institutions were fading away or recalibrating to Hispanic demands. New peoples and even ecosystems had already penetrated much of the productive farmland in the region—so much so that by 1606 the viceroy Montesclaros was moved to declare that if any stranger were to invade the "lands and haciendas" traditionally held by the "ancient populations" of Tetzcoco, they were to be "violently" expelled and the properties restored to their original owners. This declaration is particularly striking because it came on the heels of *congregación*, the forced consolidation of outlying or depopulating tlaxilacalli into new, sometimes purpose-built spatial arrangements.[11]

As with many actions of the Hispanizing administration, congregación appears to have been rather patchily applied across New Spain—particularly as tlaxilacalli also redeployed on their own, similarly around local chapels. Nevertheless, involuntary centrally mandated congregación did affect the lives of Acolhua commoners around the turn of the seventeenth century. A Nahuatl document from 1608, for example, contains a petition from two "former residents" of the tlaxilacalli of San Esteban Metepec in Tetzcoco, which describes how "people were transferred to other houses by the order of the king, our tlatoani," and how they themselves moved to the tlaxilacalli of San Miguel Tlaixpan, "abandoning our own land there in San Esteban Metepec." Resigned to the fact that "we will never work that milpa of ours again," the couple sold their field to Juan Bautista de Pomar's Spanish widow, doña María de Ibargueren. Another Nahuatl sale describes how tlaxilacalli officials in San Idelfonso Sultepec "consulted" about the sale of a "large" (200 square tlalquahuitl) milpa to the same doña María, deciding that this sale "greatly helps us with the problem of the cocoliztli epidemic and our worry about money. This helps us ... It doesn't belong to us anymore, but we have so much of our beloved land."[12]

Our beloved land: it is clear that Sultepec treasured its territorial continuity and that arriving at the decision to sell was difficult. Nevertheless, it made this wrenching choice and decided to sell to its "neighbor" doña María, who bordered the milpa in question on two sides. Facing the ongoing ravages of epidemic attack and the increasingly insistent Hispanic demand for silver tribute, this tlaxilacalli assayed its still significant holdings and decided to tactically divest a field. It was a dangerous move, but one Sultepec made with a certain amount of deliberated care.

Across the turn of the seventeenth century, a fair number of tlaxilacalli strategically sold certain collective lands, often to meet pressing needs for specie. These were hard choices, unsustainable in the long term, but they differed from the mass noble land sales of a generation before: whereas in the earlier case land transactions facilitated the wider divestment of nobles from "their" rural communities, in the latter, such sales constituted desperation moves to staunch the financial and territorial hemorrhaging of the early Hispanic period. The main difference lay in the operating logic of these two types of sale: for the local nobility—particularly those secondary nobles not in line for cacicazgo or mayorazgo inheritance—rural divestment could facilitate entry into urban networks of Hispanic sociability. For local communities, collective land sales were taken as a loss and an affront to regional spatial logics, so tlaxilacalli-sized holes came to appear in local documents, as in the "depopulated barrio of Totolan" still haunting a map from the altepetl of San Martín Obispo, right next door to Teotihuacan (figure 6.1). Even in these absences, therefore, a certain logic of community and space could still apply.

LOGICS OF COMMUNITY

Even during the duress of Hispanic-mandated congregación, an ongoing spatial logic of tlaxilacalli regimes remained powerfully at work; when Hispanic zeal for

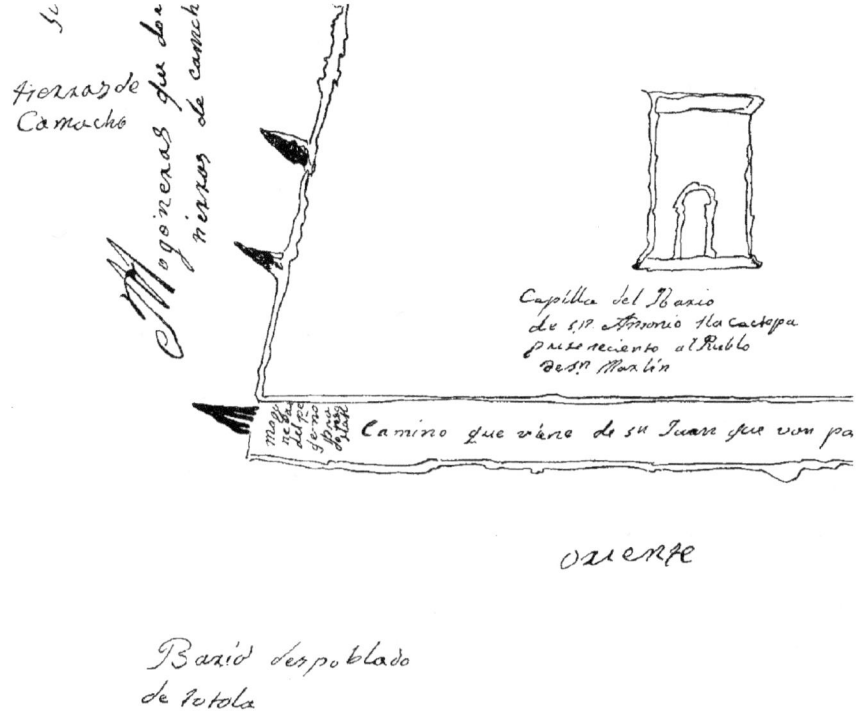

FIGURE 6.1. Two tlaxilacalli in San Martín Obispo, the active San Antonio Tlacactecpan with its chapel and the "depopulated" barrio of Totola. In Gamio, *La poblacion* ..., image 142.

congregación dissipated after only a few decades, more durable local arrangements rushed in once again to fill available spatial and political voids. In Tepetlaoztoc, for example, although lands in Chimalpan tlaxilacalli were once again dispersed to Spaniards during congregación in 1607, by 1615 tlaxilacalli were once again mounting successful and robust defenses of communal lands.[13]

In that year, the Spaniard don Diego de Ochandiano requested a large grant of six caballerías of land in the tlaxilacalli of San Martín Tetlicac, San Gabriel Atlitic, and San Gerónimo Chimalpan, arguing that the lands were abandoned and therefore ripe for grazing. The various tlaxilacalli countered instantly, invading Ochandiano's claim and violently destroying the waterwheel the interloper had already raised over the Tepetlaoztoc-Papalotla river (now called Río Hondo). Together with this physical assault, the tlaxilacalli filed both joint and individual lawsuits in Hispanic court, sometimes signed by local officials, other times in the name of a cofradía. In addition, they enlisted the aid of a local priest, fray Juan Nuñez, to argue on their behalf.

In other words, these were fully functioning Hispanic tlaxilacalli: local communities for commoners to live in hierarchical order, producing for themselves and their bosses; sites to bury their dead and mark identity; places to live and worship collectively. The viceroy understood as much and quickly confirmed tlaxilacalli claims to local exclusivity.[14]

This vigorous and detailed defense of community lands—accompanied by an impressive full-color map, including the seven named tlaxilacalli—shows how these institutions still structured the defense of local landholding in rural Acolhuacan and remained the defining spatial anchors of the surrounding landscape. Tepetlaoztoc's 1615 litigation map shows little of the spatial clustering often assumed to correlate with campaigns of congregación; in fact, it can be read as an immediate post-congregación response to centralizing pressure (figure 6.2). Here, tlaxilacalli and their dependent household groups continue to flood the landscape.[15]

Arguments for community also proved convincing to the local priest, even if he did not completely understand the full import of the various tlaxilacalli-based assertions. In his letters of support, fray Juan Nuñez jumped confusedly between the tlaxilacalli—confusing Atlicac (In the Water) for Tetlicac (In the Rock)—but nevertheless supported their joint case for lands. He knew what he thought he needed to: that the lands were collectively managed by a local cofradía for the benefit of the community and its cult. He could err a bit on geography because what mattered more was legality and precedent.[16] A similarly amusing case comes from neighboring Teotihuacan in 1605, when the love-struck Baltasar de Ortega made up a tlaxilacalli in his native Spain called "De la Villa" (From the Town) to fit the Nahuatl-language conventions of his bride and her local hierarchies.[17]

At least in certain instances in these northern Acolhua lands, Spanish administrators appear to have tired of wrangling with tlaxilacalli, local institutions that they only partially comprehended and struggled to control. Congregación was perhaps their most concerted attempt to decouple these polities from both traditional landscapes and official Hispanic politics, but tlaxilacalli-derived centers of gravity—the hierarchical ties binding one commoner to others—remained robust through the period. Local community still superseded regional politics.

NEEDING A COMMUNITY

Commoners doubled down on tlaxilacalli administration due to, among other reasons, of a lack of better options, among other reasons. Besides the ongoing pull of out-migration to mines or cities, which continued at a slow trickle across this period, few avenues apart from tlaxilacalli regimes presented themselves to macehualtin looking to make a way in the Acolhua countryside. They could personally serve

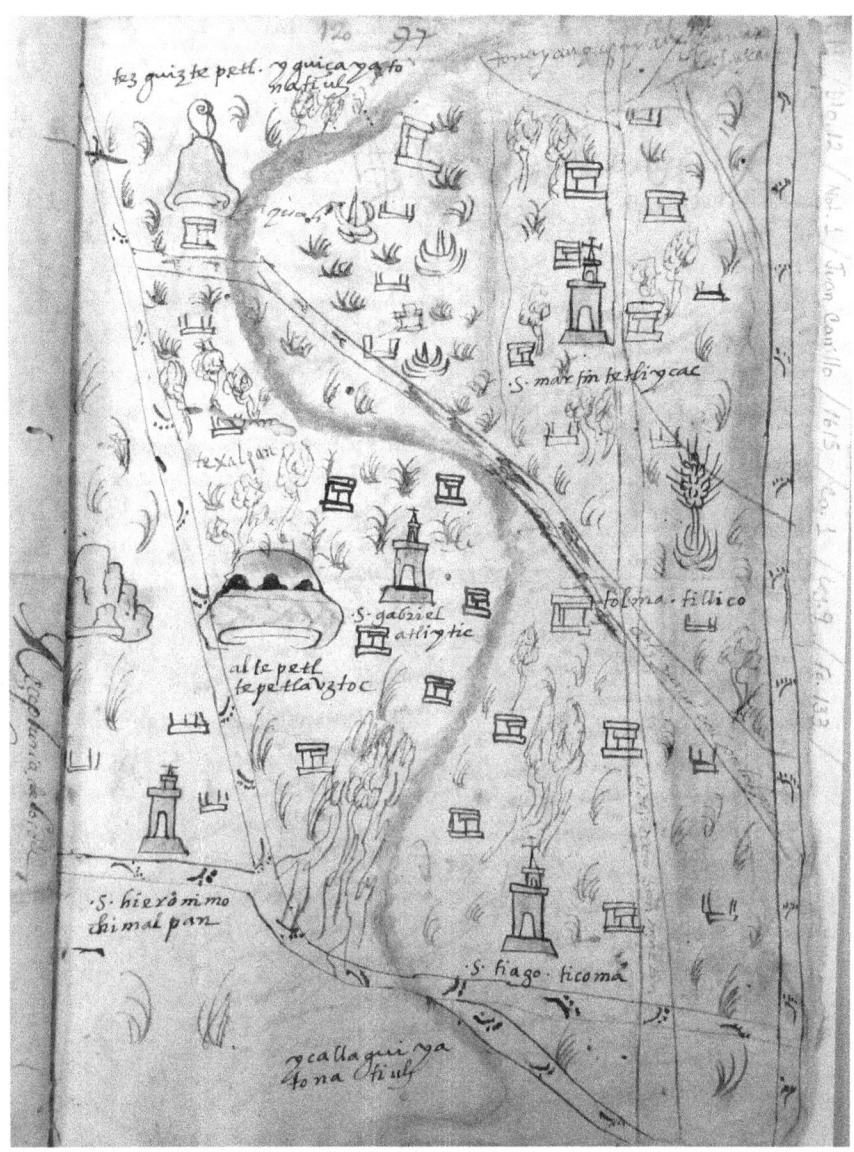

FIGURE 6.2. The vibrant and scattered tlaxilacalli of Tepetlaoztoc, together with (unnamed) altepemaitl: San Gerónimo Chimalpan, San Gabriel Atlitic, Texalpan, Santiago Ticoman, Toliman Tillico, San Martín Tetlicac, San Mateo Tlachihuacan. AGNM-T, caja 1, leg. 9, f. 121r. *Courtesy,* Archivo General de Notarías del Estado de México, Toluca.

Hispanizing households or chapels; they could join sweatshops (*obrajes*) or other factories (such as gunpowder in Teotihuacan); they could escape to marginal hideouts, like the hillside "bandits" mentioned by Fernando de Alva Ixtlilxochitl; or they could become full-time logistical or marketplace intermediaries—market women, muleteers—transporting and selling the goods of others in place of their own.[18]

Each of these avenues attracted small but noticeable numbers of commoners across the seventeenth century, but tlaxilacalli retained their majoritarian status well into this period and beyond. For some vocations, outside conditions limited additional entry—there were only so many mountain hideouts, mule trains, and market stalls available—while for others, the ferocity of Hispanic-oriented factory labor and domestic service served as a deterrent. In 1610, for example, ten sweatshop "elders" (huehuetque) wrote a detailed protest to the Mexican Inquisition denouncing the obraje owner, Jácome Passalli, as a sadistic heretic. They accused this owner, a personal friend of Juan Bautista de Pomar's wife, of locking the sweatshop's eighty-one workers in to keep them from attending Mass and feast days; of making death threats and engaging in excessive violence; of misappropriating collective labor levies; of blaspheming; and of buying off priests and tribute judges in exchange for trouble-free reports to regional officials.[19]

Such corruption appears to have been an effective strategy, for Passalli weathered not only this complaint but many others, including a 1611 investigation into the murder of the commoner Miguel Juárez in his sweatshop. Indeed, both Passalli and his laborers understood Spanish colonial labor regimes as antithetical to compulsive communal hierarchies such as tlaxilacalli. The sweatshop petitioners mark both a spatial and a social division between Passalli's obraje and the altepetl of Tetzcoco despite their inter-penetrating spatial proximity. Similarly, on a later occasion Passalli sent thugs to threaten the gobernador of Huexotla to "avoid problems with Jácome" and force him to sign a document. Tlaxilacalli were Hispanizing along with the rest of central Acolhuacan, but they changed in very particular ways: by the early seventeenth century, local hierarchies had grown to pattern themselves into oppositional counterpoints to Spaniards and their official regional administration.[20]

This dialectical patterning looked different at different levels. As Brian Owensby and others have shown, altepetl and their attached Hispanic institutions (such as cabildos) became increasingly skillful at negotiating concessions within the architecture of Spanish administration, mastering the arts of dialogue and bureaucratic wrangling.[21] At the level of the often-ignored tlaxilacalli, colonial adaptation took a different path, reinforcing a communitarian and often oppositional outlook, offering identities and political frameworks to increasingly marginalized rural macehualtin.

Tlaxilacalli therefore continued to assert their central place in commoners' lives across this period, vigorously defending their lands against foreign interlopers and negotiating various business deals (mostly rental arrangements) with other local actors. As traditional institutions such as the nobility buckled and transformed and new ones simultaneously showed themselves to be increasingly predatory, commoners labored ceaselessly to reinforce their unequal but increasingly communitarian tlaxilacalli. More than before, these institutions carried the brunt of local politics—proving themselves robust enough to even withstand the rending of their ties to specific landscapes and geoforms. Further, under increasing territorial duress, tlaxilacalli became surprisingly portable, retaining their hierarchical and collective ties even as they found themselves occasionally dislodged from traditional landscapes. Remarkably, this added flexibility often strengthened their local power and influence.

WARRING TLAXILACALLI

The most powerful displays of oppositional commoner politics during this period came from just outside Acolhuacan, 30 kilometers to the east, during the ferocious Mexico City uprising of 1624 in which "the plebe, with swords drawn" forced the viceroy Gelves to escape from his burning palace in the shabby clothes of his valet, himself calling for government overthrow. As Gibran Bautista y Lugo has shown, the shared experience of Hispanic mis-administration joined various, often conflicting commoner groups—market women, indigenous construction workers, Afro-Mexicans, students and poor clerics, Tetzcoca migrants, and local tlaxilacalli members, among many others—into an insurrectionary force of perhaps 30,000 that not only expelled Gelves but also hobbled the next ten viceroys in their attempts to restore centralizing power in New Spain.[22] Most striking for purposes here, however, was the organized participation of what witnesses called "neighborhood Yndians"—note once again the customary if imprecise usage—particularly from Mexico City's northern tlaxilacalli in Santiago Tlatelolco, in the rebellion. Here is the narration of the capital city's anti-Gelves cabildo of Spanish mercantile elites, which can stand for many examples of this genre: "Indians from the neighborhood of Santiago had come to inform, and it was said publicly that 4,000 or 5,000 Indians were armed and in the main plaza, this not counting others who could come from the other neighborhoods and those who could be organized outside the city."[23]

Santiago was not itself a tlaxilacalli but rather the long-suppressed northern altepetl of Tlatelolco, and the slippage of terms between various levels of local hierarchy is characteristic for Spanish documentation from the period. Nevertheless, other sources also mention workers who "were coming down from the highlands of Mexico with lances and daggers" together with "4,000 or 5,000 Indian archers from the outskirts" of the city, all heading for the viceregal complex in the center city. These large and organized detachments of archers appear to have been the most troublesome and fear-inducing for Spanish authorities—a fear caused much more by their comprehensive logistical operations than by their traditional but now inadequate weaponry.[24]

As in the later 1692 Mexico City uprising of almost comparable strength, the underlying organizational power of Tlatelolco's nineteen constituent tlaxilacalli proved fundamental to the overthrow of Viceroy Gelves. The large numbers of transitory rebels certainly played important roles in barring access to Spanish forces seeking to retake the city center; but, at least as far as the one-sided narrations of this battle permit, the main fight of this rebellion took place between well-armed but confused palace guards and outgunned but better-organized tlaxilacalli fighters in the main square. The palace guards eventually won, but not before long-lasting damage was done to Spanish administrative power in New Spain: arms mattered, but collective organization mattered more.[25]

Indeed, the weakness and confusion of the official administration in Mexico City during this time proved so embarrassing to the King of Spain that he officially forbade the 1624 sack of the viceregal palace to be called a "tumult, commotion, or uprising" and proclaimed rather that it should only be understood as a "jurisdictional dispute" between civil and religious authorities. Nahuatl annals described the episode differently. They called the episode war, *yaoyotl*. In many ways, this was a war that central Mexicans fought and won on their own terms. A later popular refrain about this period, collected in the mid-nineteenth century, perhaps reflects something of this feeling: "now we live in our own law, for the viceroy has fled"—"*Ahora vivimos en nuestra ley, que no hay virrey.*"[26]

ANCHORS OF POSESSION

The idea of a separate law, of a different localizing order, was not new in the seventeenth century; indeed, such a premise underlay tlaxilacalli regimes since at least the start of Acolhua imperial expansion. Nevertheless, the practice of local law and administration took on a new shading after the 1624 uprising and its aftermath, forcing even greater decentralization across many areas of activity. As has been shown elsewhere, the 1624 rebellion catalyzed a succession of administrative failures by centralizing Spanish administrators, culminating in the devastating five-year flood of Mexico City and its surrounding regions (including lakeside Acolhua altepetl such as Tetzcoco and Atenco) between 1629 and 1634. Local histories of this period are similarly evocative, with one Nahuatl-language source declaring that during this flood "the viceroy turned into a fish," while a Spanish-language one has the king's chief representative stating insultingly that "it doesn't take much water to drown a creole [a locally born Spaniard] . . . If the water had been atole [a widely consumed central Mexican drink], the creoles would have drunk themselves dry fast enough."[27]

More so than even the earlier capital-city rebellion, this catastrophic flood forced the Spanish administration into accommodating and sometimes even dependent relationships with local commoner populations, particularly in the water-carrying northeastern section of the Basin of Mexico, in and around Acolhuacan. Vera Candiani has shown how altepetl and tlaxilacalli around Huehuetoca, just northwest of Acolhua territory, effectively managed large sections of the principal drainage lines leading into Mexico City over centuries; and documents from the small Acolhua altepetl of Chiautla show ongoing use of the tlaxilacalli-based coatequitl tribute musters to provide the "Castilian topile" with labor in the decades after the 1629 flood.[28] The progressive decentralization of the central Mexican regional administration fortified both the altepetl and the tlaxilacalli—even as these two interrelated and inter-penetrating hierarchies themselves underwent profound change.

EXPANSIVE TLAXILACALLI

Not all changes were peaceful. As the seventeenth century deepened, both altepetl-based cabildos and their constituent tlaxilacalli became more self-assertive and obstreperous. Sometimes it was local desperation forcing breaks in traditional administration, but more often it was simply a story of vigorous institutions expanding outward to exploit available opportunities. The cases are multiple and often led by a tlaxilacalli: in 1679, for example, officials in Papalotla tlaxilacalli blocked the main watercourse into the urban core of Tetzcoco, choking the center for their own monetary needs.[29] Sometimes these actions were unofficial and even illegal, such as cattle rustling and butchering in the tlaxilacalli of San Mateo, Huexotla, and Santísima Trinindad, Atenco.[30] Tlaxilacalli administration also continued to both compel participation, as in the case of some officials in Tetzcoco who took hostages to muster tribute payments in 1688,[31] and to mediate community business, as when officials of the community of Tepetitlan mediated the aftermath of a drunken brawl, provoking the conflicting parties to pull their case out of Hispanic courts and settle matters themselves. The claimants praised this intervention, declaring that "both our injuries and our friendships are healed through the mediation of some great people."[32] Local justice provoked unique actions and attitudes, behaviors centralizing forces were unable or unwilling to evoke.

Indeed, even as they coordinated their actions through the cabildo and other institutions, tlaxilacalli, as often as not, now acted as polities unto themselves. Scholars of central Mexican regions have noted the ways legal emancipations of "subject towns"—growing out of, and still often defined as, rural tlaxilacalli—served both to fracture wider altepetl-based politics and to produce new patterns of Hispanic-oriented political patronage. Most studies concentrate on the eighteenth century, and Bernardo García Martínez estimates that a large majority of the more than 1,000 legally defined pueblos present in central Mexico at the end of the Hispanic period had been created only a few decades earlier by breakaway commoner groups. This eighteenth-century process appears to have begun early in Acolhuacan, so in 1707, for instance, the robust Tetzcoca tlaxilacalli of Tlailotlacan blithely referred to itself as an "altepetl." Independence-minded tlaxilacalli were clearly on the rise.[33]

Even more striking are a series of interconnected wills and titles from the tlaxilacalli of San Gabriel Tlailotlacan, in the altepetl of Huexotla. The first document, written in 1632, provides a full accounting of an extended local hierarchy: "My name is Francisco Pérez. I am a resident (*nichane*) here in (the altepemaitl of) San Lorenzo Acxotlan. My tlaxilacalli is (San Gabriel) Tlailotlacan. My altepetl is San Luis Huexotla." In this will, despite the robust presence of tlaxilacalli throughout, the altepetl still received special reverence, for the testator requested to be buried "at the feet of my beloved father San Luis Obispo," patron saint of Huexotla. Forty years later, Francisco Pérez's son, Juan Diego, wrote his own will, also mentioning the broader hierarchies of altepemaitl (where he located his lands), tlaxilacalli (where he claimed residence: "my calpolli of San Gabriel"), and altepetl (whose saint he also specifically reverenced). So far, the documents lined up as expected.[34]

Then things become interesting: the next document in the Huexotla papers records an apocryphal land title, likely from the late seventeenth century but dating itself to Christmas Day, 1531, which it wrongly correlates to the mangled Mesoamerican year "Rabbit," given without the customary number prefix. (Although, interestingly, December 25, 1531, did fall within the thirteen-day trecena of 1 Rabbit). This title largely consisted of a spatial reckoning of tlaxilacalli lands, distributed and confirmed by the "tlatoani regidor of the cabildo palace." Some lands belonged to Francisco Pérez, the self-same individual as the testator above, who hierarchically locates himself in a manner reminiscent of his 1632 will: resident (chane) of the altepemaitl of San Lorenzo Acxotlan, tlaxilacalli of Tlailotlacan, altepetl of Huexotla. Other notables in the same document, however, were more assertive in their affiliations, promoting San Lorenzo Acxotlan to the status of "our calpolli," although they were also still interested in making sure that these land titles "please the altepetl of San Luis Obispo Huexotla."[35]

The final document of this sequence, a letter written (or recopied) in the same hand as the transcription of the apocryphal land title, completes this transformation, describing the onetime tlaxilacalli of San Gregorio Tlailotlacan as an "altepetl" while describing San Luis Huexotla as "our home" (*tochantzinco*). All this presents a question: when this final author, a certain Antonio Martínez, referenced the speech of "the altepetl's residents" (*altepehuaque*), was he talking about the people in the striving onetime tlaxilacalli of San Gregorio Tlailotlacan or about everyone in the traditionally inferred San Luis Huexotla? Contextual clues—references to landholding and its regulation, close-in reports of damaging local gossip—seem to suggest the latter. If true, Tlailotlacan now considered itself independent, even if it still required administrative confirmation from Huexotla in certain circumstances.[36]

REWRITING HISPANIC ADMINISTRATION

The seventeenth-century map underlying the apocryphal land titles of the Huexotla collection—called, somewhat extravagantly, the Códice de los Señores de San Lorenzo Axotlan y San Luis Huexotla—places disconnected slivers of individual landholding into the broad spatial array of the "tlaxilacalli" of San Lorenzo Acxotlan within the "altepetl" of Tlailotlacan. The codex flaunts the newfound autonomy of these local hierarchies with all the symbols of administrative independence: a name glyph, a council chamber, and a church bell. In this graphic landscape, a figure who earlier might have been a subordinate alcalde or juez is now a sovereign juez gobernador, complete with a crown and a thick archive full of administrative ledgers. Four lower-level administrators, once perhaps tepixque, now give orders as tlaxilacalli-level "tlatoque," seated on the small boxlike throne of delegated authority and striking the traditional pose for rulerly speech as they face each other. Administratively and graphically, this onetime sub-district (altepemaitl) declared its autonomy from the traditional hierarchies of Huexotla, hitching its fortunes to the newly assertive "altepetl" of Tlailotlacan. Autonomy was now more local than ever.[37]

On a deeper level, however, much less seems to have changed. Indeed, the greater autonomy of former tlaxilacalli often retrenched and even deepened many of the most characteristic patterns of local politics over the 300-year cycle of Acolhua colonialism. Area administrators, be they imperial calpixque managing their subordinate tlaxilacalli or a latter-day juez gobernador guiding a largely autonomous micro-polity, still trafficked in the key exchange of land for labor, as the Codex Axotlan explicitly states in its entry for Gabriel Álvarez: "they gave us the land so that we can work it." Another individual, Juan de Santa María, "of the calpolli of Santa María Cuixtenco, in Tepozcaltitlan," also took advantage of a place in Acxotlan to store a local church bell. Compulsion—laced always with cooperation—remained a core organizing principle.[38]

So, too, did kinship, as both an intensive and an extensive institution. Gabriel Álvarez worked his lands next door to his relatives (his brothers?) Marcos and Gaspar. All three are connected in the codex by a black line of relation, which also tied them

FIGURE 6.3. Connected landholding, perhaps in two commoner tlacamecayotl. Codex Axotlan. *Courtesy*, Instituto Nacional de Antropología e Historia, Mexico City.

to an unnamed pitched-roof house that could represent either a collective household holding or a low-level tribute boss (figure 6.3). The Álvarez household lived next door to Pedro de San Juan, who appears to have had similar kin relations, although some core information is hidden by the Codex Axotlan's poor conservation.

Kinship also operated intensively in the struggles of one generation to pass its advantages on to the next. This is most strikingly shown in the holdings of Francisco Pérez and his grandson Agustín (figure 6.4). In the codex, Pérez continues to work one field at bottom center but indicates that he "has shown" his grandson how it is to be worked. In addition, Agustín Pérez had begun to work a second field on the road to Tetzcoco. This field is particularly noteworthy because its ownership can be traced through four exchanges of the Pérez inheritance, beginning with Francisco's sister-in-law, Francisca Juana, then passing to Francisco himself after he purchased the land, then to his son, Juan Diego, and daughter-in-law, María Francisca. Juan Diego and María Francisca seem to have then lost this field—perhaps Francisco changed his will to favor his grandson Agustín, or perhaps some other circumstance

FIGURE 6.4. Landholding across generations. Codex Axotlan. *Courtesy*, Instituto Nacional de Antropología e Historia, Mexico City.

alienated the couple from this plot. Regardless, kin arrangements and their ongoing permutations were anchored in land and labor, which continued to flow through local hierarchies even as these hierarchies changed administrative status within wider regional frameworks.[39]

Spatial frameworks also retained their relevance as centralizing politics fractured. In the Codex Axotlan, Agustín Pérez delineated his lands in almost exactly the same as had his grandfather Francisco: a sliver of the altepemaitl Tetzcacohuac toward the east along a barranca, individual lands at the west, Xochicaltenco to the north, the church of San Lorenzo Acxotlan toward the south. Territorial divisions were even more pronounced in the entry for Acxotlan's juez gobernador, who delineated the boundaries of all the lands of his "tlaxilacalli," beginning in the east and in all likelihood moving in the customary counterclockwise direction, which would give this orientation: Quauhxacalencan to the east until the barranca of Tetzcacohuan, Xochicaltenco to the north, then San Marcos Puchtlan and Xochpan to the west, inter-penetrating with San Pedro Coatepanco to the south. Despite the various administrative promotions and emancipations in this region, the cited territorial divisions were minuscule—locally important but almost invisible to central administration.[40]

The Códice de los Señores de San Lorenzo Axotlan y San Luis Huexotla is remarkable in its inter-penetrating detail, providing a total (if now slightly deteriorated) picture of a small but aspirational new-style "tlaxilacalli." Nevertheless, this document did not produce its desired outcome, either juridically or historically. Acxotlan was unable to secure firm title to its lands despite robust documentary production; and the codex has usually joined the scholarly genre of primordial titles, those hopeful post facto attempts to create adequate local histories in the absence of earlier documentary evidence.[41] There is another way to view this codex from the year "Rabbit" or "1531," however. As tlaxilacalli such as Acxotlan became more and more independent, they required new local histories corresponding to their ambitious moves toward

FIGURE 6.5. Repurposing documents. Codex Axotlan. *Courtesy*, Instituto Nacional de Antropología e Historia, Mexico City.

altepetl status. A modular history of the constituent parts of this polity—here counting individuals instead of tlaxilacalli but retaining the semiautonomous and segmentary nature of earlier annals—fit the needs of this genre almost perfectly.[42]

Still more illustrative is the way the Codex Axotlan was produced: small cracks in the document show the multiple layers of paper used to make the thick stock used for this spatial history—including printed Spanish documents (figure 6.5). Considering the restricted availability of both movable type and licenses to print, it seems clear that the creators of this document reused expired or ignored official decrees for more pressing local ends. The aspirational history of this tlaxilacalli was literally written on the back of the officious Spanish administration.

TLAXILACALLI USURPATIONS

Tlatoani privelege did not completely disappear; and despite their reduced power, late tlatoque continued to claim special tributes and prerogatives. Mid-century cabildos and their ruling "tlatoque" occasionally bristled at these demands from the traditional elite, but rarely did they show their disrespect with such vigor as in the altepetl of Atenco in 1669. In this year, the cabildo of Atenco and its individual members sent a series of forceful and pungent letters to the putative tlatoani of the altepetl, don Domingo de Haro Bravo San Román Ixtlilxochitl. The first cabildo letters begin in February by alerting the tlatoani that "the commoners are suffering" with hard tribute levies during an ongoing cocoliztli epidemic and reminding him of "his beloved responsibility" to care for them. Haro seemingly ignored these appeals because the next letter, written by don Diego Francisco, the juez alcalde of the deeply rooted tlaxilacalli of Tlailotlacan, describes the "lying words" of outside tribute collectors who showed up on three consecutive days to demand payments and eventually steal the produce set aside for "our lord"—likely the local patron saint. For don Diego Francisco, local reverences superceded customary submission.[43]

Haro reacted against these rebellious actions and had don Diego Francisco jailed within two weeks of receiving his letter. The tlatoani would not be denied his expected due, regardless of other tlaxilacalli commitments. In a subsequent letter sent from jail, don Diego Francisco relented to Haro's demands, offering to kiss the tlatoani's hands and personally deliver the tributes were it not for the ongoing sicknesses and pain he was experiencing. He then confessed that "I still haven't collected from the natives that which they still owe: the natives and the alcaldes and officials who went along with me. They still have to fulfill their debts, since the natives still owe you. If they had been collected, we wouldn't be in the situation we now find ourselves."[44] Despite don Diego Francisco's assurances, it is clear that Tlailotlacan had priorities beyond the tlatoani's tribute—especially during a time of disease and famine.

A closer illustration of the vast distances separating vestigial nobles such as Haro and the local tlaxilacalli-based administration comes in the envelope carrying don Diego Francisco's second letter to Haro, which lists the far-detached tlatoani's home residence as Mexico City, 30 kilometers away across a shrinking lake. Further, the envelope also shows Francisco scrambling to belatedly muster the tlatoani's tribute, together with a schematic map (likely of a section of Tlailotlacan) on the far left and a series of payment calculations on the far right (see figure 6.6). Later, in a final letter where he assumes the title "juez pasado," Francisco shifted the blame for tribute delays to two other tlaxilacalli, Purificación Tenochco and Xalapango, even as he accused Haro of "tyrannizing" him, stealing payments, and sending spies to make it "impossible for us to go anywhere." It is clear that this tlaxilacalli official knew where and how to muster the demanded tribute; he was just reluctant to do so.[45]

Other local officials were also jailed by Haro. A separate letter, likely written only a few days later by Tlailotlacan's pugnacious alcalde, don Diego Francisco, includes the names of seven "currently serving" alcaldes also pleading to be freed from prison to return to their work of fulfilling their tribute responsibilities. "If we are allowed," they declare, "we will leave to go around mustering up what remains of the macehualtin's tribute . . . each one in his own calpolli." Despite these offers of collaboration, however, Haro appears to have disengaged even further from the local administration as epidemiological and nutritional crises deepened. Later letters by these same seven alcaldes are ignored by Haro: "many times we sent a messenger to your home in Tetzcoco, and nobody answered." They then scheduled a meeting with Haro in the tlaxilacalli of Alpanocan, but the tlatoani never showed up. Soon thereafter, the alcaldes once again jointly expressed their disappointment to Haro: "You should know, oh tlatoani, that when we came upon your esteemed words [promising] that you would bring yourself, that you would come to us here in beloved Alpanocan, your dear children were [left] waiting for you. And now when you say you will come, we will no longer believe you. Please be true to us, oh tlatoani."[46]

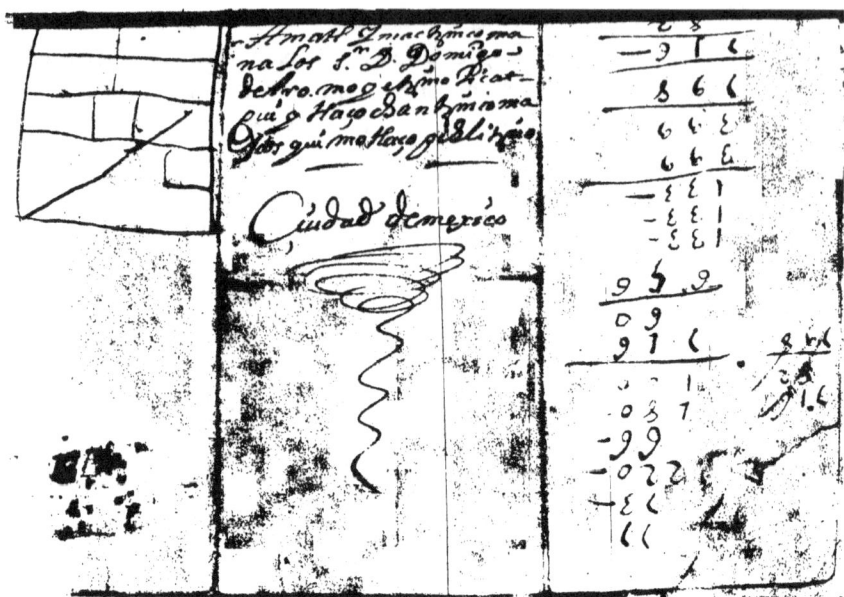

FIGURE 6.6. Back-of-the-envelope tribute estimates, containing a map and calculations. Tlailotlacan tlaxilacalli, Texcoco, 1669. *Courtesy,* Archivo General de la Nación, Mexico City.

Tensions continued to mount between tlaxilacalli officials and Hispanizing administrators, so much so that this war of words soon escalated into aggressive physical acts. Specifically, the commoners of Atenco—led by at least two of the tlaxilacalli officials writing above, Sebastián de la Cruz and Gaspar Antonio—invaded the lands claimed by Haro and also appropriated the legal titles attached to these fields. Remarkably, they appear to have held this claim for at least thirteen years, until 1683, when Haro began what would be a twenty-year lawsuit. By the time land title was reclaimed by his heir, Haro the tlatoani had died. The cabildo and its alcaldes, meanwhile, continued to robustly defend their interests, even copying some of Haro's tactics, such as imprisoning intermediaries to force the compliance of their associates and relatives.[47]

A final striking example of the rising power of tlaxilacalli and their increasingly combative nature comes in the famous Mexico City insurrection of 1692. Here, as Natalia Silva Prada has extensively shown, various centers of revolt quickly and diffusely joined the mounting June 8 rebellion: drinking houses (*pulquerías*), sweat baths (*temazcaltin*), artisanal guilds (ruff makers, cobblers, construction workers), kinship bundles (tlacamecayotl of the nobles of Tlatelolco), and tlaxilacalli officials (*fiscales y principales* in the communities of Santa Cruz and San Sebastian), among other institutions. These links reached across altepetl boundaries, with a particularly strong conspiratorial node between tlaxilacalli in Tetzcoco and others in the northern and eastern sections of Mexico City, Santiago Tlatelolco and Zoquiapan.[48]

Many points of insurrection built toward the burning of the viceregal palace in June 1692, but two such intertwining conspiracies can illustrate the thick commoner networks threading across tlaxilacalli. These communities were far from the only institutions supporting such conspiracies, but it is hard to imagine the diffuse and interlinked planning of insurrection without their root-level functioning. In one case, Felipe de la Cruz (nickname "El Ratón") from the tlaxilacalli of Tomatlan[49] confessed to having conspired with other shoemakers to "burn the palace." This planning occurred over months in pulquerías around the tlaxilacalli of Trinidad,[50] where he now resided. Both tlaxilacalli were on the eastern edge of Mexico City, providing easy water access to Tetzcoco.[51]

In those pulquerías, "El Ratón" also stated that he had heard porters from the neighboring tlaxilacalli of Santa Cruz and San Pablo likewise planning insurrection. Among this second group of insurrectionists were two Tetzcoca brothers who were likely using the home of a relative in that neighboring altepetl as a safehouse. This relative, an alcalde in Tetzcoco named either Salvador or Sebastián de la Cruz, also had lodgings in Tomatlan, the home tlaxilacalli of "El Ratón," where Spanish silver stolen during the insurrection was later recovered. Another habitation of that same Tetzcoca alcalde in the tlaxilacalli of Santa Cruz housed stolen clothing.[52]

These two lines of attack—one by shoemakers in Trinidad, the other by porters in Santa Cruz with the help of a Tetzcoca official—converged on June 8, when they joined many other organized groups to assault the viceregal palace and its environs. As Silva Prada has shown, this uprising was far from spontaneous. Local officials, including gobernadores from Santiago Tlatelolco and San Juan Tenochtitlan, exercised important leadership roles; and certain northern and eastern tlaxilacalli (such as Tomatlan and Santa Cruz) played outsized roles in the uprising.[53] Tlaxilacalli did not plan this coordinated attack on viceregal power, but they did channel and catalyze the insurrection.

REGIONAL NETWORKS, LOCAL CELEBRATIONS

In both informal conspiracies and official celebrations, the interactions among increasingly autonomous Acolhua tlaxilacalli retained a remarkable level of coordination, even as their relationships to both the Spanish administration and local elites shifted. This dance of autonomy and interdependence among current and former (i.e., nouveau "altepetl") tlaxilacalli is particularly evident in the robust fiesta circuit of mid- and late-century Acolhuacan, whereby each local hierarchy celebrated its own distinct feast days and also invited a wide swathe of neighboring polities to join in the celebrations. For large feast cycles such as Holy Week and Corpus Christi, tlaxilacalli pooled their resources for more centralized celebrations while also maintaining local celebrations.

Holy Week consisted of a series of sequential fiestas, celebrated collectively by people from across Tetzcoco's wider hinterland and sponsored jointly by Tetzcoco's cabildo, an unnamed "Yndian" cofradía (described only as "la Hermandad de los Yndios" in the documentation) and the Hispanizing Archcofradía of the Holy Sacrament. Corpus Christi was different: logbooks from the Franciscan convent in Tetzcoco show sixteen separate communities celebrating individual fiestas of the Holy Sacrament immediately following the large collective celebration of Corpus, which also required broad participation across the tlaxilacalli. If Holy Week represented a high tide of centralizing local coordination, Corpus saw this joint energy flow back out into the separate tlaxilacalli of Tetzcoco's raucous hinterland.[54]

Indeed, there seem to have been many more festivities in the backlands than in the altepetl regional center. For the thirty-two separate fiestas recorded for the close-in tlaxilacalli of Tetzcoco in the late seventeenth century, there were fifty-eight "in the bush" (*en el monte*), farther away still from the Franciscans and their convent. Further, despite the important concurrent fiestas of Corpus Christi and the Holy Sacrament, the Birth of the Virgin, and the feast day of St. James (patron of the Spanish empire), there were still thirty separate celebrations in the countryside compared with twenty-one for Tetzcoco proper. (All told, Fransciscans in the Tetzcoco region, center and bush, officiated forty-one separate feast days.) Most of these unique fiestas celebrated the feast day of one or another of the twenty-seven tlaxilacalli listed in the Franciscan legers. These were not just outside impositions or formalities: communities collected and paid for their fiestas. The basic Franciscan rate seems to have been 23 pesos in total to cover wine, bread, chickens, and fruit. Embellishments such as sung Masses and processions following the stations of the cross were extra. Figure 6.7 illustrates, the tlaxilacalli-based Tetzcoco fiesta circuit around 1660.[55]

Franciscans surely saw these festivities as anchoring Christian belief across their ecclesiastical jurisdiction, but these celebrations also evoked a broad and pulsating network of inter-tlaxilacalli sociability.[56] Commoners often celebrated marriages during these events (which the Franciscans grudgingly officiated); but the wider meanings were celebration, community, and "custom"—*costumbre*, the active remaking of tradition through vigorous action. A later vignette from Tetzcoco illustrates much of this activity: as costumbre dictated, during the fiesta of this altepetl's patron saint, a local couple from the tlaxilacalli of La Resurreción went out to observe the *bailadores*, or formal dancers, from the various local communities. They partied, celebrating the briefly joined diversity of the arrayed local tlaxilacalli,

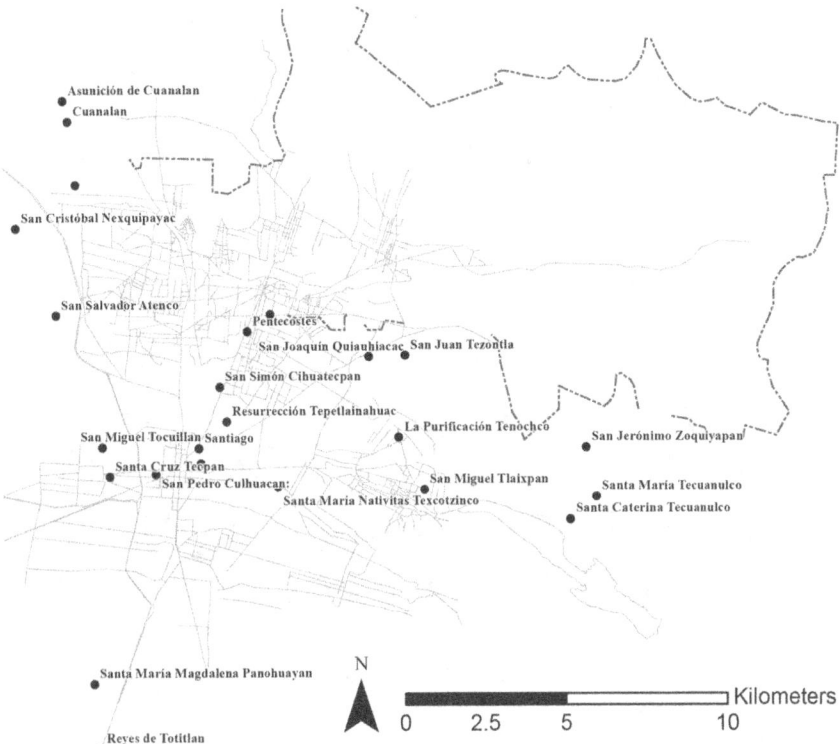

FIGURE 6.7. The tlaxilacalli-based Texcoco party circuit. Note the fiesta-less gaps in the map, which correspond to other altepetl: Chiautla and Tepetlaoztoc to the north, Huexotla to the south. Lake Texcoco bordered on the west. Map by Bill and Kris Keegan.

and then on their return, "halfway on the road back to our neighborhood"—notice once again the penetration of Spanish concepts by this later stage—"we saw my precious mother, doña Antonia Gertrudis, already drunk and lost. When we arrived at our house, my wife and I, we asked around for her and found out that she had left with the dancers around nine at night."[57]

Not only had doña Antonia gone out drinking and dancing without notifying her son and daughter-in-law (with whom she presumably lived), she had a ready group of bailadores to join her in separate festivities. As a whole, therefore, this festive mother stood at the intersection of a number of often contradictory webs of association, including present and extended kin relations, housemates and neighbors, drinking buddies, and competing tlaxilacalli dance groups—in addition to all the other connections of tribute, labor, marketing, churchgoing, and sociability that clung to nearly every rural Acolhua during this period.

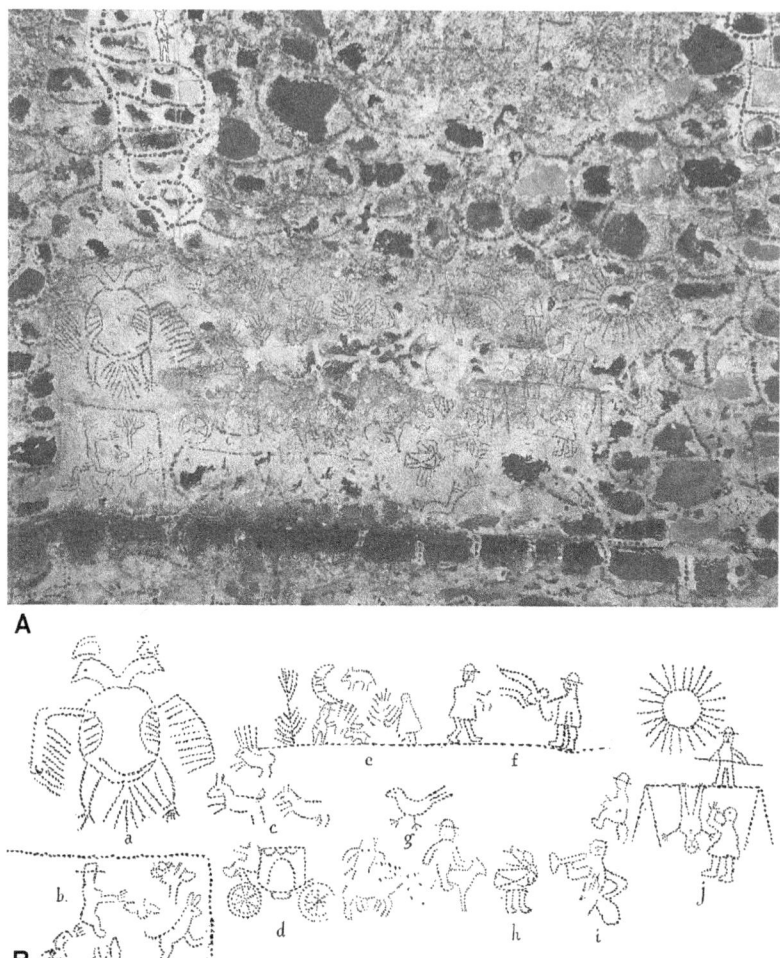

FIGURE 6.8. Church graffiti, San Sebastián Xolalpan. *A*: a current photo; *B*: a drawing from the 1920s: Gamio, ed., *La población del valle de Teotihuacán*, 2:645.

Finally, consider the parties of the tlaxilacalli of San Sebastián Xolalpan, Teotihuacan, as they were etched into the walls of its church around this same time (figure 6.8). Among a veritable plethora of images—including everything from the Habsburg royal crest to a late-night rendezvous between a man and a woman to a chicken running across a field—a wider scene of action and festivity unfolds. An important official arrives in town to celebrate a fiesta, parading down the road by coach. Drummers drum and trumpeters play as the sun shines down brightly.

Someone dances, someone else walks a balance beam, and a third man hangs festively upside down. As the fancy coach approaches drawn by two horses, a local woman raises her thumb to her nose and wiggles her fingers in disrespect, perhaps giving an accompanying jeer for good measure. Here, finally and vulgarly, the interface of centralizing power and local response comes to life as the recently arrived administrator's coach ambles through a scene that was built before he arrived and will continue after he leaves. Meanwhile, tlaxilacalli, and the occasionally impertinent women and men who built them, were there to stay.[58]

NOTES

1. "muchos yndios prinçipales y naturales della que estaban juntos y congregados para oir missa en el patio y sementerio del monasterio del Senor San [F]ranCo." AGNM-T, caja 1, leg. 9, f. 24v.

2. "juntamente con los demas de dho varrio." AGNM-T, caja 1, leg. 9, ff. 68r–69r. On graveyards, see Claudio Lomnitz, *Death and the Idea of Mexico* (New York: Zone Books, 2005).

3. "governador, alcaldes, principales del dho pueblo y sotros muchos yndios y yndias congreagados en la yglesia del pueblo despues de missa." AGNM-T, caja 1, leg. 9, 23v.

4. "los naturales de san min san gabriel san geriono y estos de sus congregacion dexaron al tempho della algunas tierras y maguayles en sus puestos antiguos ... que se junta los sabados de vespera de salude y fiesta solemnda de nuestra senora y otros dias senalados de para deçir o aser deçir las missa universales y para los entierros de los hnos donde se gasta muncho." AGNM-T, caja 1, leg. 9, f. 3r, 40r. Literature on cofradías is comparatively diffuse. A good place to start is Alicia Bazarte Martínez and Clara Garcia Ayluardo, *Los costos de la salvación: Las cofradías y la Ciudad de México, siglos XVI al XIX* (Mexico City: CIDE, 2001).

5. "las dhas tierras passadas la yglesia de san martin en la puerta de la sierra de san martin arriba yendo asia el monte a mano yzquierda esta una arboleda y unas casas que parecen ser de la comunidad del pueblo." AGNM-T, caja 1, leg. 9, f. 27v.

6. "el gobernador alcaldees rregidores por si y por todos los hernos que en ella estan y por todo el pueblo y comund que en ella se ban [uniendo?]." AGNM-T, caja 1, leg. 9, f. 39v. For other cofradía responsibilities see, among other pages, AGNM-T, caja 1, leg. 9, ff. 5r, 20r, 26r.

7. On the unlikeliness of hiring a priestly religious specialist for all doings, recall that much was spent, "se gasta muncho," at cofradía functions. AGNM-T, caja 1, leg. 9, f. 3r, 40r.

8. "los naturales son pobres y no tienen para poder continuar limosnas y sustentar la cofradía." AGNM-T, caja 1, leg. 9, ff. 3r, 40r. On cofradías as sites of financial concentration, see two chapters in María del Pilar Martínez López-Cano, Gisela von Wobeser, and Juan Guillermo Muñoz Correa, eds., *Cofradías, capellanías y obras pías en la América Colonial* (Mexico City: UNAM, 1998): Asunción Lavrin, "Cofradías novohispanas: Economía

material y spiritual," 49–64, and Alicia Bazarte Martínez, "Las limosnas de las cofradías: su administración y destino," 65–74.

9. In contemporary usage, "neighborhood" has become the customary term used to refer to the modern descendants of tlaxilacalli communities.

10. For a fuller discussion of current church niches, see Rivera Pérez, "Acolhuacán septentrional," 87–89.

11. "sean entereados de todas las Tierras y haciendas que en sus poblaciones antiguas gosaran y tenían antes de mandarse de ellas y que si algunas personas de cualquiera calidad o condición que sean, se les han en las dichas Tierras y haciendas hora sea Violentemente hona por merced particular de los Virreyes de estos reynos luego que lo tal se verificare, sean despojados de las dichas tierras y haciendas y en ellas se entere a los Yndios para que las posean y tengan como las tenian." AHMTEX, Notaría, FS2.

12. "Canican. otichancatca. sant Esteuā. metepec. auh y nihquac. otecalihquaniloc. ynitencopatzinco. totlahtocauh. Rey . . . . auh yntlalli yn tixcoyan ynoticchihua ya ynōcan. sant Esteuā metepec. oticcauhque . . . ynoticteneuhque. totlal. ypampa. canelaocmo hueltic chi huazq." BNAH-3PS, leg. 7, exp. 2–42, f. 25r; "yc tech mopalehui lia çen ca miyac tlamantli yca coco liz tli yhuanto tlayyohuilizypan yhuan tomin y cotech mopa lehuili . . . auh atle onpouh qui ypan pa oc hualca yntic topialilia yto tlaçotlaliztzin." BNAH-3PS, leg. 3, exp. 1–20.

On congreación more generally, see Federico Fernández Christlieb and Pedro Sergio Urquijo Torres, "Los espacios del pueblo de indios tras el proceso de Congregación, 1550–1625," *Investigaciones geográficas* 60 (2006): 145–58.

13. The 1607 loss was to Juan Games de Chavarría. AGN, Tierras, vol. 2739, exp. 1.

14. AGNM-T, caja 1, leg. 9, ff. 1r–4r.

15. AHMTEX, Notaría, FS2. On San Jeronimo, see AGNM-T, caja 1, leg. 9.

16. AGNM-T, caja 1, leg. 9, ff. 12r–v.

17. "balthasar de urtega telpochtli ychan castilla ynitlaxilacal de la villa." BNAH, Archivo Teotihuacán, Matrimonios, lib. 1, 1605–25, f. 28r.

18. Ixtlilxochitl, *Obras* (1952), 2:38.

19. Here is a rather extensive Nahuatl recitation of Passalli's alleged crimes: "Ycan tzauhcan nican . . . Otlica oquizaincilu altepehuaque . . . toteyeahuan topilhuan maquimamachilti . . . Canitlatohuan yn nehuatl Diego Xacome ynaquin amoyciuhca tequitiz nimin Miquiz quimictizuque ynnocalpixcahuan yn manel xiquilliuca Rey tleyn nechi huiliz çantomin: micmacaz Cayc notlacatl . . . Auh yniquac tlacamo yciuhca tlani nima quinmecahuitqui yn Señora yninamic xacome. Auh yncteci Cihuatztzintin atley yn tlaxtlahui . . . Oquinilhui ynix Quichtin nican nochan tequiti yndios yhuan ynin Namichhuan mochintin xiquinhuitequcan . . . Yn ixquichtin nican nochan tequiti yndios yhuan ynin namichuan mochintin xiquinhuitequican . . . Oquinmilhui namechnahuatia yn itlilticahua cquintin. I quimilhuui namechnahuatia yninteccopa yn indios yn ica tequiti chicahua . . . xicmictica xoquinpopoztequilican ymoniniuil yntla . . . yey tlacatl yn indios . . . Ynican Ynipan

Altepetl San Anthonio Tetzcoco ... ynmanelye Ce semana monenei yn ipan Altepetl ... ynican ychan tazuhcan nican ... oquizaincili altepehuaque ... que llevasse el diablo las fiestas y los domingos que le quitauan toda la ganancia ... en los demas dias proque en las dhas fiestas los Yndios comian y no trabajauan." AGN, Inquisición, vol. 301, exp. 19, ff. 1r–4v.

20. "le dijo que no tuviera problemas con Jácome Passalli y que Hernando Ortiz le dio un papel a firmar." AGNM-T, caja 4, leg. 3, ff. 145v–146v. The murder accusation is in AGN, Tierras, vol. 2948, exp. 115.

21. Cf. Owensby, *Empire of Law*. See also Haskett, *Indigenous Rulers*.

22. Gibran I.I. Bautista y Lugo, "Los indios y la rebellion de 1624 en la Ciudad de México," in *Los indios y las ciudades de Nueva España*, ed. Felipe Castro Gutiérrez (Mexico City: UNAM, 2013), 197–216.

23. "los indios del barrio de Santiago habían venido á avisar, y se decía públicamente, estaban armados más de cuatro o cinco mil indios, sin los que podían venir de los demás barrios, y estaban en la plaza, y los que se les agregaran de fuera de la ciudad." "Carta de la Ciudad de México, en que se hace relación a S.M. del suceso del tumulto del 15 de enero de 1624," in *Documentos relativos al tumulto de 1624*, ed. Mariano Fernández de Echeverría y Veytia (Mexico City: Imprenta de F. Escalante y Cía, 1855), vol. 2, doc. 21.

24. "corria voz echadiza que bajaban los labradores de los altos de México con lanza y adarga, y que venían cuatro o cinco mil indios flecheros de los contornos, al allanamiento de las casas reales." Juan Gutiérrez Flores and Juan de Lormendi, "Relación sumaria y puntual del tumulto y sedición que hubo en México," in Echeverría y Veytia, vol. 1, doc. 2.

25. The various tlaxilacalli of Tlatelolco were, in alphabetical order by their Nahautl names: Acozac, Apohuacan, Atenantitech, Atenantitlan, Azococolocan, Aztecapan, Calpotitlan, Cohuatlan, Hueypantonco, Iztatlan, Mecamalinco, Nonoalco, Tecpolcaltitlan, Teocaltitlan, Tepiton, Tlatelolco, Tlaxoxiuhco, Tolquechiuhca, and Xolalpan.

26. "En 25 de diziembre 1627 años dia de pasqua de navidad sabado entre las quarto y cinco de la tarde se publico la Real Cedula de su magestad en que ordena y manda no se de nombre de tumulto conmocion o alçamiento lo sucedido de 15 de henero de 1624 años sino que se entienda fue competencia de juridizion entre justicia secular y eclesiastica." Constantino Medina Lima, ed. and trans., *Libro de los guardianes y gobernadores de Cuauhtinchan (1519–1640)* (Mexico City: CIESAS, 1995), 118; "1624 Nican ypa xihuitl yn oquichihuilique yaoyotl biRey gelbes yhuan quitlatiliq palasio." Camilla Townsend, ed. and trans., *Here in This Year: Seventeenth-Century Nahuatl Annals of the Tlaxcala-Puebla Valley* (Stanford: Stanford University Press, 2010), 90. Refrain quoted in Vicente Riva Palacio, ed., *México a través de los siglos* (Mexico City: Ballescá y compañía, 1888–89), 2:581.

27. "Rey MiChin moCuep," in Townsend, *Here in This Year*, 176. The Gelves quote comes from Louisa Hoberman, "Bureaucracy and Disaster: Mexico City and the Flood of 1629," *Journal of Latin American Studies* 6, no. 2 (November 1974): 220. The citation given by the

author is Archivo General de Indias, Mexico, 3. For a compelling overall study of flooding and drainage in New Spain, see Candiani, *Dreaming of Dry Land*.

28. Candiani, *Dreaming of Dry Land*. "v yhua oticpopoloque yniquac oytlacauh Cohuatequitl huehuetoCa otechanaCo Castilteca topile otictlaxtla huique ome peSo—2 pos." "1638 Anos . . ." DNT, doc. 30.

29. AHMTEX, Justicia, Gobierno Administrativo, Real Cédula de Parte, 29 octubre 1679.

30. AHMTEX, Justicia, Robo de Ganado, 6 julio 1693.

31. AGNM-T, caja 4, leg. 1, f. 89.

32. "estamos buenos de las eridas y amistades mediate algunas personas de buen selo." AHMTEX, Justicia, Crimen, Eridas, 21 septiembre 1688. Hostage taking: AHMTEX, Justicia, Averiguación, 7 mayo 1688.

33. "yn paniAltepetl Sta M^a tlaylotlaca." DNT, doc. 34. García Martínez, "Pueblos de indios, pueblos de castas," 107; also Stephen M. Perkins, "'Macchuales' and the Corporate Solution: Colonial Secessions in Nahua Central Mexico," *Mexican Studies/Estudios Mexicanos* 21, no. 2 (2005): 277–306; Danièle Dehouve, "The 'Secession' of Villages in the Jurisdiction of Tlapa (Eighteenth Century)," in *The Indian Community of Colonial Mexico: Fifteen Essays on Land Tenure, Corporate Organizations, Ideology, and Village Politics*, ed. Arij Ouweneel and Simon Miller (Amsterdam: CEDLA, 1990), 47–58.

34. "Yn nehuatl notoca Fran.co Peres nican nichane Sa Lorenço Acxotlan notlaxilacaliya tlaylotlacan auh in notltepeuh San Luis huexotla." "auh ca ycxitlantzinco ninotocaz ynotlaçomahuiztatzin San Luis Obipo . . . nocalpolpan San Gabriel." AGN, Tierras, vol. 1520, exp. 6, ff. 8v, 12r.

35. "yn tlatoan Regidor caytocatzin Don Fran^{co} Val . . . tocalpolpa Sn Lorenço Acxotlan yn altepetl Sn Luis Huexotla . . . yn tlatoani recidor cabildo de palacio . . . yn nehautl notoca Don franco peres nica nicane San lorenço acxotla tocalpolantlaylotlacan auh ynoaltepetzin San luis obispo huexotla . . . ypan xihuitl tochtli ypan mestli yn omochiuh a 25 de diciembre de 1531 años . . . Cayc pacti es yn nalteptl yn San luis obislpo huexotla." AGN, Tierras, vol. 1520, exp. 6, ff. 8v, 13r.

36. "quitohua yn altepehuaq . . . nica yn altepetl Sn grio tohantzinco San Luis huexlotlan." AGN, Tierras, vol. 1520, exp. 6, f. 14r.

37. The Codex Axotlan is available online at http://www.codices.inah.gob.mx/pc/contenido.php?id=43, accessed December 9, 2015.

38. "gabriel alVares ynic otechtlalmacaque yn tehuan ynic titotequipanolque . . . nocalpolpa Santa maria cuixtenco inic teposcaltitla." Codex Axotlan.

39. The earlier titles are in AGN, Tierras, vol. 1520, exp. 6, f. 8v.

40. Given the shape of the plots, there might be some slight error in correlating these boundary markers to the cardinal directions.

41. Cf. Haskett, *Visions of Paradise*. Also, for later texts, see Ethelia Ruiz Medrano, Claudio Barrera Gutiérrez, and Florencio Barrera Gutiérrez, *La lucha por la tierra: Los títulos primordiales y los pueblos indios en México, siglos XIX y XX* (Mexico City: FCE, 2013).

42. On primordial titles, see María de los Ángeles Romero Frizzi and Michel R. Oudijk, "Los títulos primordiales: Un género de tradición mesoamericana: Del mundo prehispánico al siglo XXI," *Relaciones: Estudios de Historia y Sociedad* 24, no. 95 (2003): 19–48; Margarita Menegus Bornemann, "Los títulos primordiales de los pueblos de indios," in *Dos décadas de investigación en historia económica comparada de América Latina: Homenaje a Carlos Sempat Assadourian*, ed. Margarita Menegus Bornemann (Mexico City: El Colegio de México, 1999), 137–61.

43. "motolinia yn cuitlapiltin atlapaltin . . . ymotlaçotequitzin . . . iztlacatlatolli . . . yn itlatquitzin N˜r S.r." AGN, Tierras, vol. 1740, exp. 1, f. 100r.

44. "Cuix moçhi onechmo[?] maçehualli caoquintechonoc y[?] yninoAldes hua yn otloc o nech[?] oncatqui yn tleyn ycmopale[hui?] caça yehuatl ynimach[?]alltzin[?] camochi quipia yntechonoc cay[?] moechich[?] çaonoytzq[ui?] ynaxcan . . . no e cobrado de los naturales que todavia deven assi naturales como alcaldes Y oficiales que anduvieron Conmigo que asta agora tienen de que balersse Como consta que los naturales lo deben todavia si se ubiera Cobrado no nos bieramos como nos vemos agora." AGN, Tierras, vol. 1740, exp. 1, f. 189r.

45. "[?]chmixnahelhuia . . . Auh ynaxcan casa huel teyxpipi[a] yn amo ca huel toyasque." AGN, Tierras, vol. 1740, exp. 1, f. 102r.

46. "yn axcan tlatequipanohua . . . yn cuix tihuelititzque ynic tiquiçazque ynipantitlatotihui yn oc çequi quipia maçehualli yn itlacalaquil . . . yn oc cequi [?]ma ypan tlatotin yn tlein calpolpan." AGN, Tierras, vol. 1740, exp. 1, ff. 120r–v; "auh ca ye [?]titi yn ottlatitlani ymochantzine tetzcuco ayaca tec[?]toquillа." AGN, Tierras, vol. 1740, exp. 1, f. 102v; "Auh maxicmomachiltzitzino tlahtohuanie ca yniquac ynoticaque ymotlaçotlatoltzin ynica tihualmohuicazquia ca otitechiaya yn onca ynipa Alpanoctzin, omitzmochialia ymopilhuatzitzin Auh yn axca yniqui tihualmohuicaz ma huel quali ticacquizque ymotlaçotaltoltzin yhuan ma xic[?]machiltzino tlahtohuanie." AGN, Tierras, vol. 1740, exp. 1, f. 100r.

47. AGN, Tierras, vol. 1740, exp. 1.

48. Silva Prada, *La política*, chapter 5, especially 364–410.

49. Tomatlan is called a tlaxilacalli in Chimalpan, *Annals of His Time*, 50: "ypan tlaxilacalli tomatlan."

50. Trinidad was a subdivision of the tlayacatl of Zoquiapan and therefore a tlaxilacalli. See Eugenia Acosta Sol, "El barrio de la Santísima Trinidad y su contexto urbano," *Boletín de Monumentos Históricos*, 3rd epoch, 24 (2012): 12–15.

51. Silva Prada, *La política*, 269–72, 397–98, 408–9.

52. Silva Prada, *La política*, 397–98, 408–9.

53. See in particular Cuadros 3, 4, 15–19, and 24 and Plano 3 in Silva Prada, *La política*.

54. AHDT, *Libro de la disposición de Este conu.to de San Ant.o de Texcoco* . . . *1664*, ff. 9r–10r.

55. AHDT, *Libro de la disposición de Este conu.to de San Ant.o de Texcoco* . . . *1664*, ff. 9r–10r.

56. Complex and interlocking celebrations are still a feature of the region. See Rivera Pérez, "Bandidos" 111–16, for both the various "localidades" of contemporary Tepetlaoxtoc de Hidalgo and the "municipios" of the wider region of Acolhuacan.

57. "ybamos para ñro barrio a la mitad del camino, vimos a mi madrecita doña antonia gertrudis ya ebria perdida yegamos a nra casa yo estando con mi muger cuando la buscamos a la dha mi madre ya se abia salido juntamente con los bayladores serca de las nuebe de la noche." AGN, Indiferente virreinal, caja. 4799, exp. 6, f. 1r.

58. Indigenous authorship is also suggested by Ignacio Marquina, the architectural analyst who describes the graffiti in *La población del valle de Teotihuacán*, tomo 1, 2:643–44. Marquina also notes that at least part of the graffiti can be dated to the later seventeenth century because of the presence of the Habsburg eagle among the motifs. On colonial graffiti more generally, see Russo, *Untranslatable*, chapter 6.

CONCLUSION

Tlaxilacalli and Barrio

On May 11, 1692, less than a month before the major Mexico City uprising that would again set the viceregal palace aflame, the residents of Cuauhtepoztlan—the tlaxilacalli in Tepetlaoztoc profiled in chapter 3—once more assayed the territorial extension of their tlaxilacalli. Echoing the contents of the Asunción Land Title elaborated 150 years earlier, this Nahuatl-language "repeat title of possession" (*ocsepa posesion*) evoked the political and metaphysical boundaries of the tlaxilacalli.[1] Like its predecessor, this title of "barrio property" (*yn barrio tlatquitl*) listed a run of sacred mountains encircling this community from the north as well as a set of tlaxilacalli surrounding it on all sides but the west.[2]

More than 170 years into Hispanic administration and over a century since massive demographic and ecological shifts forced the retrenchment of local tlaxilacalli, the continuities in this recapitulation come clearly to the fore. Despite Cuauhtepoztlan's partial adoption of the term *barrio* as a complement to both calpolli and tlaxilacalli,[3] its five defining mountains (Ayauhcalli, Xoxoqui Tepetl, Huei Tepetl, Ocoyo,[4] and Tetepayo) retained their function as spatial anchors on the landscape, now part of an even more extensive accounting of the surrounding sierra. The same nearby tlaxilacalli continued to jostle residents of Cuauhtepoztlan on all sides except the now-depopulated west, and a cross still marked the shift from mountains to communities along the tlaxilacalli's outer perimeter. Most foundationally, residents persisted in seeking ultimate resolution from "calpolli leaders in Cuauhtepoztlan" (*ȳ calpoleque ȳ Cuauhtepoztlan*)—even after tentatively appealing to higher altepetl-wide officials, such as the tlatoani and the local priest.[5]

The second Asunción Land Title[6] compels attention for a number of reasons, especially its assertive use of the term *barrio* to evoke the collectivity of Cuauhtepoztlan. In the first analysis, such usage could constitute prime evidence for social and political change, describing a well-known process of redefinition and transculturation, characteristic of deeper Hispanic penetration on the local level.[7] In this reading, the use of "barrio" could suggest that Cuauhtepoztlan changed so drastically over the seventeenth century that a new term was necessary to fill the semantic gap once occupied by the tlaxilacalli. Such a move from expansive Acolhua tlaxilacalli to circumspect Hispanic neighborhood could only be described as a demotion.

Such a transformation does not seem to be the case, however, for Cuauhtepoztlan. In both the documentation specific to this community and also across the available corpus of later Nahuatl texts, *tlaxilacalli* continued to predominate as the main term of local identification.[8] Recent scholarship even shows an expansion of tlaxilacalli roles in central Mexico entering the eighteenth century.[9] Further, returning to the second Asunción title, the term *barrio* appears only in particular circumstances, coalescing around the repeated phrases *tibarrio tlacatl*, "we, the barrio people," and *yn barrio tlatquitl*, both of which evoked the work of locals to defend their claims in a wider altepetl full of competing tlaxilacalli.

Pueblos within Pueblos has argued against a false equivalency between tlaxilacalli and neighborhood, highlighting time and again the autonomous and communal nature of these remarkable institutions. Entering the eighteenth century, however, local tlaxilacalli began to adopt the term *barrio* as their own. Such an adoption demanded a profound redefinition of this once-Spanish term. Unlike Spanish neighborhoods, eighteenth-century Acolhua barrios owned land collectively, ran their affairs independently, and anchored local identities in historical and religious landscapes that retained their sharply Mesoamerican flavor despite sincere Catholic devotion.[10]

Collective identity remained local and distinct. "Barrio people" were understood as separate from neighboring others, such as the "Belén people" mentioned in the second Asunción title, and each carried its own distinctive history. Multiple texts from the later Cuauhtepoztlan corpus evoke both "our fathers and grandfathers" and "our children and grandchildren," carrying local affiliation across a century through mention of these five generations. Saints were also domesticated, as in one text mentioning "the tlaxilacalli of our beloved, honored mother, Santa María Asunción Cuauhtepoztlan."[11] Here, locals fused the traditional locative to the widespread saint's name, making this Santa María theirs and theirs alone. Both in Cuauhtepoztlan and also more generally, "barrio" became much more like an Acolhua tlaxilacalli and much less like a Hispanic neighborhood.

Of all the tlaxilacalli profiled in this book, Cuauhtepoztlan is the best-documented. Archaeological research uncovered its initial formation in the fusion of three modest settlements around the twelfth century. During 1543–44, in the aftermath of invasion, the Codex Asunción profiled its entire territorial extent and political hierarchy. A decade later, the Memorial de los Indios de Tepetlaoztoc showed its tributary linkages to specific local elites. The Asunción Land Title of approximately 1570 shows an early redeployment around its sacred hills, one of which now housed a chapel to the patron saint, Santa María Asunción of Cuauhtepoztlan. By the mid-seventeenth century, locals could evoke both the tlaxilacalli and its territory simply through reference to this local Santa María, and this identification stretched across the later Hispanic period into modern, republican times.[12] Indeed, residents still reference Cuauhtepoztlan's defining mountains when discussing local boundaries; and the official website for the contemporary Municipio of Tepetlaoxtoc includes reference to the mountains Cuajio,[13] Ocoyo, and Tetepayo in its description of the barrio of Asunción.[14] The historian Mariano Cando Morales, a current resident of Asunción Cuauhtepoztlan, also lists the "hills on the west of Tepetlaoztoc that almost form a circle to the north of the barrio of La Asunción," citing twelve mountains in counterclockwise order: Totopoyo, Zozocuasto, Tlalcos, Huei Tepetl, Portezuelo, Tlapitzahuayan, Zautepec (or Muerto), Ocoyo, Minas, Ayacal (Ayauhcalli), Tetepayo, and Choncuicuil.[15] In a later conversation he connected the history of his community to wider questions of history and power, of what is recorded and what is ignored: "This is our barrio, where the Codex Santa María Asunción was born. If many barrios or pueblos had done this (produced codices), we would have a lot—right? But the Spaniards burned so much: large paintings (*biombos*) and such. I don't think it was only at that time (around the Spanish invasion) that (locals) invented (such documents). Many of the symbols we still can't interpret."[16]

In their robust autonomy, local tlaxilacalli proved a persistent torment to centralizing powers, who tried over centuries to erase their influence from official history. Few canonical sources describe their functions and none their historical importance. Nevertheless, tlaxilacalli members have asserted time and again the power of their local communities. Across two empires and more than 400 years, *Pueblos within Pueblos* has traced the persistence of tlaxilacalli and their symbols. Perhaps now tlaxilacalli can receive more of the attention they deserve.

NOTES

1. "ynbarrio tlaca Asumcion mochi ynin tlal ynin meuh ymaxca yn tlatqui conanaocsepa posesion yn Canin tlantica ynquaxochi yn barrio tlatquitl ycpehua tecatitlan yc tlamelahua silan yx topatl yc moselohua tlamelhua xolal ochpanco niman tla tohua ytenco ynacxotlan

yc tlamelahua yc tlecotlamelhua yr[?] tla yntlalcostepetl yc tlacolohua ynepantla tlapitzaha yany tleco ynacastla yn huei tepetl conamiqui yn tepetl quachichiqu niman yc tlacolohua ynonca muetztica cruz ytech tlantica—tlamelahua onca motepanamiqui yn belentlaca niman tlecozqu nepantla yn xoxoquitepetl yc temo ypan ynacastla amyalte niman yctelco ynepantla ynocoyo yc hual mopilhua yquanep tla ynyauhcalo yc tlamelahua yquanepantla tetepayo yn temo= cohuamiltenco= mochi ynin tlal ynin maxca qnin quaxoch barrio tlaca." AGN, Tierras, vol. 1610, exp. 3, f. 11v.

2. The mountains listed are Ayauhcalli, Tlalcoztepetl, Xoxoqui Tepetl, Amayaltepetl, Huei Tepetl, Quachichiqui Tepetl, Ocoyo, and Tetepayo. The tlaxilacalli are Tzillan and Acxotlan (also called Ochpanco) to the east; Belén, over the northern mountain range toward Otumba; and Coamiltenco to the southeast. Tzillan was one of the most prestigious names for Acolhua tlaxilacalli, evoking core tlatoani lands in Tetzcoco. This evocation of the huei tlatoani's lands likely corresponds in Tepetlaoztoc, therefore, to the "land of the tlatoani don Martín Sevilla" in the Asunción Title. Acxotlan is mentioned in the earlier title and Belén is not, likely because of the distance across the mountains. Given its connection to Tetepayo mountain, it is possible that Coamiltenco is the tlaxilacalli of "San Vicente" in the Asunción Title.

3. This run of documents uses "barrio," "calpolli," and "tlaxilacalli" interchangeably but favors the final term—especially when referring to the collectivity, as in "our tlaxilacalli of Santa Martía Asunción Cuauhtepoztlan" (totlaxilacal Sta Maria asuncio quauhtepoztlan). AGN, Tierras, vol. 1610, exp. 3, f. 7r.

4. This geoform is termed Coyotianguiztli in the first Asunción Title. Ocoyo remains its modern name.

5. AGN, Tierras, vol. 1610, exp. 3, f. 17v. The officials were Pedro Cabeza (priest) and Juan de Escalona (tlatoani).

6. There is a series of interlinking but distinct Nahuatl documents surrounding this title; all are discussed in this section.

7. In addition to the adoption of "barrio" and other later terms, other "Stage Three" phenomena in this document include the use of "pia" in a meaning similar to the Spanish "tener" and the use of "pasado" to indicate past officeholding.

8. Comments regarding the wider corpus of later Nahuatl texts are somewhat impressionistic, since there is no corpus analysis of late Nahuatl comparable to Frances Karttunen and James Lockhart, *Nahuatl in the Middle Years* (Berkeley: University of California Press, 1976).

9. Cf. Pizzigoni, *Life Within*, esp. 115–17.

10. See, for example, the two definitions of "saint" in Evonne Levy and Kenneth Mills, eds., *Lexikon of the Hispanic Baroque* (Austin: University of Texas Press, 2014); Jodi Bilinkoff, "Saint," 287–90, for Spain and William B. Taylor, "Saint," 291–94, for Hispanic America. See also Stresser-Péan, *Sol-Dios y Cristo*.

11. "itlaxilacaltzin totlaçomahuiznantzin Sta ma asusio Cuauhtepoztla." AGN, Tierras, vol. 1610, exp. 3, f. 51r. The phrasing of this term means it cannot be translated as "St. Mary of Cuauhtepoztlan."

12. "itlalpantzinco totlaçomahuiznantzin st^a m^a açopsio." AGN, Tierras, vol. 1610, exp. 3, f. 50r.

13. This hill was not mentioned in the first Asunción Title but appears in the second as Quachichiqui Tepetl.

14. "Cerros como el Cuajio, el Ocoyo, el Tetepayo entre otros son los que conformar la parte de las elevaciones de la Sierra Patlachique en el Municipio de Tepetlaoxtoc y que son un gran atractivo para realizar el ecoturismo." Tepetlaoztoc, "Barrio La Asunción," accessed March 9, 2016, http://tepetlaoxtoc.gob.mx/comunidades_detalle?CM=94.

15. "estos cerros del oeste de Tepetlaoxtoc forman casi un círculo en el norte del barrio de La Asunción." Cando Morales, *Tepetlaoztoc*, 28.

16. "Este es nuestro barrio, donde nació el códice Santa María Asunción. Si hubieran hecho muchos barrios o pueblos eso; tuvieramos mucho, verdad? Pero los españoles quemaron muchísimo, que serian biombos, o. . . . Porque ese trabajo no creo que haya sido en ese momento que lo inventaron. Y muchos símbolos que a lo mejor ni interpretamos." Interview, Mariano Cando Morales, Tepetlaoxtoc, Estado de Mexico, August 27, 2015.

List of Acronyms Used Frequently in This Book

AGN	Archivo General de la Nación, Mexico City
AGNM-T	Archivo General de Notarías del Estado de México, Toluca–Notaría Texcoco no. 1
AHMTEX	Archivo Histórico Municipal de Texcoco
BnF-MM	Bibliothèque nationale de France, Paris Manuscrits Mexicains
BNAH-3PS	Biblioteca Nacional de Antropología e Historia—3a Série de Papeles Sueltos
BNM	Biblioteca Nacional de México, Mexico City
DNT	*Documentos nahuas de Tezcoco*
FCE	Fondo de Cultura Económica
INAH	Insituto Nacional de Antropología e Historia, Mexico City
SEP	Secretaría de Educación Pública
UNAM	Universidad Nacional Autónoma de México

Bibliography

Acosta, Virginia García, Juan Manuel Pérez Zevallos, and América Molina del Villar. *Desastres agrícolas en México: Catálogo histórico*. Mexico City: FCE, 2003.

Acosta Sol, Eugenia. "El barrio de la Santísima Trinidad y su contexto urbano." *Boletín de Monumentos Históricos*, 3rd epoch, 24 (2012): 12–15.

Acuña, René, ed. *Relaciones geográficas del siglo XVI*. 10 vols. Mexico City: UNAM, 1984–88.

Acuña-Soto, Rodolfo, Leticia Calderón Romero, and James H. Maguire. "Large Epidemics of Hemorrhagic Fevers in Mexico, 1545–1815." *American Journal of Tropical Medicine and Hygiene* 62, no. 6 (2000): 733–39.

Aguirre Beltrán, Gonzalo. *La población negra de México: Estudio etno-histórico*. Mexico City: Fuente Cultural, 1946.

Aguirre Beltrán, Gonzalo. "El gobierno indígena en México y el proceso de aculuración." *America Indigena* 12 (1952): 271–97.

Aguirre Beltrán, Gonzalo. *Formas de gobierno indígena*. Mexico City: Imprenta Universitaria, 1953.

Alberro, Solange. *Inquisición y sociedad en México, 1571–1700*. Mexico City: FCE, 1988. https://doi.org/10.4000/books.cemca.2601.

Alberti Manzanarez, Pilar. "Mujeres sacerdotisas aztecas: Las cihuatlamacazque mencionadas en dos manuscritos inéditos" *Estudios de cultural náhautl* 24 (1994): 171–217.

Alcalá, Gerónimo de. *Relación de Michoacán*. Edited by Claudia Espejel Carbajal. Accessed August 9, 2017. http://etzakutarakua.colmich.edu.mx/proyectos/relaciondemichoacan/default.asp.

Alcántara Rojas, Berenice, and Federico Navarrete Linares, eds. *Los pueblos amerindios más allá del Estado*. Mexico City: UNAM, 2011.

Alva, Bartolomé de. *A Guide to Confession Large and Small in the Mexican Language, 1634*. Edited and translated by Barry D. Sell, John Frederick Schwaller, and Lu Ann Homza. Norman: University of Oklahoma Press, 1999.

Alva Ixtlilxochitl, Fernando de. *Obras históricas*. 2 vols. Edited by Alfredo Chavero. Mexico City: Editorial Nacional, 1952.

Alva Ixtlilxochitl, Fernando de. *Obras históricas*. 2 vols. Edited by Edmundo O'Gorman. Mexico City: UNAM, 1975.

Alvarado Tezozomoc, Hernando. *Crónica mexicáyotl*. Edited and translated by Adrian León. Mexico City: Imprenta Universitaria, 1949.

Alvarado Tezozomoc, Hernando. *Crónica mexicana*. Edited and translated by Gonzalo Díaz Migoyo and Germán Vázquez Chamorro. Madrid: Dastin, 2001.

Amith, Jonathan D. "Place Making and Place Breaking: Migration and the Development Cycle of Community in Colonial Mexico." *American Ethnologist* 32, no. 1 (February 2005): 159–79. https://doi.org/10.1525/ae.2005.32.1.159.

Amith, Jonathan D. *The Möbius Strip: A Spatial History of Colonial Society in Guerrero, Mexico*. Stanford: Stanford University Press, 2005.

Amith, Jonathan D. *Nahuatl Learning Environment*. Accessed October 20, 2010. www.balsas-nahuatl.org.

Amoxcalli website. Accessed February 2, 2011. http://amoxcalli.org.mx.

Anderson, Arthur J.O. "Los 'Primeros memoriales' y el *Códice florentino*." *Estudios de Cultura Nahuatl* 24 (1994): 49–91.

Anderson, Arthur J.O., Frances Berdan, and James Lockhart. *Beyond the Codices: The Nahua View of Colonial Mexico*. Berkeley: University of California Press, 1976.

Arnauld, M. Charlotte, Linda R. Manzanilla, and Michael E. Smith, eds. *The Neighborhood as a Social and Spatial Unit in Mesoamerican Cities*. Tucson: University of Arizona Press, 2012.

Aubin, J.M.A., ed. *Mapa Tlotzin: Historia de los reyes y de los estados soberanos de Acolhuacan*. Mexico City: Imprenta del Museo Nacional, 1886.

Baber, R. Jovita. "The Construction of Empire: Politics, Law, and Community in Tlaxcala, New Spain, 1521–1640." PhD dissertation, University of Chicago, 2005.

Baquedano, Elizabeth. "Tezcatlipoca as Warrior: Wealth and Bells." In *Tezcatlipoca: Trickster and Supreme Deity*. Edited by Elizabeth Baquedano, 113–33. Boulder: University Press of Colorado, 2014.

Barlow, Robert H. "La Crónica 'X': Versiones colonials de la historia de los Mexica Tenocha." *Revista mexicana de estudios antropológicos* 7 (1945): 65–87.

Barlow, Robert. "Chalchiuhnenetzin." *Tlalocan* 1 (1947): 73–75.

Barlow, Robert H. *The Extent of the Empire of the Culhua Mexica*. Berkeley: University of California Press, 1949.

Baskes, Jeremy. *Indians, Merchants, and Markets: A Reinterpretation of the Repartimiento and Spanish-Indian Economic Relations in Colonial Oaxaca, 1750–1821*. Stanford: Stanford University Press, 2000.
Batalla Rosado, Juan José. "Los códices mesoamericanos: problemática actual de su censo." In *Escritura Indígena en México*. Edited by Alfonso Lacadena et al., 85–103. Madrid: Cuadernos del Instituto de México en España, 1995.
Batalla Rosado, Juan José. "Las falsificaciones de códices mesoamericanos." In *Actas de Primer Congreso Internacional Escrituras Silenciadas en la época de Cervantes*. Edited by Manuel Casado Arboniés, Antonio Castillo Gómez, Paulina Numhauser, and Emilio Sola, 363–85. Alcalá de Hanares, Spain: Universidad de Alcalá de Henares, 2005.
Batalla Rosado, Juan José. "The Scribes Who Painted the Matrícula de Tributos and the Codex Mendoza." *Ancient Mesoamerica* 18, no. 1 (2007): 31–51. https://doi.org/10.1017/S0956536107000077.
Bautista y Lugo, Gibran I.I. "Los indios y la rebelión de 1624 en la Ciudad de México." In *Los indios y las ciudades de Nueva España*. Edited by Felipe Castro Gutiérrez, 197–216. Mexico City: UNAM, 2013.
Bazarte Martínez, Alicia. "Las limosnas de las cofradías: su administración y destino." In *Cofradías, capellanías y obras pías en la América Colonial*. Edited by Pilar Martínez López-Cano, Gisela von Wobeser, and Juan Guillermo Muñoz Correa, 65–74. Mexico City: UNAM, 1998.
Bazarte Martínez, Alicia, and Clara García Ayluardo. *Los costos de la salvación: Las cofradías y la Ciudad de México, siglos XVI al XIX*. Mexico City: CIDE, 2001.
Benaducci Boturini, Lorenzo. *Idea de una nueva historia general de la América septentrional*. Edited by Miguel León-Portilla. Mexico City: Porrúa, 1974.
Benavente (Motolinia), Toribio de. *Historia de los indios de la Nueva España*. Edited by Edmundo O'Gorman. Mexico City: Porrúa, 1969.
Benavente (Motolinia), Toribio de. *Memoriales; o, Libro de las cosas de la Nueva España y de los naturales de ella*. Edited by Edmundo O'Gorman. Mexico City: UNAM, 1971.
Benton, Bradley. *The Lords of Tetzcoco: The Transformation of Indigenous Rule in Postconquest Central Mexico*. Cambridge: Cambridge University Press, 2017.
Berdan, Frances. *The Aztecs of Central Mexico: An Imperial Society*. New York: Holt, Rinehart, and Winston, 1982.
Berdan, Frances F., ed. *Ethnic Identity in Nahua Mesoamerica: The View from Archaeology, Art History, Ethnohistory, and Contemporary Ethnography*. Salt Lake City: University of Utah Press, 2008.
Berdan, Frances F., and Patricia Rieff Anawalt, eds. *Codex Mendoza*. 4 vols. Berkeley: University of California Press, 1992.
Berdan, Frances F., and Patricia Rieff Anawalt, eds. *The Essential Codex Mendoza*. Berkeley: University of California Press, 1997.

Berdan, Frances F., Richard E. Blanton, Elizabeth Hill Boone, Mary G. Hodge, Michael E. Smith, and Emily Umberger, eds. *Aztec Imperial Strategies*. Washington, DC: Dumbarton Oaks Research Library, 1996.

Bernal, Ignacio. "Durán's *Historia* and the Crónica X." In *The History of the Indies of New Spain*. Edited by Diego Durán, trans. Doris Heyden, 565–78. Norman: University of Oklahoma Press, 1994.

Bernal García, Manuela Cristina. "Encomienda y sociedad: Auge y declive de una institución colonial." In *Entre Puebla de los Ángeles y Sevilla: Estudios americanistas en homenaje al Dr. José Calderón Quijano*. Edited by María Justina Sarabia Viejo, 435–48. Seville: Universidad de Sevilla, 1997.

Bethell, Leslie. Edited by *The Cambridge History of Latin America*. 11 vols. New York: Cambridge University Press, 1984–2008.

Bierhorst, John. *Cantares Mexicanos: Songs of the Aztecs*. Stanford: Stanford University Press, 1985.

Bierhorst, John, ed. and trans. *Ballads of the Lords of New Spain*. Austin: University of Texas Press, 2009.

Bierhorst, John, ed. and trans. *Codex Chimalpopoca: The Text in Nahuatl*. Tucson: University of Arizona Press, 1992.

Bilinkoff, Jodi. "Saint." In *Lexikon of the Hispanic Baroque*. Edited by Evonne Levy and Kenneth Mills, 287–90. Austin: University of Texas Press, 2014.

Biskowski, Martin. "Maize Preparation and the Aztec Subsistence Economy." *Ancient Mesoamerica* 11, no. 2 (2000): 293–306. https://doi.org/10.1017/S0956536100112040.

Biskowski, Martin, and Karen D. Watson. "Changing Approaches to Maize Preparation at Cerro Portezuelo." *Ancient Mesoamerica* 24, no. 1 (2013): 213–23. https://doi.org/10.1017/S0956536113000126.

Blanton, Richard E. "Texcoco Region Archaeology." *American Antiquity* 40, no. 2, part 1 (April 1975): 227–30. https://doi.org/10.2307/279620.

Blanton, Richard E. *Houses and Households: A Comparative Study*. New York: Plenum, 1994. https://doi.org/10.1007/978-1-4899-0990-9.

Blanton, Richard E., and Lane Fargher. *Collective Action in the Formation of Pre-Modern States*. New York: Springer, 2008. https://doi.org/10.1007/978-0-387-73877-2.

Boone, Elizabeth Hill. *Stories in Red and Black: Pictorial Histories of the Aztecs and Mixtecs*. Austin: University of Texas Press, 2000.

Boone, Elizabeth Hill, Louise M. Burkhart, and David Tavárez. *Painted Words: Nahua Catholicism, Politics, and Memory in the Atzaqualco Pictorial Catechism*. Cambridge, MA: Harvard University Press, 2016.

Boornazian Diel, Lori. *Tira de Tepechpan: Negotiating Place under Aztec and Spanish Rule*. Austin: University of Texas Press, 2008.

Borah, Woodrow. *New Spain's Century of Depression*. Berkeley: University of California Press, 1951.

Borah, Woodrow. *Justice by Insurance: The General Indian Court of Colonial Mexico*. Berkeley: University of California Press, 1983.

Borah, Woodrow, ed. *El gobierno provincial en la Nueva España, 1570–1787*. Mexico City: UNAM, 1985.

Boyer, Richard. "Mexico in the Seventeenth Century: Transition of a Colonial Society." *Hispanic American Historical Review* 57, no. 3 (August 1977): 455–78. https://doi.org/10.2307/2514025.

Boyer, Richard. *Lives of the Bigamists: Marriage, Family, and Community in Colonial Mexico*. Albuquerque: University of New Mexico Press, 1995.

Boyer, Richard, and Geoffery Spurling, eds. *Colonial Lives: Documents on Latin American History, 1550–1850*. New York: Cambridge University Press, 2000.

Bracamonte y Sosa, Pedro. *Amos y sirvientes: las haciendas de Yucatán, 1789–1860*. Mérida: Universidad Autónoma de Yucatán, 1996.

Bracamonte y Sosa, Pedro. *La conquista inconclusa de Yucatán: Los mayas de las montañas, 1560–1680*. Mexico City: Porrúa, 2001.

Bracamonte y Sosa, Pedro. *Los mayas y la tierra: La propiedad indígena en el Yucatán colonial*. Mexico City: Porrúa, 2003.

Bracamonte y Sosa, Pedro. *Una deuda histórica: Ensayo sobre las condiciones de pobreza secular entre los mayas de Yucatán*. Mexico City: Porrúa, 2007.

Bracamonte y Sosa, Pedro, and Gabriela Solís. *Espacios mayas de autonomía: El pacto colonial en Yucatán*. Mérida: Universidad Autónoma de Yucatán, 1996.

Brading, David A. *Miners and Merchants in Bourbon Mexico, 1763–1810*. Cambridge: Cambridge University Press, 1971.

Brading, David A. *Haciendas and Ranchos in the Mexican Bajío, Léon, 1700–1860*. Cambridge: Cambridge University Press, 1978.

Brading, David A. *The First America: The Spanish Monarchy, Creole Patriots, and the Liberal State*. Cambridge: Cambridge University Press, 1991.

Brading, David A. *Mexican Phoenix: Our Lady of Guadalupe, Image and Tradition across Five Centuries*. Cambridge: Cambridge University Press, 2001.

Brian, Amber. "The Alva Ixtlilxochitl Brothers and the Nahua Intellectual Community." In *Texcoco: Prehispanic and Colonial Perspectives*. Edited by Jongsoo Lee and Galen Brokaw, 201–18. Boulder: University Press of Colorado, 2014. https://doi.org/10.58/6/9781607322849.c009.

Brian, Amber. *Alva Ixtlilxochitl's Native Archive and the Circulation of Knowledge in Colonial Mexico*. Nashville: Vanderbilt University Press, 2016.

Brokaw, Galen, and Jongsoo Lee, eds. *Fernando de Alva Ixtlilxochitl and His Legacy*. Tucson: University of Arizona Press, 2015.

Bronner, Fred. "Urban Society in Colonial Spanish America: Research Trends." *Latin American Research Review* 21, no. 1 (1986): 7–72.

Brumfiel, Elizabeth M. "Figurines and the Aztec State: Testing the Effectiveness of Ideological Domination." In *Gender and Archaeology*. Edited by Rita P. Wright, 143–66. Philadelphia: University of Pennsylvania Press, 1996.

Brumfiel, Elizabeth M. "The Quality of Tribute Cloth: The Place of Evidence in Archaeological Argument." *American Antiquity* 61, no. 3 (July 1996): 453–62. https://doi.org/10.2307/281834.

Bueno Bravo, Isabel. "La importancia del faccionalismo en la política mesoamericana." *Revista de Indias* 64, no. 232 (2004): 651–72.

Burkhart, Louise. *The Slippery Earth: Nahua-Christian Moral Dialogue in Sixteenth-Century Mexico*. Tucson: University of Arizona Press, 1989.

Burkhart, Louise. *Before Guadalupe: The Virgin Mary in Early Colonial Nahuatl Literature*. Austin: University of Texas Press, 2001.

Cabeza de Vaca, Álvar Nuñez. *Naufragios*. Accessed December 9, 2014. http://www.cervantesvirtual.com/obra-visor/naufragios-0/html/feddcf8e-82b1-11df-acc7-002185ce6064_2.html#I_0_.

Cabrera y Quintero, Cayetano. *Escudo y armas de México*. Edited by Víctor M. Ruiz Naufal. Mexico City: IMSS, 1981.

Calderón, Francisco R. *Historia económica de la Nueva España en tiempo de los Austurias*. Mexico City: FCE, 1988.

Calvo, Thomas. "Concubinato y mestizaje en el medio urbano: el caso de Guadalajara en el siglo XVII." *Revista de Indias* 44, no. 173 (1984): 203–12.

Calvo, Thomas. *Guadalajara y su región en el siglo XVII: Población y economía*. Guadalajara: Centro de Estudios Mexicanos y Centroamericanos, 1992.

Calvo, Thomas. *La plebe según los virreyes de América (siglos XVI–XVIII)*. Mexico City: CONDUMEX, 2003.

Calvo, Thomas, and Woodrow Borah, eds. *Historia y población en México: Siglos XVI–XIX*. Mexico City: Colegio de México, 1994.

Candiani, Vera. *Dreaming of Dry Land: Environmental Transformation in Colonial Mexico City*. Stanford: Stanford University Press, 2014. https://doi.org/10.11126/stanford/9780804788052.001.0001.

Cando Morales, Mariano. *Tepetlaoxtoc: Monografía municipal*. Toluca: Gobierno del Estado de México, 1999.

Cañizares-Esguerra, Jorge. *How to Write the History of the New World: Histories, Epistemologies, and Identities in the Eighteenth-Century Atlantic World*. Stanford: Stanford University Press, 2001.

Cañizares-Esguerra, Jorge. *Nature, Empire, and Nation: Explorations of the History of Science in the Iberian World*. Stanford: Stanford University Press, 2006.

Canny, Nicholas, and Anthony Pagden, eds. *Colonial Identity in the Atlantic World, 1500–1800*. Princeton: Princeton University Press, 1987.

Carballo, David M. "Advances in the Household Archaeology of Highland Mesoamerica." *Journal of Archaeological Research* 19, no. 2 (2011): 133–89. https://doi.org/10.1007/s10814-010-9045-7.

Carballo, David M. "Labor Collectives and Group Cooperation in Pre-Hispanic Central Mexico." In *Cooperation and Collective Action: Archaeological Perspectives*. Edited by David M. Carballo, 243–74. Boulder: University Press of Colorado, 2013.

Carballo, David M., Paul Roscoe, and Gary M. Feinman. "Cooperation and Collective Action in the Cultural Evolution of Complex Societies." *Journal of Archaeological Method and Theory* 21, no. 1 (2014): 98–133. https://doi.org/10.1007/s10816-012-9147-2.

Carmagnani, Marcelo. "The Inertia of Clio: The Social History of Colonial Mexico." *Latin American Research Review* 20, no. 1 (1985): 149–66.

Carmagnani, Marcelo. *El regreso de los dioses: El proceso de reconstitución de la identidad étnica en Oaxaca, siglos XVII y XVIII*. Mexico City: FCE, 1988.

Carrasco, Davíd. *Aztec Ceremonial Landscapes*. Niwot: University Press of Colorado, 1999.

Carrasco, Davíd. *Quetzalcoatl and the Irony of Empire*. 2nd ed. Boulder: University Press of Colorado, 2000.

Carrasco, Davíd, and Scott Sessions, eds. *Cave, City, and Eagle's Nest: An Interpretive Journey through the Mapa de Cuauhtinchan No. 2*. Albuquerque: University of New Mexico Press, 2007.

Carrasco, Pedro. "The Civil-Religious Hierarchy in Mesoamerican Communities: Pre-Spanish Background and Colonial Development." *American Anthropologist* 63, no. 3 (June 1961): 483–97. https://doi.org/10.1525/aa.1961.63.3.02a00020.

Carrasco, Pedro. "El barrio y la regulación del matrimonio en un pueblo del Valle de México en el siglo XVI." *Revista Mexicana de Estudios Antropológicos* 25, no. 98 (1975): 175–203.

Carrasco, Pedro. "La transformación de la cultura indígena durante la colonia." *Historia Mexicana* 25, no. 98 (1975): 175–203.

Carrasco, Pedro. "Los mayeques." *Historia Mexicana* 39, no. 1 (July–September 1989): 123–66.

Carrasco, Pedro. *Estructura oolítico territorial del imperio tenocha: La triple alianza de Tenochtitlan, Tetzcoco y Tlacopan*. Mexico City: FCE, 1996.

Carrasco, Pedro, and Johanna Broda, eds. *Estratificación social en la Mesoamérica prehispánica*. Mexico City: INAH, 1976.

Carrasco, Pedro, and Johanna Broda, eds. *Economía política e ideología en el México prehispánico*. Mexico City: Editorial Nueva Imagen, 1978.

Carreón Flores, Jaime Enrique. *Nahuas de Texcoco*. Mexico City: Comisión Nacional para el Desarrollo de los Pueblos Indígenas, 2007.

Carrera Stampa, Manuel. "El obraje novohispano." *Memorias de la Academia mexicana de la historia* 20 (1961): 148–71.

"Carta de la Ciudad de México, en que se hace relación a S.M. del suceso del tumulto del 15 de enero de 1624." In *Documentos relativos al tumulto de 1624*. Edited by Mariano Fernández de Echeverría y Veytia, doc. 21, 2:146. Mexico City: Imprenta de F. Escalante y Cía, 1855.

Caso, Alfonso. "Definición del indio y los indios." *America Indigena* 8, no. 4 (1948): 239–47.

Caso, Alfonso. "Los barrios antiguos de Tenochtitlan y Tlatelolco." *Memorias de la Academia Mexicana de la Historia* 15, no. 1 (1956): 7–63.

Castañeda de la Paz, María. "Dos parcialidades étnicas en Azcapotzalco: Mexicapan y Tepanecapan." *Estudios de Cultura Nahuatl* 46 (2013): 223–48.

Castañeda de la Paz, María. "Nahua Cartography in Historical Context: Searching for Sources on the Mapa de Otumba." *Ethnohistory* 61, no. 2 (2014): 301–27. https://doi.org/10.1215/00141801-2414181.

Castañeda Delgado, Paulino. "La condición miserable del indio y sus privilegios." *Anuario de Estudios Americanos* 28 (1971): 245–335.

Castillo, Cristóbal del. *Historia de la venida de los mexicanos y otros pueblos; e, Historia de la conquista*. Edited and translated by Ferderico Navarrete Linares. Mexico City: CONACULTA, 2001.

Castro Gutiérrez, Felipe. "Indeseables e indispensables: los vecinos españoles, mestizos y mulatos en los pueblos de indios de Michoacán." *Estudios de Historia Novohispana* 25 (July–December 2001): 59–80.

Castro Gutiérrez, Felipe, ed. *Los indios y las ciudades de Nueva España*. Mexico City: UNAM, 2010.

Chalhoub, Sidney. *Trabalho, lar e boteuqim: O cotidiano dos trabalhadores no Rio de Janeiro da belle époque*. 2nd ed. Campinas: UNICAMP, 2005.

Chamberlain, Robert S. "The Concept of the *Señor Natural* as Revealed by Castlian Law and Administrative Documents." *Hispanic American Historical Review* 19, no. 2 (1939): 130–37. https://doi.org/10.2307/2507437.

Chance, John K. "Indian Elites in Late Colonial Mesoamerica." In *Caciques and Their People: A Volume in Honor of Ronald Spores*. Edited by Joyce Marcus and Judith Francis Zeitlin, 45–65. Ann Arbor: University of Michigan Press, 1994.

Chance, John K. *Race and Class in Colonial Oaxaca*. Stanford: Stanford University Press, 1978.

Chance, John K. *Conquest of the Sierra: Spaniards and Indians in Colonial Oaxaca*. Norman: University of Oklahoma Press, 1989.

Chance, John K. "The Barrios of Colonial Tecali: Patronage, Kinship, and Territorial Relations in a Central Mexican Community." *Ethnology* 35, no. 2 (Spring 1996): 107–39. https://doi.org/10.2307/3774073.

Chance, John K. "The Noble House in Colonial Puebla, Mexico: Descent, Inheritance, and the Nahua Tradition." *American Anthropologist* 102, no. 3 (September 2000): 485–502. https://doi.org/10.1525/aa.2000.102.3.485.

Chance, John K., and William B. Taylor. "Estate and Class in a Colonial City: Oaxaca in 1792." *Comparative Studies in Society and History* 19, no. 4 (October 1977): 454–87. https://doi.org/10.1017/S0010417500012020.

Chance, John K., and William B. Taylor. "Estate and Class: A Reply." *Comparative Studies in Society and History* 21, no. 3 (July 1979): 434–42. https://doi.org/10.1017/S0010 417500013086.

Chance, John K., and William B. Taylor. "Cofradías and Cargos: An Historical Perspective on the Mesoamerican Civil-Religious Hierarchy." *American Ethnologist* 12, no. 1 (1985): 1–26. https://doi.org/10.1525/ae.1985.12.1.02a00010.

Charlton, Thomas H. "Population Trends in the Teotihuacan Valley, AD 1400–1969." *World Archaeology* 4, no. 1 (June 1972): 106–23. https://doi.org/10.1080/00438243.197 2.9979523.

Charlton, Thomas H. "Texcoco Region Archaeology and the Codex Xolotl." *American Antiquity* 38, no. 4 (October 1973): 412–23. https://doi.org/10.2307/279146.

Charlton, Thomas H. "On Agrarian Landholdings in Post-Conquest Rural Mesoamerica." *Ethnohistory* 50, no. 1 (Winter 2003): 221–30. https://doi.org/10.1215/00141801-50-1-221.

Chevalier, François. *La formation des grands domaines au Mexique; Terre et société aux XVIe–XVIIe siècles.* Paris: Institut d'ethnologie, 1952.

Chimalpahin, Domingo. *Codex Chimalpahin: Society and Politics in Mexico Tenochtitlan, Tlatelolco, Texcoco, Culhuacan, and Other Nahua Altepetl in Central Mexico: The Nahuatl and Spanish Annals and Accounts.* 2 vols. Edited and translated by Arthur J.O. Anderson, Susan Schroeder, and Wayne Ruwet. Norman: University of Oklahoma Press, 1997.

Chimalpahin, Domingo. *Las ocho relaciones y el memorial de Culhuacán.* 2 vols. Edited and translated by Rafael Tena. Mexico City: CONACULTA, 1998.

Chimalpahin, Domingo. *Diario.* Edited and translated by Rafael Tena. Mexico City: CONACULTA, 2001.

Chimalpahin, Domingo. *Annals of His Time: Don Domingo de San Antón Muñón Chimalpahin Quauhtlehuanitzin.* Edited and translated by James Lockhart, Susan Schroeder, and Doris Namala. Stanford: Stanford University Press, 2006.

Chimalpahin, Domingo, and Francisco López de Gómara. *Chimalpahin's Conquest: A Nahua Historian's Rewriting of Francisco López de Gómara's La conquista de México.* Edited by Susan Schroeder, Anne J. Cruz, Cristián Roa-de-la-Carrera, and David Tavárez. Stanford: Stanford University Press, 2010.

Chowning, Margaret. *Wealth and Power in Provincial Mexico: Michoacán from the Late Colony to the Revolution.* Stanford: Stanford University Press, 1999.

Chowning, Margaret. *Rebellious Nuns: The Troubled History of a Mexican Convent, 1752–1863.* Oxford: Oxford University Press, 2006.

Christian, William. *Local Religion in Sixteenth-Century Spain.* Princeton: Princeton University Press, 1981.

Clavijero, Francisco Javier. *Historia antigua de México*. Edited by Mariano Cuevas. Mexico City: Porrúa, 1965.

Clendinnen, Inga. *Ambivalent Conquests: Maya and Spaniard in Yucatan, 1517–1570*. New York: Cambridge University Press, 1987.

Clendinnen, Inga. *Aztecs: An Interpretation*. Cambridge: Cambridge University Press, 1991.

Clendinnen, Inga. *The Cost of Courage in Aztec Society: Essays on Mesoamerican Society and Culture*. New York: Cambridge University Press, 2010.

Cline, Howard F. "Civil Congregations of the Indians in New Spain, 1598–1606." *Hispanic American Historical Review* 29, no. 3 (1949): 349–69. https://doi.org/10.2307/2508456.

Cline, Howard F. "The Oxtoticpac Lands Map of Texcoco, 1540." *Quarterly Journal, Library of Congress* 23 (1966): 77–115.

Cline, Howard F. "The Oztoticpac Lands Maps." In *A la Carte, Selected Papers on Maps and Atlases*. Edited by Walter W. Ristow, 62–98. Washington, DC: Library of Congress, 1972.

Cline, Sarah L. *The Book of Tributes: Early Sixteenth-Century Nahuatl Censuses from Morelos*. Los Angeles: UCLA Latin American Center, 1993.

Coatsworth, John H. *Los orígenes del atraso: Nueve ensayos de historia económica de México en los siglos XVIII y XIX*. Translated by Juan José Utrilla. Mexico City: Alianza Editorial, 1990.

Coatsworth, John H. "Political Economy and Economic Organization." In *The Cambridge Economic History of Latin America*. Edited by Victor Bulmer-Thomas, John H. Coatsworth, and Roberto Cortés Conde, 1:237–74. Cambridge: Cambridge University Press, 2006.

Codex en Cruz. 2 vols. Edited by Charles E. Dibble. Salt Lake City: University of Utah Press, 1981.

Collier, George A., Renato I. Rosaldo, and John D. Wirth, eds. *The Inca and Aztec States 1200–1800: Anthropology and History*. New York: Academic, 1982.

Colston, Stephen A. "A Comment on Dating the 'Cronica X.'" *Tlalocan* 7 (1977): 371–77.

Cook, Noble David. *Born to Die: Disease and New World Conquest, 1492–1650*. New York: Cambridge University Press, 1998.

Cook, Sherburne F., and Woodrow Borah. *The Indian Population of Central Mexico, 1531–1610*. Berkeley: University of California Press, 1960.

Cook, Sherburne F., and Woodrow Borah. *Essays in Population History*. 3 vols. Berkeley: University of California Press, 1971–79.

Cope, R. Douglas. *The Limits of Racial Domination: Plebeian Society in Colonial Mexico City, 1660–1720*. Madison: University of Wisconsin Press, 1994.

Cordova, Carlos. "Landscape Transformation in Aztec and Spanish Colonial Texcoco, Mexico." PhD dissertation, University of Texas, Austin, 1997.

Cordova, Carlos. "Pre-Hispanic and Colonial Flood Plain Destabilization in the Texcoco Region and Lower Teotihuacan Valley, Mexico." *Geoarchaeology: An International Journal* 32 (2017): 64–89.

Cordova, Carlos, and Jeffrey Parsons. "Geoarchaeology of an Aztec Dispersed Village on the Texcoco Piedmont of Central Mexico." *Geoarchaeology: An International Journal* 12, no. 3 (1997): 177–210. https://doi.org/10.1002/(SICI)1520-6548(199705)12:3<177::AID-GEA1>3.0.CO;2-#.

Cortés, Hernán. *Letters from Mexico*. Edited and translated by Anthony Grafton. New Haven: Yale University Press, 1986.

Cortés, Hernán. "Cartas de relación: Primera relación (Carta de Veracruz)." *Early Modern Spain*. Accessed February 4, 2014. http://www.ems.kcl.ac.uk/content/etext/e014.html.

Cortés, Hernán. "Cartas de relación: Segunda relación." *Early Modern Spain*. Accessed February 4, 2014. http://www.ems.kcl.ac.uk/content/etext/e015.html.

Cortés, Hernán. "Cartas de relación: Tercera relación." *Early Modern Spain*. Accessed February 4, 2014. http://www.ems.kcl.ac.uk/content/etext/e016.html.

Cortés, Hernán. "Cartas de relación: Cuarta relación" *Early Modern Spain*. Accessed February 4, 2014. http://www.ems.kcl.ac.uk/content/etext/e017.html.

Cortés, Hernán. "Cartas de relación: Quinta relación." *Early Modern Spain*. Accessed February 4, 2014. http://www.ems.kcl.ac.uk/content/etext/e018.html.

Couvreur, Aurélie. "La description du Grand Temple de Mexico par Bernardino de Sahagún (Codex de Florence, annexe du Livre II)." *Journal de la Société des Americanistes* 88, no. 88 (2002): 9–46. https://doi.org/10.4000/jsa.2742.

Crapo, Richley H., and Bonnie Glass-Coffin, eds. *Anónimo Mexicano*. Logan: Utah State University Press, 2005.

Crider, Destiny L. "Shifting Alliances: Epiclassic and Early Postclassic Interactions at Cerro Portezuelo." *Ancient Mesoamerica* 24, no. 1 (2013): 107–30. https://doi.org/10.1017/S0956536113000047.

Crosby, Alfred W. *The Columbian Exchange: Biological and Cultural Consequences of 1492*. Westport: Greenwood, 1972.

Crosby, Alfred W. *Ecological Imperialism: The Biological Expansion of Europe, 900–1900*. New York: Cambridge University Press, 1986.

Cruces Carvajal, Ramón. *Semblanza histórica de la ciudad de Tezcoco, 1551–1981*. Tezcoco: Private printing, 1986.

De Vos, Jan. *Los enredos de Remesal: ensayo sobre la conquista de Chiapas*. Mexico City: CONACULTA, 1992.

Dehouve, Danièle. "The 'Secession' of Villages in the Jurisdiction of Tlapa (Eighteenth Century)." In *The Indian Community of Colonial Mexico: Fifteen Essays on Land Tenure, Corporate Organizations, Ideology, and Village Politics*. Edited by Arij Ouweneel and Simon Miller, 47–58. Amsterdam: CEDLA, 1990.

Dehouve, Danièle. "Las funciones rituales de los altos personajes mexicas." *Estudios de Cultura Nahuatl* 45 (2013): 42–43.

Dehouve, Danièle. "El Fractal: ¿Una noción útil para la antropología americanista?" *Desacatos* 53, no. 4 (January–April 2017): 130–49.

Díaz del Castillo, Bernal. *Historia verdadera de la conquista de la Nueva España: Manuscrito de Guatemala*. Mexico City: UNAM, 2005.

Díaz Polanco, Héctor. *El fuego de la inobediencia: Autonomía y rebelión india en el obispado de Oaxaca*. Mexico City: CIESAS, 1996.

Dibble, Charles E., ed. *Códice Xolotl*. 2 vols. Mexico City: UNAM, 1951.

Dibble, Charles E. "Apuntes sobre la plancha X del Códice Xólotl." *Estudios de Cultura Nahuatl* 5 (1965): 103–6.

Dibble, Charles E., ed. *Códice Xolotl*. 2 vols. Mexico City: UNAM–Instituto de Investigaciones Históricas, 1980.

Dibble, Charles E., ed. *Codex en Cruz*. 2 vols. Salt Lake City: University of Utah Press, 1981.

Douglas, Eduardo de Jesús. *In the Palace of Nezahualcoyotl: Painting Manuscripts, Writing the Pre-Hispanic Past in Early Colonial Period Tetzcoco, Mexico*. Austin: University of Texas Press, 2010.

Durán, Diego. *Historia de las Indias de Nueva España y islas de la Tierra Firme*. 2 vols. Edited by Rosa Carnelo and José Rubén Romero. Mexico City: CONACULTA, 1995.

Duverger, Christian. *La fleur létale: Économie du sacrifice aztèque*. Paris: Éditions du Seuil, 1979.

Duverger, Christian. *Cortès*. Paris: Fayard, 2003.

Duverger, Christian. *El primer mestizaje: La clave para entender el pasado mesoamericano*. Mexico City: CONACULTA, 2007.

Duverger, Christian. *Cortès et son double: Enquête sur une mystification*. Paris: Le Seuil, 2013.

Earle, Timothy. "Archaeology, Property, and Prehistory." *Annual Review of Anthropology* 29 (2000): 39–60.

El Códice de Xicotepec: Estudio e interpretación. Edited by Guy Stresser-Péan. Puebla: Gobierno del estado de Puebla, 1995.

El libro de las tasaciones de pueblos de la Nueva España, siglo XVI. Mexico City: AGN, 1952.

Escalante Gonzalbo, Pablo. "La polémica sobre la organización de las comunidades de productores." *Nueva Antropologia* 11, no. 38 (1990): 147–62.

Escalante Gonzalbo, Pablo. *El arte cristiano-indígena del siglo XVI novohispano y sus modelos europeos*. Cuernavaca: Centro de Investigación y Docencia en Humanidades del Estado de Morelos, 2008.

Escalante Gonzalbo, Pablo. *El México antiguo*. Mexico City: CIDE, 2009.

Escalante Gonzalbo, Pablo. *Los códices mesoamericanos antes y después de la conquista española*. Mexico City: FCE, 2010.

Escalante Gonzalbo, Pablo, Bernardo García Martínez, Luis Jáuregui, Josefina Zoraida Vázquez, Elisa Speckman Guerra, Javier Garciadiego, and Luis Aboites Aguilar. *Nueva historia mínima de México*. Mexico City: Colegio de México, 2004.

Escobar Ohmstede, Antonio, and Teresa Rojas Rabiela, eds. *Estructuras y formas agrarias en México: Del pasado y del presente*. Mexico City: Registro Agrario Nacional, 2001.

Evans, Susan Toby. "Sexual Politics in the Aztec Palace: Public, Private, and Profane." *Res: Anthropology and Aesthetics* 33 (Spring 1998): 166–83. https://doi.org/10.1086/RESv33n1ms20167007.

Evans, Susan Toby. "Aztec Palaces and Other Elite Residential Architecture." In *Palaces of the Ancient New World*. Edited by Susan Toby Evans and Joanne Pillsbury, 7–58. Cambridge, MA: Harvard University Press, 2009.

Evans, Susan Toby, and Joanne Pillsbury, eds. *Palaces of the Ancient New World*. Cambridge, MA: Harvard University Press, 2009.

Fargher, Lane, Verenice Heredia Espinosa, and Richard E. Blanton. "Alternative Pathways to Power in Late Postclassic Highland Mesoamerica." *Journal of Anthropological Archaeology* 30, no. 3 (2011): 306–26. https://doi.org/10.1016/j.jaa.2011.06.001.

Farriss, Nancy M. *Maya Society under Colonial Rule: The Collective Enterprise of Survival*. Princeton: Princeton University Press, 1984.

Feijoo, Rosa. "El Tumulto de 1624." *Historia Mexicana* 14, no. 1 (July–September 1964): 42–70.

Fernández Christlieb, Federico, and Ángel Julián García Zambrano, eds. *Territorialidad y paisaje en el altepetl del siglo XVI*. Mexico City: FCE, 2006.

Fernández Christlieb, Federico, and Pedro Sergio Urquijo Torres. "Los espacios del pueblo de indios tras el proceso de Congregación, 1550–1625." *Investigaciones Geográficas* 60 (2006): 145–58.

Fernández de, Echeverría y Veytia, Mariano, ed. *Documentos relativos al tumulto de 1624*. 2 vols. Mexico City: Imprenta de F. Escalante y Cía, 1855.

Fernández de Recas, Guilleromo S. *Cacicazgos y nobiliario indígena de la Nueva España*. Mexico City: Instituto Bibliográfico Mexicano, 1961.

Fisher, Andrew Bryan. "Worlds in Flux, Identities in Motion: A History of the Tierra Caliente of Guerrero, Mexico, 1521–1821." PhD dissertation, University of California, San Diego, 2002.

Florentine Codex. World Digital Library. Accessed May 6, 2016. https://www.wdl.org/en/item/10096/.

Florescano, Enrique. *Precios del maíz y crisis agrícolas en México, 1708–1810: Ensayo sobre el movimiento de los precios y sus consecuencias económicas y sociales*. Mexico City: Colegio de México, 1969.

Florescano, Enrique. *Origen y desarrollo de los problemas agrarios de México, 1500–1821*. Corrected edition. Mexico City: Era, 1976.

Gage, Thomas. *A Survey of the Spanish-West Indies*. London: Thomas Horne, 1642. Reproduced in *Eighteenth Century Collections Online*. Gale Group. Accessed October 18, 2010. https://archive.org/details/surveyofspanishwo0gage.

Gálvez, José de. *Informe sobre las rebeliones populares de 1767: Y otros documentos inéditos.* Edited by Felipe Castro Gutiérrez. Mexico City: UNAM, 1990.

Gamio, Manuel, ed. *La población del Valle de Teotihuacán: Representativa de las que habitan las regiones rurales del Distrito Federal y de los estados de Hidalgo, Puebla, México y Tlaxcala.* 3 vols. Mexico City: Dirección de Talleres Gráficos, 1922.

García, Genaro, and Carlos Pereyra. *Documentos ineditos o muy raros para la historia de Mexico.* 36 vols. Mexico City: Viuda de C. Bouret, 1905–11.

García Ayluardo, Clara. *De tesoreros y tesoros: La administración financiera y la intervención de las cofradías novohispanas,* vol. 1. Mexico City: CIDE, 2002.

García Ayluardo, Clara, and Manuel Ramos Medina, eds. *Manifestaciones religiosas en el mundo colonial americano.* Mexico City: INAH, 1993.

García Ayluardo, Clara, and Manuel Ramos Medina, eds. *Ciudades mestizas: Intercambios y continuidades en la expansión occidental, siglos XVI a XIX.* Mexico City: Condumex, 2001.

García Figueroa, Francisco. *Documentos para la historia de Méjico.* 21 vols. Mexico City: Imprenta de J. R. Navarro, 1853–57.

García Icazbalceta, Joaquín. *Vocabulario de mexicanismos.* Accessed April 22, 2010. http://www.cervantesvirtual.com/servlet/SirveObras/12584961023489384321435/p0000002.htm.

García Icazbalceta, Joaquín, ed. *Nueva colección de documentos para la historia de México.* Mexico City: Editorial Salvador Chávez Hayhoe, 1941.

García Martínez, Bernardo. *Los pueblos de la sierra: El poder y el espacio entre los indios del norte de Puebla hasta 1700.* Mexico City: El Colegio de México, 1987.

García Martínez, Bernardo. "Pueblos de indios, pueblos de castas." In *The Indian Community of Colonial Mexico: Fifteen Essays on Land Tenure, Corporate Organizations, Ideology, and Village Politics.* Edited by Arij Ouweneel and Simon Miller, 103–16. Amsterdam: CEDLA, 1990.

García Martínez, Bernardo, and Gustavo Martínez Mendoza. *Señoríos, pueblos, y municipios: Banco preliminar de información.* CD-Rom. Mexico City: El Colegio de México, 2012.

García Quintana, Josefina, Carlos Martínez Marín, and Mario de la Torre, eds. *Lienzo de Tlaxcala.* Mexico City: Cartón y Papel, 1983.

García Zambrano, Ángel Julián. "Zahuatlan el Viejo y Zahuatlan el nuevo: Trasuntos del poblamiento y la geografía sagrada del altepetl de Yecapixtla." In *Territorialidad y paisaje en el altepetl del siglo XVI.* Edited by Frederico Fernández Christlieb and Ángel Julián García Zambrano, 422–78. Mexico City: FCE, 2006.

Garraty, Christopher P. "Aztec Teotihuacan: Political Processes at a Postclassic and Early Colonial City-State in the Basin of Mexico." *Latin American Antiquity* 17, no. 4 (December 2006): 363–87. https://doi.org/10.2307/25063064.

Gerhard, Peter. "Congregaciones de indios en la Nueva España antes de 1570." *Historia Mexicana* 26, no. 103 (1970): 347–95.

Gerhard, Peter. *A Guide to the Historical Geography of New Spain*. Cambridge: Cambridge University Press, 1972.

Gibson, Charles. *Tlaxcala in the Sixteenth Century*. New Haven, CT: Yale University Press, 1952.

Gibson, Charles. "The Aztec Aristocracy in Colonial Mexico." *Comparative Studies in Society and History* 2, no. 2 (January 1960): 169–96. https://doi.org/10.1017/S0010417 500000657.

Gibson, Charles. *The Aztecs under Spanish Rule*. Stanford: Stanford University Press, 1964.

Gillespie, Susan D. *The Aztec Kings: The Construction of Rulership in Mexica History*. Tucson: University of Arizona Press, 1988.

Gonzablo Aizpuru, Pilar. *Historia de la educación en la época colonial*. 2 vols. Mexico City: Colegio de México, 1990.

Gonzablo Aizpuru, Pilar. *Familia y orden colonial*. Mexico City: Colegio de México, 1998.

Gonzablo Aizpuru, Pilar. *Vivir en la Nueva España: Orden y desorden en la vida cotidiana*. Mexico City: Colegio de México, 2009.

Gonzalbo Aizpuru, Pilar, and Cecilia Rabell, eds. *La familia en el mundo iberoamericano*. Mexico City: UNAM, 1994.

González González, Carlos Javier. *Xipe Tótec: Guerra y regeneración del maíz en la religión mexica*. Mexico City: FCE, 2011.

González Hermosillo Adams, Francisco. *Gobierno y economía en los pueblos indios del México colonial*. Mexico City: INAH, 2001.

González Obregón, Luis, ed. *Proceso inquisitorial del cacique de Texcoco*. Mexico City: AGN, 1910.

González Sánchez, Isabel. *Situación social de indios y castas en las fincas rurales*. Mexico City: UNAM, 1963.

González y González, Luis. *Jerónimo de Mendieta: Vida, pasión y mensaje de un indigenista apocalíptico*. Zamora: El Colegio de Michoacán, 1996.

Gran Diccionario Nahuatl. Accessed December 2, 2015. www.gdn.unam.mx/termino/search.

Granados, Luis Fernando. "*Calpultin* decimonónicos: Aspectos nahuas de la cultura política de la ciudad de México." In *Actores, espacios y debates en la historia de la esfera pública en la ciudad de México*. Edited by Cristina Sacristán and Pablo Piccato, 41–66. Mexico City: Instituto Mora, 2005.

Granados, Luis Fernando. "Cosmopolitan Indians and Mesoamerican Barrios in Bourbon Mexico City." PhD dissertation, Georgetown University, Washington, DC, 2008.

Graulich, Michel. *Myths of Ancient Mexico*. Translated by Bernard R. Ortiz de Montellano and Thelma Ortiz de Montellano. Norman: University of Oklahoma Press, 1997.

Graulich, Michel. *Ritos Aztecas: Las fiestas de las veintenas*. Mexico City: Instituto Nacional Indigenista/INAH, 1999.

Greenleaf, Richard E. *Zumárraga and the Mexican Inquisition, 1536–1543*. Washington, DC: American Academy of Franciscan History, 1961.

Greenleaf, Richard E. *The Mexican Inquisition of the Sixteenth Century*. Albuquerque: University of New Mexico Press, 1969.

Grijalva, Juan de. *Cronica de la Orden de N.P.S. Agustin en las prouincias de Nueua España: En quatro idades desde el año de 1553 hasta el de 1592*. Mexico City: Porrúa, 1985.

Gruzinski, Serge. *Les hommes-dieux du Mexique: Pouvoir indien et société coloniale XVIe–XVIIIe siècles*. Paris: Éditions des Archives Contemporaines, 1985.

Gruzinski, Serge. "La segunda aculturación: El estado ilustrado y la religiosidad indígena en Nueva España (1775–1800)." *Estudios de Historia Novohispana* 8, no. 8 (1985): 175–201.

Gruzinski, Serge. *El poder sin límites: Cuatro respuestas indígenas a la dominación española*. Mexico City: INAH, 1988.

Gruzinski, Serge. *La colonización de lo imaginario: Sociedades indígenas y occidentalización en el México español, siglos XVI–XVIII*. Translated by Jorge Ferreiro. Mexico City: FCE, 1991.

Gruzinski, Serge, and Nathan Wachtel. "Cultural Interbreedings: Constituting the Majority as a Minority." *Comparative Studies in Society and History* 39, no. 2 (April 1997): 231–50. https://doi.org/10.1017/S0010417500020600.

Guthrie, Chester L. "Riots in Seventeenth-Century Mexico City: A Study of Social and Economic Conditions." In *Greater America: Essays in Honor of Herbert Eugene Bolton*. Edited by Adele Ogden and Engel Sluiter, 243–58. Berkeley: University of California Press, 1945.

Gutiérrez, Ramón. "Honor, Ideology, Marriage Negotiation, and Class-Gender Domination in New Mexico, 1690–1846." *Latin American Perspectives* 12, no. 1 (1985): 81–104. https://doi.org/10.1177/0094582X8501200105.

Gutiérrez, Ramón. *When Jesus Came, the Corn Mothers Went Away: Marriage, Sexuality, and Power in New Mexico, 1500–1846*. Stanford: Stanford University Press, 1991.

Gutiérrez Flores, Juan, and Juan de Lormendi. "Relación sumaria y puntual del tumulto y sedición que hubo en México." In *Documentos*. Edited by Fernández de Echeverría y Veytia, doc. 2, 1:1–36.

Hanks, William F. *Converting Words: Maya in the Age of the Cross*. Berkeley: University of California Press, 2010. https://doi.org/10.1525/california/9780520257702.001.0001.

Haring, C. H. "Ledgers of the Royal Treasurers in Spanish America in the Sixteenth Century." *Hispanic American Historical Review* 2, no. 2 (May 1919): 173–87. https://doi.org/10.2307/2505904.

Harvey, Herbert R., ed. *Land and Politics in the Valley of Mexico: A Two Thousand Year Perspective*. Albuquerque: University of New Mexico Press, 1991.

Harvey, Herbert R., and Hanns J. Prem, eds. *Explorations in Ethnohistory: Indians of Central Mexico in the Sixteenth Century*. Albuquerque: University of New Mexico Press, 1984.

Haskett, Robert. *Indigenous Rulers: An Ethnohistory of Town Government in Colonial Cuernavaca*. Albuquerque: University of New Mexico Press, 1991.

Haskett, Robert. *Visions of Paradise: Primordial Titles and Mesoamerican History in Cuernavaca*. Norman: University of Oklahoma Press, 2005.

Hassig, Ross. *Aztec Warfare: Imperial Expansion and Political Control.* Norman: University of Oklahoma Press, 1995.
Hernández, Francisco. *Antigüedades de la Nueva España.* Madrid: Dastin, 2003.
Hernández de León-Portilla, Ascensión. *Obras clásicas sobre la lengua náhuatl.* CD-Rom. Madrid: Fundación Histórica Tavera, 1998.
Herrera Meza, María del Carmen, Alfredo López Austin, and Rodrigo Martínez Baracs. "El nombre náhuatl de la Triple Alianza." *Estudios de Cultura Nahuatl* 46 (2013): 8–35.
Herzog, Tamar. *Defining Nations: Immigrants and Citizens in Early Modern Spain and Spanish America.* New Haven: Yale University Press, 2003. https://doi.org/10.12987/yale/9780300092530.001.0001.
Herzog, Tamar. *Upholding Justice: Society, State, and the Penal System in Quito, 1650–1750.* Ann Arbor: University of Michigan Press, 2004. https://doi.org/10.3998/mpub.17644.
Hicks, Frederic. "Tetzcoco in the Early 16th Century: The State, the City and the 'Calpolli.'" *American Ethnologist* 9, no. 2 (1982): 230–49. https://doi.org/10.1525/ae.1982.9.2.02a00020.
Hicks, Frederic. "Labor Squads, Noble Houses, and Other Things Called 'Barrios' in Aztec Mexico." *Nahua Newsletter* 49 (2012): 13–21.
Hicks, Frederic. "Governing Smaller Communities in Aztec Mexico." *Ancient Mesoamerica* 23, no. 1 (2012): 47–56. https://doi.org/10.1017/S095653611200003X.
Hicks, Frederic. "Texcoco 1515–1519: The Ixtlilxochitl Affair." In *Chipping Away on Earth: Studies in Prehispanic and Colonial Mexico in Honor of Arthur J.O. Anderson and Charles E. Dibble.* Edited by Eloise Quiñones-Keber, 235–39. Lancaster, CA: Labrynthos, 1995.
Hinz, Eike, Claudine Hartau, and Marie-Louise Heimann-Koenen, eds. *Aztekischer Zensus: Zuer indianischen Wirtschaft und Gessellschaft im Marquesado um 1540: Aus dem "Libro de Tributos" (Col. Ant. Ms. 551) im Archivo Histórico, Mexico.* 2 vols. Hamburg: Verlag für Ethnologie, 1983.
Hoberman, Louisa. "Bureaucracy and Disaster: Mexico City and the Flood of 1629." *Journal of Latin American Studies* 6, no. 2 (November 1974): 211–40. https://doi.org/10.1017/S0022216X00008968.
Horcasitas, Fernando. "Los descendientes de Nezahuapilli: Documentos del cacicazgo de Texcoco, 1545–1855." *Estudios de Historia Novohispana* 6 (1978): 145–86.
Horcasitas, Fernando, ed. *Teatro náhuatl.* 2 vols. Mexico City: UNAM, 2004.
Horn, Rebecca. *Postconquest Coyoacan: Nahua-Spanish Relations in Central Mexico, 1519–1650.* Stanford: Stanford University Press, 1997.
Huerta Preciado, María Teresa, and Patricia Palacios. *Rebeliones indígenas de la época colonial.* Mexico City: INAH, 1976.
Humboldt, Alexander von. *Ensayo político del reino de la Nueva España.* 4 vols. Translated by Vicente Gonzalez Arnao. Paris: Rosa, 1822.

Isendahl, Christian E., and Michael E. Smith. "Sustainable Agrarian Urbanism: The Low-Density Cities of the Mayas and Aztecs." *Cities* 31 (2013): 132–43. https://doi.org/10.1016/j.cities.2012.07.012.

Israel, Jonathan I. *Race, Class, and Politics in Colonial Mexico, 1610–1670*. Oxford: Oxford University Press, 1975.

Jiménez Moreno, Wigberto, José Miranda, and María Teresa Fernández. "La historiografía tezcocana y sus problemas." *Sociedad Mexicana de Antropología* 17 (1962): 81–96.

Johanssen K., Patrick. "Tamoanchan: una imagen verbal del origen." *Estudios de Cultura Nahuatl* 49 (2015): 59–92.

Johnson, Benjamin D., trans. *Documetos nahuas de Tezcoco*, vol. 1. Edited by Javier Eduardo Ramírez López. Texcoco: Diócesis de Texcoco, A.R., 2017.

Jorge, María del Carmen, Barbara J. Williams, Clara E. Garza-Hume, and Arturo Olvera. "Mathematical Accuracy of Aztec Land Surveys Assessed from Records in the Codex Vergara." *Proceedings of the National Academy of Sciences of the United States of America* 108, no. 37 (2011): 15053–57. https://doi.org/10.1073/pnas.1107737108.

Juana Inés de la Cruz, Sor. *Obras completes*. 14th ed. Mexico City: Porrúa, 2004.

Karttunen, Frances. *An Analytical Dictionary of Nahuatl*. Norman: University of Oklahoma Press, 1992.

Karttunen, Frances, and James Lockhart. *Nahuatl in the Middle Years*. Berkeley: University of California Press, 1976.

Karttunen, Frances, and James Lockhart, eds. *The Art of Nahuatl Speech: The Bancroft Dialogues*. Los Angeles: University of California Press, 1987.

Katz, Friedrich. *The Ancient American Civilizations*. London: Weidenfeld and Nicolson, 1972.

Katz, Friedrich, ed. *Riot, Rebellion, and Revolution: Rural Social Conflict in Mexico*. Princeton: Princeton University Press, 1987.

Kellogg, Susan. *Law and the Transformation of Aztec Culture, 1500–1700*. Norman: University of Oklahoma Press, 1995.

Kellogg, Susan. *Weaving the Past: A History of Latin America's Indigenous Women from the Prehispanic Period to the Present*. Oxford: Oxford University Press, 2005.

Kellogg, Susan, and Matthew Restall. *Dead Giveaways: Indigenous Testaments of Colonial Mesoamerica and the Andes*. Salt Lake City: University of Utah Press, 1998.

Kirchoff, Paul, Lina Odena Güemes, and Luis Reyes García, eds. *Historia tolteca-chichimeca*. Mexico City: INAH, 1976.

Klein, Cecilia F. "Teocuitlatl, 'Divine Excrement': The Significance of 'Holy Shit' in Ancient Mexico." *Art Journal* 52, no. 3 (1993): 20–27.

Klor de Alva, J. Jorje. "Nahua Colonial Discourse and the Appropriation of the (European) Other." *Archives de Sciences Sociales des Religions* 77, no. 1 (January–March 1992): 15–35. https://doi.org/10.3406/assr.1992.1513.

Kourí, Emilio H. *A Pueblo Divided: Business, Property, and Community in Papantla, Mexico*. Stanford: Stanford University Press, 2004.

Lacadena, Alfonso. "Regional Scribal Traditions: Methodological Implications for the Decipherment of Nahuatl Writing." *PARI Journal* 8, no. 4 (2008): 1–22.

Lafaye, Jacques. *Quetalcoatl and Guadalupe: The Formation of Mexican National Consciousness, 1532–1813*. Chicago: University of Chicago Press, 1976.

Launey, Michel. *Introduction à la langue et à la littérature aztèques*. 2 vols. Paris: L'Harmattan, 1979–80.

Launey, Michel. *An Introduction to Classical Nahuatl*. Edited and translated by Christopher Mckay. Cambridge: Cambridge University Press, 2011. https://doi.org/10.1017/CBO9780511778001.

Lavrin, Asunción. "Cofradías novohispanas: Economía material y spiritual." In *Cofradías, capellanías y obras pías en la América Colonial*. Edited by María del Pilar Martínez López-Cano, Gisela von Wobeser, and Juan Guillermo Muñoz Correa, 49–64. Mexico City: UNAM, 1998.

Lavrin, Asunción. *Brides of Christ: Conventual Life in Colonial Mexico*. Stanford: Stanford University Press, 2008. https://doi.org/10.11126/stanford/9780804752831.001.0001.

Lavrin, Asunción, ed. *Latin American Women: Historical Perspectives*. Westport: Greenwood, 1978.

Lavrín, Asunción, ed. *Sexuality and Marriage in Colonial Latin America*. Lincoln: University of Nebraska Press, 1989.

Lee, Jongsoo. *The Allure of Nezahualcoyotl: Pre-Hispanic History, Religion, and Nahua Poetics*. Albuquerque: University of New Mexico Press, 2008.

Lee, Jongsoo. "Colonial Writings and Indigenous Politics in New Spain: Alva Ixtlilxochitl's Chronicles and the Cacicazco of San Juan Teotihuacan." In *Ixtlilxochitl and His Legacy*. Edited by Galen Brokaw and Jongsoo Lee, 122–52. Tucson: University of Arizona Press, 2015.

Lee, Jongsoo, and Galen Brokaw, eds. *Texcoco: Prehispanic and Colonial Perspectives*. Boulder: University Press of Colorado, 2014. https://doi.org/10.5876/9781607322849.

León-Portilla, Miguel. *Visión de los vencidos: Relaciones indígenas de la conquista*. Mexico City: UNAM, 1959.

León-Portilla, Miguel. *Toltecáyotl: Aspectos de la cultura náhuatl*. Mexico City: FCE, 1980.

León-Portilla, Miguel, and Carmen Aguilera. *Mapa de México-Tenochtitlan y sus contornos hacia 1550*. Mexico City: Celanese, 1986.

Lesbre, Patrick. "Illustrations acolhua de facture européenne (Codex Ixtlilxochitl, ff. 105–112)." *Journal de la Société des Américanistes* 84, no. 2 (1998): 97–124. https://doi.org/10.3406/jsa.1998.1719.

Lesbre, Patrick. "Historiografía acolhua: seudo-rebelión e intereses coloniales (Ixtlilxochitl)." In *Actas del II Congreso Europeo de Latinoamericanistas*. Edited by Thomas Brenner and Susanne Schütz. CD-Rom. Halle: Universität Halle-Wittenberg, 1999.

Lesbre, Patrick. "Oublis et censures de l'historiographie acolhua coloniale: Nezahualcoyotl." *C.M.H.L.B. Caravelle* 72, no. 1 (1999): 11–30. https://doi.org/10.3406/carav.1999.2831.

Lesbre, Patrick. "Un représentant de la première génération métisse face à l'aristocratie acolhua: Juan Bautista Pomar, Tezcoco (fin XVIe–début XVIIe siècle)." In *Transgressions et stratégies du métissage en Amérique colonial*. Edited by Bernard Lavallé, 183–200. Paris: Sorbonne Nouvelle, 1999.

Lesbre, Patrick. "Nezahualcoyotl entre historia, leyenda y divinización." In *El héroe entre el mito y la historia*. Edited by Federico Navarrete and Guilhem Olivier, 21–55. Mexico City: UNAM, 2000. https://doi.org/10.4000/books.cemca.1319.

Lesbre, Patrick. "¿Influencias occidentales en el Mapa Quinatzin?" *Revista Española de Antropologia Americana* 38, no. 2 (2008): 173–97.

Lesbre, Patrick. "Dos manuscritos pictográficos tezcocanos desconocidos del siglo XVI— escrituras y nobleza acolhua colonial: Tezcoco y Atenco, 1575." *Estudios de Cultura Nahuatl* 41 (2010): 231–57.

Lesbre, Patrick. "Le Mexique central à travers le Codex Xolotl et Alva Ixtlilxochitl: Entre l'espace préhispanique et l'écriture colonial." *e-Spania* 14 (2012). Accessed December 2, 2015. https://e-spania.revues.org/22033. https://doi.org/10.4000/e-spania.22033.

Lesbre, Patrick. "El Templo Mayor de Tetzcoco según las fuentes históricas." II Coloquio de Historia Regional, Texcoco, May 9, 2015.

Lewis, Leslie. "Colonial Texcoco: A Province in the Valley of Mexico, 1570–1630." PhD dissertation, University of California, Los Angeles, 1978.

Lockhart, James. "Y la Ana lloró: Cesión de un sitio para casa, San Miguel Tocuilán, 1583." *Tlalocan* 8 (1980): 21–33.

Lockhart, James. "And Ana Wept: Grant of a Site for a House, San Miguel Tocuillan, 1583." In *Nahuas and Spaniards*. Edited by Lockhart, 66–74.

Lockhart, James. *Nahuas and Spaniards: Postconquest Central Mexican History and Philology*. Stanford: Stanford University Press, 1991.

Lockhart, James. *The Nahuas after the Conquest: A Social and Cultural History of the Indians of Central Mexico, Sixteenth through Eighteenth Centuries*. Stanford: Stanford University Press, 1992.

Lockhart, James. *We People Here: Nahuatl Accounts of the Conquest of Mexico*. Berkeley: University of California Press, 1993.

Lockhart, James. *Of Things of the Indies: Essays Old and New in Early Latin American History*. Stanford: Stanford University Press, 2000.

Lockhart, James, and Stuart B. Schwartz. *Early Latin America: A History of Colonial Spanish America and Brazil*. Cambridge: Cambridge University Press, 1983.

Loera Chávez, Margarita. *Murmillos de antiguos muros: Los inmuebles del siglo XVI que se conservan en el Estado de México*. Toluca: Instituto Mexiquense de Cultura, 1994.

Lomnitz, Claudio. *Death and the Idea of Mexico*. New York: Zone Books, 2005.

Lopes Don, Patricia. "Franciscans, Indian Sorcerers, and the Inquisition in New Spain, 1536–1543." *Journal of World History* 17, no. 1 (March 2006): 27–48. https://doi.org/10.1353/jwh.2006.0025.

Lopes Don, Patricia. "The 1539 Inquisition and Trial of don Carlos of Texcoco in Early Mexico." *Hispanic American Historical Review* 88, no. 4 (November 2008): 573–606. https://doi.org/10.1215/00182168-2008-001.

Lopes Don, Patricia. *Bonfires of Culture: Franciscans, Indigenous Leaders, and the Inquisition in Early Mexico, 1524–1540*. Norman: University of Oklahoma Press, 2010.

López Austin, Alfredo. *Tamoanchan y tlalocan*. Mexico City: FCE, 1994.

López Austin, Alfredo. *Cuerpo humano e ideología*, 2nd ed. 2 vols. Mexico City: UNAM, 2004.

López Caballero, Paula, ed. *Los títulos primordiales del centro de México*. Mexico City: CONACULTA, 2003.

López Corral, Aurelio. "Los glifos de suelo en códices acolhua de la Colonia temprana: un reanálisis de su significado." *Desacatos* 37 (2011): 145–62.

López y Magaña, Juan. "Aspects of the Nahuatl Heritage of Juan Bautista Pomar." MA paper in Latin American Studies. University of California, Los Angeles, 1980.

Love, Edgar P. "Legal Restrictions on Afro-Indian Relations in Colonial Mexico." *Journal of Negro History* 55, no. 2 (April 1970): 131–39. https://doi.org/10.2307/2716446.

Madajczak, Julia. "La carrera de Ixtlilxochitl: Una comparación entre fuentes pictográficas y escritas." In *Códices del centro de méxico análisis comparativa y estudios indivduales*. Edited by Miguel Ángel Ruz Barrio and Juan José Batalla Rosado, 43–54. Warsaw: University of Warsaw Press, 2013.

Madajczak, Julia. "Nahuatl Kinship Terminology as Reflected in Colonial Written Sources from Central Mexico: A System of Classification." PhD dissertation, University of Warsaw, 2014.

Magazine, Roger. *The Village Is Like a Wheel: Rethinking Cargos, Family, and Ethnicity in Highland Mexico*. Tucson: University of Arizona Press, 2012.

Magazine, Roger, and Martínez Saldaña, eds. *Texcoco en el nuevo milenio*. Mexico City: Universidad Iberoamericana, 2010.

Marcus, Joyce. *Mesoamerican Writing Systems: Propaganda, Myth, and History in Four Ancient Civilizations*. Princeton: Princeton University Press, 1992.

Marquez Morfin, Lourdes, Robert McCaa, Rebecca Storey, and Andes del Angel. "Health and Nutrition in Pre-Hispanic Mesoamerica." In *The Backbone of History: Health and Nutrition in the Western Hemisphere*. Edited by Richard H. Steckel and Jerome C. Rose, 307–40. Cambridge: Cambridge Unviersity Press, 2005.

Martínez, Hildeberto. *Tepeaca en el siglo XVI: Tenencia en la tierra y organización de un señorío*. Mexico City: CIESAS, 1984.

Martínez, María Elena. *Genealogical Fictions: Limpieza de Sangre, Religion, and Gender in Colonial Mexico*. Stanford: Stanford University Press, 2008.

Martínez Baracs, Rodrigo. *Convivencia y utopía: El gobierno indio y español de la 'ciudad Mechuacan,' 1521–1580*. Mexico City: INAH, 2005.

Martínez Vargas, Enrique, and Ana María Jarquín Pacheco. "El sacrificio de negros al inicio de la conquista de México." *Arqueología Mexicana* 21, no. 119 (January 2013): 28–35.

Matrícula de tributos. Edited by María Teresa Sepúlveda y Herrera. CD-Rom. Mexico City: CONACULTA, 2007.

Matrícula de tributos (Códice de Moctezuma). Edited by Frances Berdan and Jacqueline de Durand-Forest. Graz: Akademische Druck- u. Verlagsanstalt, 1980.

Mayanez, Pilar. "Documentos de Tezcoco: Consideraciones sobre tres manuscritos en mexicano del ramo 'tierras.'" *Estudios de Cultura Nahuatl* 22 (1992): 325–43.

Mayer, Enrique. *The Articulated Peasant: Household Economies in the Andes*. Boulder: Westview, 2002.

McAffee, Byron, and R. H. Barlow. "The Titles of Tetzcotzinco (Santa María Nativitas)." *Tlalocan* 2, no. 2 (1946): 110–27.

McCaa, Robert. "Modeling Social Interaction: Marital Miscegenation in Colonial Spanish America." *Historical Methods* 15, no. 2 (Spring 1982): 45–66. https://doi.org/10.1080/01615440.1982.10594080.

McCaa, Robert. "Calidad, Clase, and Marriage in Colonial Mexico: The Case of Parral, 1788–90." *Hispanic American Historical Review* 64, no. 3 (August 1984): 477–501. https://doi.org/10.2307/2514936.

McCaa, Robert. "Marriageways in Mexico and Spain, 1500–1800." *Continuity and Change* 9, no. 1 (1994): 11–43.

McCaa, Robert. "Spanish and Nahuatl Views on Smallpox and Demographic Catastrophe in Mexico." *Journal of Interdisciplinary History* 25, no. 3 (Winter 1995): 397–431. https://doi.org/10.2307/205693.

McCaa, Robert. "The Peopling of Mexico from Origins to Revolution." In *The Population History of North America*. Edited by Richard Steckel and Michael Haine. Cambridge: Cambridge University Press, 1997. Accessed October 18, 2010. http://www.hist.umn.edu/~rmccaa/mxpoprev/cambridg3.htm.

McCaa, Robert. "The Nahua Calli of Ancient Mexico: Household, Family, and Gender." *Continuity and Change* 18, no. 1 (2003): 23–48. https://doi.org/10.1017/S0268416 00300448X.

McCaa, Robert. "Revisioning Smallpox in Mexico-Tenochtitlan, 1520–1950." Accessed October 18, 2010. http://www.hist.umn.edu/~rmccaa/mexico/poxcity.doc.

McCaa, Robert, and Stuart B. Schwartz. "Measuring Marriage Patterns: Percentages, Cohen's Kappa, and Log-Linear Models." *Comparative Studies in Society and History* 25, no. 4 (October 1983): 711–24.

McCaa, Robert, Stuart B. Schwartz, and Arturo Grubessich. "Race and Class in Colonial Latin America: A Critique." *Comparative Studies in Society and History* 21, no. 3 (July 1979): 421–33. https://doi.org/10.1017/S0010417500013074.

McDonough, Kelly S. *The Learned Ones: Nahua Intellectuals in Postconquest Mexico*. Tucson: University of Arizona Press, 2014.

Medina Lima, Constantino, ed. and trans. *Libro de los guardianes y gobernadores de Cuauhtinchan (1519–1640)*. Mexico City: CIESAS, 1995.

Megged, Amos. *Exporting the Catholic Reformation: Local Religion in Early-Colonial Mexico*. New York: E. J .Brill, 1996.

Megged, Amos. *Social Memory in Ancient and Colonial Mesoamerica*. Cambridge: Cambridge University Press, 2010.

Megged, Amos, and Stephanie Wood, eds. *Mesoamerican Memory: Enduring Systems of Remembrance*. Norman: University of Oklahoma Press, 2012.

Melville, Elinor G.K. *A Plague of Sheep: Environmental Consequences of the Conquest of Mexico*. Cambridge: Cambridge University Press, 1994. https://doi.org/10.1017/CBO9780511571091.

Mendieta, Gerónimo de. *Historia eclesiástica Indiana*. 2 vols. Edited by Antonio Rubial García. Mexico City: CONACULTA, 1997.

Menegus, Margarita. *Del señorío indígena a la república de indios: El caso de Toluca, 1500–1600*. Mexico City: CONACULTA, 1994.

Menegus, Margarita, and Rodolfo Aguirre Salvador, eds. *El cacicazgo en Nueva España y Filipinas*. Mexico City: Plaza y Valdés, 2005.

Menegus Bornemann, Margarita. "Economía y comunidades indígenas: El efecto de la supresión del sistema de reparto de mercancías en la intendencia de México, 1786–1810." *Estudios mexicanos* 5, no. 2 (1989): 201–19. https://doi.org/10.2307/1052087.

Menegus Bornemann, Margarita. *Del señorío indígena a la república de indios: El caso de Toluca, 1500–1600*. Mexico City: CONACULTA, 1994.

Menegus Bornemann, Margarita. "Los títulos primordiales de los pueblos de indios." In *Dos décadas de investigación en historia económica comparada de América Latina: Homenaje a Carlos Sempat Assadourian*. Edited by Margarita Menegus Bornemann, 137–61. Mexico City: El Colegio de México, 1999.

Mendieta, Gerónimo de. *Historia eclesiástica indiana*. Cervantes Virtual. Accessed April 23, 2013. http://www.cervantesvirtual.com/obra-visor/historia-eclesiastica-indiana-0/html/.

Mikulska, Katarzyna. *Tejiendo destinos: Un acercamiento al sistema de comunicación gráfica en los códices adivinatorios*. Zinacantepec: El Colegio Mexiquense, 2015.

Minc, Leah D. "Style and Substance: Evidence for Regionalism within the Aztec Market System." *Latin American Antiquity* 20, no. 2 (June 2009): 343–74. https://doi.org/10.1017/S1045663500002674.

Miño Grijalva, Manuel. *Obrajes y tejedores de Nueva España, 1700–1810*. Madrid: Instituto de Cooperación Iberoamericana, 1990.

Miño Grijalva, Manuel. *La manufactura colonial: La constitución técnica del obraje*. Mexico City: Colegio de México, 1993.

Miño Grijalva, Manuel. *La protoindustria colonial hispanoamericana*. Mexico City: FCE, 1993.

Miño Grijalva, Manuel. *El mundo novohispano: Población, cuidades y economía, siglos XVII y XVIII*. Mexico City: Colegio de México, 2001.

Miño Grijalva, Manuel, ed. *Mundo rural, ciudades y población del Estado de México*. Toluca: Colegio Mexiquense, 1990.

Miño Grijalva, Manuel, ed. *Haciendas, pueblos y comunidades: Los valles de México y Toluca entre 1530 y 1916*. Mexico City: CONACULTA, 2001.

Miño Grijalva, Manuel, ed. *Núcleos urbanos mexicanos, siglos XVIII y XIX: Mercado, perfiles sociodemográficos y conflictos de autoridad*. Mexico City: Colegio de México, 2006.

Miranda, José. *El tributo indígena en la Nueva España durante el Siglo XVI*. Mexico City: Colegio de México, 1952.

Miranda, José. *La función económica del encomendero en los orígenes del regimen colonial de Nueva España*. Mexico City: UNAM, 1965.

Mohar Betancurt, Luz María. *El tributo mexica en el siglo XVI: Análisis de dos fuentes pictográficos*. Mexico City: SEP, 1987.

Mohar Betancurt, Luz María, ed. *Códice Mapa Quinantzin: Justicia y derechos humanos en el México antiguo*. CD-Rom. Mexico City: Porrúa, 2004.

Molina, Alonso de. *Vocabulario en lengua castellana y mexicana y mexicana y castellana*. Edited by Miguel León-Portilla. Mexico City: Porrúa, 1977.

Molina, Alonso de. *Confesionario mayor en la lengua mexicana y castellana*. Edited by Roberto Moreno. Mexico City: UNAM, 1984.

Montes de Oca, Mercedes. *Los difrasismos en el náhuatl del siglo xvi y xvii*. Mexico City: UNAM, 2013.

Morris, Mark. "Language in Service of the State: The Nahuatl Conterinsurgency Broadsides of 1810." *Hispanic American Historical Review* 87, no. 3 (2007): 433–70. https://doi.org/10.1215/00182168-2007-001.

Mulhare, Eileen M. "Barrio Matters: Toward an Ethnology of Mesoamerican Customary Social Units." *Ethnology* 35, no. 2 (Spring 1996): 93–106. https://doi.org/10.2307/3774072.

Munch, Guido. *El cacicazgo de San Juan Teotihuacan durante la colonia*. Mexico City: INAH, 1976.

Mundy, Barbara E. *The Mapping of New Spain: Indigenous Cartography and the Maps of the Relaciones Geograficas*. Chicago: University of Chicago Press, 2000.
Mundy, Barbara E. *The Death of Aztec Tenochtitlan, the Life of Mexico City*. Austin: University of Texas Press, 2015.
Muñoz Camargo, Diego. *Historia de Tlaxcala*. Edited by Alfredo Chavero. Mexico City: Secretaría de Fomento, 1892.
Muñoz Camargo, Diego. *Suma y epíloga de toda la descripción de Tlaxcala*. Edited by Andrés Martínez Baracs and Carlos Sempat Assadourian. Tlaxcala: Universidad Autónoma de Tlaxcala, 1994.
Nahautl Dictionary/Diccionario del náhuatl. Accessed November 1, 2014. http://whp.uo regon.edu/dictionaries/nahuatl/index.lasso.
Nájera Coronado, Martha Ilia. "El rito del 'palo volador': Encuentro de significados." *Revista Espanola de Antropologia Americana* 38, no. 1 (2008): 51–73.
Navarette Linares, Federico. "Chichimecas y toltecas en el valle de México." *Estudios de Cultura Nahuatl* 42 (2011): 19–50.
Navarette Linares, Federico. "Las dinámicas históricas y culturales de ciclos de concentración y dispersión en las sociedades amerindias." In *Los pueblos amerindios más allá del Estado*. Edited by Berenice Alcántara Rojas and Federico Navarrete Linares, 169–99. Mexico City: UNAM, 2011.
Navarrete Linares, Federico. "Los libros quemados y los nuevos libros: Paradojas de la autenticidad en la tradición mesoamericana." In *La abolición del arte: El Coloquio Internacional de Historia del Arte*. Edited by Alberto Dallad, 53–71. Mexico City: UNAM, 1998.
Navarette Linares, Federico. *Los orígenes de los pueblos indígenas del valle de México: Los altépetl y sus historias*. Mexico City: UNAM, 2011.
Nesvig, Martin Austin, ed. *Local Religion in Colonial Mexico*. Albuquerque: University of New Mexico Press, 2006.
Nichols, Deborah. "Merchants and Merchandise: The Archaeology of Aztec Commerce at Otumba, Mexico." In *Merchants, Markets, and Exchange in the Pre-Columbian World*. Edited by Kenneth G. Hirth and Joanne Pillsbury. Washington, DC: Dumbarton Oaks, 2013, 49–84.
Nicholson, H. B. "The Mesoamerican Pictorial Manuscripts: Research, Past and Present." In *34th International Congress of Americanists, Vienna*. Edited by Herbert Baldus. Horn-Vienna: Ferdinand Berger, 1962, 199–215.
Nicholson, H. B. "Pre-Hispanic Central Mexican Historiography." In *Investigaciones contemporáneas sobre historia de México*. Mexico City: UNAM, 1971, 38–81.
Nicholson, H. B. *Topiltzin Quetzalcoatl: The Once and Future Lord of the Toltecs*. Boulder: University Press of Colorado, 2001.
Noguez, Xavier. "El Mapa de Oztoticpac de la Biblioteca del Congreso de Washington: Una edición facsimilar." In *Códices y Documentos sobre México: Segundo Simposio*. Edited

by Salvador Rueda Smithers, Constanza Vega Sosa, and Rodrigo Martínez Baracs, 2:301–10. Mexico City: INAH, 1997.

Noguez, Xavier, and Stephanie Wood, eds. *De tlacuilos y escribanos: Estudio sobre documentos indígenas coloniales del centro de México*. Zamora: Colegio de Michoacán, 1998.

Novo, Salvador. *La guerra de las gordas*. Mexico City: FCE, 1963.

Offner, Jerome A. "A Reassessment of the Extent and Structuring of the Empire of Techotlalatzin, Fourteenth Century Ruler of Texcoco." *Ethnohistory* 26, no. 3 (1979): 231–41. https://doi.org/10.2307/481560.

Offner, Jerome A. "Archival Reports of Poor Crop Yields in the Early Postconquest Texcocan Heartland and Their Implications for Studies of Aztec Period Population." *American Antiquity* 45, no. 4 (October 1980): 848–56. https://doi.org/10.2307/280155.

Offner, Jerome A. "Aztec Political Numerology and Human Sacrifice: The Ideological Ramifications of the Number Six." *Journal of Latin American Lore* 6, no. 2 (1980): 205–15.

Offner, Jerome A. "On the Inapplicability of 'Oriental Despotism' and the 'Asiatic Mode of Production' to the Aztecs of Texcoco." *American Antiquity* 46, no. 1 (1981): 43–61. https://doi.org/10.2307/279985.

Offner, Jerome A. *Law and Politics in Aztec Texcoco*. Cambridge: Cambridge Unviesity Press, 1983.

Offner, Jerome A. "The Distribution of Jurisdiction and Political Power in Aztec Texcoco: Subgroups in Conflict." In *Five Centuries of Law and Politics in Central Mexico*. Edited by Ronald Spores and Ross Hassig, 5–14. Nashville: Vanderbilt University Publications in Anthropology, 1984.

Offner, Jerome A. "Dueling Rulers and Strange Attractors: Some Patterns of Disorder and Killing in Aztec Society." *Political and Legal Anthropology Review* 16, no. 2 (June 1993): 65–74. https://doi.org/10.1525/pol.1993.16.2.65.

Offner, Jerome A. "Ixtlilxochitl's Ethnographic Encounter: Understanding the Codex Xolotl and Its Depdendent Alphabetic Texts." In *Fernando de Alva Ixtlilxochitl and His Legacy*. Edited by Galen Brokaw and Jongsoo Lee, 77–121. Tucson: University of Arizona Press, 2015.

Offner, Jerome A. "The Future of Aztec Law." In *Legal Encounters on the Medieval Globe*. Edited by Elizabeth Lambourn and Carol Symes, 2, no. 3, article 3. Kalamazoo: ARC Humanities Press, 2016.

Offner, Jerome A. "Apuntes sobre la plancha X del Códice Xolotl: Cincuenta años más tarde." Translated by Agnieszka Brylak. In *Códices del Centro de México: Análisis comparativos y estudios individuales*, vol. 2. Edited by Miguel Ánge Ruz Barrio and Juan José Batalla Rosado. Warsaw: University of Warsaw, in press.

Olivera, Mercedes. *Pillis y macehuales: Las formaciones sociales y los modos de producción de Tecali del siglo XII al XVI*. Mexico City: INAH, 1978.

Olivier, Guilhem. *Tezcatlipoca: Burlas y metamorfosis de un dios azteca.* Mexico City: FCE, 2004.

Olivier, Guilhem. "Tlantepuzilama: Las peligrosas andanzas de una diedad con dientes de cobre en Mesoamérica." *Estudios de Cultura Nahuatl* 36 (2005): 245–71.

Olivier, Guilhem. *Cacería, sacrificio y poder en Mesoamérica: Tras las huellas de Mixcóatl, "serpiente de nube."* Mexico City: FCE, 2015.

Olko, Justyna. "El 'otro' y los estereotipos étnicos en el mundo nahua." *Estudios de Cultura Nahuatl* 44 (2012): 165–98.

Olko, Justyna. *Insignia of Rank in the Nahua World: From the Fifteenth to the Seventeenth Centuries.* Boulder: University Press of Colorado, 2013.

Oudijk, Michel R. "La toma de posesión: Un tema mesoamericano para la legitimación del poder." *Relaciones: Estudios de Historia Social* 23, no. 91 (2002): 97–131.

Ouweneel, Arij. "From Tlahtocayotl to Gobernadoryotl: A Critical Examination of Indigenous Rule in 18th-Century Central Mexico." *American Ethnologist* 22, no. 4 (November 1995): 756–85. https://doi.org/10.1525/ae.1995.22.4.02a00060.

Ouweneel, Arij. *Shadows over Anáhuac: An Ecological Interpretation of Crisis and Development in Central Mexico, 1730–1800.* Albuquerque: University of New Mexico Press, 1996.

Ouweneel, Arij. *The Flight of the Shepherd: Microhistory and the Psychology of Cultural Resilience in Bourbon Central Mexico.* Amsterdam: Aksant, 2005.

Ouweneel, Arij, and María Cristina Torales Pacheco, eds. *Empresarios, indios y estado: Perfil de la economía mexicana, siglo XVIII.* Mexico City: Universidad Iberoamericana, 1992.

Owensby, Brian P. *Empire of Law and Indian Justice in Colonial Mexico.* Stanford: Stanford University Press, 2008.

Oxford English Dictionary. Accessed January 8, 2014. oed.com.

Palerm, Ángel, and Eric Wolf. "El desarrollo del área clave del imperio texcocano." *Revista mexicana de estudios antropológicos* 14, no. 1 (1954–55): 337–49.

Palerm, Ángel, and Eric Wolf. "Irrigation in the Old Acolhua Domain, Mexico." *Southwestern Journal of Anthropology* 2, no. 3 (1955): 265–81.

Parsons, Jeffrey R., with Richard E. Blanton and Mary H. Parsons. *Prehistoric Settlement Patterns in the Texcoco Region, Mexico.* Ann Arbor: University of Michigan Museum of Anthropology, 1971.

Paso y Troncoso, Francisco del. *Description, historia y exposición del códice pictórico de los antiguos Náuas que se conserva en la Biblioteca de la Cámara de diputados de Paris.* Florence: Salvador Landi, 1899.

Paso y Troncoso, Francisco del, ed. *Códice Kingsborough: Memorial de los indios de Tepetlaoztoc al monarca español contra los encomenderos del pueblo.* Madrid: Hauser y Menet, 1912.

Pastor, María Alba. *Crisis y recomposición social: Nueva España en el tránsito del siglo XVI al XVII.* Mexico City: FCE, 1999.

Pastor, María Alba, and Alicia Mayer, eds. *Formaciones religiosas en la América colonial.* Mexico City: UNAM, 2000.

Pastor, Rodolfo. *Campesinos y reformas: La Mixteca, 1700–1856.* Mexico City: Colegio de México, 1987.

Pastrana Flores, Miguel. *Entre los hombres y los dioses: Acercamiento al sacerdocio de calpulli entre los antiguos nahuas.* Mexico City: UNAM, 2008.

Peñafiel, Antonio. *Nomenclatura geográfica de México*, vol. 2. Mexico City: Secretaria de Fomento, 1897.

Peñafiel, Antonio, ed. *Manuscritos de Texcoco.* Mexico City: Innovación, 1979.

Peperstraete, Sylvie. "La 'Chronique X': Reconstitution et analyse d'une source perdue fondamentale sur la civilisation Aztèque, d'après l'Historia de las Indias de Nueva España de D. Durán (1581) et la Crónica mexicana de F. A. Tezozomoc (ca. 1598)." BAR International Series 1630. Oxford: Archaeopress, 2007.

Pérez-Lizaur, Marisol. *Población y sociedad: Cuatro comunidades del Acolhuacan.* 2nd ed. Mexico City: Universidad Iberoamericana, 2008.

Pérez Rocha, Emma, and Rafael Tena, eds. *La nobleza indígena del centro de México después de la conquista.* Mexico City: INAH, 2000.

Perkins, Stephen M. "'Macehuales' and the Corporate Solution: Colonial Secessions in Nahua Central Mexico." *Mexican Studies/Estudios Mexicanos* 21, no. 2 (2005): 277–306. https://doi.org/10.1525/msem.2005.21.2.277.

Phelan, John Leddy. *The Millennial Kingdom of the Franciscans in the New World.* Berkeley: University of California Press, 1970.

Pietschmann, Horst. *Las reformas borbónicas y el sistema de intendencias en Nueva España: Un estudio político administrativo.* Translated by Roland Meyer Misteli Rolf. Mexico City: FCE, 1996.

Pilar Aizpuru, Gonzalbo, ed. *Historia de la vida cotidiana en México.* 5 vols. Mexico City: Colegio de México, 2004–7.

Pitarch, Pedro. *La cara oculta del pliegue: Ensayos de antropología indígena.* Mexico City: Artes de Mexico, 2013.

Pitarch Román, Pedro. *Ch'ulel: Una etnografía de las almas tzeltales.* Mexico City: FCE, 1996.

Pizzigoni, Caterina. *Testaments of Toluca.* Stanford: Stanford University Press, 2007.

Pizzigoni, Caterina. *The Life Within: Local Indigenous Society in Mexico's Toluca Valley, 1650–1800.* Stanford: Stanford University Press, 2012. https://doi.org/10.11126/stanford/9780804781374.001.0001.

Pomar, Juan Bautista de. "Relación de la ciudad y provincia de Tezcoco." In *Relaciones geográficas del siglo XVI.* Edited by René Acuña, 7:23–116. Mexico City: UNAM, 1986.

Poole, Stafford. *Our Lady of Guadalupe: The Origins and Sources of a Mexican National Symbol, 1531–1797.* Stanford: Stanford University Press, 1996.

Prado, Osvaldo F. *The Origins of Mexican Catholicism: Nahua Rituals and Christian Sacraments in Sixteenth-Century Mexico.* Ann Arbor: University of Michigan Press, 2004. https://doi.org/10.3998/mpub.17681.

Prem, Hanns. *Milpa y hacienda: Tenencia de la tierra indígena y española en la cuenca del Alto Atoyac, Puebla, México, 1520–1650.* Mexico City: CIESAS, 1988.

"Procesos de indios idolatras y hechiceros." In *Publicaciones de la Comisión Reorganizadora del Archivo General y Público de la Nación*, vol. 3. Edited by Luis González Obregon. Mexico City: AGN, 1912.

Pulido Acuña, Rodolfo. *Texcoco: Monografía Municipal.* Toluca: Instituto Mexiquense de Cultura, 2001.

Quiñones Keber, Eloise, ed. *Codex Telleriano-Remensis: Ritual, Divination, and History in a Pictorial Aztec Manuscript.* Austin: University of Texas Press, 1995.

Quiñones Keber, Eloise. "The Tlailotlaque in Acolhua Pictorial Histories: Imitators or Inventors?" *Journal de la Société des Américanistes* 84, no. 2 (1998): 83–96. https://doi.org/10.3406/jsa.1998.1718.

Quiroz, Bernardino de Jesús, ed. *Códice Aubin: Manuscrito azteca de la Biblioteca Real de Berlin.* Mexico City: Editorial Innovación, 1980.

Ramírez López, Javier Eduardo, ed. *De Catemahco a Tezcoco: origen y desarrollo de una ciudad indígena.* Texcoco: Diócesis de Texcoco, 2017.

Rao, Narayana, David Shulman Velcheru, and Sanjay Subrahmanyam. *Textures of Time: Writing History in South India, 1600–1800.* Delhi: Permanent Black, 2001.

"Relación de Tequizistlan y su partido." In *Relaciones.* Edited by René Acuña, 2:211–51. Mexico City: UNAM, 1984–88.

Restall, Matthew. "Heirs to the Heiroglyphs: Indigenous Writing in Colonial Mesoamerica." *Americas* 54, no. 2 (1997): 239–67. https://doi.org/10.2307/1007743.

Restall, Matthew. *The Maya World: Yucatec Culture and Society, 1550–1850.* Stanford: Stanford University Press, 1999.

Restall, Matthew. *Seven Myths of the Spanish Conquest.* Oxford: Oxford University Press, 2003.

Restall, Matthew. *The Black Middle: Africans, Mayas, and Spaniards in olonial Yucatan.* Stanford: Stanford University Press, 2009.

Restall, Matthew. "The New Conquest History." *History Compass* 10, no. 2 (February 2012): 151–60. https://doi.org/10.1111/j.1478-0542.2011.00822.x.

Restall, Matthew, Lisa Sousa, and Kevin Terraciano. "Nahuatl Grant of a House Site in San Miguel Tocuillan, 1583." In *Mesoamerican Voices: Native-Language Writings from Colonial Mexico, Oaxaca, Yucatan, and Guatemala.* Edited by Matthew Restall, Lisa Sousa, and Kevin Terraciano, 100–102. New York: Cambridge University Press, 2005.

Reyes, Alfonso. "Visión de Anáhuac." In *Obras completes*, 1:13–34. Mexico City: UNAM, 1956.

Reyes García, Luis. "El término *calpulli* en los documentos del siglo XVI." In *Documentos nauas de la ciudad de México del siglo XVI*. Edited by Luis Reyes García, Eustaquio Celestino Solís, Armando Valenica Ríos, Constantino Medina Luna, and Gregorio Guerrero Díaz, 21–67. Mexico City: AGN, 1996.

Reyes García, Luis. *¿Cómo te confundes? Acaso no somos conquistados? Anales de Juan Bautista*. Estudio, transcripción y traducción de Luis Reyes García. Mexico City: Biblioteca Lorenzo Boturini Insigne/Nacional Basílica de Guadalupe/CIESAS, 2001.

Reyes García, Luis, Eustaquio Celestino Solís, Armando Valenica Ríos, Constantino Medina Luna, and Gregorio Guerrero Díaz, eds. *Documentos nauas de la ciudad de México del siglo XVI*. Mexico City: AGN, 1996.

Reyes Valerio, Constantino. *El pintor de conventos: Los murales del siglo XVI en la Nueva España*. Mexico City: INAH, 1989.

Ricard, Robert. *La "conquête spirituelle" du Mexique: Essai sur l'apostolat et les méthodes missionaires des ordres mendiants en Nouvelle-Espagne de 1523–24 à 1572*. Paris: Institut d'ethnologie, 1933.

Riva Palacio, Vicente, ed. *México a través de los siglos: historia general y completa del desenvolvimiento social, político, religioso, militar, artístico, científico y literario de México desde la antigüedad más remota hasta la época actual*. 3 vols. Mexico City: Ballescá y compañía, 1888–89.

Rivera Pérez, Roberto. "Bandidos, arrieros y machos contempoáneos del Acolhuacán septentrional: Múltiples espacios para la construcción de la masculinidad." PhD dissertation, Universidad Autónoma Metropolitana-Iztapalapa, 2013.

Robertson, Donald. *Mexican Manuscript Painting of the Early Colonial Period: The Metropolitan Schools*. New Haven: Yale University Press, 1959.

Rodríguez Rojo, Alma Rosa. *San Juan Tezontla: Lucha por el agua*. Mexico City: Iberoamericana, 1995.

Rodríguez Vázquez, Elías, and Pascual Tinoco Quesnel. *Graffitis Novohispanos de Tepeapulco, Siglo XVI*. Pachuca: Universidad Autónoma del Estado de Hidalgo, 2006.

Rojas, Jose Luis de. *Cambiar para que yo no cambie: La nobleza indígena en la Nueva España*. Buenos Aires: Editorial SB, 2010.

Rojas Rabiela, Teresa, Elsa Leticia Rea López, and Constantino Medina Lima, eds. *Vidas y bienes olvidados: Testamentos indígenas novohispanos*. 4 vols. Mexico City: CIESAS, 1999.

Romero Frizzi, María de los Ángeles, and Michel R. Oudijk. "Los títulos primordiales: Un género de tradición mesoamericana: Del mundo prehispánico al siglo XXI." *Relaciones: Estudios de Historia y Sociedad* 24, no. 95 (2003): 19–48.

Romero Galván, José Rubén. "La historia según Chimalpain." *Journal de la Société des Americanistes* 84, no. 2 (1998): 183–95.

Roniger, Luis, and Tamar Herzog, eds. *The Collective and the Public in Latin America: Cultural Identities and Political Order*. Brighton: Sussex Academic Press, 2000.

Ruiz de Alarcón, Hernando. *Treatise on the Heathen Superstitions That Today Live among the Indians Native to This New Spain*. Edited and translated by J. Richard Andrews and Ross Hassig. Norman: University of Oklahoma Press, 1984.

Ruiz Medrano, Carlos Rubén. "Alevosos, ingratos y traidores ¿queréis sacudir el yugo del monarca más católico? El discurso de la contrainsurgencia en la Nueva España durante el siglo XVIII." *Hispanic American Historical Review* 87, no. 3 (2007): 471–97. https://doi.org/10.1215/00182168-2007-002.

Ruiz Medrano, Ethelia. *Gobierno y sociedad en Nueva España*. Zamora: Colegio de Michoacán, 1991.

Ruiz Medrano, Ethelia. *Mexico's Indigenous Communities: Their Lands and Histories, 1500–2010*. Boulder: University Press of Colorado, 2010.

Ruiz Medrano, Ethelia. "Don Carlos de Tezcoco and the Universal Rights of Emperor Carlos V." In *Texcoco: Prehispanic and Colonial Perspectives*. Edited by Jongsoo Lee and Galen Brokaw, 165–85. Boulder: University Press of Colorado, 2014.

Ruiz Medrano, Ethelia, Claudio Barrera Gutiérrez, and Florencio Barrera Gutiérrez. *La lucha por la tierra: Los titulos primordiales y los pueblos indios en México, siglos XIX y XX*. Mexico City: FCE, 2013.

Russo, Alessandra. *The Untranslatable Image: A Mestizo History of the Arts in New Spain, 1500–1600*. Austin: University of Texas Press, 2014.

Ruz Barrio, Miguel Ángel, and Juan José Batalla Rosado, eds. *Códices del Centro de México: Análisis comparativos y estudios individuales*. 2 vols. Warsaw: University of Warsaw, 2013–17.

Saether, Steiner. "Bourbon Absolutism and Marriage Reform in Late Colonial Spanish America." *Americas* 59, no. 4 (2003): 475–509. https://doi.org/10.1353/tam.2003.0056.

Sahagún, Bernardino de. Primeros Memoriales. Edited and translated by Thelma D. Sullivan, H. B. Nicholson, Arthur J.O. Anderson, Charles E. Dibble, Eloise Quiñones-Keber, and Wayne Ruwet. Norman: University of Oklahoma Press, 1997.

Sahagún, Bernardino de, ed. *General History of the Things of New Spain: Florentine Codex*. 13 vols. Edited and translated by Arthur J.O. Anderson and Charles E. Dibble. Salt Lake City: University of Utah Press, 1950–55.

Sahagún, Bernardino de, ed. *Códice florentino*. Mexico City: Secretaría de Gobernación, 1979.

Salomon, Frank. "Unethnic Ethnohistory: On Peruvian Peasant Historiography and Ideas of Autochthony." *Ethnohistory* 49, no. 3 (Summer 2002): 475–506. https://doi.org/10.1215/00141801-49-3-475.

Salvucci, Richard J. *Textiles and Capitalism in Mexico: An Economic History of the Obrajes, 1539–1840*. Princeton: Princeton University Press, 1987.

Salvucci, Richard J. "Some Thoughts on the Economic History of Early Colonial Mexico." *History Compass* 8, no. 7 (2010): 626–35. https://doi.org/10.1111/j.1478-0542.2010.00690.x.

Sanders, William T., and Barbara J. Price. "The Native Aristocracy and the Evolution of the Latifundio in the Teotihuacán Valley, 1521–1917." *Ethnohistory* 50, no. 1 (Winter 2003): 69–88. https://doi.org/10.1215/00141801-50-1-69.

Schroeder, Susan. *Chimalpahin and the Kingdoms of Chalco*. Tucson: University of Arizona Press, 1991.

Schroeder, Susan, and David Cahill, eds. *The Conquest All Over Again: Nahuas and Zapotecs Thinking, Writing, and Painting Spanish Colonialism*. Sussex: Sussex Academic Press, 2009.

Schroeder, Susan, Anne Cruz, Cristián Roa-de-la-Carrera, and David Tavárez. Chimalpahin's Conquest: A Nahua Historian's Rewriting of Francisco López de Gómara's La conquista de México. Stanford: Stanford University Press, 2010.

Schroeder, Susan, Stephanie Wood, and Robert Haskett, eds. *Indian Women of Early Mexico*. Norman: University of Oklahoma Press, 1997.

Sedano, Francisco. *Noticias de México: Crónicas de los siglos XVI al XVII*. Mexico City: Secretaría de Obras y Servicios, 1974.

Seed, Patricia. "Social Dimensions of Race: Mexico City, 1753." *Hispanic American Historical Review* 62, no. 4 (November 1982): 569–606. https://doi.org/10.2307/2514568.

Seed, Patricia. *To Love, Honor, and Obey in Colonial Mexico: Conflicts of Marriage Choice, 1574–1821*. Stanford: Stanford University Press, 1988.

Seed, Patricia, and Philip F. Rust. "Estate and Class in Colonial Oaxaca Revisited." *Comparative Studies in Society and History* 25, no. 4 (October 1983): 703–10. https://doi.org/10.1017/S0010417500010689.

Sell, Barry D. "Friars, Nahuas, and Books: Language and Expression in Colonial Nahuatl Publications." PhD dissertation, University of California, Los Angeles, 1993.

Sell, Barry D., and Louise M. Burkhart, eds. *Nahuatl Theater*. 4 vols. Norman: University of Oklahoma Press, 2004–9.

Sempat Assadourian, Carlos. *El sistema de la economía colonial: el mercado interior, regiones y espacio económico*. Mexico City: Editorial Nueva Imagen, 1983.

Sigal, Pete. "Queer Nahuatl: Sahagún's Faggots and Sodomites, Lesbians and Hermaphrodites." *Ethnohistory* 54, no. 1 (2007): 9–34.

Silva Prada, Natalia. *La política de una rebelión: los indígenas frente al tumulto de 1692 en la Ciudad de México*. Mexico City: Colegio de México, 2007.

Smith, Michael E. "Houses and the Settlement Hierarchy in Late Postclassic Morelos: A Comparison of Archaeology and Ethnohistory." In *Prehispanic Domestic Units in Western Mesoamerica*. Edited by Robert S. Stanley and Kenneth G. Hirth, 191–206. Boca Raton: CRC, 1993.

Smith, Michael E. "The Aztec Empire and the Mesoamerican World System." In *Empires: Perspectives from Archaeology and History*. Edited by Susan Alcock, 128–54. New York: Cambridge University Press, 2001.

Smith, Michael E. *The Aztecs*, 2nd ed. Malden: Blackwell, 2003.

Smith, Michael E. *Aztec City-State Capitals*. Gainesville: University of Florida Press, 2008.
Smith, Michael E., and Frances F. Berdan, eds. *The Postclassic Mesoamerican World*. Salt Lake City: University of Utah Press, 2003.
Smith, Raymond, ed. *Kinship, Ideology, and Practice in Latin America*. Chapel Hill: University of North Carolina Press, 1984.
Socolow, Susan Migden. *The Women of Colonial Latin America*. Cambridge: Cambridge University Press, 2000. https://doi.org/10.1017/CBO9780511840074.
Spain. *Leyes de indias*. Lima: Congreso de la República del Perú. Accessed October 18, 2010. http://www.congreso.gob.pe/ntley/LeyIndiaP.htm.
Stavig, Ward. "Living in Offense of Our Lord: Indigenous Sexual Values and Marital Life in the Colonial Crucible." *Hispanic American Historical Review* 75, no. 4 (1995): 597–622. https://doi.org/10.2307/2518037.
Stern, Steve J. *Peru's Indian Peoples and the Challenge of Spanish Conquest: Huamanga to 1640*, 2nd ed. Madison: University of Wisconsin Press, 1993.
Stern, Steve J. *The Secret History of Gender: Women, Men, and Power in Late Colonial Mexico*. Chapel Hill: University of North Carolina Press, 1995.
Stresser-Péan, Guy. *Sol-Dios y Cristo: La cristianización de los indios de México vista desde la Sierra de Puebla*. Mexico City: FCE, 2011. https://doi.org/10.4000/books.cemca.2264.
Sullivan, John, Eduardo de la Cruz Cruz, Abelardo de la Cruz de la Cruz, Delfina de la Cruz de la Cruz, Victoriano de la Cruz Cruz, Sabina Cruz de la Cruz, Ofelia Cruz Morales, Catalina Cruz de la Cruz, and Manuel de la Cruz Cruz. *Tlahtolxitlauhcayotl: Chicontepec, Veracruz*. Warsaw: University of Warsaw, 2016.
Sweet, David G., and Gary B. Nash, eds. *Struggle and Survival in Colonial America*. Berkeley: University of California Press, 1981.
Szuchman, Mark, ed. *The Middle Period in Latin America: Values and Attitudes in the Seventeenth–Nineteenth Centuries*. Boulder: Lynne Rienner, 1989.
Tavárez, David. *The Invisible War: Indigenous Devotions, Discipline, and Dissent in Colonial Mexico*. Stanford: Stanford University Press, 2011. https://doi.org/10.11126/stanford/9780804773287.001.0001.
Taylor, William B. *Landlord and Peasant in Colonial Oaxaca*. Stanford: Stanford University Press, 1972.
Taylor, William B. *Drinking, Homicide, and Rebellion in Colonial Mexican Towns*. Stanford: Stanford University Press, 1979.
Taylor, William B. "The Virgin of Guadalupe in New Spain: An Inquiry into the Social History of Marian Devotion." *American Ethnologist* 14, no. 1 (1987): 9–33. https://doi.org/10.1525/ae.1987.14.1.02a00020.
Taylor, William B. *Magistrates of the Sacred: Priests and Parishioners in Eighteenth-Century Mexico*. Stanford: Stanford University Press, 1996.

Taylor, William B. "Saint." In *Lexikon of the Hispanic Baroque*. Edited by Evonne Levy and Kenneth Mills, 291–94. Austin: University of Texas Press, 2014.

Tena, Rafael, ed. and trans. *Anales de Tlatelolco*. Mexico City: CONACULTA, 2004.

Tepetlaoztoc. "Barrio La Asunción." Accessed March 9, 2016. http://tepetlaoxtoc.gob.mx /comunidades_detalle?CM=94.

Terraciano, Kevin. *The Mixtecs of Colonial Oaxaca: Ñudzahui History, Sixteenth through Eighteenth Centuries*. Stanford: Stanford University Press, 2001.

Tetlacuilolli. Accessed March 9, 2016. http://www.tetlacuilolli.org.mx.

Therrell, Matthew D., David W. Stahle, and Rodolfo Acuña Soto. "Aztec Drought and the 'Curse of One Rabbit.'" *Bulletin of the American Meteorological Society* 85, no. 9 (2004): 1263–72. https://doi.org/10.1175/BAMS-85-9-1263.

Thouvenot, Marc. "Codex Xolotl: Étude d'une des composantes de son écriture: Les glyphs: Dictionnaire des éléments constitutifs des glyphes." PhD dissertation, École des hautes études en sciences sociales, Paris, France, 1987.

Tinajero Morales, José Omar. *Imágenes del silencio: Iconología de Tepetlaoztoc*. Mexico City: CEASDP, 2002.

Tlachia. Accessed November 11, 2016. tlachia.lib.unam.mx.

Torquemada, Juan de. *Monarquía Indiana*. 2nd ed. Madrid: Nicolás Rodríguez Franco, 1723.

Torquemada, Juan de. *Monarquía indiana*. 3 vols. Edited by Miguel León-Portilla. Mexico City: Porrúa, 1969.

Townsend, Camilla. *Malintzin's Choices: An Indian Woman in the Conquest of Mexico*. Albuquerque: University of New Mexico Press, 2006.

Townsend, Camilla. "Glimpsing Native American Historiography: The Cellular Principle in Sixteenth-Century Nahuatl Annals." *Ethnohistory* 56, no. 4 (2009): 625–50. https://doi.org/10.1215/00141801-2009-024.

Townsend, Camilla, ed. and trans. *Here in This Year: Seventeenth-Century Nahuatl Annals of the Tlaxcala-Puebla Valley*. Stanford: Stanford University Press, 2010.

Trigger, Bruce G., Wilcomb E. Washburn, Richard E.W. Adams, Murdo J. MacLeod, Frank Salomon, and Stuart B. Schwartz, eds. *Cambridge History of the Native Peoples of the Americas*. 3 vols. New York: Cambridge University Press, 1996–2000.

Tutino, John. *From Insurrection to Revolution in Mexico: Social Basis of Agrarian Violence, 1750–1940*. Princeton: Princeton University Press, 1986.

Tutino, John. *Making a New World: Founding Capitalism in the Bajío and Spanish North America*. Durham: Duke University Press, 2011. https://doi.org/10.1215/9780 822394013.

Twinam, Ann. *Public Lives, Private Secrets: Gender, Honor, Sexuality, and Illegitimacy in Colonial Spanish America*. Stanford: Stanford University Press, 1999.

Urquiza Vázquez del Mercado, Gabriela. *Convento Huexotla: Reflejo de la mística franciscana*. Mexico City: Plaza y Valdéz, 1993.

Urton, Gary. *The History of a Myth: Pacariqtambo and the Origin of the Inkas*. Austin: University of Texas Press, 1990.

Valle, Perla, ed. *Memorial de los indios de Tepetlaóztoc o códice Kingsborough: A cuatrocientos cuarenta años*. Mexico City: INAH, 1992.

Van Young, Eric. *Hacienda and Market in Eighteenth-Century Mexico: The Rural Economy of the Guadalajara Region, 1675–1820*. Berkeley: University of California Press, 1981.

Van Young, Eric. "Mexican Rural History since Chevalier: The Historiography of the Colonial Hacienda." *Latin American Research Review* 18, no. 3 (1983): 5–61.

Van Young, Eric. "Conflict and Solidarity in Indian Village Life: The Guadalajara Region in the Late Colonial Period." *Hispanic American Historical Review* 64, no. 1 (February 1984): 55–79. https://doi.org/10.2307/2514465.

Van Young, Eric. "Agrarian Rebellion and Defense of Community: Meaning and Collective Violence in Late Colonial and Independence-Era Mexico." *Journal of Social History* 27, no. 2 (Winter 1993): 245–69. https://doi.org/10.1353/jsh/27.2.245.

Van Young, Eric. *The Other Rebellion: Popular Violence, Ideology, and the Struggle for Mexican Independence, 1810–1821*. Stanford: Stanford University Press, 2001.

Van Young, Eric. "Beyond the Hacienda: Agrarian Relations and Socioeconomic Change in Rural Mesoamerica." *Ethnohistory* 50, no. 1 (Winter 2003): 231–45. https://doi.org/10.1215/00141801-50-1-231.

Velazco, Salvador. "Visiones de Anáhuac: Historiografía y etnicidad en el México colonial: Fernando de Alva Ixtlilxochitl, Diego Munoz Camargo y Hernando Alvarado Tezozomoc." PhD dissertation, University of Michigan, Ann Arbor, 1996.

Vetancurt, Agustín de. *Chrónica de la provincia del Santo Evangelio de México*. Mexico City: Doña María Benavides, 1697.

Vetancurt, Agustín de. *Teatro mexicano*. Mexico City: Porrúa, 1971.

Villa-Flores, Javier. "'To Lose One's Soul': Blasphemy and Slavery in New Spain, 1596–1669." *Hispanic American Historical Review* 82, no. 3 (August 2002): 435–68. https://doi.org/10.1215/00182168-82-3-435.

Villa-Flores, Javier. *Dangerous Speech: A Social History of Blasphemy in Colonial Mexico*. Tucson: University of Arizona Press, 2006.

Villella, Peter B. "The Last Acolhua: Alva Ixtlilxochitl and Elite Native Historiography in Early New Spain." *Colonial Latin American Review* 23, no. 1 (2014): 18–36. https://doi.org/10.1080/10609164.2013.877249.

Vinson, Ben, III, and Matthew Restall, eds. *Black Mexico: Race and Society from Colonial to Modern Times*. Albuquerque: University of New Mexico Press, 2009.

Vinson, Ben, III, and Bobby Vaughan. *Afroméxico: El pulso de la población negra en México, una historia recordada, olvidada y vuelta a recorder*. Mexico City: FCE, 2004.

Viqueira, Juan Pedro. ¿*Relajados o reprimidos? Diversiones públicas y vida social en la ciudad de México durante el Siglo de las Luces*. Mexico City: FCE, 1987.

Viqueira, Juan Pedro. "Tributo y sociedad en Chiapas (1680–1721)." *Historia Mexicana* 94, no. 174 (1994): 237–67.

Viqueira, Juan Pedro. *Indios, rebeldes e idólatras: Dos ensayos históricos sobre la rebelión india en Cancuc, Chiapas, acaecida en al año 1712*. Mexico City: CIESAS, 1997.

Wauchope, Robert, ed. *Handbook of Middle American Indians*. 16 vols. Austin: University of Texas Press, 1964–76.

Whitmore, Thomas M. "A Simulation of the Sixteenth-Century Population Collapse in the Basin of Mexico." *Annals of the Association of American Geographers* 81, no. 3 (September 1991): 464–87. https://doi.org/10.1111/j.1467-8306.1991.tb01705.x.

Whitmore, Thomas M. *Disease and Death in Early Colonial Mexico: Simulating Amerindian Depopulation*. Boulder: Westview, 1992.

Whitmore, Thomas M., and Barbara J. Williams. "Famine Vulnerability in the Contact-Era Basin of Mexico: A Simulation." *Ancient Mesoamerica* 9, no. 1 (1998): 83–98. https://doi.org/10.1017/S0956536100001863.

Whittaker, Gordon. "The Study of North Mesoamerican Place-Signs." *Indiana* 13 (1993): 9–38.

Whittaker, Gordon. "The Principles of Nahuatl Writing." *Göttinger Beiträge zur Sprachwissenschaft* 16 (2009): 47–81.

Whittaker, Gordon. "Nahuatl Hieroglyphic Writing and the Beinecke Map." In *Painting a Map of Sixteenth-Century Mexico City: Land, Writing, and Native Rule*. Edited by Mary E. Miller and Barbara E. Mundy, 137–57. New Haven: Beinecke Library, 2012.

Whittaker, Gordon. "The Identities of Fernando de Alva Ixtlilxochitl." In *Fernando de Alva Ixtlilxochitl and His Legacy*. Edited by Galen Brokaw and Jongsoo Lee, 29–76. Tucson: University of Arizona Press, 2015.

Williams, Barbara J. "Mexican Pictorial Cadastral Registers: An Analysis of the Códice de Santa María Asunción and the Codex Vergara." In *Explorations in Ethnohistory: Indians of Central Mexico in the Sixteenth Century*. Edited by H. R. Harvey and Hanns J. Prem, 103–25. Albuquerque: New Mexico University Press, 1984.

Williams, Barbara J. "Contact Period Rural Overpopulation in the Basin of Mexico: Carrying-Capacity Models Tested with Documentary Data." *American Antiquity* 54, no. 4 (October 1989): 715–32. https://doi.org/10.2307/280678.

Williams, Barbara J. "Aztec Soil Knowledge: Classes, Management, and Ecology." In *Footprints in the Soil: People and Ideas in Soil History*. Edited by Benno P. Warkentin, 17–41. Oxford: Elsevier, 2006.

Williams, Barbara J., and H. R. Harvey, eds. *The Códice de Santa María Asunción: Facsimile and Commentary: Households and Lands in Sixteenth-Century Tepetlaoztoc*. Salt Lake City: University of Utah Press, 1997.

Williams, Barbara J., and H. R. Harvey. "Content, Provenience, and Significance of the *Codex Vergara* and the *Códice de Santa Maria Asuncion*." *American Antiquity* 53, no. 2 (1988): 337–51.
Williams, Barbara J., and Frederic Hicks, eds. *El códice Vergara: Edición facsimilar con comentario*. Mexico City: UNAM, 2011.
Williams, Barbara J., and Janice K. Pierce. "Evidence of Acolhua Science in Pictorial Land Records." In *Texcoco: Prehispanic and Colonial Perspectives*. Edited by Jongsoo Lee and Galen Brokaw, 147–64. Boulder: University Press of Colorado, 2014. https://doi.org/10.5876/9781607322849.c006.
Wolf, Eric R. "Closed Corporate Peasant Communities in Mesoamerica and Central Java." *Southwestern Journal of Anthropology* 13, no. 1 (Spring 1957): 1–18. https://doi.org/10.1086/soutjanth.13.1.3629154.
Wolf, Eric R. "The Vicissitudes of the Closed Corporate Peasant Community." *American Ethnologist* 13, no. 2 (May 1986): 325–29. https://doi.org/10.1525/ae.1986.13.2.02a00080.
Wood, Stephanie. "Corporate Adjustments in Colonial Mexican Indian Towns: Toluca Region." PhD dissertation, University of California, Los Angeles, 1984.
Wood, Stephanie. *Transcending Conquest: Nahua Views of Spanish Colonial Mexico*. Norman: University of Oklahoma Press, 2003.
Wright Carr, David Charles. "Hñahñu, Ñuhu, Ñhato, Ñuhmu: Precisiones sobre el término 'otomí.'" *Arqueología Mexicana* 12, no. 73 (May 2005): 19–20.
Wright Carr, David Charles. "La sociedad prehispánica en las lenguas náhuatl y otomí." *Acta Universitaria* 18 (2008): 15–23.
Wright Carr, David Charles. "Los otomíes: cultura, lengua, y escritura." PhD dissertation, El Colegio de Michoacán, 2005.
Yannakakis, Yanna. *The Art of Being In-Between: Native Intermediaries, Indian Identity, and Local Rule in Colonial Oaxaca*. Durham: Duke University Press, 2008. https://doi.org/10.1215/9780822388982.
Yannakakis, Yanna. "Witnesses, Spatial Practices, and a Land Dispute in Colonial Oaxaca." *Americas* 65, no. 2 (October 2008): 161–92. https://doi.org/10.1353/tam.0.0031.
Zantwijk, Rudolf van. "La entronización de Acamapichtli de Tenochtitlan y las características de su gobierno." *Estudios de Cultura Nahuatl* 15 (1982): 17–26.
Zantwijk, Rudolf van. *The Aztec Arrangement: The Social History of Pre-Spanish Mexico*. Norman: University of Oklahoma Press, 1985.
Zantwijk, Rudolf van. "Tlen Quihtoznequi 'Chichimecatl.'" *Estudios de Cultura Nahuatl* 25 (1995): 131–47.
Zantwijk, Rudolf van, ed. *Anales de Tula: Museo Nacional de Antropología, Mexico City (Cod. 35–9)*. Graz: Akademische Druck- und Verlagsanstalt, 1979.
Zavala, Silvio. *La encomienda indiana*. Mexico City: Porrúa, 1992.

Zavala, Silvio, and María Castelo, eds. *Fuentes para la historia del trabajo en la Nueva España*. 8 vols. Mexico City: FCE, 1939.

Zorita, Alonso de. *Relación de la Nueva España: relación de algunas de las muchas cosas notables que hay en la Nueva España y de su conquista y pacificación y de la conversión de los naturales de ella*. Edited by Ethelia Ruiz Medrano, Wiebke Ahrndt, and José Mariano Leyva. Mexico City: CONACULTA, 1999.

Index

Acolhua: administration in Cuauhtepoztlan tlaxilacalli, 58–59; death rates in Tlanchiuhcan altepemaitl, 80–82; differences with Mexica, 19–20, 35(n55); documentary tradition, 20–23, 35(n56), 35(n57), 37(n62), imperialism, 77

Acolhuacan: changes to elite landholding in, 159; Chichimeca rulers, 45–47; defined, 19, 34(n54); evangelization, 131; hierarchical founding narratives, 45–45; hunger in, 115(n2), 116(n3); long term population trends, 40–41; patron deity cared for by Huiznahuac tlaxilacalli, 51; role in Aztec empire, 64–65; scholars of, 22–23, 38(n69); spatial history, 72(n43)

Acxotlan, San Lorenzo (altepemaitl in Huexotla), land inheritance, 186–90

Acxotlan (tlaxilacalli), 206(n2); general characteristics, 14; merchants, 12

administration: Acolhua, 77–79; Aztec, 64–65; comparative Mexican empires, 4–5; difficulty of Spanish centralism, 27(n8); hierarchy of elites, 59; offices, 24; ongoing local logics, 19; tlaxilacalli, 4–5, 19. *See also* calpixqui; tepixqui; teuctli; teuctlatoani; tlatoani; topile

Agustinians, expelled from Teotihuacan, 135–39

altepemaitl: hierarchy, 116(n7), 120(n33); map of Tlanchiuhcan, 54, 55–57; Spanish definitions of, 13, 54; as sub-district of tlaxilacalli, 119(n30)

altepetl: definitions of, 10; as pueblo, 12–13; relation to huei altepetl, 4; relation to tlaxilacalli, 4, 9–10; Spanish definitions of, 13; tlaxilacalli self-defining as, 10

Alva Ixtlilxochitl, Fernando de. *See* Ixtlilxochitl, Fernando de Alva

Ana of Tocuillan, 87–89, 95(n32), 105

Asunción Land Title (from Cuauhtepoztlan tlaxilacalli): first, 115; second, 204–5

Aztec: administration, 4–5, 16–17; empire, 64, 73(n56); problematic but useful term, 25(n3)

barrio. *See* neighborhood

Benavente, fray Toribio de. *See* Motolinia

Calla Tlaxoxouhco (altepemaitl in Tepetlaoztoc), 106; lords of, 108–9; new habitational center, 83–84, religious imagery of, 177

calli: definitions, 13, 24; function, 99–100

calpixqui: coercive land sale, 157–58; definition, 24; function, 106–7; in Teotihaucan rebellion, 137

calpolli: cognate of tlaxilacalli, 11, 25(n2), 31(n31), 31(n32), 31(n38); Spanish definitions of, 13

247

celebrations, 17, 124, 139–40, 175, 193–97, 202(n56). *See also* volador dance

Chichimeca: in Codex Xolotl, 68(n17); early rulers of Acolhuacan, 45–47; learning to farm tlaxilacalli-style, 47–49; opposition to Acolhua consolidation, 51–52; transculturation, 49–50

Chimalpahin, Domingo (Nahua historian), praise of Tlailotlacan tlaxilacalli, 8

Chimalpan (tlaxilacalli): boundary with Cuauhtepoztlan in Tepetlaoztoc, 113, 115; conspiracy against Ixtlilxochitl Ometochtzin, 61–62; continuous occupation of Tetzcoca hillside in dispute with Pomar, 160–62; contribution of head priest to Tetzcoco, 32(n42); devotion to Huitzilopochtli, 12; early integration into Tetzcoca politics, 60; early presence in Tetzcoco, 5–7, 50; general characteristics of, 14; glyph in Codex Xolotl, 62; Hñähnu death rate in Tepetlaoztoc, 81; influence on Codex Xolotl, 8; making peace with Nezahualcoyotl, 75–76; partial reconstruction of, 28(n12); political calculations in the Codex Xolotl, 30(n26); reconsolidating around Calla Tlaxoxouhco altepemaitl in Tepetlaoztoc, 83–84; religious imagery, 177; resistance to congregación in Tepetlaoztoc, 179–80; spatial interpenetration in Coatlinchan, 86; teuctlatoani of in Tepetlaoztoc, 108–10

Christianity. *See* evangelization; Inquisition

Cihuatecpan (tlaxilacalli), general characteristics of, 14

Coanacoch (tlatoani of Tetzcoco), flight, 77

Coapanco, San Joaquín (tlaxilacalli in Tetzcoco): burial rites in, 174; conflict with Tetlicac over land, 175–75

Coatlinchan (altepetl), 14–15, 34(n54), 47, 62, 69(n25), 70(n36), 85–86

codex (painted manuscript), colonial situation of production, 20

Codex Chimalpahin, 77, 78, 79–80

Codex en Cruz, famine, 65

Codex Kingsborough. *See* Memorial de los Indios de Tepetlaoztoc

Codex Mendoza, 11, 17

Codex San Juan Teotihuacan, 135, 137–39

Codex Santa María Asunción: 22, 28(n11), 80, 88, 97, 98, 99, 100, 105, 113, 115(n1), 123, 142(n5), 205; earliest land survey in Americas, 5; plotting of tlaxilacalli, 54, 55–57

Codex Telleriano-Remensis, 65

Codex Vergara, 22, 28(n11), 80, 88, 98, 113, 115(n1); earliest land survey in Americas, 5

Codex Xolotl, 38(n67), 154; Chimalpan and Tlailotlacan make peace in, 75–76; credibility as a historical source, 60; narration of early Tetzcoca tlaxilacalli, 5–6; narration of founding of Acolhuacan, 45–46; narration of Ixtlilxochitl Ometochtzin's fall, 60–61; privileging of Chichimeca narrations, 68(n17); tlaxilacalli authorship, 8; tlaxilacalli-based narration of Nezahualcoyotl saga, 62

Códice de los Señores de San Lorenzo Acxotlan y San Luis Huexotla, 187–90

cofradía, 70(n36), 112–13, 122(n54), 194, 197(n4), 197(n6–n8)

Colhuacan (tlaxilacalli): Colhua affiliation, 50; devotion to Tlaloc, 50; early presence in Tetzcoco, 5–7, 50; general characteristics, 14; integrated into Tetzcoca politics, 60

collective action theory, tlaxilacalli role in, 17–19

comunidad (legal term), 157, 166

congregación (resettlement), 177–79

Conquest. *See* War for Mexico

Cortés, Hernán, 4, 21, 24, 77–79, 159

Cozcacuauhco (tlaxilacalli in Tetzcoco), land sales in, 157–59, 170(n26)

"Crónica X," 22, 37(n60)

Cuauhtepoztlan (tlaxilacalli in Tepetlaoztoc): broad history, 203–5; demographic decline, 80–83; founding, 41–43; hierarchy of hunger, 97–99, 116(n7); modern cofradía in, 70(n36), 112–13, 122(n54); naming patterns in, 114; partially mapped, 54–57, 71(n40); political hierarchy, 110–11; reconsolidating around Calla Tlaxoxouhco altepemaitl, 83–84; religious practice, 113–14, 123–24, 177; spatial history, 56–58, 115, 203; territorial interpenetration with Chimalpan, 113

Durán, fray Diego (evangelist): description of famine aftermath, 62–63; narration of harvest practice, 134; narration of "St. Lucas" tlaxilacalli, 18

evangelization, 142(n5), 146(n38); Acolhua, 127–28, 131; story of "St. Lucas" tlaxilacalli, 18; tlaxilacalli role in Tepetlaoztoc, 84–84, 128

famine: in Acolhuacan, 115(n2), 116(n3); One Rabbit, 65–66
fiestas. *See* celebrations
Franciscans: convent in Tepepulco, 139–42, 151; Teotihuacan, 134–39; Tetzcoco fiesta circuit, 194; translation of Quetzalmamalitzin's will, 153, 155, 168(n5). *See also* Motolinia; Torquemada

gender, 96(n38), 117(n15–n17); within household, 100–102, 118(n22)

Hñähñu: death rates in Tlanchiuhcan altepemaitl, 80–82; definitions, 71(n41); in Cuauhtepoztlan tlaxilacalli, 56–57, 98, 100, 103–5, 116(n5), 120(n36); privation, 98, 116(n6); revolt in Mexico City, 17; volador dance, 139; word for altepemaitl, 13, 119(n30)
huei altepetl, 12, 78, 119; relation to altepetl, 4; Spanish definitions of, 13
huei tlatoani, 37, 60, 65, 75, 77, 152, 206(n2)
Huexotla (altepetl), 14–15, 60, 62, 69(n25), 148(n53), 182, 185–89, 195
Huitznahuac (tlaxilacalli): Colhua affiliation, 50; devotion to Tezcatlipoca, 12, 50; early presence in Tetzcoco, 5–7, 50; exclusion by Techotlalatzin, 60; general characteristics of, 14; ongoing care for Tetzcoca patron deity, 51; role in destroying Aztec religious architecture, 128; role in War for Mexico, 7; soldier, 11

Inquisition, 33, 144; case of don Carlos Ometochtzin, 125–28, destruction of archives, 21–22; Jácome Passalli denounced before, 182
Ixtlilxochitl, Fernando de Alva (historian), 12, 63, 93(n10), 95; complaint against rural "bandits," 51, 182; description of Acolhua elite demotions, 154; exoticizing view of tlaxilacalli, 5–7; historiography of work, 29(n17); narration of Chimalpan tlaxilacalli's conspiracy against Ixtlilxochitl Ometochtzin, 61; narratives of Hernando Ixtlilxochitl's administration, 77; transfer of personal archive, 154, 168(n10); use of "pueblo" for both tlaxilacalli and altepetl, 12; verification of his work by seven tlaxilacalli, 22
Ixtlilxochitl, Hernando (tlatoani of Tetzcoco): putative conspiracy of, 77; role in early Hispanic administration, 77, 78–79, 81, 159

Ixtlilxochitl Ometochtizn (tlatoani of Tetzcoco): conspiracy by tlaxilacalli against, 60–62, 92(n3); supported by Tlailotlacan tlaxilacalli, 60, 72(n46)

kinship, 89–90, 96(n38), 117(n14), 187–89. *See also* tlacamecayotl

land: changing valuation of, 163–64; inheritance, 186–90; productivity, 99, 116(n3), 117(n9); noble, 152–60, 178; reclamation by tlaxilacalli, 43–45; tlaxilacalli apportionment, 87–88, 119(n28); uncertainty of form of tlaxilacalli holding, 159–60
Lockhart, James, 25(n2), 31(n31), 95(n34), 121(n42), 142(n5), 155, 169(n19), 206(n8)

Mapa de Coaltinchan, 85–86
Mapa Quinatzin, 154
Mapa Tlotzin, 154
Map of Mexico 1550, 90–91, 93(n43)
maye (mayeque), 58, 72(n42), 99
Memorial de los Indios de Tepetlaoztoc, 22, 51, 133; maps, 52–55, 70(n36)
Mendieta, fray Gerónimo de, 135–37, 148(n53), 149(n58)
Mexica, 5, 12, 14, 22, 37(n62), 50, 60, 62, 65, 66, 72(n49), 77; defined, 25(n3); distinct from Acolhua, 19–20, 35(n55), 35(n57)
Mexicapan (tlaxilacalli): devotion to Huitzilopochtli, 50; early presence in Tetzcoco, 6–7, 50; general characteristics, 14; home to Mexica, 12; integrated into Tetzcoca politics, 60; role in Mexica control of Azcapotzalco, 72(n49)
Mexico City, 79, 81, 125, 126, 134, 135, 151, 154, 191; Hñähñu rebellion, 17; rebellion of 1624, 4, 7, 27(n7), 27(n8), 183–84; rebellion of 1692, 4, 7, 27(n7), 184, 192–93, 203
Mexico-Tenochtitlan, 7, 13, 14–15, 16, 20, 21, 25(n3), 33(n46), 35(n57), 64, 67, 71, 76, 77, 81, 97, 125, 126, 127, 154; tlaxilacalli founding of, 5, 47–48. *See also* Mexico City
Mixcoatl, Andrés (ritual specialist), 126–27, 144(n16)
Motolinia (missionary): 127, 130, 131, 134
Moyotlan (tlayacatl): administration in, 11, 17, 33(n46); Inquisition targeting of, 125

Nahua, 139; ethnic majority in Cuauhtepoztlan tlaxilacalli, 56–58; institutions, 13; thought, 107, 116, 117(n14)
Nahuatl, 10, 25(n1–n2), 26(n5), 29(n13), 45, 50, 73(n59), 78, 86, 89, 93, 95(n34), 116(n6), 118(n20), 119(n27), 119(n30), 132, 134, 151–52, 157–59, 166, 174–76, 180, 184, 196(n19), 203, 204, 206(n8); popular expressions, 65; in Tetzcoco, 35(n56)
names: passing of, 101–2, 118(n21); religious connections to Tezcatlipoca, 114
neighborhood, conflated with tlaxilacalli, 10, 26(n5), 30(n23), 203–5
Nezahualcoyotl (huei tlatoani of Tetzcoco), 13, 35(n57), 60, 130, 159, 163, 170, 173; administration by tlaxilacalli, 43, 46, 78, 159; dictate cited in Hispanic court, 166; early land divisions, 79, 93(n8); hiding in Poyauhtlan tlaxilacalli, 17; reincorporation of Chimalpan tlaxilacalli, 75–77; reliance on tlaxilacalli in war, 62–63; response to famine, 65; rule in Acolhuacan, 64–65, 75–76
Nezahualpilli (huei tlatoani of Tetzcoco), 21, 35(n57), 155–57, 160, 164
nobility, 21, 28(n12), 30(n26), 35(n57), 45, 49, 51, 63, 65, 71(n42), 80, 91, 94(n15), 102, 118(n17), 119(n28), 120(n38), 127, 130, 151, 166, 170(n31); following tlaxilacalli, 78–79, 93(n12); landholding, 54–58, 84, 106, 108–9, 152–60, 178; role in Teotihuacan rebellion, 135–38, 149(n60); of Tepetlaoztoc, 59–60; tribute shares, 59; vestigial, 45, 80, 154, 159, 190–92. *See also* pilli; teuctli; teuctlatoani; tlatoani

Ocelotl, Martín (ritual specialist), 126, 143(n13)
Ocotoch (Chichimeca war captain): Acolhua tributary and administrator, 51; rebellion against Quinatzin, 51–52
Ometochtzin, don Carlos (Tetzcoco noble), 127–28, 130, 145(n23), 157
Otomí, *See* Hñähñu
Oztoticpac (tlaxilacalli), 49; general characteristics of, 14; glyph in Codex Xolotl, 62; Lands Map, 108, 121(n45); prestige in Tetzcoco, 12–13; seed of Tetzcoco altepetl, 47, 69(n26); support of Nezahualcoyotl, 62; teteuctin of, 108

Passalli, Jácome (obraje owner), 157, 169(n22), 199(n20); alleged crimes, 182, 198(n19)
patio block, 103–5, 117(n12)
pilli, 108. *See also* nobility
Pochtlan (tlaxilacalli), 189; general characteristics of, 14; merchants, 17, 33(n47), 86
Pomar, Juan Bautista de (historian): association with Spaniards, 170(n23); claims to tlaxilacalli land, 159–62, 164–67, 175; compilation of *Romances de los Señores de la Nueva España*, 151; description of destroyed Acolhua archives, 21–22; research work, 22; role in land sales by Tetzcoca elite, 156–59
population collapse, 67(n12), 78, 80–82, 86–86
Primeros Memoriales, 103, 139
pueblos: altepetl understood as, 12–13; tlaxilacalli understood as, 10, 12–13

Quecil, Ciprían (tepixqui in Cuauhtepoztlan), 81; part of wider tlaxilacalli hierarchy, 98–99, 103–5, 117(n12); plot mapped, 54, 71(n39)
Quetzalmamalitzin, don Francisco Verdugo (tlatoani of Teotihuacan): role in rebellion, 135–37; will as example of Hispanic translation, 152–53, 155–56, 159–60, 168(n7)
Quinatzin (huei tlatoani of Tetzcoco): aid in settling Tlailotlacan tlaxilacalli, 12; building Tetzcoco altepetl from Oztoticpac tlaxilacalli, 47, 49, 69(n25); settling of final two founding Tetzcoca tlaxilacalli, 50; war with Yacatzotzolotl, 51

religion: Aztec transculturation, 131–33; practice, 147(n40). *See also* evangelization; Inquisition

San Antonio, Juan de: letter, 70(n37), 79–80
Spaniards, 4, 67, 91, 95(n31), 129, 139, 153, 156–58, 170(n23), 179, 182, 185, 205; claiming an invented home tlaxilacalli, 180; misunderstanding of tlaxilacalli names, 7, 9–10, 12, 144(n17), 144(n18)

Techotlalatzin (huei tlatoani of Tetzcoco): tolerance of tlaxilacalli religion, 51–52; welcome of new tlaxilacalli, 5–6
Teotihuacan: elite disarticulation in, 152–54; hierarchy, 149(n60); rebellion, 134–39, 149(n58); ruling elite, 148(n52), 159; Spaniard inventing tlaxilacalli for, 180

Tepaneca, 66, 77; conspiracy against Ixtlilxochitl Ometochtzin, 61–62, 72(n51), 92(n5)

Tepanecapan (tlaxilacalli), 6; ambiguity of glyph in Codex Xolotl, 60–61, 72(n49); early presence in Tetzcoco, 5–7, 50; general characteristics of, 15; marginalization of, 60; opposition to Tetzcoca rulers, 60

Tepepulco (altepetl); religion in, 125, 132–33, 139–42, 151; site of Primeros Memoriales, 96(n37), 139

Tepetlaoztoc (altepetl), 14, 15, 22, 24, 26(n5), 28(n12), 42, 67(n8), 68(n19), 69(n25), 79, 90, 91, 94(n10), 96(n38), 97, 100, 116(n3), 119(n28), 195; disease in, 80–83, 87; elite hierarchy, 59–60, 101, 110, 119(n23); religion in, 123, 126, 128–29, 133–34, 139, 177; separation from Acolhua power, 49, 51–52; spatial history of tlaxilacalli, 53–58, 70(n36), 94(n26), 121(n51), 122(n54), 142(n2), 174–77, 179–81, 203–5; tlaxilacalli reassigned in, 54, 70(n37), 80–81, 939(n9)

tepixqui, 24, 110, 117(n11), 137; assuming title of "tlatoani," 187; function, 102–5, 123

Tetlicac, San Martín (tlaxilacalli): conflict with Coapanco over land, 174–75; identity as cofradía, 175–77

Tetzcacohuac (tlaxilacalli), general characteristics of, 15

Tetzcoco (altepetl): evangelization, 127–28; fiesta circuit, 193–95; foundational tlaxilacalli, 5–7; growth from Ozototicpac tlaxilacalli, 47, 49; marginalization during Hispanic period, 155; versions of its name, xiii–xiv

Tetzcotzinco (tlaxilacalli), 46, 62, 149(n58); religious reconstruction in, 128–30; support of Nezahualcoyotl, 62; titles of, 93(n8), 128–29

teuctlatoani, 59, 72(n44), 87, 107, 120(n38)

teuctli, 59, 72(n44)

Tezcatlipoca, 12, 14, 50–51, 70(n32), 88, 96(n37), 114, 133

Tezcatzonco Tlanelocan (tlaxilacalli), defense of lands though archives, 164–69

Tezozomoc (huei tlatoani of Azcapotzalco), imperial tlaxilacalli strategies, 60–63, 159

Tira de Tepechpan, 154

tlacamecayotl (kin group), 30(n26), 60, 89–90, 99, 107, 109, 188, 192

Tlacochcalco (tlaxilacalli): general characteristics, 15; legendary migrations, 12

Tlailotlacan (tlaxilacalli): aspiring to altepetl status, 186; cited in *Romances de los Señores de la Nueva España*, 151; communication specialists, 12; conflicts with tlatoani, 190–92; devotion to Tezcatlipoca, 50; dynastic history, 8–9; early integration into Tetzcoca politics, 60; early presence in Tetzcoco, 5–7, 50; elite land sales in, 156; general characteristics of, 15; influence on Codex Xolotl, 8, 30(n27); land inheritance in, 186–90; likely origins in Puebla/Mixteca region, 50; making peace with Nezahualcoyotl, 75–76; political calculations, 30(n26); recovery of Ixtlilxochitl Ometochtzin's body for burial, 60; role in destruction of Aztec religious architecture, 128; semantic reach of term, 33(n43); spread across Acolhuacan, 12, 60; support for Tetzcoca rulers, 60; Tlailotlaca affiliation, 50

Tlalcocomoco (tlaxilacalli), role in founding of Mexico-Tenochtitlan, 5

tlalquahuitl (Acolhua measurement), 87, 95(n34), 100, 119(n29)

Tlanchiuhcan (altepemaitl): death rates, 80–82; glyph, 105–6; mapped, 54–57, 71(n40); noble landholding in, 109; spatial history, 56–58

Tlaquilcan, San Gregorio (tlaxilacalli), land fight with Pomar and Tezcatzonco, 164–67

tlatoani, 59–60, 77–80, 96, 101, 102, 103, 107, 108, 110, 115, 120(n37), 121(n41), 126, 127, 130, 131–38, 152–55, 165–67, 178, 186, 190–92, 204, 206(n2), 206(n5)

Tlaxcala (huei altepetl), 7, 14–15, 19, 21, 24, 27(n7), 35(n56), 61–62, 77, 79, 82, 87, 93(n11), 121(n42)

tlaxilacalli: cognate of calpolli, 11, 25(n2), 31(n31), 31(n32), 31(n380); conflated with neighborhood, 10, 26(n5), 30(n23), 203–5; defined, 3–4, 10, 25(n2); diversity, 17, 44(n33); ecology, 43–45, 67(n8)–67(n10); first emergence, 40–45; hierarchy of Coatlinchan, 85–86; list of common names and features, 14–15; map of spatial array in Tetzcoco, xii; misunderstandings of, 7, 9–12; partial dismemberment of, 177–78; redefined as altepetl, 10; regional array, 4, 32(n41); reintroduction of maize agriculture in Acolhuacan, 46–47, 67(n12); relation to altepetl, 4, 9–10; religious practice, 123–25, 142(n2); response to One Rabbit famine, 62–63; role in early Hispanic imperialism, 78–79; role in Mexico City revolts, 7; silenced in conventional histories, 5; Spanish definitions, 13; studies, 27(n10); uncertainty about land ownership in, 159–60; understood as pueblo, 10, 13

tlayacatl: expanded functions of tlaxilacalli, 16, 33(n45); Hñähñu revolt based in, 17; Moyotlan as example of, 11, 17; role in Aztec administration, 16; Spanish definitions of, 13; in Tetzcoco, 50

Tocuillan (tlaxilacalli), 87–88, 95(n32), 105

"Tolteca" (post-Tolteca groups still identified by this imperial term): early tlaxilacalli farmers, 45, 47–49; transculturation, 49–50

topile, 24, 103, 107, 109, 110, 123, 124, 135, 154, 185; function, 105–6, 95(n34); role in Teotihuacan rebellion, 137–38

Torquemada, fray Juan de, 46–47

Tzillan (tlaxilacalli): destruction of palace archives in, 21; glyph in Codex Xolotl, 62

volador dance, 139–40

War for Mexico: destruction of Acolhua archives, 21–22; "New Conquest" historiography, 26(n4); tlaxilacalli continuing to function after, 19; tlaxilacalli influence in battles, 7. *See also* Cortés; evangelization; Ixtlilxochitl, Hernando; Tlaxcala

Xolalpan, San Sebastían (tlaxilacalli), fiesta graffiti, 196–97

Yacanex. *See* Yacatzotzolotl

Yacatzotzolotl (Chichimeca war leader), 69(n25); opposition to Quinatzin, 49–51

Yopico (tlaxilacalli): particular features, 13–16; role in case of Carlos Ometochtzin, 127–28; role in founding of Mexico-Tenochtitlan, 5

Zapotlan (tlaxilacalli): general characteristics of, 15; home to Zapoteca, 12

www.ingramcontent.com/pod-product-compliance
Lightning Source LLC
Chambersburg PA
CBHW071153070526
44584CB00019B/2774